BAPHOMET
GUARDIAN OF THE KEY TO THE TEMPLE

BAPHOMET

GUARDIAN OF THE KEY
TO THE TEMPLE

by

Joel Bernard Brady

In Perpetuity Publishing

First Printing, 2026
Paperback ISBN 978-0-6451039-8-4
Hardback ISBN 978-1-7645007-7-7

Ordo Templi Orientis
GPO Box 1936
Adelaide, SA 5001
AUSTRALIA

www.otoaustralia.org.au
inperpetuitypublishing.com

Editor: Padraig Maclain
Cover Design and Layout: Annette Eustace @luxlovesnox_design

CONTENTS

For

K 2 X

who understood

Division of the North wind and the South,
The lightning of the armies of the Lord;
East rolled asunder from the rended West;
Height clove the depth ; the Voice begotten
        Said:
"Divided be thy ways and limited!"
Answered the reflux and the indrawn breath:
"Let there be Life, and Death!"

ALEISTER CROWLEY

Tannhauser

Acknowledgements

Firstly, I would like to thank Stephen J. King (Frater Shiva X° of the Australian Grand Lodge of Ordo Templi Orientis) for his initial encouragement when shown a very early draft of my original Baphomet essay, and for his inspired guidance and counsel over many years. He also encouraged me to expand this work into book form, as well as suggesting new avenues of research and editorial advice.

Brendan Walls and Padraig MacIain worked tirelessly to edit and prepare the first volumes of *Ora et Labora* and went above and beyond to help bring Baphomet to print. Brendan also worked closely with me as editor of this work. His constant energy, encouragement and enthusiasm has been a great inspiration for me.

Gordan Djurdjevic also provided me with encouragement and welcome criticism, and also suggested that my original work had the potential to be expanded into book form after his review of the original paper.

Thanks also goes to Shawn Gray, who provided some important clarifications into the kanji used by the enigmatic Massaki Hatsumi sensei.

I would like to thank and remember Brother J.P. Lund who gave me invaluable fraternal guidance, encouragement, and assistance over many years.

Finally, I would like to thank and remember J. Daniel Gunther whose works were a godsend to a struggling aspirant. I will never forget his generosity of spirit.

"Binario Verbum Vitae Mortem et Vitam Aequilibrans"[1]

---

1   Binary Word of Life, Death and Life Balancing

And Freedom stands, re-risen from the
rod,
A goodlier godhead than the broken God.

Aleister Crowley
The Triumph of Man

Editorial Note

Do what thou wilt shall be the whole of the Law.

Baphomet: Guarding of the Key to the Temple is the third monograph to be published by *In Perpetuity Publishing*. The first was *Living in the Sunlight* by Steve King; the second was *Descent from the Cross: Transformation of a Masochistic Woman* by Elaine Simard LaForêt, published from her graduate paper. These monographs allow authors to engage with a subject in greater depth than is possible in our compendiums, such as *The Best of OZ* or *Ora et Labora*, and enable readers to focus directly on a single topic.

As the newly appointed editor of *In Perpetuity Publishing*, this is the first book over which I have editorial control. As with many things in the universe, it has not been a simple work to prepare for print. Many books proceed in a linear fashion, moving from a general idea or question, through a series of proofs, and culminating in a concluding answer. *Baphomet*, however, does not follow a linear narrative. Instead, it is a collection of threads arising from different directions, woven together into a whole that forms a tapestry describing the modern image of Baphomet—as both an archetype and an instruction.

I would like to thank Brendan Walls for all of his previous work with *In Perpetuity Publishing*, tirelessly editing and collating material. Like Joel, I would also like to thank him for the editorial work he did on this title before it was handed over to me. I would further like to wholeheartedly thank Stephanie Williams for her extensive and exacting proofreading. I also extend a thank you to Zac Duggan for his initial phase of proofreading. Finally, I'd like to give a huge thank you to Annette

Eustace for her typesetting and cover design. All this work and all these contributions have been invaluable.

Any remaining typographical issues are entirely my fault.

Love is the law, love under will.

Yours,
Pàdraig MacIain
Editor, *In Perpetuity Publishing*

INTRODUCTION

Do what thou wilt shall be the whole of the Law.

My first version of *Baphomet* appeared in Volume 1 of *Ora et Labora*, the research journal of the Grand Lodge of Ordo Templi Orientis (OTO) in Australia[1]. It was the result of many years of research, reflection, and meditation on this enduring mystery. Yet, there was also an undeniable sense of immediacy—perhaps even inspiration—behind its creation. True to the spirit of *Ora et Labora*, the essay was never intended as an academic paper. The journal was a platform for work produced by OTO members that had, until then, remained unpublished or circulated only in limited circles.

That original essay was never meant to be definitive. Rather, it was a snapshot of a process—my own unfolding exploration of the enigmatic Templar idol that continues to captivate so many. At the time, I felt as though I were trying to contain something far larger than myself. The result was a piece that lacked structural coherence and included Qabalistic and symbolic material that may have confused some readers. It was, in essence, a "download." I published it with considerable hesitation, but as the ever-patient editor Brendan Walls reminded me, it was a case of 'art for art's sake'—a need to release these ideas that had been circulating in my mind and give them some form, however provisional. To give them shape, yes—but also to expose them to wider scrutiny.

This book is both a continuation and a reworking of that initial effort. It aims to expand the scope of the original essay

---

1   "Work and Pray". Ed. Walls, IPP, 2001.

while bringing a clearer structure and greater coherence to the material. It is, admittedly, still a work in progress—how could it be otherwise? The figure of the "Goat of Mendes" resists finality, and I anticipate continuing to explore and write about these mysteries. I also hope others will take up the thread—as many already are—and contribute their own insights and interpretations.

This work should be read alongside the original *Ora et Labora* essay, as some of the initial ideas remain exclusive to that piece. Interestingly, my original intent was simply to expand upon that essay. Yet, despite numerous attempts, I found myself unable to begin. In the end, I started anew—with a blank page—and as I did, I felt that same spark of inspiration return.

Over time, Baphomet has come to represent different things to different people. Various groups have adopted the figure for different reasons, and it has gradually entered popular culture. Baphomet has even entered contemporary politics, being used in America by The Satanic Temple to emphasise reason and science, as well as values such as compassion and justice.[2] It has also become fodder for conspiracy theorists[3] and anti-satanic crusaders. It is a glyph that has lost none of its impact, but instead seems to grow and transform.

In the following pages I will be exploring the concept of Baphomet as representing a state of transformed consciousness, a field[4] of experience or consciousness, and "a faculty

---

2   Laycock, 'What The Satanic Temple Is and Why It's Opening a Debate about Religion', Oxford University Press. 2020.

3   After the publication of my essay, I also became the target of conspiracy theorists who managed to shape my writing to fit their extremist world view.

4   'It is logical to suggest that there is a neutral place where the two realms remain undivided. Like the *tao*, this 'place' is elusive and very likely not a place at all but rather a non-local prior, which accords with the idea that there

of the mind which is 'above the Abyss'"[5] - and "...its name is Compassion."[6] This is married with a term I have called in this work, the "kingly power" - the mysterious energy described under various names. In order to wield the kingly power effectively and purely, one needs to have attained this Baphomet consciousness; one needs to stand silent and still between contending forces so that their operation can be properly observed and controlled from a transcendent point of view.[7] As described by Joseph Campbell (1904–1987), 'It is there, which is no "where," that the Eye opens of Transcendent Vision, which in the way of art is of that instant (once again to quote James Joyce) "wherein that supreme quality of beauty, that

---

exists behind this world a neutral domain in which mind and matter are unified, or to be more precise, have not yet separated.' (Browne, 'Examining Coincidences', 133.)

5 Crowley, *The Book of Thoth*, 64.

6 Crowley, Neuburg, and Desti, *The Vision & the Voice with Commentary and Other Papers: The Collected Diaries of Aleister Crowley, 1909-1914 E.V.*, 149.

7 This becomes more fascinating when we consider the implications of quantum physics. 'Thus we inhabit, according to Wheeler, a participatory universe that is shaped not only by physical forces but also the observations in a kind of loop effect, where the universe shapes the observer, and the observers shape the universe.' (Browne, 'Examining Coincidences', 120.) According to Nick Mansfield (born 1959) 'We can no longer consider objects as independently existing entities that can be localised in well-defined regions of spacetime. They are interconnected in ways not even conceivable using ideas from classical physics... These are instantaneous interconnections. These quantum correlations reveal that nature is non-causally unified in ways we only dimly understand... It will take time for this view of nature to be fully understood and to penetrate the collective psyche. Nevertheless, it certainly provides a much more congenial world within which to understand synchronicity than the Newtonian world of independently and separately existing entities acting causally upon each other within an absolute space and time.' (Browne, 123.)

clear radiance of the esthetic image, is apprehended luminously by the mind which has been arrested by its wholeness and fascinated by its harmony...the luminous silent stasis of esthetic pleasure...The last [*Happiness in Tranquillity* – The Peaceful] is not, like the others, to be separately developed in distant compositions, but to underlie the experiences of all as a kind of drone, or ground, over which they play. It is the experience of the "permanent state"...'[8] Or in the words of The Master Therion:

> Thou must (1) Find out what is thy Will, (2) Do that Will with (a) one-pointedness, (b) detachment, (c) peace. Then, and then only, art thou in harmony with the Movement of Things, thy will part of, and therefore equal to, the Will of God. And since the will is but the dynamic aspect of the self, and since two different selves could not possess identical wills; then, if thy will be God's will, *Thou* art *That*.[9]

As proposed by James Jeans (1877–1946) '...the universe begins to look more like a great thought than like a great machine. Mind no longer appears as an accidental intruder into the realm of matter; we are beginning to suspect that we ought rather to hail it as the creator and governor of the realm of matter – not, of course, our individual minds, but the mind in which the atoms out of which our individual minds have grown exist as thoughts.'[10]

I believe, however, that the mysteries of Baphomet are open to all no matter where they are on their path in eternity or their inward journey (the paths of the OTO and A∴A∴ respec-

---

8   Campbell, *The Inner Reaches of Outer Space*, 137-139.

9   Crowley, "The Message of the Master Therion" *The Equinox*, III:10, Weiser, 1986.

10   Browne, 'Examining Coincidences', 132.

tively). Baphomet represents a marriage of Heaven and Earth, and a glyph of the reconciliation of opposites. Similar to the teachings of Shingon Buddhism in Japan, where 'The material world, be it body or object, was reinstated as an integral part of truth and reality...The absolute speaks through the material world and we respond to it through our bodies.'[11] Or as Aleister Crowley would say, 'The new Aeon is the worship of the spiritual made one with the material.'[12] In many ways this is a reflection of my own magical character and experience as both an Aspirant to the A∴A∴, and initiate of the OTO. I often feel in sympathy with Karl Germer (1885 –1962), when he wrote in 1958, 'You should also know that I am not of the traditional type of occultist; I am 'blind' in a peculiar way; I have never studied the Qabalah, The Tree of Life, "777", Magick, or what have you. I cannot practice rising on the planes in the technical sense. In fact, I seem to be set apart. A.C. saw this in me in 1925. And yet...!'[13] Sometimes I feel like I am reaching into the deeper strata of myself, consciousness and existence, in the act of writing. Writing is, for me, one of the vehicles of transcendence, but also a link to the material (it is a fixing of the volatile). As Eliphas Lévi would write, 'The torch of intelligence burning between the horns is the magical light of universal equilibrium; it is also the type of the soul exalted above matter, even while cleaving to matter, as the flame cleaves to the torch.'[14]

As this is based on my personal, and perhaps idiosyncratic, engagement with Baphomet some links may still seem obscure (and even I grapple with the subtleties), but I have tried to con-

---

11 Silk et al., 'Brill's Encyclopedia of Buddhism', 1032.

12 Crowley, *The Equinox of the Gods*, 136.

13 Germer, 'Karl Germer to Brother Williams', 24 June 1958.

14 Lévi, *Transcendental Magic*, 309.

nect these concepts as well as I can. It should be kept in mind that this book, like the original paper, is also not an academic work – it is, in essence, a magical document. I hope it is not completely without rigour, but I also hope I will be excused for the use of some "imaginal logic" [15] and that it will be appreciated in that context. Unfolding the nature of Baphomet consciousness is a recognition of the repeating pattern throughout human history, and human spiritual experiences, of the place of silence and stillness between two contending forces. I suggest the reader build up an accumulative field of consciousness and understanding throughout the reading of this, at times, difficult, book, rather than be bound to individual concepts.

I am also aware that there has already been a book published on Baphomet by Tracy R. Twyman and Alexander Rivera. I have deliberately not referred to this work, or read it, as I am unsure about the context in which it was written, and I suspect our purposes for writing are quite different. I also wanted to map out my own course in my exploration of these mysteries as much as possible. I am sure, however, that there will be overlap with the research presented in that work, and areas explored there which I have overlooked. I was unaware of her work when I produced my original paper. I have, however, made reference to the English translation of *Mysterium Baphometis Revelatum* that Twyman commissioned, edited and annotated, although with some caution.

Although I present Baphomet, 'Two-In-One Love',[16] with a degree of trepidation, it is my hope that it will at least further the discourse around Baphomet, and its importance to both the OTO and the A∴A∴ I also acknowledge that others have

---

15   Marvell, 65.

16   Crowley, Neuburg, and Desti, *The Vision & the Voice with Commentary and Other Papers: The Collected Diaries of Aleister Crowley, 1909-1914 E.V.*, 77.

explored this theme to greater and lesser extents and through different lenses. I view the presentation of this material to readers as the fulfilment of an obligation.

I would also like to note that in many ways this work represents the thoughts of many others, and I feel like somewhat of a compiler. But to quote Australian musician, writer, and visual artist Nick Cave, 'Nothing you create is ultimately your own, yet all of it is you. Your imagination, it seems to me, is mostly an accidental dance between collected memory and influence, and is not intrinsic to you, rather it is a construction that awaits spiritual ignition.'[17]

The inmost is the home of God. He moulds
Infinity,
The great within the small, one stainless
unity!

Aleister Crowley
Aceldama[18]

Love is the law, love under will.

Joel Brady, Sunday 25th May, 2025

Canberra, Australian Capital Territory
Adelaide, South Australia
Asakusa, Tokyo, Japan
Bridport, Tasmania

---

17 Cave, 'Nick Cave – The Red Hand Files – Issue #181 – How or When or Do You Shut the Voices of All Your Influences (Your Heroes, Your Parents, Your Jesus, Your Music) to Listen to Yourself, to Become You or to Believe That What You Create Is Your Own?'

18 Crowley, *The Collected Works of Aleister Crowley*, I:4.

THE TEMPLARS

Item, that in each province they had idols, namely heads, of which some had three faces, and some one, and others had a human skull. Item, that they adored these idols or that idol, and especially in their great chapters and assemblies. Item, that they venerated [it] as God, as their Savior... Item, that they said that the head could save them and make them rich... Item, that they believed or touched or kissed the head...[1]

Therefore, reverend brothers, it is your obligation most of all because having despised the light of the present life and having ignored the suffering of your bodies you have promised to count as vile the raging world for the love of God, nourished and filled by divine food, and learned and strengthened by the teachings of the Lord after the consummation of the divine mystery. Let no one fear battle, and let him be ready for the crown.[2]

The origin of the name, and conception of Baphomet has its genesis with the Knights Templar, and the trials of 1307, which marked the end of the order and its descent or integration into the imaginal world. It seems fitting to start here.

---

1   Translated from Latin records of the Inquisition, as cited in Barber, Malcolm, *The Trial of the Templars* (Cambridge University Press, 1978), p. 248.

2   Wojtowicz, 'The Original Rule of the Knights Templar: A Translation with Introduction', 36.

The order was properly '*Pauperes Commilitones Christi Templique Salomonici*' ("Poor Fellow-Soldiers of Christ and of the Temple of Solomon"). The simplified name of Templars comes from their headquarters being located on Temple Mount in Jerusalem. They were 'a fighting force sworn to the service of the Church, a religious order which offered salvation as a reward for valour in war. The dual nature of the Temple was symbolised by its banner, which was piebald – the white signifying gentleness towards friends of Christ, the black ferocity towards his enemies.'[3]

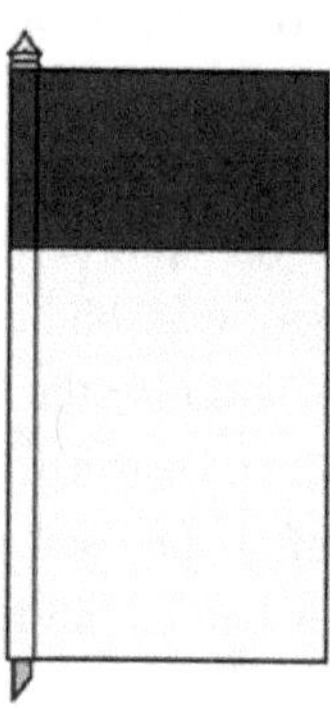

The Templars lived under the religious rule of St. Augustine, 'and they had guidance from the canons[4] of the Church of the Holy Sepulchre of Jerusalem.'[5] This combination of the military and the religious may seem natural to a modern reader, due to the presence of the Templars in our cultural narratives. However, at the time this was a very controversial initiative.

---

3   Cohn, *Europe's Inner Demons*, 76.

4   Canons are priests who live in a community under religious rule. The Canons Regular of the Holy Sepulchre were a Catholic order of canons regular of the Rule of St. Augustine. It is said that they were founded in the Church of the Holy Sepulchre. The order was recognised in 1113 by Pope Pascal II.

5   Partner, *The Murdered Magicians: The Templars and Their Myth*, 3.

'The Templars seemed to introduce confusion into one of the basic distinctions of medieval society, between the 'religious order' and 'military order.'[6] The division between priesthood and kingdom was confused. 'Far from idealising chivalry, religious leaders usually represented knightly life as lawless, licentious, and bloody.'[7]

Documents released by the Vatican in 2007 showed that 'Pope Clement was convinced that while the Templars had committed some grave sins, they were not heretics.'[8] Despite this, some Templars were burnt at the stake as heretics. It should be noted, however, that this point is disputed by some historians, such as Helen Nicholson, who argues that Papal absolution was quite normal in heresy trials. However, in the *Faciens misericordiam,*[9] the Pope described the Templar practices as 'extremely serious heresies'.[10] I hope this work, however, will show that the Templars were not heretics, but for the most part loyal to humanity, as well as to the divinity of Jesus, who they believed suffered and died for humankind. At the same time, they were human, and suffered from the same faults found within institutions, large and small, throughout history.

Michael Turnbull points out in relation to the Templar trial in 1309 at Holyrood Abbey, 'Although forty-one witnesses were ordered to appear, sworn to tell the truth and legally examined (including abbots, priests and domestic servants of the Templars and Sir Henry St Clair), their summarised report did

---

6 Partner, 6.

7 Partner, 6.

8 Pullella, 'Knights Templar Win Heresy Reprieve after 700 Years'., Reuters, 2007.

9 "Granting forgiveness". This was a papal bull issued by Pope Clement V in 1308.

10 Nicholson, 'The Changing Face of the Templars', 658.

not testify to any significant evidence of heresy or immorality, other than a culture of unnecessary secrecy, a tendency to avarice and an uncaring attitude towards the poor whom they neglected in favour of the great and the wealthy.'[11] Charges were levied against the Templars despite a lack of material evidence to substantiate them. A fifth of these accusations were that the Templars venerated an idol or a head.

Thirty-six of the two hundred and thirty-one Templars underwent torture and died during these trials, which indicates the extreme cruelty of this process, and the psychological pressure the Templars were subjected to. As Partner explains, 'The torture of the accused was carried out with a barbarity which even medieval men found shocking.'[12] The royal letter opening the trials is chilling when you consider what awaited the arrested Templars: '...if some among them are innocent, it is expedient that they should be assayed like gold in the furnace, and purged by proper judicial examination.'[13] Proper, indeed.

---

11   Turnbull, 'Who Were the Templars?', 7.

12   Partner, *The Murdered Magicians: The Templars and Their Myth*, 60.

13   Partner, 61.

The Torture of the Templars

Despite the perception of secrecy mentioned above, Nicholson argues that the Templars were not necessarily the secret organisation they are often portrayed as, but rather the organisation was quite open to local people and travellers, and their faith was the same as that of the people they were sworn to protect.[14] She also stresses that relying on the confessions of the Templars, based on what we now know of the psychological effects of torture, is unreliable and should be viewed cautiously.

Under torture, or the threat of it, the Templars were unable to consistently explain the allegedly blasphemous initiation ritual attributed to their order. The few who did offer explanations disagreed on its meaning and purpose, suggesting the ritual may have been a fabrication of their accusers. However, as with many such allegations—both historical and contemporary—it is possible they were built around a kernel of truth.

The Templars were highly influential in France. The Paris temple, in particular, became the centre of European Finance...'[15] The king of France, Philip the Fair, was in some ways a megalomaniac and religious fanatic, who had intentions for himself to become *Bellator Rex* ("Warrior King"), a role proposed by Raymond Lull (1232–1315/1316) after the loss of Jerusalem. A king who, in the end, would become the king of Jerusalem. 'To Philip the religious megalomaniac the existence of the Temple presented an infuriating obstacle, while to Philip the politician the destruction of the Temple offered financial

---

14   Norman Cohn, however, does highlight that 'The temple had always cultivated secrecy, no doubt in the first place for military reasons; but this bull [*Omne datum optimum*] encouraged the habit. Chapter meetings from which all outsiders were rigorously excluded, and every crack in door or wall was carefully blocked, symbolized the Templars' sense of being a race apart.' (Cohn, *Europe's Inner Demons*, 78.)

15   Cohn, 81.

relief... Philip knew that as long as the Temple survived as an autonomous institution, it would block even the first steps to his becoming *Bellator Rex*.'[16] Philip already had a precedent: In July 1306, Jews in France were imprisoned, their money seized, Jewish businesses transferred to Italian banks, their goods auctioned, and the Jews expelled. 'The royal publicists presented this last expedient as a great victory for Christ. They were to say the same, a couple of years later, of the destruction of the Temple.'[17]

The persecution of the Templars, the accusations of heresy, and the style of accusations certainly had precedent, and had been used for the purposes of power and wealth, driven by a religious fanaticism. In Germany, Henry VII (1211–1242) issued a decree regarding the disposal of the property of people condemned of heresy, which left some of this property to the heirs of the accused.[18] The inquisitors went further to propose that 'the whole of the property should be confiscated and divided amongst the various overlords, including the king; the heirs would receive nothing.'[19] This gained support and 'the shady characters Conrad Torso and Johannes attached themselves to the genuine fanatic Conrad of Marburg, and the resulting combination proved astonishingly powerful.'[20] Torso (along with the mysterious one armed man called "Johannes") claimed to be able to identify a heretic on sight, and these people were often burned alive within the day they were accused. In the beginning it was lower class people that were the subject of the

---

16 Cohn, 82–83.

17 Cohn, 82.

18 It is interesting that Henry intervened against some inquisition measures, which led to his excommunication by Pope Gregory IX.

19 Cohn, *Europe's Inner Demons*, 26.

20 Cohn, 26.

accusations and punishment, but due to the redistribution of property, heresy began to be found amongst the wealthy and the influential 'and rival members of the aristocracy... People began to abuse the system, accusing rivals of heresies so they'd be burned or humiliated.'[21]

After the assassination of Torso, a Papal Bull was released called *Vox in Rama,*[22] which detailed the events described by the Inquisitor (which said more about their own minds than those of the accused). 'It spoke of initiation rites of the heretics which involved a giant toad and culminated with kissing a cat on the arse before engaging in the customary orgy.'[23] This sounds familiar, and is another example of the "social contagion" that we saw during the persecution of the Templars, and also a phenomenon that continues to this day in various forms.

> This is perhaps the most alarming aspect of the European witch hunts, that once the narrative was embedded in people's minds and simply accepted as fact, it took on a life of its own. And an atrocity industry, build [sic] on delusion, greed and fanaticism, continued to grow and sustain itself far into the future.[24]

There are numerous texts that deal with the history of the Templars (from the purely historical to the fanciful) and their dramatic downfall, so there is no need to go into a great deal of detail here. However, I would encourage readers to familiarise

---

21 Stantonian, 'Witch Hunts and the Weaponisation of Moral Panic'.

22 "Voice in Rama". See, Jeremiah 31:15 AV "A voice is heard in Ramah, mourning and great weeping, Rachel weeping for her children and refusing to be comforted, because they are no more".

23 Stantonian, 'Witch Hunts and the Weaponisation of Moral Panic'.

24 Stantonian.

themselves with this history—both historical and fanciful—in order to understand the ongoing fascination with this order of religious warriors, and perhaps to gain some indication of the spiritual practices taught to their initiates. The issues with the credibility of the Templars' testimonies does not necessarily mean that there were not forms of worship or religious practice that the Templars undertook. Perhaps their testimonies reflected elements of religious practice also found outside the order, with which they were familiar. There is an interesting artefact that may point to this form of worship (or what is being referenced by the Templars), and a connection between the Templars and the description of "a head" given during the trials. This is the "Templecombe Head" which is kept within the Church of St. Mary at Templecombe in Somerset, southwest England, but was discovered in a Templar Preceptory (the *Combe Templariorum*, 1185-1307).

Head of Christ from Templecombe, Somerset, England,
13th-14th century

The head 'may have been a Templar object',[25] and it has been associated with both Jesus and John the Baptist, who will be dealt with in more detail later. This artwork also shares some similarities with the *Johannesschüssel*; a representation of John the Baptist which was used as an object of worship and meditation. The *Johannesschüssel* also shares characteristics with the well-known Shroud of Turin. These fascinating objects will also be explored in more detail.

Eliphas Lévi (the occultist and artist who created the most widely known image of Baphomet) taught that 'The avowed object of the Templars[26] was to protect Christians on pilgrimage to the holy places; their concealed end was to rebuild the Temple of Solomon on the model foreshewn by Ezekiel.'[27] Ezekiel was a prophet in exile in Babylon and had a vision of a future Temple, future priests and of a future prince. In his vision Ezekiel saw the return of the Shekinah[28] glory to the Temple (the Shekinah not considered present in the second Temple).

With the advent of the New Aeon, the Shekinah did return. The Temple has been rebuilt and the Templar archetype continues to guard pilgrims. In other words, the work of the OTO continues its obligation to transform society globally, so that people may be free to pursue their own Great Work, whatever this may be, free from persecution and bigotry.

---

25   Churton, *The Mysteries of John the Baptist*, 251.

26   For contemporary OTO members who partake of the Templar archetype in our mysteries, it would be worthwhile to meditate on what it means to protect pilgrims in the context of Thelema and the modern world as we find it.

27   Levi, *The History of Magic: Including a Clear and Precise Exposition of Its Procedure, Its Rites and Its Mysteries*, 265.

28   The Shekinah is the presence of God and means "dwelling" or "settling". Shekinah is a feminine word.

Neo-Templarism

Although countless words have been written about the Templars, and their supposed survival beyond their persecution and dissolution, '...there is not a single serious historical fact to support it.'[29] And, as Pierre Mollier further writes, 'to study links between Freemasonry and the Templars is to turn legend into history.'[30] It is these legends surrounding the Templars that this book is primarily interested in. It is the archetypal nature that the different legends of the Templars have taken on; and how these have become a vehicle for carrying other mysteries – moral, mystical and magical. In a similar way, the Buddha became much more than just an enlightened man once his teachings were developed in Mahayana Buddhism – freed as they were from the rigours of dry history and into the realm of the archetypes and human imagination. Although we must separate the rigours of pure historical analysis and historical and theological speculation, both these rationalisations and the archetypal essences are equally important to the human psyche. The Templar archetype was born of the human imagination; therefore, it must serve a purpose for us – it must fulfil a psychological need.

This is, of course, a two-edged sword: Tortured histories used as a vehicle to delude; and verifiably false evidence and narratives presented as fact. But there is also something interesting in the human tendency to want to believe these fantastic tales – to suspend disbelief. 'In all human behaviour there is a rational and an irrational element, neither of which can be entirely suppressed.'[31] This is akin to what we can observe con-

---

29 Bogdan and Snoek, *Handbook of Freemasonry*, 82.

30 Bogdan and Snoek, 83.

31 McIntosh, *Eliphas Levi and the French Occult Revival*, 45.

temporarily in the prevalence of conspiratorial thinking across the world. People willing to accept and fabricate grand narratives in order to make sense of the world and manage their own insecurities, and perhaps, for them, make the world a more interesting place (a strange form of entertainment), or make themselves feel more important or relevant within the grand narrative. We see something similar play out in the perception of the Japanese samurai (another warrior class), when the historical record shows them in an often different, and very human light. Much of the concepts around *bushido*[32] were the products of minds who had never known war - 'The concept of a code of conduct for the samurai was a product of the seventeenth and eighteenth centuries, when Japan was at peace, not the medieval "Age of the Country at War."'[33] The samurai of past ages became a vehicle for more contemporary needs, as did the Templars in the West.

Peter Partner argues that prior to the Reformation it was probable that 'the memory of the Templars would survive only as a murky footnote to crusading history.'[34] This fate was altered after the publication of Henry Cornelius Agrippa's (1486–1553) *De occulta philosophia*, published in 1531. In this work he makes a brief reference to the Templars alongside writing about witches, Gnostic magicians and the rites of

---

32   Much of what was known of Bushido in the West was based on the writings of Nitobe Inazo (1862-1933). Primarily his *Bushido– The Soul of Japan*. It should be noted that this work was written in English, and that Nitobe was a Christian, and his Bushido is, in many ways, a tract on Western philosophy and morality which he is attempting to reconcile with his Japanese heritage. '...some critics have even charged that Nitobe fabricated the term "bushido" and its definition. Today, however, the word "bushido" exists in every country on the planet.' (Masahiro, 'Nitobe Inazo and Bushido', 41.)

33   Friday, 'The Historical Foundations of Bushido'.

34   Partner, *The Murdered Magicians: The Templars and Their Myth*, 91.

Priapus – 'Nor were they much different, if what we read is truth and not just fantasy [*fabula*], from the detestable heresy of the Templars; and similar things are known about the witches and their senile craziness in wandering into offences of this sort.'[35] Although Agrippa is vague regarding the Templars, 'the passage was potentially lethal to Templar reputation, because in the occult world qualities are transmitted by sympathetic contagion, not established argument. Templar proximity to the witches was going to make Agrippa's less critical readers accept the Order as Wizards.'[36] This connection, however, did not become more commonly seen until the eighteenth century.[37]

It should also be noted that bookseller, Freemason, and Illuminatus, Christoph Friedrich Nicolai (1733–1811) was also most likely influenced by the writings of Agrippa. It was Nicolai who first proposed that Baphomet was derived from the Greek βαφη μητϚς, *baphe metous* (*Taufe der Weisheit*), "Baptism of Wisdom". Nicolai also thought the Templars were inheritors of a doctrine that originated with the Gnostics. 'Nicolai and Starck must between them bear the main responsibility for the modern reputation of the Templars for practicing some form of sorcery or satanism.'[38]

Mollier traces the absorption of the Templars into Freemasonry via the concept of chivalry, and he believes that, de-

---

35 Partner, 92.

36 Partner, 93.

37 Another Renaissance writer, Guillaume Paradin, also wrote about the Templars and associated them with magical activities. According to him 'Templar novices were brought into a "cave" where they were compelled to worship an image covered with human skin and having glowing carbuncled eyes. Here they were made to renounce Christ and to blaspheme and desecrate the cross; then when the lights were extinguished an orgy took place with the women who had been – inexplicably – admitted...' (Partner, 94.), among other familiar accusations.

38 Partner, 129.

spite the Templar theme being a later arrival in Scotland, it was supporters of the house of Stuart who promoted the transformation of Masonry into a chivalric order.[39] 'Even though the last of the knights had disappeared in the second half of the fourteenth century, the ideal—or if we are to remain neutral on the subject, the image—of chivalry survived them.'[40] Chivalry was in fashion, many books were published and 'imagination reveal[ed] itself to be infinitely more resilient than the real world.'[41] Once the link to chivalry was made within Freemasonry, the Templars followed. In 1746, we read, 'The Free-masons have, like the Templars, such vital and secret points that they would rather lose their life than reveal them.' And in 1752, 'on examining [the sect] of the Templars in their final days, it seems to live on in its entirety within that of the Masons.'[42] Jean-Baptiste Willermoz also wrote that, 'I mysteriously taught those upon whom I conferred that 4th degree of the [lodge] that they had become heirs to Kni[ght] T[emplars] and their wisdom.'[43]

Following the introduction of the Templar archetype into Freemasonry, the rites, and the legends grew and developed into 'truly an imaginary world.'[44] The Templars had taken on a life of their own within and without the Masonic fraternity. In the first Masonic rite to include the Templars, a version of the degree of 'Knight Kadosh', from 1750, 'The 'Elect Knights' are, therefore, the descendants of the Templars. Members of the most illustrious Order of Chivalry of the Middle Ages, their

---

39   Bogdan and Snoek, *Handbook of Freemasonry*, 85.

40   Bogdan and Snoek, 86.

41   Bogdan and Snoek, 86.

42   Bogdan and Snoek, 87.

43   Bogdan and Snoek, 87.

44   Bogdan and Snoek, 87.

name is associated with the mysteries of their wealth and supposed heresy...'[45]

It is through its origins in Freemasonry, and this "imaginary world", that the OTO also carried on the Templar archetype, with Crowley assuming the title of their idol, clearly indicating that he, like Eliphas Lévi, saw this as a vehicle for the mysteries taught within the Order (Mysteries concealed within Freemasonry). The OTO's VI° initiates are 'Illustrious Knights Templar of the Order of Kadosh & Companions of the Holy Grail.' Kadosh means holy or consecrated. In his *Encyclopedia of Freemasonry*, Mackey writes that 'the doctrine of the Kadosh system is that the persecutions of the Knights Templars by Philip the Fair of France, and Pope Clement V., however cruel and sanguinary in its results, did not extinguish the Order, but it continued to exist under the forms of Freemasonry. That the ancient Templars are the modern Kadoshes, and that the builder at the Temple of Solomon is now replaced by James de Molay...'[46]

As mentioned, the Templar legend first appears in a Masonic rite in 1750, in the degree titled "Knight Kadosh" (from documents relating to a 'Sublime Order of Elect Knights'). This rite is found to be, however, a reworking of the 'Elect of IX'. If we look at this from the perspective of the Masons of the time, and the connection between the 'Sublime Order of Elect Knights' and the existing 'Elect Master' the rite may have seemed like a revelation. 'This degree, which every Freemason in the first half of the eighteenth century thought they knew, is in fact—it was claimed—the vestige and surviving remains of one of the

---

45 Bogdan and Snoek, 89.

46 Mackey, *Encyclopedia of Freemasonry and Its Kindred Sciences Comprising the Whole Range of Arts, Sciences and Literature as Connected with the Institution*, 444.

most illustrious Orders of Chivalry. A 'Sublime Order', but one extinguished as a result of an injustice. On closer examination we note that the legend of the degree of 'Elect Knight' is made up of several parts. Firstly, the 'Elect Knights' are descendants of the Templars. Secondly, the Order of the Temple was itself nothing other than the extension of a long line of initiates.'[47] The new ritual shows a new vengeance, not for the death of Hiram, but the death of Jacques de Molay – 'the election avenges innocence'.[48]

The degree also taught that the Templars survived in Scotland, which seems of significance to Thelemites. Boleskine house, located on the picturesque shores of Loch Ness, is considered the Kaaba described in *The Book of the Law*. This is the place to which we orient ourselves, which is both a physical location and an "invisible house", connected intimately to the current Aeon. 'The Templar myths supposed that after the execution of the heads of the Templar Order in 1314 the hidden wisdom was carried by some surviving Templars in exile to Scotland.'[49]

> But your holy place shall be untouched throughout the centuries: though with fire and sword it be burnt down & shattered, yet an invisible house there standeth, and shall stand until the fall of the Great Equinox; when Hrumachis shall arise and the double-wanded one assume my throne and place. Another prophet shall arise, and bring fresh fever from the skies; another woman shall awake the lust & worship of the Snake; another soul of God and beast shall mingle in the globèd priest; another sacrifice shall stain the tomb; anoth-

---

47   Bogdan and Snoek, *Handbook of Freemasonry*, 88–89.

48   Bogdan and Snoek, 89.

49   Partner, *The Murdered Magicians: The Templars and Their Myth*, 112.

er king shall reign; and blessing no longer be poured To the Hawk-headed mystical Lord!

Liber CCXX, III:34[50]

This concept of the Templar secrets being carried to Scotland 'led to the advanced degrees being referred to as "Scottish"'.[51] The Templar legend, and its connection to Scotland were further embellished over time in new rites. In the degree of *Chevalier de Dieu et de son Temple*[52] we read:

> These noble Templars on whose head there was a price, were led by their friends, the knights of Saint Andrew of the Thistle, to the caves near Heredon, where they were safe from the searches carried out by the enemies of their order; they were fed and kept safe by their friends for several years while they remained hidden in the caves. Eventually the persecution gradually diminished and the knights of Saint Andrew of the Thistle joined the 9 knights of the T. who had sought refuge in Scotland in the caves of Heredon. Even the very name of Templars was forgotten and the two orders became as one ... they created the Order of Freemasonry.[53]

Additionally, it was taught that the Templars possessed great wealth because they were alchemists[54] – 'We have several

---

50   Crowley, *The Holy Books of Thelema*, 123.

51   Partner, *The Murdered Magicians: The Templars and Their Myth*, 108.

52   "Knight of God and his Temple"

53   Bogdan and Snoek, *Handbook of Freemasonry*, 93.

54   In Germany one of the central figures in introducing the Templars into Freemasonry was Karl Gotthelf von Hund (1722-1776), appealing to the German's more hierarchical tendency rather than the equality of the blue lodges. He introduced the concept of "Unknown Superiors", an unidentified authority to which 'Hund demanded complete and unquestioning obedience, espe-

members who believe in natural philosophy, and working with nature, they are learned in her secrets.'[55]

The teachings that developed around the Templars within a Masonic context, like the writings of Lévi, took on both an esoteric or occult leaning, as well as a political one (it was both occult and revolutionary). Cadet de Gassicourt wrote of the Templars in connection with the French Revolution and the Enlightenment, but also, in order to avenge themselves against Philip the Fair, the Templars were devoted to 'uncovering the secrets of nature, transmuting metals and finding the universal agent ...'[56]

Within the Masonic tradition, and 'On the margins of the orthodoxy of the churches and secular history, the Templar legend has created a place where the most diverse speculations can find a home. The same causes produce the same effects: for three centuries, be it in literature or in esoteric movements, the Templars hide in the folds of their cloaks the quest of men who, today just as before, find themselves strangers in a world become too secular.'[57]

Frater Shiva X° of the Australian OTO has lectured about the Templar archetype, its relationship to Freemasonry, and its transmission to initiates of the OTO.[58] Regardless of the real

---

cially in regards the delivery of scientific information about alchemical operations...His organisation acted as a big clearing house for information about alchemical research..." (Partner, *The Murdered Magicians: The Templars and Their Myth*, 118.)

55 Bogdan and Snoek, *Handbook of Freemasonry*, 93.

56 Bogdan and Snoek, 96.

57 Bogdan and Snoek, 96.

58 'They are described as a mighty guard [Liber 418, 11th Aethry], the legions of eternal vigilance, the armies of Light – the new LVX – set against the outermost Abyss, set against the terror of things, set against the horror of emptiness and the demon of dispersion, keeping watch and ward throughout

historical facts, this archetype is embedded in the psyche of the Western world. Both the image of the Templars and Baphomet (in various forms) still play out in our culture. It should be noted that the connection between warriors and a religious or spiritual dimension is certainly not isolated to the Western world. This is perhaps explained by a warrior's proximity to death, and the need for philosophical and religious structures to assist them to cope with the psychological stress this creates.

For initiates of both the OTO and the A∴A∴, the mysteries of Baphomet and the mysteries of the Templars are our mysteries, which many claim to understand without having committed to the life of service that truly illuminates them (i.e. it is service that connects us to that which is external to us, it is what we give out as an expression of our Light). These mysteries have flowed to us from various streams, with Freemasonry being one of their central catchments. These mysteries not only show us how to transform ourselves, our consciousness, but also transform the world in which we find ourselves. 'For, in True Things, all are but images one of another; man is but a map of the universe, and Society is but the same on a larger scale.'[59] However, in order to be able to transform those things external to ourselves, we must have first undertaken our own internal transformation. We must have reconciled the contradictions within ourselves and forged a link between the highest

---

the aeons. There in purple flashes of lightning has the Secret Master written the word Eternity, the path of the Templars. It is there that you might look to find the mystical or spiritual impulse behind the battle against superstition, tyranny and oppression which every OTO member swears to uphold. Here again we see Templars protecting pilgrims, throughout the flights of the Bennu Bird.' (Shiva X°, 'Aspiring to the Holy Order'.)

59 Crowley, 'Liber CXCIV, An Intimation with Reference to the Constitution of the Order', 173.

and the lowest. We must have achieved Baphomet consciousness and become true Templars.

> [I]t is the true Nature of Man to dwell upon the Earth, so that
> his Flights are oft but Phantasy; yea, the Eagle also is bound
> to his Eyrie, nor feedeth upon Air. Therefore, this goat, mak-
> ing each leap with Fervour, yet all Times secure in his own
> Element,[60] is a true Hieroglyph of the Magician.[61]

As highlighted by Peter Partner, '[s]ince the occult world
is a continuum which in many ways defies time and space, the
Templars are not in this view mere carrion for university pro-
fessors to feed on, but a living tradition of hidden knowledge
that may be shared by the elect. And, since the concealment
of his great wealth is one of the typical acts of the worldly
magician, the Templars may ...have scattered great deposits of
riches which those who can decipher their mysteries may recov-
er.'[62] Freemasonry became one vehicle for the transmission of
the Templars and their idol over time; an ark to carry mysteries
that can be found by those who have eyes to see.

---

60   In describing the Path of Ayin, Crowley also writes that 'Mark also, this
Path sheweth One continuous in Exaltation upon a Throne, and so is it the
Formula of the Man...' (Crowley, *Liber Aleph Vel CXI: The Book of Wisdom
or Folly*, 174.) A Throne being the seat of a King, and here we could read this
as the earth itself.

61   Crowley, 174.

62   Partner, *The Murdered Magicians: The Templars and Their Myth*, xvii.

Mosaic Cornice Freemasons United Grand Lodge of England

Mohammad and the Kaaba

Through the midnight thou art dropt, O my child, my conqueror, my sword-girt captain, O Hoor! and they shall find
thee as a black gnarl'd glittering stone, and they shall
worship thee.

Liber LXV, V:6

One of the first historical references to Baphomet is from 1195 in a poem titled '*Senhors, per los nostres peccatz*'; a crusaders song written by Gavaudan (1195-1215) who was a soldier and troubadour:

> *Profeta sera.n Gavaudas*
> *Gavaudan shall be a prophet*
> *qu'el dig er faitz, e mortz als cas!*
> for his words shall become a fact. Death to those dogs!
> *e Dieus er honratz e servitz*
> God shall be honoured and worshipped
> **on Bafometz era grazitz.**
> where Mahomet is now served.[1]

As can be seen in the translation Baphomet (*Bafometz*) is likely a corruption of Mahomet or Mohamed, the founder and prophet of Islam (and Saint in the *Ecclesia Gnostica Catholica*), who was known to meditate for weeks at a time in a cave on *Jabal an-Nour* ("The Mountain of Light or Enlightenment"),

---

1   Kastner, 'Gavaudan's Crusade Song. (Bartsch, Grundriss, 174, 10)'.

and it was here that he was said to have been visited by the Angel Gabriel and received his first revelation.

Although false charges were brought against other enemies of King Philip, Baphomet seems to have been unique to the Templars. Some modern scholars propose that the name Baphomet is indeed an Old French corruption of Muhammad, and that the charges against the Templars stem from the integration of some Islamic elements into their beliefs due to their time spent in the Holy Land (which to me seems, to an extent, unavoidable).

A Provençal Templar, Ricaut Bonomel, was also recorded to have stated, 'In truth, anyone who has eyes to see realises that God upholds them [the Infidels]. For God, who should be waking, is sleeping, and Baphomet [Mahomet] uses all his power for the benefit of the Melicadeser [Balibars].'[2]

In six of the testimonies given by the Templars an association was made between the idol and Islamic portraits. The head was called *Magometum* (or *baffometum*), *Maguineth* and *Mandaguorra*. The idol was also said to have been made *in figura baffometi*, and addressed by the word "*Yalla*" (possibly a rendering of *Allah*).

During one of the inquests held in Tuscia it was stated that, 'there had been a real theological discussion to deny the dogmas of Christianity, and the idol, a figure of Allah, as the centre of this debate: he said that brother Alberto made him deny Christ and told him that he should not believe in him. "And in whom should I believe then?".... "In that great and single God that the Saracens worship."'[3] Another interesting claim was 'this supposed *Machomet* had horns!'[4] This horned iconogra-

---

2   Demurger, *The Last Templar*, 36.

3   Frale, *The Templars and the Shroud of Christ*, 70.

4   Frale, 72.

phy does correspond to some representations of Moses that will be looked at later, but unlikely to reflect any real influence of Islam on the Templars.[5] The idea that the image worshipped by the Templars is an image of Mohammed becomes more unlikely if we consider that Islam forbids images of the Prophet. The only images of the Prophet show just the body with the face concealed by holy fire. The Koran also forbids representations of God.

* * *

In Islamic tradition the stone placed at the Kaaba by the Prophet dates back to the time of Adam and Eve, and is said to have fallen from "*Jannah*"[6] to show Adam and Eve where to build an altar (the first temple on Earth), becoming a link between heaven and earth.[7] In another tradition it is said that the stone is an Angel who had previously been placed by God in the Garden of Eden to protect Adam. This angel was punished for being absent when the forbidden fruit was eaten and was turned into the black stone. Its black colour[8] is said to represent the extinction of the ego needed to progress towards God. The stone has been worn smooth by the generations of Muslim

---

5   It is also interesting that Pope Innocent the III considered the Prophet Muhammad to be the beast of the Apocalypse, 'whose number is concluded in 666.' (Partner, *The Murdered Magicians: The Templars and Their Myth*, 18.)

6   جنة - "Literally a garden" (Paradise)

7   Author and commenter Karen Armstrong (who describes religion as "ethical alchemy") writes that 'the Kaaba indicated a location where the sacred world intersected with the profane. The Black Stone is a symbol of this as a link between heaven and earth.' (Armstrong, *Jerusalem: One City, Three Faiths*, 221.)

8   '...hence blackness is also attributed to the sun, according to a certain long-hidden tradition. One of the shocks for candidates in the "Mysteries" was the revelation "Osiris is a *black* god".' (*Crowley, The Book of Thoth*, 118.)

pilgrims, who have touched it for the expiation of their Sins. However, the Kaaba and the black stone predates Islam, and was once a pilgrimage site for the Nabateans.[9]

Similar temples and acts of worship can be seen at other Nabatean sites such as Petra in Jordan. Semitic cultures in the Middle East were known to use unusual stones to indicate religious sites or sites of worship.

An illustration from 1315 from the Jami al-Tawarikh

In the above image the Prophet can be seen lifting the black stone (الأسود) into its position in the *Kaaba* based on *Ibn Ishaq's*

---

9   '**Nabataean**, member of a people of ancient Arabia whose settlements lay in the borderlands between Syria and Arabia, from the Euphrates River to the Red Sea.' ('Nabataean | Arabian, Petra & Trade | Britannica'.)

Sirah Rasul Allah ("The Life of Muhammad").[10] Two men lift the black curtain to reveal the door to the sanctuary. It shows the elders of the clans holding the corners of a cloth in which the stone was placed at Mohammad's request. Here we may see disordered elements (the clan elders who could not decide who should place the stone back in the rebuilt Kaaba) joined by a unifying influence (spirit) represented both by the black stone and the Prophet. Herein is also the element of chance (or perhaps some would argue fate), as the elders decided to wait for the first person to walk through the gate and ask that person to make the decision for them. This may represent Muhammad's role—and that of Islam's—in uniting warring clans and forging a cohesive society from a fragmented tribal one.

A symbolic connection between the sacredness of stones, Mohammad's Kaaba and Baphomet is seen in Lévi's glyph. Baphomet is seated on the cubic stone. Although the black stone itself is not cubical, the Kaaba, in which the stone is kept, is cubical in shape and the word Kaaba means cube in Arabic (أَلْكُعْبَة).

In Islamic tradition it is believed that the Kaaba was built by Abraham (Ibrahim) and his son. Some authors also posit that prior to Islam the Kaaba was the site of fertility rites, and that the word Kaaba is derived from the old Semitic KBA, which referred to the female genitals.[11] Alfred Guillaume (1888–1965), makes a claim that the Kaaba might have been referred to in the feminine form, with circumambulation performed naked by men and almost naked women.[12]

---

10 Ishaq, *The Life of Muhammad*, 84–87.

11 Zalewski, *The Crucible of Religion*, 269.

12 Ishaq, *The Life of Muhammad*, 88–89.

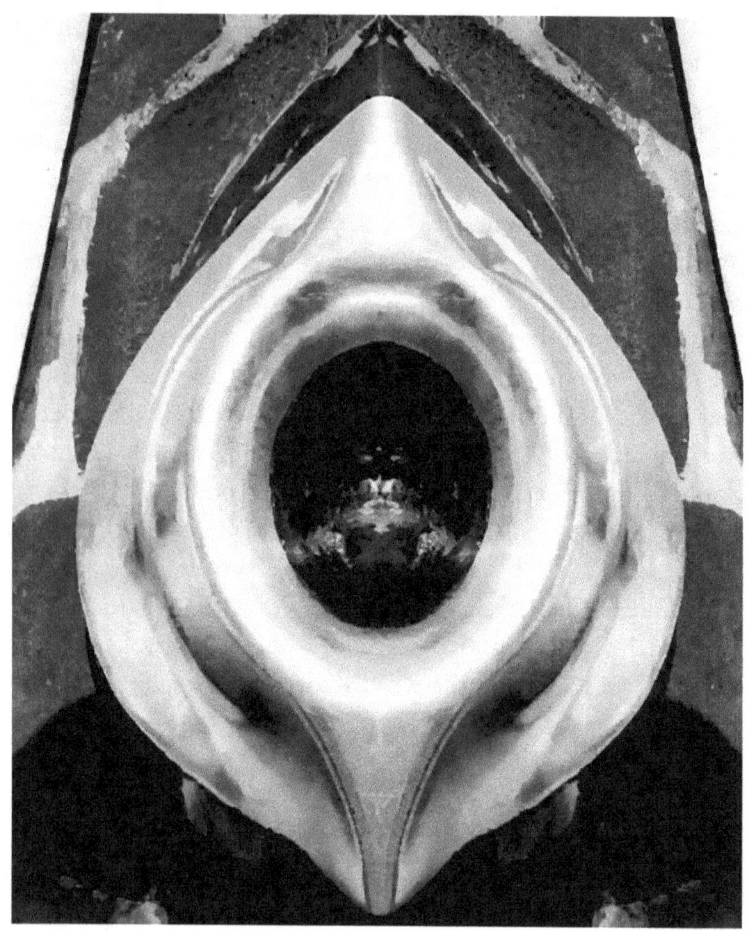

The Black Stone (الحجر الأسود)

The Kaaba was also associated with the pre-Islamic deity Hubal, before which arrows were tossed as a form of divination in cases of death, virginity and marriage. Little is clearly known about Hubal, but he has been associated with the Moon, and was possibly a warrior god and a god of rain.

The position of the Kaaba also means that, at the midpoint of the day just before and after the Northern Hemisphere summer solstice, the cube casts no shadow. When the Sun is either in the East or West, it casts a shadow, but when these two meet, when there is a marriage between them at 'the point of the day at which the sun is at the zenith of Heaven directly overhead—there are no shadows, just pure light.'[13] When the lands of death and rebirth are reconciled we can see clearly. Our consciousness is illuminated. Tom Bree describes this wedding of East and West, this moment of harmony and balance as the "coronation" of the Sun[14] – 'in union their conjoined light shines vertically downwards from Heaven to earth.'[15]

Consider also one of Crowley's instructions on Baphomet, 'Now the Path of Ayin is a Link between Mercury and the Sun, and in the Zodiac importeth a Goat. This Goat is called also Strength, and standeth in the Meridian at the Sunrise of Spring, and it is his Nature to leap upon the Mountains.'[16] A meridian (from the Latin *meridies*) means "midday". At solar noon (midway between sunrise and sunset) the sub-solar point passes through the meridian. The sub-solar point is where the Sun is perceived to be directly overhead. Additionally in John St. John Crowley writes, 'Abide in the meditation; unite all thy symbols into the form of a Lion, and be lord of thy jungle, travelling through the servile Universe even as Mau the Lion[17] very lordly,

---

13 Bree, 'Symbolism as Marriage and the Symbolism of Marriage', 136.

14 'This repeats the doctrine of the danger of Binah. The attack on Tiphareth is to be regarded as a reference to the "Fall," death of Hiram at high noon, etc, etc.' (Crowley, *Tao Te King*, 55.)

15 Bree, 'Symbolism as Marriage and the Symbolism of Marriage', 136.

16 Crowley, *Liber Aleph Vel CXI: The Book of Wisdom or Folly*, 174.

17 The sign of Leo, the Lion, is ruled by the Sun. 'Those who have this sign rising at birth will come under the dominion of the fiery, fixed, executive and magnetic sign Leo, symbolised by the Lion, which is ruled by the Sun, the "giver of life". As the Sun is the centre and archetype of his entire system, the native of Leo is the most complete and balanced representative of humanity.'

the Sun in His strength that travelleth over the heaven of Nu in His bark in the mid-career of Day.'[18]

Campbell also writes of the Sun, '…for the sun, as Ramakrishna has told, is of consciousness absolute and eternal, disengaging from space-time and temporal life. It is a blaze of sheer spirit, whose full force is more than corporal life can stand.'[19]

The pre-Islamic Kaaba also has one of its sides oriented towards the sunrise on the summer-solstice. The word solstice means "the sun standing still". The sun in stillness, crowning from above, and casting no shadows, which shows that nothing is veiled, or hidden from its light.[20] This is a moment 'of complete revelation where the heavenly face gazes downwards at a fully illuminated and unveiled earthly face "and it is light upon light."'[21] In a similar vein Crowley writes in relation to one of the verses in *The Book of the Law* that refers to the concept of Kingship, 'We must abolish the shadows by the Radiant Light

---

(Crowley and Adams, *The General Principles of Astrology*, 86.)

18   Crowley, *Aleister Crowley and the Practice of the Magical Diary*, 20.

19   Campbell, *The Inner Reaches of Outer Space*, 72.

20   This seems in alignment with Crowley's statement in a diary entry from 1926 where he writes. 'It's in this sense that I have succeeded in my life's work, that at last I am received among the Brethren of the Star, the Star which the ignorant call Silver, the learned call still or shining. I never heard that calling a star names interfered with it. (Laugh). I have attained my life's asymptote, & instead of falling into the sere & yellow, I am going to shine & in order to get the strength for shining, I'm going through the Hell I've been through…' (Crowley, *The Magical Diaries of Aleister Crowley: Tunisia 1923*, 54.) The term "sere & yellow" are colours associated with an autumn leaf, and therefore a person near the end of life. 'I have liv'd long enough: my way of life Is fall'n into the sear, the yellow leaf;" (Shakespeare, 'Macbeth – Entire Play | Folger Shakespeare Library'.)

21   Bree, 'Symbolism as Marriage and the Symbolism of Marriage', 136.

of the Sun. Real things are only thrown into brighter glory by His effulgence.'[22]

This symbolism has its reflection in the Christian marriage ceremony we are familiar with in the West. The veiled bride appears at the West of the Church – a veiled light. She moves Eastwards towards the groom, who stands still at his station at the altar.

These glories are a mirror shining through a veil;
If the mirror were unveiled, how would it be?

Rumi[23]

St. Paul writes in 1 Corinthian 13:12, 'Now we see but a poor reflection as in a mirror;[24] then we shall see face to face. Now I know in part; then I shall know fully even as I am known'. There is a similar concept taught in Sufism regarding "reflecting like a mirror", 'The mystic, empty of self, then has the capacity to reflect the Divine to the Divine. The mystic has been unveiled so that light comes to reflect light...'[25] By becoming a polished mirror, the divine light is reflected. This is somewhat inverted in the solar-centric consciousness of the Thelemite, who instead radiates their own inner light, which is then reflected back, like a mirror, but still 'light comes to reflect light'.

---

22 Crowley, *The Law Is for All*, 132.

23 Bree, 'Symbolism as Marriage and the Symbolism of Marriage', 135.

24 Sometimes translated as "a glass".

25 Bree, 'Symbolism as Marriage and the Symbolism of Marriage', 134.

Now let us consider what has happened. In order to get this mental picture of the ever-shining Sun, what did you do? You identified yourself with the Sun. You stepped out of the consciousness of this planet; and for a moment you had to consider yourself as a Solar Being.[26]

In relation to veils, Crowley writes, 'The uninitiate is a "Dark Star," and the Great Work for him is to make his veils transparent by "purifying" them. This "purification" is really "simplification"; it is not that the veil is dirty, but that the complexity of its folds makes it opaque. The Great Work therefore consists principally in the solution of complexes. Everything in itself is perfect, but when things are muddled, they become "evil." ...The Doctrine is evidently of supreme importance, from its position as the first "revelation" of Aiwass.'[27]

In Christianity, with the Church as "The Bride of Christ" (a holdover from the concept of Israel being the "Bride of God"), the final wedding, the final union between the human and the divine will take place at the end of time. At the end of time Revelation describes the Heavenly Jerusalem,[28] a cube like the Kaaba, is dressed 'as a bride adorned for her husband' (Revelation 21:2). The cube can be seen as the end of a cycle that began with the sphere, the two seen as opposites. The circle and the cube also have an inverse relationship:

If a sphere is cut along three of its circular planes or more spe-

---

26   Achad, 'Stepping Out of the Old Aeon and Into the New'.

27   Crowley, *The Law Is for All*, 32.

28   The concept of the Heavenly Jerusalem has its origins in Judaism, most likely due to the trauma following the destruction of the Temple by the Romans in 70 C.E. Influenced by Plato and the idea that all "real" objects exist in an ideal metaphysical form, it would not have been far to move to the idea that the Temple that was destroyed still existed in an ideal form in heaven.

cifically the three circular planes whose intersections mark the axial coordinates of three dimensional space (length, breadth and depth), we end up with eight identical sections of sphere. If each of these sections is then inverted, effectively turning the sphere inside out, we end up with a cube.[29]

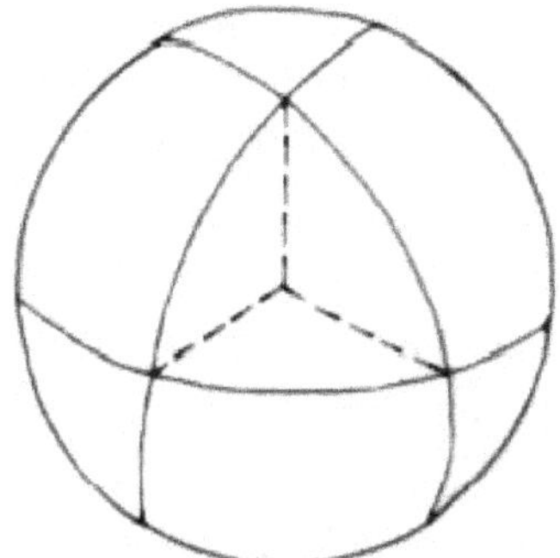 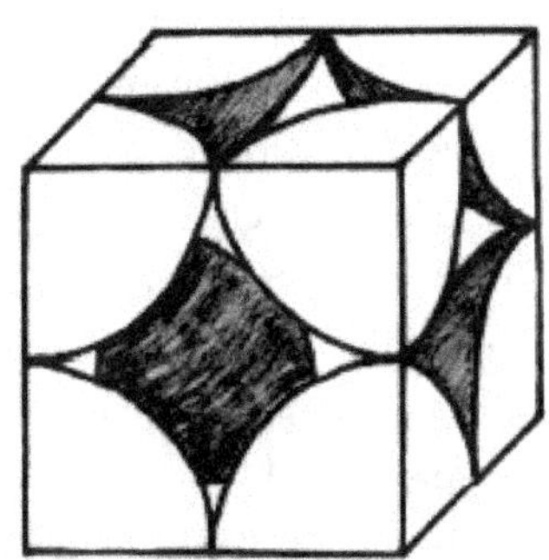

The Circle Squared

The circle in divided into 8[30] and the eight corners, now externalised in the form of the cube, were concealed in the central point[31] of the circle. The "New Jerusalem"; a time in which

---

29 Bree, 'Symbolism as Marriage and the Symbolism of Marriage', 132.

30 Of the number 8, Edinger writes, 'The ascending soul had to ascend the seven steps of the planetary ladder in order to reach the eighth step – which was the sphere of the fixed stars and, therefore, the eternal.' (Edinger, *Archetype of the Apocalypse*, 57.). Similarly, in relation to the 4, which we can associate with the cube, '..."four" is the number of wholeness beyond space and time (which are, by the way, categories of consciousness) and thus tends to represent "Eternity." (Edinger, 58.) Eternity is perhaps seen here in connection to 'the sun standing still'. This is the still sun, the consciousness of the aspirant experiencing eternity as '*a permanent now*', as described by Thomas Hobbes (1588-1679) (Melamed, 'Eternity in Early Modern Philosophy', 129.)

31 'One of his greatest strokes of genius was expanding the notion of the

the internal has become external – the bride is dressed for the bridegroom.

Nu! the hiding of Hadit

Liber AL II:1

This relation between the circle and the square could be seen as a relationship between Nu and Hadit[32] – 'It is the "veils" mentioned previously in this comment that obstruct the relation between Nuit and Hadit.'[33] In this same section Crowley writes further about Light, the "Inmost Light" and the "Light of Infinite Space" – 'the Light of Space is what men call Darkness; its nature is utterly incomprehensible to our un-initiated minds.'[34]

Bree writes that 'This inverse relationship has, as its inter-mediary, the very coordinates of three dimensional space itself, which is sometimes referred to as the "six armed three dimen-sional cross."'[35] The Calvary Cross being one of the symbols of Tiphareth (as is the cube itself – the cross hidden within the form of the cube), acting as an intermediary between the state that is represented by the circle, and the state that is represented by the cube. The concept of the Sun rising in the West is found

---

point. Beneath his gaze, the humble dot was no longer a dimensionless posi-tion; it swelled with a complex inner structure. Where others had seen a sim-ple locus without depth, size or breath, Grothendieck saw an entire universe.' (Labatut, *When We Cease to Understand the World*, 67.)

32 Noting the difference between Nuit, and Nu as explained by Gunther, Nu represents the personal, whereas Nuit represents the collective.

33 Crowley, *The Law Is for All*, 33.

34 Crowley, 33.

35 Bree, 'Symbolism as Marriage and the Symbolism of Marriage', 133.

within Islam and is connected with the end of time – everything has become inverted; the Sun rises in the West.

> In Her blood I inscribed the secret riddles of the Sphinx of the Gods, that none shall understand, - save only the pure and voluptuous, the chaste and obscene, the androgyne and the gynander that have passed beyond the bars of the prison that the old Slime of Khem set up in the Gates of Amennti.
>
> *Liber LXV, V:44*[36]

This must have seemed like somewhat of an excursion away from the Kaaba, but here we can see that the Kaaba, with its form as a cube,[37] and the proposed connection between the stone and the female genitals, which in itself could be seen as a form of the circle or intersecting circles. These two symbols form two of the elements of the throne of Baphomet, the foundation of the glyph (the other a "triangular stool").[38] Additionally, its connection to the solstice, and the Sun at its zenith as a symbol of consciousness in balance, harmony, and stillness – illuminated. Opposites have been reconciled in a sacred marriage, and the circle squared – we are unveiled and able to see, unobstructed, the Radiance of the Sun. Here we see a representation of the Baphomet consciousness. The contending of opposites reconciled into a state of harmony. It is in this state, a state of purity, where our complexes are purified and simplified, that we may radiate our true creative energy, unhindered; the creative light of the Sun.

---

36 Crowley, *The Holy Books of Thelema*, 80.

37 Noting the Crowley considered the cube a phallic and solar symbol. 'It is thus like the Sun in the Zodiac, which is no more than the field for His fulfilment in His going.' (Crowley, *The Law Is for All*, 93.)

38 'The Triangle and the Square is also the Key to "Squaring the Circle…' (Gunther, *Initiation In the Aeon of the Child*, 83.)

"Muhammad at the Ka'ba" from the Siyer-i Nebi., c. 1595.

Gone are the four arms of the Cross limited by law; the creative energy of the Cross expands freely; its rays pierce in every direction the body of Our Lady of the Stars.[39]

---

39 Crowley, *The Book of Thoth*, 114.

ÉLIPHAS LÉVI

There is only one dogma in magic, and it is this: the visible is the manifestation of the invisible, or, in other terms, the perfect Logos bears in things which are appreciable to our senses and invisible to our eyes. The Magus raises one hand to heaven and points the other to earth, and he says:-"Above immensity! below, immensity also! Immensity is equivalent to immensity." This is true in the order both of the seen and the unseen.[1]

Alphonse Louis Constant (1810–1875), better known as Éliphas Lévi or Éliphas Lévi Zahed, 'is known today as the founder of occultism',[2] or in the words of Hymenaeus Beta, he 'was probably the first truly modern writer on magick'.[3] Lévi would heavily influence the likes of Helena Blavatsky (1831–1891)[4] and Aleister Crowley (1875–1947), and therefore, it could be argued, most (if not all) magic writing and practice that has followed.

---

1   Lévi, *The Mysteries of Magic: A Digest of the Writings of Eliphas Lévi*, 61.

2   Strube, 'Socialist Religion and the Emergence of Occultism: A Genealogical Approach to Socialism and Secularization in 19th-Century France', 371.

3   Crowley, Desti, and Waddell, *Magick. Liber ABA. Book Four. Parts I-IV*, xliv.

4   It should be noted that, despite his great influence on her, Blavatsky later turned on Lévi when there became a split between "Eastern occultism" (Theosophical Society) and the "Western Kabbalists", which she saw as inferior (or at least stated so publicly, possibly for political reasons).

He was the son of a Paris shoemaker ('apparently of meagre circumstances'[5] according to A.E Waite (1857–1942)) and entered the Saint-Sulpice seminary in 1832. He was eventually ordained a deacon, but left the seminary in 1836, supposedly a week before his ordination as a priest. A hint of the reasons for his departure can be read in the A.E. Waite translation of *Dogme et ritual de la Haute Magie*, titled *Transcendental Magic*:

> The existing accounts of his expulsion are hazy, and incorporate unlikely elements, as, for example, that he was sent by his ecclesiastical superiors to take duty in country places, where he preached with great eloquence what, however, was doctrinally unsound.[6]

Lévi was 'delicate in his childhood, and received no regular education, but his aptitude for learning and his avidity for picking up stray bits of knowledge were so great that at last the neighbours used to talk of him as "the clever lad."'[7]

He was described as 'a first-rate Hebrew scholar', but Waite includes a footnote to this claim stating that, 'his [Lévi's] published writings do not exhibit a profound acquaintance with later Jewish literature.'[8] Strube, however, states that, 'His [Lévi's] own concept of Kabbalah, however, was as exceptional as it was fascinating because of its Neo-Catholic background. For Constant, "Kabbalah" meant nothing else but *tradition*, and for him, the one and only true tradition had always been

---

5   Lévi, *The Mysteries of Magic: A Digest of the Writings of Eliphas Lévi*, 1.

6   Lévi, *Transcendental Magic*, xix.

7   Lévi, *The Mysteries of Magic: A Digest of the Writings of Eliphas Lévi*, 2.

8   Lévi, 2.

Catholicism.[9] Lévi's Catholicism has caused a level of confusion for people who have engaged with his work. Although Lévi may have walked away from his engagement with the Catholic Church as an institution, he never walked away from his Catholicism. While Lévi and his contemporaries acknowledged a "universal revelation"[10] in all religions, 'only Catholicism was, thanks to the revelation of Christ, the heir of the pure and eternally true divine revelation.'[11] Additionally, this was 'guided by the idea of vast lines of transmission of a presupposed tradition of absolute truth.'[12] These lines of transmission are found across countries, cultures, and religions throughout history.

As highlighted by McIntosh, Lévi is far from an easy writer to understand, and trying to find coherence in his books and teachings 'is like trying to fit together a puzzle whose pieces are constantly changing shape and colour.'[13] This evolved over time (not helped by a lack of proofing), and Lévi may not have ever found complete coherence in his writings, but did find 'a method and a point of view.'[14] It is these that we are attempting to uncover – the consistent threads within the jungle of his writing.

It should also be noted that, aside from his religious vocation and his writing, Lévi was an artist—a painter and illustrator. At times when he was unable to earn a living from writing,

---

9   Strube, 'Socialist Religion and the Emergence of Occultism: A Genealogical Approach to Socialism and Secularization in 19th-Century France', 376.

10   Often referring to the '*révélation primitive*'

11   Strube, 'Socialist Religion and the Emergence of Occultism: A Genealogical Approach to Socialism and Secularization in 19th-Century France', 377.

12   Winter, 'Looking out for Magic in Ancient China: The Yijing, Its Trigrams and the Figurist Tradition in Eliphas Levi', 38.

13   McIntosh, *Eliphas Levi and the French Occult Revival*, 141.

14   McIntosh, 142.

he worked as an artist, producing works such as paintings for the Church in Choisy-le-Roi.[15] It is thanks to his gifts as an artist that he was able to convey his teachings in symbols (such as Baphomet) as well as words.

More than just an occultist and artist, Lévi was also a political animal, and we cannot separate this aspect of Lévi from his occultism. In the 1840s 'he was known as one of the most notorious socialist radicals'[16] and railed against the French principles of Liberty, Equality and Fraternity, which he called 'a triple Lie' and 'full of shadow.'[17] Lévi was even imprisoned for his political convictions (in 1841 and 1847).[18] Despite his transformation into the occultist known today, 'both socialism and Catholicism remained the main pillars of his self-understanding...'[19]

An indication of the form of liberty acceptable to Levi can be found in his *The Key of the Mysteries*:

Q. What is liberty?'
A. The right to do one's duty, with the possibility of not doing it.[20]

Lévi claimed to represent a form of "true" Catholicism, in opposition to what he saw as the corruption of the estab-

---

15   McIntosh, 88.

16   Strube, 'The "Baphomet" of Eliphas Lévi: Its Meaning and Historical Context', 40.

17   Churton, *Occult Paris*, 89.

18   Winter, 'Looking out for Magic in Ancient China: The Yijing, Its Trigrams and the Figurist Tradition in Eliphas Levi', 37.

19   Winter, 37.

20   Levi, 'The Key of the Mysteries', 104.

lished Churches.[21] This he 'vehemently identified with "true" socialism.'[22] Lévi needs to be understood not just in terms of a continuation of traditions of occult teaching and practice (real or otherwise), but also the social and political context in which he lived. Lévi 'not only developed his "occultist" ideas in a socialist context, but[...]his "occultism" was directly derived from his socialist and Neo-Catholic ideas.'[23] It is also interesting to note that the discourse around socialism in France in the 1830s and early 1850 saw 'the socialists as the heirs of a heretical tradition that included the theosophists of the eighteenth century, medieval groups such as the Templars and the Cathars, and eventually the very same protagonists of the School of Alexandria, most notably the Gnostics.'[24] Strube also argues that there has been a general focus on Marxism in the study of the historical process of secularisation, and that, 'Even scholars without a Marxist background tend to perceive the history of socialism through the lens of such narratives and dismiss the central role that "religion" played in socialist theories prior to Marxism...A wide variety of recent scholarship has convincingly illustrated that "religion" was not only intrinsic to the vast majority of socialist theories, but that it lay at their

---

21   'Constant had explained that the "Catholic authority and hierarchy" was necessary before everybody would eventually become a priest and the *association universelle* would be realized.' (Strube, 'Socialist Religion and the Emergence of Occultism: A Genealogical Approach to Socialism and Secularization in 19th-Century France', 378.)

22   Strube, 'The "Baphomet" of Eliphas Lévi: Its Meaning and Historical Context', 40.

23   Strube, 'Socialist Religion and the Emergence of Occultism: A Genealogical Approach to Socialism and Secularization in 19th-Century France', 373.

24   Strube, 'The "Baphomet" of Eliphas Lévi: Its Meaning and Historical Context', 57.

very core.'[25] Until the emergence of Marxism, socialist theories were rooted in religion, and religion was seen as the foundation stone of a well-functioning society. For Lévi, the predominance of the Marxist form of socialism, stripped of religion, would have been an anathema.

Just as Lévi's writings need to also be considered in a political context, equally 'His Baphomet has to be seen as an iconic representation of this "true" doctrine, as the Knights Templar were considered to be the successors of the very same heretical revolutionary tradition that reached back to the "Gnostics" of the late ancient School of Alexandria, the environment where the momentous separation between "true" and "false" religion supposedly took place. In this light, the Baphomet is not only a magnetistic symbol representing Lévi's theory of magic, but first and foremost an embodiment of the one and only true tradition whose ultimate goal is the establishment of a perfect social order.'[26]

Again, it could be seen that this vision of a "perfect social order" also took root in the mind of Crowley, and his reformulation and reconstitution of the OTO.

> Thus we balance the Triads, uniting Three in One; thus we gather up the threads of human passion and interest, and weave them into an harmonious tapestry...[27]

Lévi also emphasized that the true meaning of the Temple was 'a social utopia and a symbol for the perfect government,

---

25   Strube, 'Socialist Religion and the Emergence of Occultism: A Genealogical Approach to Socialism and Secularization in 19th-Century France', 360.

26   Strube, 'The "Baphomet" of Eliphas Lévi: Its Meaning and Historical Context', 40.

27   Crowley, 'Liber CXCIV, An Intimation with Reference to the Constitution of the Order'.

based on an egalitarian hierarchy of intelligence and merit.'[28] This concept of a 'hierarchy of intelligence and merit', as opposed to a hierarchy based on inheritance or hereditary claim, I would argue is a key principle that would also later inform the thought of Crowley and his vision of the Order of the Temple, and its governance structure.

There is also something prophetic and resonant with Thelema in the writing of Lévi when he states, 'The ecclesiastical hierarchy is only temporary and must end when the time of the virility of humanity has come, the age of force and reason" which will bring "the second coming of Christ'.[29] One must not assume, however, that Lévi and the other socialists, grounded in a religious or occult paradigm, were passively waiting for the Second Coming, but 'envisioned the creation of the Kingdom of God on Earth and rejected the passive expectation of a transcendent ideal state.'[30]

Tobias Churton proposes that, 'Lévi's essential contribution to Occult Paris of the late nineteenth and early twentieth centuries was in effect to redefine Magic as an "occult science" enabling a process of transcendental self-perfecting, a means to connect oneself to a deeper, invisible universe by progressive initiation through symbols and signs.'[31] This work influenced and was continued in the writings and teachings of Crowley, with the primary vehicles being the A∴A∴ and the OTO. Further, 'Lévi's *Baphomet* design encapsulated this in a manner both risqué and fashionably provocative.'[32] It is the "risqué"

---

28 Strube, 'The "Baphomet" of Eliphas Lévi: Its Meaning and Historical Context', 47.

29 Strube, 47.

30 Strube, 'Socialist Religion and the Emergence of Occultism: A Genealogical Approach to Socialism and Secularization in 19th-Century France', 381.

31 Churton, *Occult Paris*, 97.

32 Churton, 97.

and provocative nature of Lévi's Baphomet that helped carry it into the current age (perhaps a time when it is needed the most). It is also only in more recent years that there has been more acknowledgement in academia of the influence of *fin-de-siècle* occultism on politics, but also art and science.[33] As stated by Mark Morrison, 'If magic and the occult had been explained in terms of the science of matter and energy, the science of matter and energy was also, during the period from 1895 to 1939, invested with the tropes and concerns of the occult.'[34] A clear (if slightly later) intersection between science and the occult occurred with the formation of the Alchemical Society in 1912, a society which included members from the collapsed Golden Dawn,[35] and took a more open and public approach to the exploration of the alchemical mysteries. 'The material world, in the form of radioactive matter, had decidedly intervened in the theoretical debates of both atomic science and occultism. No scientific theory of matter that could not account for the strange properties of radioactive elements could still be taken as valid. During these early years of the science of radioactivity, theories that seemed to offer insight into radioactive transformation included those of Rutherford, Soddy, Thomson, and Ramsay—but, for some, also included those of Paracelsus, Flamel, Lully, and Vaughan.'[36]

Despite being highly critical of Lévi (to the extent one must

---

33   Strube, 'Occultist Identity Formations Between Theosophy and Socialism in Fin-de-Siècle France', 568.

34   Morrisson, *Modern Alchemy: Occultism and the Emergence of Atomic Theory*, 21.

35   The Hermetic Order of the Golden Dawn, a magical order active in the late 19th and early 20th centuries.

36   Morrisson, *Modern Alchemy: Occultism and the Emergence of Atomic Theory*, 21.

wonder why he spent so much time translating and publishing his works), Waite writes of him that 'No modern expositor of occult claims can bear any comparison with Eliphas Lévi, and among ancient expositors, though many stand higher in authority and are assuredly more sincere, all yield to him in living interest, for he is actually the spirit of modern thought forcing an answer for the times from the old oracles.'[37] Lévi would prove to be an important transitional figure; whole ideas would be matured by Crowley, and further developed by successive generations (and will continue to be developed).

The image of Baphomet most recognized today bears little resemblance to the descriptions given at the Templar trials, but is the image of Baphomet, or 'The Sabbatic Goat', that was produced by Lévi in his *Dogme et Rituel de la Haute Magie*[38] in 1854. Although in the minds of many, this rendering of Baphomet has become associated with "Satanism"[39] and anti-Christian movements, 'it is well known that Eliphas Lévi hardly qualifies as a Satanist, and that the meaning of the drawing, as ghastly as it may appear to the beholder, is neither satanic nor anti-Christian.'[40]

---

37 Lévi, *Transcendental Magic*, xxiii–xxiv.

38 Dogma and Ritual of High Magic, the original English Translation by Waite was titled *"Transcendental Magic: Its Doctrine and Ritual"*.

39 Contemporary Christians who indulge in conspiratorial thinking in relation to religious and other practice outside of their own should remember the accusations levelled at the early Church by the Romans during the Early Empire. Christians were accused of 'Depraved religion – hidden knowledge, exclusiveness of admission, suspicion of monstrous practices...' (Partner, *The Murdered Magicians: The Templars and Their Myth*, 42.). The Christians were believed to 'to practice both ritual murder and cannibalism...' (Cohn, *Europe's Inner Demons*, 8.). Accusations that are, obviously, without foundation.

40 Strube, 'The "Baphomet" of Eliphas Lévi: Its Meaning and Historical Context', 39.

There are many traceable sources that would have had an influence on Lévi, and the themes associated with the "sabbatical goat" were commonplace. Strube, however, puts forward that the primary influence for Baphomet was *"Le Diable"*[41] from the Marseille tarot deck.[42] 'Lévi mentioned the "Italian Tarot," which at the time signified the Tarot of Marseille, as well as the Tarot of Besançon, which was based on the Marseille deck.'[43]

In his writings about Baphomet, Lévi refers to the "magnetistic"[44] elements he was attempting to portray. '*Dogme et rituel* was presented and understood as a magnetistic work, which, however, wanted to distance itself from Mesmerist publications.'[45] Arguing from a historical perspective, Lévi 'dismissed the "Mesmerists" as amateurish dabblers who could only guess what powers they [were] dealing with.'[46] In his *Doctrine of Occult Force* Levi writes, 'This agent, which barely manifests under the uncertainties of the art of Mesmer and his followers, is precisely what the medieval adepts called the first matter of the *magnum opus*. The Gnostics represented it as the burning body of the Holy Ghost, and this it was which was adored in the secret rites of the Sabbath or the Temple under the symbolic figure of Baphomet, or the Androgyne Goat of Mendes.'[47]

---

41   The Devil.

42   Strube, 'The "Baphomet" of Eliphas Lévi: Its Meaning and Historical Context', 41.

43   Strube, 41.

44   Relates to magnetism or animal magnetism, which is described by Levi as 'a force analogous to that of the ordinary magnet, and permeates the whole of nature. Its characteristics are: attraction, repulsion and a balanced polarization...' (Lévi, Eliphas, *The Great Secret or Occultism Unveiled*)

45   Strube, 43.

46   Strube, 43.

47   Lévi, *The Mysteries of Magic: A Digest of the Writings of Eliphas Lévi*, 69.

Churton also writes that the concepts of the "Astral Light"[48] and "Universal Agent"[49] could be traced to Mesmer, and seventeenth-century Rosicrucianism.[50] However, Baphomet for Lévi (and for us) relates to more than just magnetism. Baphomet 'stood for a specific secret tradition that formed the key to the understanding of the true form of religion.'[51] Strube, however, traces Lévi's influence for this principle to '*La magie devoilée* by Jean Du Potet de Sennevoy (1796–1881),[52] which Lévi explicitly named as a source.'[53]

Although in his lifetime Mesmer's theories and practices were rejected by the medical establishments in both Vienna and Paris (and a panel from the Royal Medical Society), it has been noted by Jocelyn Godwin that we now live in a time with more awareness of the psychological impacts Mesmer's treatments may have had on his patients. '[I]f we have this awareness, it is thanks to those who followed in Mesmer's footsteps and developed, in the teeth of the medical establishment, the techniques of hypnosis and the theory of the unconscious mind. No one

---

48   *lumière astrale* (fr)

49   I am also of the opinion that these concepts are alive in the teachings of the OTO and A∴A∴ today. In their most approachable form these principles can be seen in the meditative / magical practice that traces its origins to Jeanne Robert Foster, or Hilarion, called "Living in the Sunlight" (King, *Living in the Sunlight*; Achad, 'Living in the Sunlight'.)

50   Churton, *Occult Paris*, 92.

51   Strube, 'The "Baphomet" of Eliphas Lévi: Its Meaning and Historical Context', 44.

52   Potet described 'Mesmer as a "great Republican"…' (Strube, 'Socialist Religion and the Emergence of Occultism: A Genealogical Approach to Socialism and Secularization in 19th-Century France', 375.)

53   Strube, 'The "Baphomet" of Eliphas Lévi: Its Meaning and Historical Context', 65.

had heard of those in 1784.'[54] We can see, however, that Lévi saw his work and practice diving much deeper than medical cures and sought to differentiate his teachings from those of the mesmerists.

As already highlighted, some of the concepts that Lévi associates with Baphomet are not necessarily original (Lévi was part of an active community and history of ideas). Jean-Marie Ragon de Bettignies (1781–1862)[55] 'did, as a matter of fact, identify the "matter of the alchemists" with, among others, the Goat of Mendes, Pan, Kabbalistic doctrines, and—perhaps most notably—with "magnétisme spécifique."'[56] This equation is very similar to Lévi's description of the Baphomet, and it is likely that this is no coincidence.'[57] But Ragon himself was drawing on existing masonic and anti-masonic sources.

After Lévi's death, no organised movement formed around his teachings. However, some of his former students continued his work until it was later taken up by a new generation of occultists, particularly those associated with Papus.[58] Nevertheless, 'It becomes clear that the memory of Lévi had faded so much by the middle of the 1880s that a "seeker" like Papus had not even been able to learn about his death.'[59] Papus also

---

54   Godwin, *The Theosophical Enlightenment*, 152.

55   Jean-Marie Ragon de Bettignies was a French Freemason, author and editor, and stated to have been, 'the most learned Mason of the nineteenth century.' (Mackey, *Encyclopedia of Freemasonry and Its Kindred Sciences Comprising the Whole Range of Arts, Sciences and Literature as Connected with the Institution*, 713.)

56   Specific magnetism.

57   Strube, 'The "Baphomet" of Eliphas Lévi: Its Meaning and Historical Context', 53.

58   Gérard Anaclet Vincent Encausse (1865–1916). French-Spanish occultist and one of the founders of the Martinist Order.

59   Strube, 'Socialist Religion and the Emergence of Occultism: A Genealog-

believed that Lévi's influence was more on an "artistic" manifestation of occultism, as opposed to the "scientific" one that he seemed to prefer and saw reflected in the writings of people such as Józef Maria Hoëné-Wro ski (1776–1853), even arguably inverting the relationship between Wronski and Lévi.

At the heart of Lévi's teaching was equilibrium. One of his students, a Mrs. Hutchinson, described her experience with him as follows; 'As soon as he saw my enthusiasm for an idea he led me to consider the opposite idea, thus producing equilibrium. Equilibrium was his aim to such a degree that I sometimes revolted against the apparent contradictions. He kept his smiling gravity, making me oscillate between Reason and Faith, knowing well that the seed thus deposited in my mind would bear fruit of its own accord.'[60]

The above resonates with one of the Tasks later codified in the A∴A∴ for the attainment of the Grade of Magister Templi – 'the emancipation from Thought by putting each idea against its opposite, and refusing to prefer either.'[61] Here we can see the continuity between Lévi's teachings and writings, and those that would be developed later within the Great Order, the A∴A∴ and the OTO. Methods of practical occultism and mysticism, but also methods to attain that balanced consciousness, that state of equilibrium and of silence, that is necessary to wield the power that is described by Lévi – the kingly power. Although the above is simple in its conception, in practice it is extremely difficult, and is essentially a work of destruction.[62]

---

ical Approach to Socialism and Secularization in 19th-Century France', 579.

60   McIntosh, *Eliphas Levi and the French Occult Revival*, 132.

61   Crowley et al., *Commentaries of the Holy Books and Other Papers*, 4:14.

62   'We ourselves must pass through this process of being ground down by the Stones of the Gods until we become like unto a very fine powder, until we learn to recognise the One undifferentiated Substance of our being.' (Achad, 'Bread of Stones': Part I'.)

* * *

Having given somewhat of an overview of Eliphas Lévi, we can now move to a deeper exploration of his Baphomet and attempt to turn the key and open the door to the mysteries of this complex and layered glyph (even if just to catch a glimpse into the sanctuary). To properly understand Baphomet, and what Lévi was trying to transmit through the figure, we need to look more broadly at his writing and other "keys" that he left for us. I must note (as already highlighted) that Lévi's ideas are not always easy to decipher. His 'writings poured from his pen in an inspired but often careless flow…'[63] There are also many errors and poor structure, but if you persevere there are common themes that appear throughout Lévi's writing that illuminate the cornerstone of the doctrine he was attempting to transmit.

Lévi wrote about Baphomet outside of the more well-known *Transcendental Magic*. In part three of *The Book of Splendours* he dedicates a section to Baphomet, interestingly called "The Flaming Star". Here he seems to clearly connect Baphomet to the Sphinx: 'Sometimes he is shown with a beard, the horns of a male goat, the face of a man, the breasts of a woman, the mane and claws of a lion, the wings of an eagle and the hooves of a bull.'[64] The creation of Baphomet as a sphinx-like creature is not surprising considering, 'Symbolists were fascinated by the image of the sphinx and depicted her in many ways.'[65] Occultist Victor-Emile Michilet[66] (1861–1938), influenced by Lévi, also clearly describes a connection between Baphomet and the

---

63   McIntosh, *Eliphas Levi and the French Occult Revival*, 9.

64   Levi, *The Book of Splendours*, 118.

65   Churton, *Occult Paris*, 95–96.

66   Michilet was a symbolist poet who was an early member of the Ordre Martiniste.

Sphinx, describing the figure as 'the Kheroub of Assyria and Israel, the Arabic Kharouff, the Egyptian and Greek Sphinx, the pentacle which combines the four animals of the Apocalypse.'[67] Levi further writes of Baphomet, 'He is a hold-over from the Cherubs of the ark and the Holy of holies'.[68]

The two cherubim, according to Philo, represented the two greatest of the heavenly powers. The first was the creative power, which was called God, and the second was the kingly power, which was the Lord. 'The divine presence was discerned between them.' Philo also stated that the name meant, 'recognition and full knowledge.'[69] Christian tradition later built on this and taught that the 'cherubim are those who know God, who are filled with Wisdom and then pour this into others.'[70]

> So he drove out the man; and he placed at the east of the garden of Eden Cherubims, and a flaming sword which turned every way, to keep the way of the tree of life.
>
> *Genesis 3:24*[71]

This trinity, the creative power, the kingly power and the divine presence, are important to understanding Baphomet (or to my way of understanding Baphomet). The creative power is the raw seed that needs the kingly power to rule over it, to intervene in its functioning, to control and provide it with structure. The divine presence is that stillness and silence. That state

---

67 Uzzel, *Eliphas Levi and the Kabbalah: The Masonic and French Connection of the American Mystery Tradition*, 46.

68 Levi, *The Book of Splendours*, 118–19.

69 Barker, *An Extraordinary Gathering of Angels*, 121.

70 Barker, 121.

71 *The KJV Study Bible*, 5. Editorial note, this is the edition that all standard Biblical quotes will come from, unless otherwise footnoted.

of reconciled consciousness – that field of experience outside of space and time that provides the right point of view. This trinity, this "One in Three and Three in One"[72] is the Baphomet consciousness.

Lévi had a somewhat idiosyncratic description of the Ark of the Covenant, teaching that there were four Cherubs, not just two. ' The Cherubin or sphinxes were, in fact, coupled by twos on each side of the ark, and their heads were turned to the four corners of the Mercy Seat, which they covered with their wings inclined archwise, thus overshadowing the crown of the golden table, which they sustained upon their shoulders, facing one another at the openings and looking at the Propitiatory...'[73] The "Propitiatory" is the cover of the Ark, and Lévi further assigns to the Ark, guarded by the Cherubin, the alchemical elements. The coffer is the realm of Mercury or Azoth, the cover the realm of Sulphur, and the base the kingdom of salt.

The Ark of the Covenant from Transcendental Magic

---

72   *Liber XV*; The Gnostic Mass, The Anthem.

73   Lévi, *Transcendental Magic*, 395.

Lévi, in *Transcendental Magic*, assigns Baphomet (Baphomet of the Temple or Prince of the Sabbath) to Sulphur. This is in the chapter titled *The Mastery of the Sun*, where is further explained the 'Living Gold, Living Sulphur or true Fire of the Philosopher.'[74] This, he explains, must be 'sought in the House of Mercury.'[75] The Ark and the Cherubs is used by Lévi as a vehicle to explain an alchemical process – 'All that is material contains Salt, and all Salt can be converted into pure gold by the combined action of Sulphur and Mercury.'[76]

In the above Lévi appears to be referencing Paracelsus:

Q. What other name is also given by the Philosophers to their living gold?
A. They also term it their living sulphur, and their true fire; they recognize its existence in all bodies, and there is nothing that can subsist without it.[77]

This perhaps becomes clearer if we look elsewhere in Paracelsus' catechism:

Q. What, therefore, must actually be accepted as the subject of our matter?
A. The seed alone, otherwise the fixed grain, and not the whole body, which is differentiated into Sulphur, or living male, and into Mercury, or living female.[78]

---

74 Lévi, 357.

75 Lévi, 357.

76 Lévi, 358.

77 Paracelsus, 'Theophrastus Paracelsus: Alchemical Catechism'.

78 Paracelsus.

Here we have the "whole body" which consists of the "living male", which is Sulphur, and the "living female", which is Mercury. The combined action of the living male and female is the action that converts the Salt, all that is material, into gold.

Below is one of Lévi's depictions of the twenty-first key of the Tarot, taken from his work titled *The History of Magic*. Elsewhere, Lévi shows similar depictions of this "Key" under the title "*Le Monde*" – The World.[79] This glyph is described as 'The Seal of Cagliostro, Seal of the Samian Juno, Apocalyptic Seal, Twelve Seals of the Cubic Stone in Masonry, with the Twenty-First Tarot Key in the centre of all.'[80]

---

79   Levi, *The Kabalistic and Occult Tarot of Eliphas Levi: A Study Guide*, 230.

80   Levi, *The History of Magic: Including a Clear and Precise Exposition of Its Procedure, Its Rites and Its Mysteries*, XXXV.

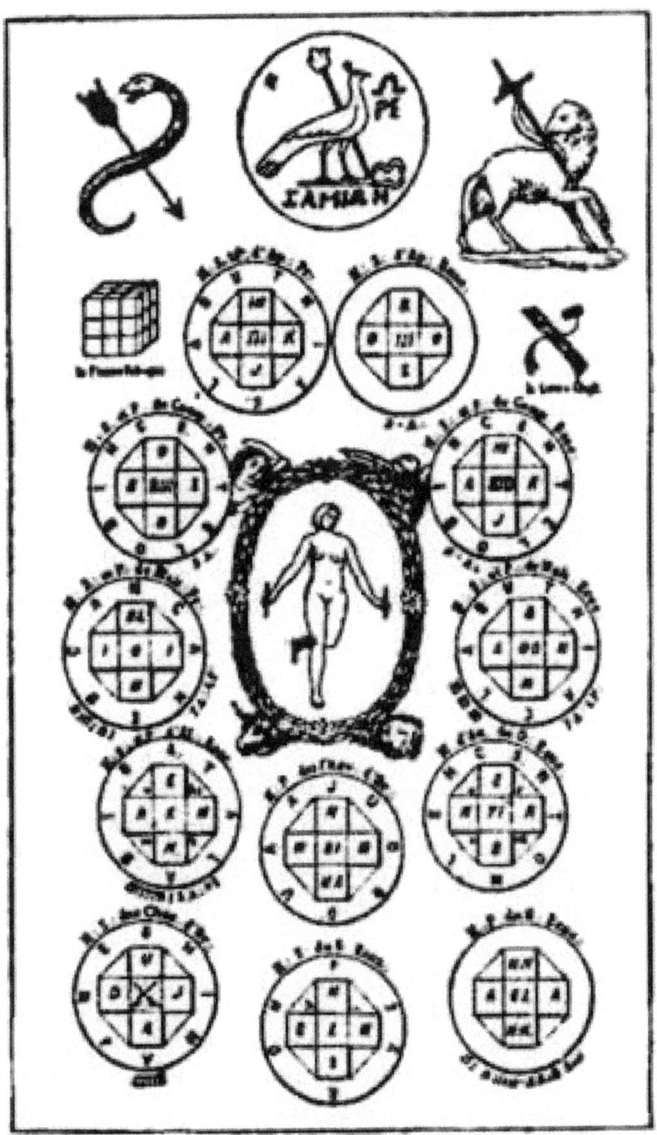

The Twenty-first Key of the Tarot, surrounded by Mystic and Masonic Seals

Lévi saw in the Cherubim and the Ark this twenty-first tarot key, and the Ark as the 'hieroglyphical synthesis of the whole kabbalistic dogma…'[81] and of this "key", that he assigned to the Hebrew letter ת[82], he writes, 'The microcosm, the sum of all in all. Hieroglyph, KETHER, or the Kabalistic Crown, between four mysterious animals. In the middle of the Crown or wreath is Truth holding a rod in each hand.'[83]

So, from the above, we can see that the Ark and the Cherubs (connected by Lévi to Baphomet) were of central importance as a 'synthesis of the whole kabbalistic dogma'. It is of note that in this representation of the symbolism of the Ark of the Covenant we see Truth within a crown holding two rods, and this figure is clearly that of a woman, holding the rods of opposing forces.

Edward Edinger writes regarding the cherubs, that they are

---

81 Lévi, *Transcendental Magic*, 394.

82 We can see a similar representation in Crowley's imagining (via Lady Frieda Harris) of the 21st key (The Universe), representing the end, as The Fool is the beginning. In her hands instead of two rods, 'she manipulates the radiant spiral force, the active and the passive, each possessing its dual polarity… The Universe, so states the theme, is the Celebration of the Great Work accomplished.' (Crowley, *The Book of Thoth*, 118–19.), remembering that Lévi connected this accomplishment with Baphomet. It is also significant that she dances with Heru-Ra-Ha. In Atu XIX (The Sun) we see him 'in his manifestation to the race of men as the Sun spiritual, moral, and physical.' (Crowley, 113.) We should also consider the Two of Disks (Change), which is ruled by Jupiter and Capricornus. This card is also 'the complete manifested Universe.' The Yin and Yang shown in opposite rotation 'represent the harmonious interplay of the Four Elements in constant movement.' (Crowley, 121.) Thus we have the balance of two inharmonious elements (Jupiter and Capricorn). It is worth noting that the serpent is also crowned, probably in reference to Jupiter (Chesed). A Mighty King, Crowned and Enthroned, balancing the raw energy of Capricorn.

83 Lévi, *Transcendental Magic*, 393.

'like guardian spirits of the threshold, [and they] express the psychological fact that the numinosum[84] manifests between opposites.'[85] It has also been proposed that the cherubs might be a manifestation of Isis and Nephthys,[86] both of whom play a role in the myths surrounding the death and resurrection of Osiris.[87]

Here beneath the winged Eros is youth, delighting in the one and the other.

He is Asar between Asi and Nepthi; he cometh forth from the veil.

Liber CCXXXI, 6[88]

---

84   This refers to a quality belonging to a visible object or the influence of an invisible presence that causes a peculiar alteration of consciousness.

85   Gilliam, 'The Angels Call', 35.

86   In a text called *The Lamentations of Isis and Nephthys*, the two sisters call to the soul of Osiris to return to the living. They call on him to return to be amongst them and invoke his son Horus to be Osiris protector in life, and sustain him with "bread, beer, oxen and fowl". Horus' sons would also protect Osiris' soul and guard his body - 'I am Nephthys, your beloved sister! Your foe is fallen, he shall not be! I am with you, your body-guard, For all eternity. Isis speaks, she says: Ho, you of On, you rise for us daily in heaven! We cease not to see your rays! (Mark, 'The Lamentations of Isis and Nephthys'). It would also be worth considering the Stolistes, who is described in a Golden Dawn Flying Roll as the Vice-regent of Nephthys (who is connected to the governing officer, the Imperator). She was also seen as a general protector of women, especially during childbirth. She was also "Lady of the Night", associated with night, death and decay – the opposite of Isis. However, Isis and Nephthys were seen to work together during birth - Isis as the midwife and Nephthys as the protector and comforter. Her chief sanctuary was in Heliopolis.

87   Gilliam, 'The Angels Call', 36.

88   Crowley, *The Holy Books of Thelema*, 201.

We can see these opposites at work in Lévi's depiction of the 21st Key (as in Baphomet). Here Truth appears between the two rods, and between the interactions of the Cherubim.

Below is (as far as I can distil) an interpretation of the Tetragrammaton that Lévi taught was "included" in the Ark:

Yod – Blossoming staff of Aaron
He – Cup (the gomor[89] containing the manna)
Vau – Two tables of the law
He – The manna

Some authors have also compared the process of the flowering and fruiting of Aaron's Rod to that of the Tetragrammaton. It is perhaps of note that Aaron was of the house of Levi. His staff was referred to as Mateh Levi (מַטֶּה לֵוִי), and if we take the first two Hebrew letters of this (מ+ל) we get, by gematria, 70 (ע), noting this number's relationship to Baphomet. The blossoming of Aaron's Rod showed that he was designated by God to be the High Priest. *Mateh Levi* equals 100, 'a square number which represents perfection or consummation...'[90]

In a footnote to the section in Book 4 (Liber ABA) regarding The Wand, and in reference to Aaron's Rod, Crowley states that, 'the word used in Exodus for a Rod of Almond is מטה השקד, adding to 463. Now 400 is *tau*, the path leading from Malkuth to Yesod. Sixty is *samekh*, the path leading from Yesod to Tiphareth; and 3 is *gimel*, the path leading thence to Kether. The whole rod therefore gives the paths from the King-

---

89 Gomor is not a vessel guardaining the manna, but a measurement of the amount of manna each Israelite was able to collect. A vessel filled with manna was placed near the Ark. It is interesting that manna, when kept overnight, putrefied, and bred worms. This may have significance in relation to AL 3:25.

90 GalEinai, 'From Essence to Actualization'.

dom to the Crown.'[91] 463 is also (תגין) – caps, crowns, diadems[92] – the ultimate crowning of the Great Work in Kether.[93]

Manna (מָן) is, of course, a substance that was provided by God to the Israelites during their 40 years of wandering. It sustained them and produced no waste. Aside from food, manna was also said to have been used as perfume.

The composite image of Lévi's twenty-first tarot key also depicts (among many obscure symbols) a serpent pierced with an arrow.[94] Lévi gives an interpretation of this glyph in his *History of Magic*, teaching that it represented the Hebrew Aleph, and was 'an image of the union between active and passive, spirit and life, will and light…equilibrated unity.'[95] This is "The Seal

---

91   Crowley, Desti, and Waddell, *Magick. Liber ABA. Book Four. Parts I-IV*, 63.

92   Crowley, *777 and Other Qabalistic Writings of Aleister Crowley*, 47.

93   "The crown of lower Egypt was formed like an open mouth with a projecting tongue, curled at the end. This symbolizes the Word of Power uttered from the kingly logos to create the universe, and by the royal Monad of man to illumine and direct the individuality…The Woman Clothed with the sun" (Rev. 12: I) wore a crown of twelve stars, symbolising the spiritual powers of the twelve zodiacal signs, all developed and shining as jewels in the perfected Higher Self. The clouds of glory in which the Adept ascends are the radiant aura, the Augoeides of the Adept, the light and splendour of the causal body, symbolised by the light and sanctuary of the temple. The crown aptly represents the actual appearance of the upper portion of the illuminated aura of a highly evolved man. The uprushing, individual aspiration and intelligence is met by the downrushing, divine response. The play of power from below and above forms the crown, which is a characteristic of certain orders of Devas, called in Hinduism 'Bright Crested'." (Hodson, *At The Sign of the Square and Compass*, 271.)

94   This symbol was later used by the Hermetic Brotherhood of Luxor (H.B.L), which also seems to borrow elements from other glyphs produced in Lévi's works; such as the Cherubim, the sun and moon, and the serpent and hexagram (these last two seen in The Great Seal of Solomon).

95   Levi, *The History of Magic: Including a Clear and Precise Exposition of Its Procedure, Its Rites and Its Mysteries*, 411.

of Cagliostro". Although Lévi wrote of Cagliostro often as an example of a cautionary tale, in *Transcendental Magic* he states that, 'It is known that he practiced evocations and that in this art he was surpassed only by the illuminated Schroepffer. It is said also that he boasted of his power in binding sympathies, and that he claimed to be in possession of the secret of the Great Work; but that which rendered him still more famous was a certain elixir of life, which immediately restored to the aged the strength and vitality of youth.'[96]

On the opposite side to the serpent and arrow is a lamb with the cross and flag, the cross appearing seeming to be in the form of a serpent, the brazen serpent, again repeating what Lévi would have seen as a representation of the positive and the negative, the volatile and the fixed. This is "the Apocalyptic Seal". This is the "Lamb of God" or "*Agnus Dei*".

> The next day John seeth Jesus coming unto him, and saith, Behold the Lamb of God,[97] which taketh away the sin of the world.
>
> *John 1:29*

---

96   Lévi, *Transcendental Magic*, 133–34.

97   Lévi would have created this from his Christian (Catholic) perspective. However, Thelemites should consider the warning given in 20th Aethyr of *The Vision and the Voice* - 'But at the top seems to be the Lamb and Flag, such as one sees on some Christian medals, and one of the lower things is a wolf, and the other a raven. The Lamb and Flag symbol is much brighter than the other two. It keeps on growing brighter, until now it is brighter than the wheel itself, and occupies more space than it did. It speaks: I am the greatest of the deceivers, for my purity and innocence shall seduce the pure and innocent, who but for me should come to the centre of the wheel. The wolf betrayeth only the greedy and the treacherous; the raven betrayeth only the melancholy and the dishonest. But I am he of whom it is written: He shall deceive the very elect.' (Crowley, Neuburg, and Desti, *The Vision & the Voice with Commentary and Other Papers: The Collected Diaries of Aleister Crowley, 1909-1914 E.V.*, 94–95.)

In the centre is depicted a peacock, standing on a caduceus, above the Greek word ΣΑΜΙΩΝ (SAMIOS). My assumption is that this is a reference to the island of Samos, considered the birthplace of Pythagoras. This has a connection to the peacock, as Pythagoras' soul was said to have moved into a peacock after his death (*palingenesis*). Peacocks symbolised immortality; it was believed that their flesh did not decay after death, and they were consequently associated with renewal and resurrection. The title of this seal given by Lévi is *Junon Samienne*, or the Seal of the Samian Juno (Samian relating to something native to Samos). Juno was a goddess of ancient Roman origin. She was seen as the protector and special counsellor of the state, and was often shown armed and wearing a goatskin cloak.

ISLANDS off IONIA, Samos. Augustus. 27 BC-AD 14. Æ (18mm, 5.52 g, 1h). Laureate head right / Peacock standing right on caduceus; transverse sceptre behind. RPC I 2681; BMC 224-5; SNG Copenhagen 1728.

Although it would be considered an abomination from an historical perspective, Lévi wrote that 'Pythagoras of Samos sought a refuge in Italy from the tyranny of Polycrates. The great promoter of the philosophy of numbers had visited all the sanctuaries of the world and had even been in Judaea, where he suffered circumcision as the price of his admission into the mysteries of the Kabbalah, communicated to him, though not without a certain reserve, by the prophets Ezekiel and Daniel. Subsequently, but again not without difficulty, he obtained Egyptian initiation, being recommended by the King Amasis. The capacities of his own genius supplemented the imperfect revelations of the hierophants, so that he became himself a master and one who expounded the mysteries.'[98]

The Pantacles of Ezekiel and Pythagoras from Transcendental Magic.

Another interesting, and important, reference Lévi makes to Pythagoras, and one that links him to this series of entwined glyphs and concepts, is his figure titled "The Pantacles of Eze-

---

98 Levi, *The History of Magic: Including a Clear and Precise Exposition of Its Procedure, Its Rites and Its Mysteries*, 92.

kiel and Pythagoras". This shows 'The four-headed Cherubim of Ezekiel's prophecy, explained by the double triangle of Solomon.'[99] At the bottom of the figure is the Wheel of Ezekiel and the pantacle of "Pythagoras" (remembering that Lévi taught that Ezekiel had instructed Pythagoras). Different associations are given to the Cherubim, and Lévi further explains that 'This symbol is analogous to that of the Egyptian sphinx, but is more appropriate to the Kabalah of the Hebrews.'[100] The hexagram is formed by the wings of the Cherubim, and if we take on Lévi's description of the Ark, then this is concealed within them.[101] To Lévi, Ezekiel's wheel and Pythagoras' pantacle shared the same mysteries. He further sees an identity between the four living creatures (the four-headed sphinx) and the Indian "Adda-Nari". This is *Ardhanarishvara* (अर्धनारीश्वर), which is a form of *Shiva*, merged with his consort, *Parvati*. This is a *coniunctio oppositorum*, a union of opposites – active (*Parvati*) and passive (*Shiva*). Hermaphroditic figures like this are often associated with the common theme in this work of growth and fertility and their connection to Baphomet. The union of these (of *Purusha*[102] and *Prikriti*[103]) are the forces in Hinduism that cause the generation of the universe.[104] *Shiva* is also associated

---

99 Lévi, *Transcendental Magic*, xiii.

100 Lévi, xiii.

101 I think it is timely here to remind the reader of Lévi's opinion that the Templars' concealed purpose was to rebuild the Temple of Solomon based on the model revealed by Ezekiel.

102 Unchanging and uncaused Universal Principle

103 Primal creative or natural force. The first power of action, which is composed of the three gunas – sattva, rajas and tamas.

104 In writing about the Ark of the Covenant and the Cherubs, Lévi states 'The four raised wings are an expression of the four celestial currents of the universal agent, extending into the four corners of the human world; and the four wings which cling to the sides of the ark show that what is below is like

with spirituality and asceticism, whereas *Parvati* is linked to the illusory and material existence. *Ardhanarishvara* harmonises and reconciles these two, seemingly conflicting, aspects of life.

> The double triangle which separates the lower wings, one white and one black, shows the duality of ideas and forms; that is, the white triangle symbolizes all that is known to us; for the reversed triangle is the shadow of God, and this shadow, for us, is light. Whereas the black triangle, its point in the air, is the light of God, which for us is shadow.[105]

---

that which is on high. If that which exists in fixed form had not first existed in volatile form, there would be no bodies, nor any of the laws governing the four kingdoms. In the interior of the ark of the universe, that is, within the latent action of the combustion of elements and their forms, rays of light combine to produce, by analogy, the directions of the raison d'être of all things, things which should be in perfect, mathematical harmony. It is there, beneath that celestial vault of aspiring souls, that causes radiate toward ideas, the mothers of form; where the benevolent action of solar splendour sends warmth and life to form the bodies for souls destined to terrestrial existence.' (Lévi, *The Mysteries of the Qabalah or Occult Agreement of the Two Testaments*, 33–34.)
105 Lévi, 34.

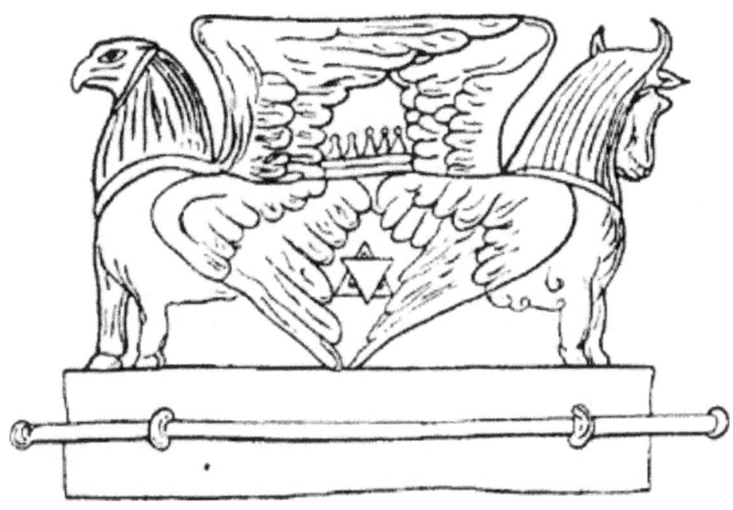

The Ark of the Covenant and the Cherubim from The Mysteries of the Qabalah

The three Seals that appear on the top of the 21st Key could be seen as a trinity of magic, reason/science, and faith.

But this purified religion will not be invented, it exists and it has always existed in humanity; but it had to be concealed by the sages, because the vulgar have been incapable of comprehending it. It is the tradition of all the great sanctuaries of antiquity, it is the philosophy of nature, it is God living in humanity and in the world, it is being demonstrated by being, it is reason proven by harmony, it is the analogy of the contraries, it is faith based on science and science elevated by faith.[106]

---

106 Strube, 'The "Baphomet" of Eliphas Lévi: Its Meaning and Historical Context', 47.

On one side of the 21st Key is also a 3×3 cube (what to us would now seem like a "Rubik's Cube"), under which is written in French "*la pierre cubique*" or "the cubic stone". Of the cubic stone Lévi states that it 'and its multiplication explains all secrets of sacred numbers, including the mystery of perpetual motion, hidden by adepts and pursued by fools under the name of squaring the circle.'[107] This is balanced on the other side by "Le Lettre Aleph", the letter aleph (א). This could, again, be a reference to the fixed and the volatile – the solid, or stationary and whirling motion. Surrounding the full image of the 21st Key are what are titled "the twelve Seals of the cubic stone". Although these seals are very much obscure to me, it is interesting that many of the Seals are assigned musical notation, giving a particular rhythm or battery, or perhaps indicating a kind of vocal incantation or mantra.

Lévi goes on further to explain that 'The plan of all great allegorical temples throughout antiquity is found in the multiplication (a) of the cube by the cross, (b) about which a circle is described, and then (c) the cubic cross moving in a globe.'[108]

In what reads like a precursor to the writing of Margaret Barker, Lévi' states 'Had not the Jews in the days of the Pharisees lost the science of that which is at once the corner-stone, the cubic stone, the philosophical stone—in a word, the fundamental stone of the Kabalistic Temple, square at the base and triangular above like the pyramids? By impeaching Jesus as an innovator did they not proclaim that they had themselves forgotten antiquity?...It will then be realised that Christianity, so far from being a heresy in Israel, was the true orthodox tradition of Jewry, while it was the Scribes and Pharisees who were

---

107 Levi, *The History of Magic: Including a Clear and Precise Exposition of Its Procedure, Its Rites and Its Mysteries*, 122.

108 Levi, 123.

sectarians... Judaism without a temple, without a High Priest and without a sacrifice survives only as a dissident persuasion; certain persons are still Jews, but the Temple and Altar are Christian.'[109]

For Thelemites, it is important to remember that it is against the cubic stone that 'the Name וְזָהֳרִי is broken in a thousand pieces.'[110] Perhaps we can also draw a parallel to Lévi's reference above to the cube, cross, circle and sphere in the comment to this 30th Aethyr – 'Without the cube – that material world – is the sphere-system of the spiritual world enfolding it.'[111] The cubic stone could be viewed as that which is unchanging, the natural principles that endure through the Aeons (the *prima materia* of the Great Work), with their application evolving with new spiritual-social perspectives that come with the evolution of the race. וְזָהֳרִי may have been broken, but it has been reformulated for the new Aeon.

The cube is also a symbol of one phase of the Rose Cross, that which expands and that which contracts. That which reflects the external and the internal and the natural phases of this action - 'Yet shall this perfect wine be the quintessence, and the elixir; and by the draught thereof shall he renew his youth; and so shall it be eternally, as age by age the worlds do dissolve and change, and the Universe unfoldeth itself as a Rose, and shutteth itself up as the Cross that is bent into the Cube.'[112]

---

109 Levi, 173.

110 Crowley, Neuburg, and Desti, *The Vision & the Voice with Commentary and Other Papers: The Collected Diaries of Aleister Crowley, 1909-1914 E.V.*, 38.

111 Crowley, Neuburg, and Desti, 31.

112 Crowley, Neuburg, and Desti, 151.

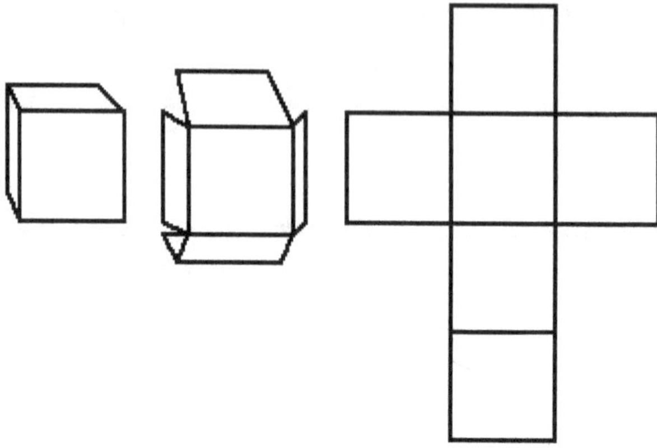

This mystery of the Rose and Cross has relevance for the individual, through successive cycles of expansion and contraction, dissolution and coagulation, but also the race (as mentioned above), as we collectively go through periods of upheaval and change, and then periods of consolidation and stability, all (we can only pray in these times) broadening our collective experience, and slowly leading to collective evolution in order to fulfill the Will of the Aeon.

We saw earlier that the Kaaba was constructed in the shape of a cube (the shape of the throne of Baphomet); this is also the form of the Holy of Holies in the Temple in Jerusalem. In Revelation, the shape of "the holy Jerusalem" is also interpreted as a cube; but this Jerusalem described in Revelation has no Temple, 'for the Lord God Almighty and the Lamb are the temple of it.' (Revelation 21:22). Frater Achad also comments that 'We must not, however, overlook the fact that the House of God should be a "Living Temple" – the Temple of our own body.'[113]

––––––––––––––––

113 Achad, 'Bread of Stones?: Part I'.

James M. Pryse (1859–1942) explains, in relation to the cube, that 'to solve this element of the puzzle it is only necessary to unfold the cube, thereby disclosing a cross, which represents the human form – a man with outstretched arms.'[114] The cube represents the material basis, humanity, but unfolded shows humanity in extension, in a state of openness.[115] The body is not separate from this process, but a natural extension and vehicle for it. Similarly, K kai 空海 (774–835), the founder of Shingon Buddhism, in his work *Sokushin j butsu gi* (即身成仏義) or "The Meaning of Attaining Buddhahood with One's Own Body" that 'Tantric practitioners were instructed to imitate the body of the Buddha with their own bodily actions, for Buddhahood was understood as a cognitive process that passes through the body.'[116]

It would also be worth remembering again that Lévi wrote of Baphomet, 'he is the guardian of the key to the temple.'[117] He also further provided an explanation of the "Templar Baphomet" which he taught should be spelt backwards. This was 'TEM. OHP. AB, *Templi omnium hominum pacis abbas*, "the father of the temple of peace of all men".[118] Putting aside Waite's criticism of Lévi's Latin, and the lack of historical support for this, what is emphasised here is the powerful archetype

---

114 Pryse, *The Apocalypse Unsealed: Being an Interpretation of the Initiation of Ioannes*, 33.

115 'There is a form of the crucifix known as "Christ Triumphant," where the figure of the Saviour is shown not broken, bleeding, naked, and with head dropped to one side, but with head erect, eyes open, body clothed, and arms outstretched as though willingly "thus come"…as the very image of a Bodhisattva in whom the agony of time and the rapture of eternity are disclosed as one and the same." (Campbell, *The Inner Reaches of Outer Space*, 72.)

116 'The Embryonic Generation of the Perfect Body', 254.

117 Levi, *The Book of Splendours*, 119.

118 Lévi, *Transcendental Magic*, 316.

of the androgyne. Lévi goes on to describe a "coffer" 'disinterred...in the ruins of an old Commandery of the Temple, and antiquaries observed upon it a baphometic figure, corresponding by its attributes to the goat of Mendes and the androgyne of Kunrath.'[119] Kunrath refers to the German physician, hermetic philosopher, and alchemist, Heinrich Khunrath (1560–1605), and an image titled "The Hermaphrodite" or "Rebis and Hermes' Bird" from his work *Amphitheatrvm Sapientiæ Æternæ, Solivs Veræ: Christiano-Kabalisticvm, Divino-Magicvm, nec non Physico-Chymicvm, Tertrivnvm, Catholicon.*

---

119 Lévi, 316.

This "baphometic figure" is described as 'a bearded figure with a female body, holding the sun in one hand and the moon in the other, attached to chains.'[120] Lévi also seems to indicate that this figure is a feature of human psychology, of the mind – 'this virile head is a beautiful allegory which attributes to thought alone the initiative and creative principle. Here the head represents spirit and the body matter. The orbs enchained to the human form, and directed by that Nature of which intelligence is the head, are also magnificently allegorical.'[121] Lévi then, strangely, moves from this "beautiful allegory" to describing the discovered figure as 'obscene and diabolical by all learned men who examined it',[122] but I cannot help but read into this a sly wink.

Lévi also seems to point at the archetypal nature of Baphomet when he writes, 'These hybrid creations of impossible animals gave to understand that the image was not an idol or reproduction of a living thing, but rather a character or representation of something having its experience in thought.'[123] As Churton rightly points out, '*Baphomet* was a composite symbol of initiation, not a thing.'[124]

In Crowley's translation of *The Key of the Mysteries*, it must be noted that there are a number of illustrations that were not included (I assume due to the difficulty of publishing such a large number of images in The Equinox). The below was included, and is instructive in relation to the above discussion about the Ark, the Cherubim and Baphomet.

---

120 Lévi, 316.

121 Lévi, 316.

122 Lévi, 316.

123 Levi, *The Book of Splendours*, 118.

124 Churton, *Occult Paris*, 96.

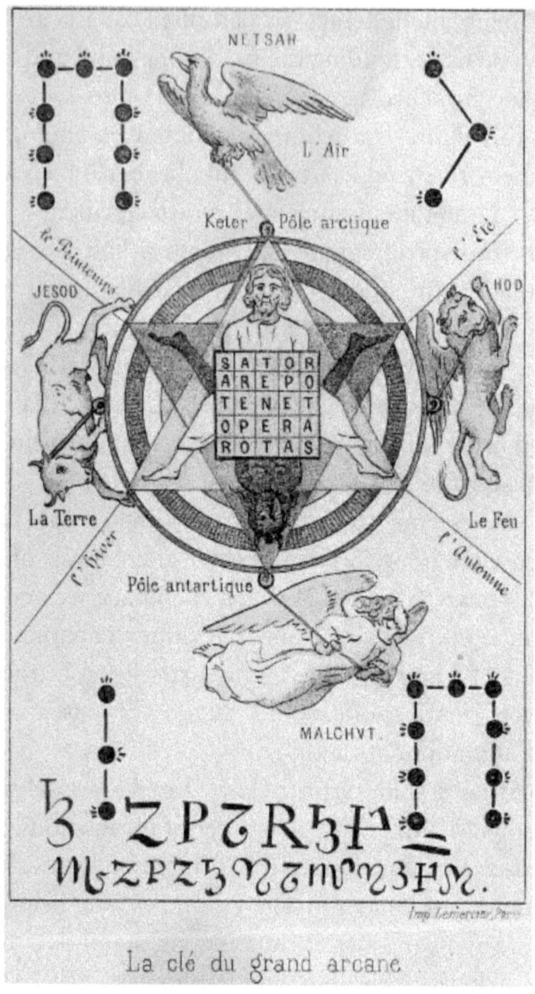

La clé du grand arcane

We can see the hexagram here is formed by the intersection of an upright, white, male figure, and an averse, black, female figure. This is *La clé du grand arcane* - "the key of the great arcane". It is also called "the Great Key of William Postel". William Postel is Guillaume Postel (1510–1581), a French linguist, astronomer, Christian Kabbalist, diplomat, polyglot, professor, and religious universalist. His writing about Mother Zuana, who he believed was a prophet, brought him to the attention of the Inquisition, but a verdict of insanity, rather than heresy, saved him from execution. He would spend the majority of his remaining life in confinement. Postel seems to be ever present in *The Key of the Mysteries* – even its frontispiece is based on an image from Postel's *Absconditorum Clavis*.

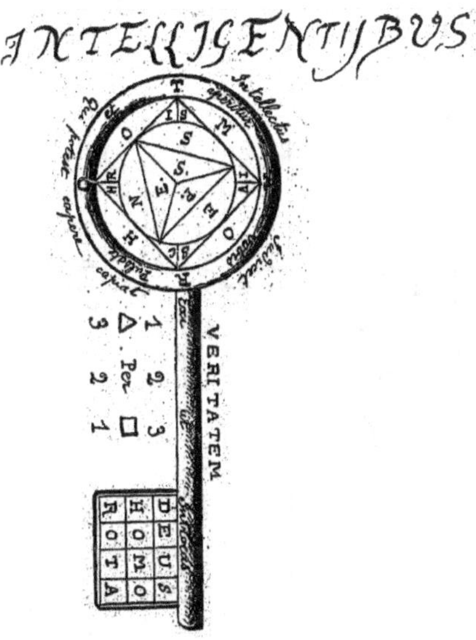

Postel provides in his writing correspondence to ROTA and the Cherubs, showing a previous consideration of these concepts (the below table was translated and compiled by Benebell Wen[125] with the original below from *Absconditorum Clavis* or "Hidden Key").

---

125 Wen, 'Postel's Key of Things Kept Secret (1547)'.

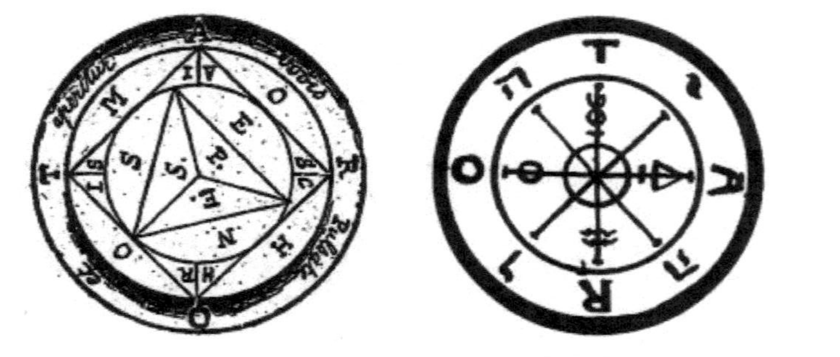

WORLD	R	O	T	A
Element	Earth	Water	Air	Fire
Direction	East	South	West	North
Season	Spring	Summer	Autumn	Winter
Human Age	Childhood	Adolescence	Adulthood	Old Age
Law	Allegiance	Charity	Faith	Amity
Scholarship	Literature	Ethics	Allegory	Analogy
Cherub	Man	Bull	Lion	Eagle
Mystery	Incarnation	Crucifixion	Resurrection	Ascension
Divine Gift	Sapience	Justice	Sanctification	Redemption
River from Eden	Pishon	Gihon	Tigris	Euphrates
Testimony	Spirit and Water	Fire and Water	Water and Blood	Spirit and Fire

		R Orient	O Méridien	T Occident	A Aquilon
M. DE DIEU / H. Naturel / R. DE LA NATURE	Monde	Orient	Méridien	Occident	Aquilon
	Année	Printemps	Eté	Automne	Hyver
	Homme	Enfant	Adolescent	Homme viril	Vieillard
	Elément	Terre	Eau	Air	Feu
E. DV PÈRE / O. Rationnel / O. DE LA LOI	Hiérarchie	Adam	Moïse	Messie	ELIaAVH
	Loi	Obédience	Charité	Foi	Concorde
	Livre	Gene-Henoch-seos	Vieux Testam	Nouv. Test.	ApOcA
	Sens	Littéral	Moral	Allégorique	Anagogique
N. DV FILS / M. Spirituel / T. DE L'EVANGILE	Evangéliste	S. Matthieu	S. Luc	S. Marc	S. Jean
	Chérub	Homme	Bœuf	LiOn	Aigle
	Mystère	Incarnation	Passion	Résurrection	Ascension
	Don	Sapience	Justice	Sanctification	Rédemption
S. DE L'ESPRIT. S. / O. DEI-forme / A. DV IVGEMENT	Visitation	de la Terre	de l'Egypte	de Jérusalem	de Babel
	Fleuve	Pischon	Gihon	Chide-Kel	Phrat
	Face	des Eaux	de Moïse	du Christ	de Jérusalem
	Témoignage	Esprit et Eau	Feu et Eau	Eau et Sang	Esprit et FEV

We can also see references in the ideas of Postel for the male and female figures that comprise the hexagram. Postel believed that the soul was divided into male and female elements[126] and 'have their separate residences in the brain and in the heart. Christ...had redeemed the male element of the soul; redemption still awaits the lower, female part, which could be raised from sin only with the help of a woman.' He goes on further, and poetically to write, 'The mind by its purity makes good errors of the heart, but the generosity of the heart must rescue the egoistic barrenness of the brain.... Religion to the majority is superstition based in fear, and those who profess such have not the woman-heart, because they are foreign to the divine enthusiasms of that mother-love which explains all religion. The power that has invaded the brain and binds the spirit is not that of the good, understanding and long-suffering God; it is wicked, imbecilic and cowardly.... The frozen and shrivelled brain weighs on the dead heart like a tombstone. What an awakening will it be for understanding, what a rebirth for reason, what a victory for truth, when the heart shall be raised by grace! ... The Word has been made man, but the world will be saved when the Word shall have been made woman.'[127] Postel was known to call himself 'male and female simultaneously.'[128]

Judith Weiss explains that Postel's system is 'formed from elaborations on a simple, quadruple structure...two upper elements, a male and a female, and two lower elements, likewise male and female.'[129] This is Chokmah and Binah, and Tiphareth

---

126 Postel also used the terms anima and animus, that would be later revived by Carl Jung as part of his theory of the collective unconscious.

127 'Guillaume Postel'.

128 Seligmann, *The History of Magic*, 328.

129 Weiss, 'Guillaume Postel's Kabbalistic Notion of Marriage, Sex, and Family', 78.

and Malkuth. For Postel the female element was central, as was the couple (male-female).

In his somewhat idiosyncratic translation of the *Zohar*, Postel has:

> "The King" indeed, "shall become delighted in God" – in the Superior and profound delight, which overflows and emanates. In what light is delight? In "Elohim". Unto it he sent life, the kind of life they call "the life of the king".[130]

Here, from one Kabbalistic perspective, "the King" is the sphere of Malkuth, and Elohim is Binah (the upper and lower feminine spheres). However, Postel saw the king as Tiphareth – 'divine profusion emanating and flowing into the lower female Sefirah.'[131] This brings to mind again the concept introduced earlier, the kingly power.

In Ms. BL Sloane 1410 (Postel's first *Zohar* Latin translation and commentary presently preserved in the British Library[132]) we can read:

> That concealed path of the holy semen's channel, which also flows unto us through the divine body, through the concealed motherhood, as the Godhead, through a concealed path, outpours its semen through a hidden path into the created wisdom. Thus all the things are from God through the male Christ, and all the things are from Christ through His lower part, and all things are from the general mother herself, through these two's firstborn son. In this manner all things are two in one. For all things are to be {united} for all eternity under the father and the mother...and [that a greater unifica-

---

130 Weiss, 79.

131 Weiss, 79.

132 Weiss, 'BL MS Sloane 1410', 136.

tion than that] of the upper and lower worlds [would exist, other] than [that which is] in the world's globe, and of [the unification of] God and the general intellect – than in one Christ, the one that consists of both the created and uncreated wisdom which arrange everything.[133]

Postel taught that there was an 'innate universal unity', a *concordia mundi,* which 'expresses the undeniable and unbreakable unity between male and female.'[134] 'God (higher male) begets everything through the male Christ (lower male); then Christ begets everything through his lower part or "general motherhood" (higher female [...]); lastly this general mother begets everything through her and Christ's firstborn son (lower female, to be identified as Postel himself).'[135]

An interesting insight into Postel's teachings about the sexual mysteries that would later be expressed by Lévi, and those influenced by him is explained by Weiss - '...prior to the actual ejaculation, a moment of inner flowing within the male "king" takes place, and it is exactly this that ensure the divine unifying quality of the male semen after its extraction and pouring into the female who is to create the foetus. In this case he chooses to accentuate the effect of child conception which he describes as the ultimate "delight of the king". This is indeed the King's delight, and not so much the intercourse itself. The same tendency recurs when Postel emphasises the outcome of the conjugation (namely, the creation of the world[136])...'[137]

---

133 Weiss, 'Guillaume Postel's Kabbalistic Notion of Marriage, Sex, and Family', 79–80.

134 Weiss, 81.

135 Weiss, 80.

136 The universal "Home".

137 Weiss, 'Guillaume Postel's Kabbalistic Notion of Marriage, Sex, and Family', 82.

In Ms. BL Sloane 1410 17.a Postel explains that, '(Him, who is The Life,[138] and this life is the light of men) the kind of life they call "the life of the king". (For it is impossible that the God would be known to live, unless he would scatter Himself in actuality into the general intellect, which is mobile in actuality. For without motion,[139] which God lacks, it is impossible for the life of Virtue to exist.)'[140]

The "delight" mentioned earlier, Weiss argues, is intercourse – 'God's intercourse with the female…an outpouring of the entire treasure of nature…'[141]

If we want a glimpse of what he saw as the benefit of the key that Lévi perceived in the writings of Postel, we need to return to *The Key of the Mysteries*, and a chapter whose title includes, 'How to Preserve and Renew Youth – The Secrets of Cagliostro – The Possibility of Resurrection…'[142] In it Lévi writes that 'the good and learned William Postel, never pretended that he possessed the great arcanum of hermetic philos-

---

138 Semen

139 Remembering the fifth power of the Sphinx is Ire, "to go", of which Crowley addresses in relation to the Tao, writing, 'And to Go is the very meaning of the name God, as elsewhere shewn in these letters; hence the Egyptian Gods were signalized as such by their bearing the Ankh, which is a Sandal-strap, and in its form the Crux Ansata, the Rosy Cross, the means whereby we demonstrate the Godhead of our Nature.' (Crowley, *Magick Without Tears*, 229.) Also, 'It is the god within, the sun, which is the centre of the Universe from the human point of view, with its own particular virtue, which is to Go.' (Crowley, *The Book of Thoth*, 277.)

140 Weiss, 'Guillaume Postel's Kabbalistic Notion of Marriage, Sex, and Family', 83.

141 Weiss, 82.

142 One cannot help but be reminded of Crowley writing about A.M.R.I.T.A. – 'This method of restoring youth and energy has been the principal secrets of the O.T.O. (Order of the Oriental Templars) for many years.' (Crowley, *Amrita*, 1.)

ophy; and yet after being seen old and broken, he reappeared with a bright complexion, without wrinkles, his beard and hair black, his body agile and vigorous.'[143] Lévi also states that Postel, after his renewal, would call himself *Postellus restitutus*, Postel the Resurrected.[144]

> Accept, O LORD, this sacrifice of life and joy, true warrants
> of the Covenant of Resurrection.[145]

Before this becomes a chapter on Postel, and not the Abbé, I would like to highlight some of Postel's other teachings that I think have relevance to Lévi, and to mysteries that have found their continuum in Thelema.

In his comment on the Genesis pericope of the *Zohar*, he writes beautifully, 'so that the "King at his repose", namely the male Sefirah Tiferet, would become stabilised within his inferior Kingship, [namely the female Sefirah Malkhut] with that secret of love and delights, which are in the superior garden [namely originating from the Sefirah Binah], and through that path which is concealed and in hiding, [the Yesod, channel of divine semen, the Malkhut] is filled from there.'[146]

---

143 Levi, 'The Key of the Mysteries', 275–76.

144 The only evidence I have been able to find regarding this is from Postel's translation of the Sefer Yetzirah, where part of the title reads, 'Vertebat ex Hebrais et commentaris illustrabad 1551, ad Babylonis ruinam et corrupti mundi finem, Gulielmus Postellus, Restitutus' ("Translated from the Hebrew and illustrated commentaries in 1551, to the fall of Babylon and the end of the corrupt world, William Postellus, Restored").

145 Crowley, Desti, and Waddell, *Magick. Liber ABA. Book Four. Parts I-IV*, 593.

146 Weiss, 'Guillaume Postel's Kabbalistic Notion of Marriage, Sex, and Family', 85.

For Postel (as expressed in the *Zohar*[147]), Tiphareth was the divine semen and Yesod the phallus, which is transferred to the female Malkuth, but this was sublimated to 'intellectual profusion emanating from higher to lower intellects within the Godhead.'[148]

Much of Lévi's writings regarding the conciliation of opposites and his concepts of a divine sexuality can be traced to the teachings of Postel. It is also not surprising that Lévi would depict "the key of the great arcane", "the Great Key of William Postel" as a hexagram composed of a male and a female figure, one could argue, in the act of copulation. Lévi also clearly shows the hexagram in other of his illustrations showing the Ark of the Covenant.

---

147 The *Zohar* is original Jewish work to explicitly utilise sex and gender in descriptions of the relationships between God, his people, and the world. The *Zohar* is also attentive to women's sexuality and sexual arousal, and arousal was 'a prerequisite for intercourse, divine and human alike.' (Weiss, 87.) This is something not always reflected in Postel's writings.

148 Weiss, 85.

The Ark of the Covenant from The Mysteries of the Qabalah

Like Postel, Lévi chose to produce a commentary on the *Zohar, The Book of Splendours,* in which he writes, 'Only one of the pre-Adamite monsters was not destroyed, the great Androgyn, male and female like the palm tree.[149] This is the pro-

---

149 'It is written in the Song of Songs: "We will make for you gold necklaces inlaid with silver." 'It is thus that, to embellish one with the other, mercy and justice are limited. And they are like the palm tree which always grows in twos; they are like brother and sister, ageing equally. Thus we know that he who separates himself from humanity by refusing to love, espousing no one, he will find no place after death in the great human synthesis, but will remain outside, a stranger to the laws of attraction and to the transformations of life.

ductive, generative force which existed before Adam and which God will not destroy.'[150]

Also shown on "The key of the great arcane", is a sphere situated behind the hexagram, which seems to represent the world, with the Arctic and Antarctic poles identified. To this "wheel" are attached by ropes the cherubim, who seem to be pulling it in an anticlockwise direction. In the middle of the hexagram is the famous SATOR square, which holds the words SATOR, AREPO, TENET, OPERA, ROTAS. These can be read top-to-bottom, bottom-to-top, left-to-right, and right-to-left. Various interpretations have been given to this square (some heavily influenced by a Christian perspective). One interesting interpretation (if a doubtful one) that relates to the image of the Cherubim is 'the sower Arepo holds the wheels with care'.[151] Some scholars have also 'suggested such widely divergent solutions as an Orphic, Mithraic, or local Italian origin for the square.'[152] Hamilton points out that, in relation to the proposed connection with the square and the Mithraic mysteries (identified with Baphomet), 'Chronos is derived from the Greek word Cronus, meaning "time". Chronos is also depicted in Greco-Roman mosaics as a man, turning the wheel of the Zodiac. This figure is also named Aeon (eternal time) in alternative renditions of the god Saturn.'[153] Time, rotation, generation, and creation.

As mentioned previously, Lévi also referred to Baphomet as 'the Baphomet of Mendes'. *Mendesis* is the Greek for the

---

And nature, ashamed of him, will cause him to disappear, as we hasten to rid ourselves of the dead.' (Levi, *The Book of Splendours*, 63–64.)

150 Levi, 48.

151 Hamilton, 'The Palindrome Paradox', IV.

152 Hamilton, V.

153 Hamilton, V–VI.

Egyptian city Djedet or Per-Banebdjedet (The Domain of the Ram Lord of Djedet). The principal gods in Djedet were the ram deity Banebdjedet (Ba of Osiris), and his consort Hatmehit, a fish goddess. With their child Har-pa-khered ("Horus the Child"), they formed the triad of Mendes.

I am certainly not the first person to identify a possible connection between Banebdjedet and Baphomet, through the influence of Lévi's writing. The title given to Banebdjedet ("goat of Mendes") is derived from the Greeks in the late period, where 'Ba-neb-Djetet' ("Ram lord of Djedet') was mispronounced and led to the naming of the city as Mendes.

E.A. Budge writes, showing the connection between Banebdjedet, fertility and sexuality, that 'At several places in the Delta...the god Pan and a goat were worshipped...Pindar says that in these places goats had intercourse with women...'[154]

---

154 Wallis Budge, *The Gods of the Egyptians: Studies in Egyptian Mythology*, 353.

Banebdjedet of Mendes

Another Egyptian deity connected to fertility who has also been proposed as a potential source for the images associated with Baphomet is "Hapi of the North". 'Hep or Hapi is always represented as a man, but his breasts are those of a woman, indicating the powers of fertility and nourishment of the god.'[155] Hapi was closely associated with balance and harmony, and sometimes referred to as the "father of the gods". Different depictions of Hapi were seen in upper and lower Egypt. 'Beginning in the 19th Dynasty, reliefs portraying two figures of Hapy, one wearing the Papyrus of Lower Egypt and the other

---

155 Stratton-Kent, *The True Grimoire: The Encyclopedia Goetica Volume One*, 155.

the heraldic plant of Upper Egypt, and binding together the two halves of Egypt (symbolised by the respective plants being used as ropes around the *sema* or 'union' hieroglyph).'[156]   Here again, we have symbolic associations with fertility, but also balance and harmony, which are all key to an understanding of Baphomet.

Throne decorations, colossal statue of Ramesses II, Luxor Temple,
19th Dynasty

Levi explores further the nature of Baphomet when he states in *The Key of the Mysteries*:

156 Richard H. Wilkinson, *The Complete Gods and Goddesses of Ancient Egypt*, 107.

...the Templars, for example, who are much less to be blamed for having worshipped Baphomet, than for allowing its image to be perceived by the profane. Baphomet, pantheistic figure of the universal agent, is nothing else than the bearded devil of the alchemists. One knows that the members of the highest grades in the old hermetic masonry attributed to a bearded demon the accomplishment of the Great Work.[157]

We can, perhaps, see further indications of these mysteries in *Transcendental Magic*, and the connection between Baphomet and Mercury, in the depiction of the Pentagram and Tetragrammaton – the Pentagram clearly depicted on the forehead of Baphomet (remembering Levi's section relating to Baphomet in *The Book of Splendours* is called 'The Flaming Star').

---

157 Levi, *The Book of Splendours*, 148.

In *Transcendental Magic* this figure is described as "The Pentagram of Faust", and in the French, the chapter in which this appears is described as 'Le microcosme et son signe. – Pouvoir sur les éléments et sur les esprits.' ("The microcosm and its sign. – Power over the elements and over the spirits").

On the forehead of the Pentagram is what appears to be one of the alchemical symbols that is used to signify lead.

Jung writes about the alchemical significance of lead in *Alchemical Studies* - 'Osiris is the name for lead and sulphur, both of which are synonyms for the arcane substance. Thus lead, which was the principal name for the arcane substance for a long time, is called "the sealed tomb of Osiris, constraining all the limbs of the god." According to legend, Set (Typhon) covered the coffin of Osiris with lead...Petasios added by way of explanation: "The lead is the water which issues from the masculine element." But the masculine element, he said, is the "sphere of fire."'[158] Here we could interpret the "masculine element" as the semen, which is both watery and fiery.[159]

In a similar way Lévi discusses the nature of the universal agent[160] in its active and passive forms – the "od" and the "ob".

---

158 Jung, *Alchemical Studies*, 13:74.

159 'Rise, O my snake, into brilliance of bloom / On the corpse of Osiris afloat in the tomb! O Heart of my mother, my sister, mine own, Thou art given to Nile, to the terror Typhon!' (*Liber LXV*, I:1)

160 Also associated with Leviathan.

These, according to Lévi, are the serpent and the fish. '[T]he serpent (with its burning bite) represents the igneous or active agent [or the "od" וד], while the fish represents the watery or passive and absorbent element [or the "ob"[161] וב].[162] Lévi further taught that these two elements (the serpent and the fish) were united in an image of "the fish of Jonah", which 'is given two heads: one which devours and the other which vomits, and thus this figure completely expresses the great arcanum of occult physics and of natural magic.'[163] Again, we could read into this the principle of polarity, of the interior and the exterior, of the shutting up and the opening out, internalising and externalising.

Lead, as the Prime Matter, has been described as "matter-cum-energy", and possibly has its origins in China, and the cults of longevity, leading to the consumption of substances such as jade due to its hardness. The colour red became associated with this principle, due to its connection to blood, and the soul. The connection between redness and the Prime Matter is through lead oxide (minium) which is produced from high purity lead.

When examining the properties of lead we find that '[w]hen gently heated it became red and when red-lead was strongly heated it became white lead. Here was a substance with redness in potential form. It was then looked upon as being body-cum-soul which was interpreted as matter-cum-energy. Being both body and soul it was conceived as the source of all metals, which thereby implied that lead was Prime Matter.'[164] In a simi-

---

161 If we add the values of "od" and "ob" we get 18, which is also the value of חמא, "the antique serpent".

162 Levi, *The Kabalistic and Occult Philosophy of Eliphas Levi*, 1:337.

163 Levi, 1:337.

164 Mahdihassan, 'Lead and Mercury Each as Prime Matter in Alchemy', 136.

lar way, mercury also became associated with the Prime Matter and longevity practices. 'Mercury gently heated became red, and red-mercury strongly heated sublimed as white mercury. The case was identical with lead, each was a metal or substance and each was potential red or soul.'[165]

In Tibetan medico-alchemical systems, mercury was used to cure disease and dispel demons that caused disease (*dön*). It is said to be needed to convert metals into gold. This redness was also connected with cinnabar (mercury sulphide). Cinnabar is also associated with the Dantian (丹田) in Chinese systems, translated as "elixir field" or "cinnabar field". Although there are three *dantian*, this term is often used to describe the lower (下丹田), which is regarded in martial arts practices and qigong (among others) as the centre of gravity of the body, giving rootedness to postures and movement. It is often interchangeably connected with the Japanese *hara* (腹), which refers to the abdomen, belly or stomach, but also carries many other connotations in the Japanese language for things such as feelings, volition and will. The lower *dantian* is the vessel in the body that contains the Jing, considered to be a person's essence, and some have connected this to our genetic inheritance, our genetic code and the wisdom inherent in this. This essence is sometimes associated with kundalini, and the foundation of a person's strength, as well as sexual power. It gives a sense of "place" and body consciousness, so it can be seen as a cognate concept for the Prime Material. This could also give a different view (from a magical perspective) of the fifth power of the Sphinx, "To Go". This is both a practical instruction on the path; but could also demonstrate a continuity of existence through generation – the march or flow of life and consciousness through time. The *dantian* is also sometimes

---

165 Mahdihassan, 136.

associated with the *svadithana* chakra, but also the *manipura*. Frater Achad writes in his lecture titled *Living in the Sunlight* '...this Kundalini (they say mystically) three and a half coils at the lower end of the spine, beneath this closed opening, and when this can be opened, the Kundalini force takes up its rightful place which is about the navel of our bodies in a certain chakra, as it is called, a nerve plexus branching off from the spine, The solar force or the Kundalini force dwells safe within, in the solar plexus and not at the base of the spine.'[166]

The alchemists, if we look at their work psychologically or spiritually, sought to create equilibrium or wholeness between mind and body (or spirit and body), but there was more to this in relation to the *prima materia* and Mercury, and also Baphomet. The *prima materia* 'contained a dual natured spirit'.[167] This was Mercurius (the messenger) that could be made volatile by fire. 'Jung interpreted this spirit as the autonomous and ambivalent power of the unconscious psyche, 'caught' as it were in matter and freed from it through an act of conscious intervention. Mercurius imparted to the adept the secret of a uniting medicant produced from two opposing principles, Sol (fire) and Luna (water), first separated from the *prima materia* and then re-combined in the wonder-working *lapis*, famously called 'the stone that is no stone'.'[168]

---

166 Achad, 'Living in the Sunlight', 326–27.

167 Williams, 'The Origin of Alchemy and the Image of God in Man'.

168 Williams.

If I do not draw
from the well of the unconscious,
it will draw from me:
Shall I choose to be drained,
or, like Egypt's earth,
yearly silted by the Nile's inundation,
Shall I choose to be fertilized?[169]

---

169 Simard LaForêt, *Descent from the Cross: Transformations of a Masoch-istic Woman*, 11.

This dual nature, and uniting medicant is indicated by Lévi when he provides instruction on the Hebrew letter shin (ש), which he connects to Ob, Od and Aour and the word Nahash[170] (נחש) - 'Thus, the word employed by Moses, read kabbalistically, gives the description and definition of that magical Universal Agent, represented in all theogonies by the serpent; to this Agent the Hebrews applied the name of OD when it manifested its active force, of OB when it exhibited its passive force, and AOUR when it exhibits itself wholly in its equilibrated power, as a producer of light in heaven and gold among metals.'[171] Lévi further shows the caduceus as a representation of this threefold operation. The right-hand side serpent is Od, the one on the left Ob. '[A]t the summit of the Hermetic Wand, there shines the golden globe which represents Aour, or equilibrated Light.'[172] Lévi also calls this trinity of the Universal Agent[173] the "medi-

---

170 This word can have multiple meanings. It can be interpreted as a serpent, but also as "the shining one" or "the one who shines", both concepts relevant to this current work.

171 Lévi, *Transcendental Magic*, 194.

172 Lévi, 194.

173 A similar substance to this "Universal Agent" is described by famous Egyptologist Gaston Maspero (1846-1916) in his work *The Dawn of Civilisation*. In describing the Gods, he writes, 'The gods, therefore, on the whole, were more ethereal, stronger, more powerful, better fitted to command, to enjoy, and to suffer than ordinary men, but they were still men. They had bones, muscles, flesh, blood; they were hungry and ate, they were thirsty and drank; our passions, griefs, joys, infirmities, were also theirs. The *sa*, a mysterious fluid, circulated throughout their members, and carried with it health, vigour, and life. They were not all equally charged with it; some had more, others less, their energy being in proportion to the amount which they contained. The better supplied willingly gave of their superfluity to those who lacked it, and all could readily transmit it to mankind, this transfusion being easily accomplished in the temples. The king, or any ordinary man who wished to be thus impregnated, presented himself before the statue of the god, and squatted at its feet with his back towards it. The statue then placed its right hand upon the nape of his neck, and by making passes, caused the fluid to

ating fire" and assigns it to the Hebrew letter shin – 'the horns of Moses and the fork of Satan.'[174]

There is some controversy over the concept of the "horns of Moses", and some argue that it is based on a mistranslation, or misunderstanding, by Jerome, of Exodus 34:29 when translated into Latin – 'And it came to pass, when Moses came down from mount Sinai with the two tables of testimony in Moses' hand, when he came down from the mount, that Moses wist not that the skin of his face shone while he talked with him.' However, we see in the Aquila and the Vulgate, "his face had horns".

Michelangelo. Moisés. 1513-1515. Pormenor.

flow from it, and to accumulate in him as in a receiver.' (Maspero, *The Dawn of Civilisation*, 109–10.)

174 Levi, *The Kabalistic and Occult Philosophy of Eliphas Levi*, 1:285.

Dr. Taylor Marshall (his conspiratorial writing aside) argues there is an important connection between these two concepts ("horned" and "shine") that also connects Moses to the altar; and I also would argue, to some of the concepts that permeate this book, i.e., the initiate giving of light. Marshall shows that the word for "horned" (*qaran*) 'refers to the 1) horns of goats/oxen, 2) a metaphor for strength, and 3) horns/corners associated with the altar/sanctuary/presence of God. As we'll see, I think the association of "horns" with the altar of God is especially important for this analysis. I fear that most miss this association of Moses' face with the altar of God.'[175] This interpretation of "shone" for "horned" could be read as a combined concept of "horns of light".

Andrea de Bonaiuto (1333-1392), Moisés. Afresco

---

175 Marshall, 'The Horns of Moses – Defending Michelangelo's Horned Moses'.

This use of the translation of "horned", instead of "shining" is also supported by biblical scholar Thomas Römer, who, in a lecture in 2009, stated that 'Almost all translations render the verbal form *qaran*, that I have not translated, as "shining, radiant", as the first Greek translators had already done. Yet this root, which appears in the Bible in the verbal form only in this account from the Book of Exodus, is apparently linked to a noun that is used more broadly, *qèrèn,* which in biblical Hebrew does indeed mean "horn". It therefore seems that Jerome's translation was right and that it ought to be rehabilitated...'[176]

And the sixth angel sounded, and I heard a voice from the four horns of the golden altar which is before God.

Revelations, 9:13

Marshall, based on the above from Revelations, makes a connection between Moses' experience speaking with God on Mt. Sinai, and his return to the people "horned" and the 'four horns of the golden altar which was before God'. In a sense, Moses had become the altar before God. His face was both "shining" and "horned," projecting horns of light that can be seen as a representation of the Law—the Commandments that Moses carried down from the mountain, the Word of God.

'In ancient Middle-Eastern iconography, horns are a common way of expressing the strength and the power of a god or of a king representing him.'[177] This is further supported by Rabbi Solomon Yitzhaki (1040–1105), who comments '[The word *qāran*] is related to the term "horns," since the light was shining and projecting in the form of a horn.' Prof. Brent A.

---

176 Römer, 'The Horns of Moses. Setting the Bible in Its Historical Context'.
177 Römer, 'The Horns of Moses. Setting the Bible in Its Historical Context'.

Strawn supports this view – 'Rashi here intuits a connection between *qāran* as "horned" and *qāran* as "shining." This is supported with what we know from ancient Near Eastern divine imagery, according to which the gods who wore horns on their heads were often associated with supernatural light.'[178] The iconography of a horned figure, representing radiance, representing light, also carried through to Lévi's Baphomet, and if we refer to the earlier references to the *od*, *ob* and *Aour*, two contrary forces reconciled in a third, a third state in which the Law (the Word) can be transmitted.

---

178 Strawn, 'Moses'.

We can also read in Deuteronomy about the end of Moses' life, that could indicate his continued radiance – 'And Moses was an hundred and twenty years old when he died: his eye was not dim, nor his natural forces abated.' (Deuteronomy 34:7) The age of Moses (120) when he died is also significant for later traditions. This was the period of time after the death of Christian Rosenkreuz that his body remained preserved. It is also the number of *Liber Cadaveris, Ritual CXX, Of Passing through the Tuat. This is the* A∴A∴ Initiation Ritual of the Zelator. *Cadaveris* (Latin) means corpse, connecting with both the death of Moses and the concealing of his body, and the preservation of the body of Christian Rosenkreuz, whose crypt is said to be located in the interior of the Earth. We should also further note the nature of the number 120, its connection to death, and the grade of Zelator in the A∴A∴, who begins 'to formulate the Foundation of his Eternal Temple.'[179]

> Your fathers did eat manna in the wilderness, and are dead. This is the bread which cometh down from heaven, that man may eat thereof, and not die.
>
> *John 6:49-50*

In a similar way Christ was transfigured on a mountain and shone with rays of light, and there he spoke with Moses and Elijah. Lévi connects these two Old Testament figures with Metatron and Sandalphon – 'he appeared placed between Metatron and Sandalphon, who were then Moses and Elias, because he summed up in himself the virtue of the Elohim.'[180] Lévi, through the number 12, assigns to Metatron "In heaven" and Sandalphon "In nature".[181] Another marriage of heaven and earth.

---

179 Gunther, *The Angel and the Abyss*, 160.
180 Levi, *The Kabalistic and Occult Philosophy of Eliphas Levi*, 1:211.
181 Levi, 1:212.

We also have an incident, recounted by Soror Virakam (Mary Desti (1871-1931)), that describes a transfiguration displayed by Crowley in relation to the writing of *Book Four* and the Ab-ul-Diz Working.[182]

At nearly midnight Virakam records that, 'Just before I had noticed a change in his face, most extraordinary, as if he were no longer the same person; in fact in the ten minutes we were talking he seemed to be any number of different people...Then quite slowly the entire room filled with a thick yellow light (deep golden, but not brilliant. I mean not dazzling, but soft). Fra. P. looked like a person I had never seen but seemed to know quite well – his face, clothes and all were of the same yellow. I was so disturbed that I looked up to the ceiling to see the cause of the light, but could only see the candles.'[183]

The above is concluded by what seems to be a description of Crowley levitating (as if throned) and appearing to Soror Virakam as 'either dead or sleeping.' Crowley was transfigured so that he was no longer recognisable to the witness, and this transfiguration was connected with a golden light.

---

182 A working from 1911 that was connected to the writing of Book 4.

183 Crowley, Desti, and Waddell, *Magick. Liber ABA. Book Four. Parts I-IV*, 85.

Azima from The Mysteries of the Qabalah

In an illustration from *The Mysteries of the Qabalah* (a manuscript not intended for publication) that was seen by Kenneth Mackenzie when visiting Lévi and later gifted to Baron Nicolas-Joseph (one of Lévi's disciples), Lévi again includes a depiction of Baphomet, but under the title of Azima.

In 1830, Jonathan Duncan (1799–1865) wrote about Azima (which I will quote at length),[184]

...it will be easy to discover, in the heavens, the origin of those divinities who assumed the attributes of the goat, male and female. Such was the famous goat adored at Mendes, in Egypt, the golden she-goat revered by the Philassians in Greece, the goat Azima of the Samaritans, and Pan, god of Arcadia...

The goat was honoured with an especial worship at Mendes in Lower Egypt, and gave its name to the whole Mendesian Nome or Prefecture. Mendes was a name common both to the sacred goat, and to the divinity represented with the feet and horns of a goat, as Herodotus declares, for the Egyptian word Mendes signified a goat... Capricornus was worshipped under the symbol of the goat, and under the name of Pan... However startling this identity may be, it is not only deducible from the fables, but it is fully confirmed by an inspection of the planisphere of Kirker, who places in the division of Taurus, to which Auriga corresponds, the figure of a man with the horns and feet of a goat, which are the true and universal attributes of Pan...The constellation of the she-goat and her kids, situate at the equinoctial borders of Spring, or in that part of the heavens to which the Sun corresponds at the time when Ether is united to the earth, and the sublunary world receives the germs of periodical generation, furnishes the Sun with one of the forms under which the heathens adored the supposed author of universal fecundity... It is on these principles that the extraordinary Samaritan reading of

---

184 Similar ideas are presented in a number of other texts, and their correctness is certainly questionable. However, these ideas are contemporary with the life and writing of Levi, and therefore quite likely influenced his thinking.

the first verse of Genesis may be explained. Instead of writing "In the beginning God created the heaven and the earth," they wrote "In the beginning the goat Azima created the universe," which is as much as to say, "In the beginning Jupiter Ægiochus,[185] or Pan, created the universe."

The Great Whole dwindled down to the humble state of a pastoral deity, as Bacchus was degraded to the subordinate condition of the god of vineyards. The shepherds of Arcadia claimed Pan as their tutelary god, and Mount Mænalus became his favorite residence. The people of Lampsacus also adopted him, but under the impure character of Priapus. The worship of Pan, however, having originated in Egypt, the true origin of his mythological character must be sought for in the institutions of that country.[186]

The more detailed description of the image of Azima produced by Lévi has 'Azima, the same as Mendes or Beelphegor. The scapegoat. Physical love.'[187] This is in agreement with aspects of Baphomet described throughout this work. Beelphegor (בַּעַל-פְּעוֹר) is a demon whose name translates as "Lord of the Gap". In The Key of Solomon the King, he is described along with others as having been one of 'the idols of the Syrians; idols without souls, idols now destroyed, and of whom the Name

---

185 This is Jupiter with the aegis, sometimes a goat skin shield with the head of a Gorgon at the centre.

186 Duncan, *The Religions of Profane Antiquity; Their Mythology, Fables, Hieroglyphics and Doctrines. Founded on Astronomical Principles*, 286–90.

187 Lévi, *The Mysteries of the Qabalah or Occult Agreement of the Two Testaments*, 44.

alone remaineth.'[188] He is the Chief of the adversaries to the Spirits of Tiphereth, the Malachim, or the Kings.

There is also a similarity between the image shown on the stomach of "Azima" and the one Lévi produced to represent "Nisroch", which is described as "The Phallus".[189]

Nisroch from The Mysteries of the Qabalah

---

188 MacGregor Mathers, *The Key of Solomon the King (Clavicula Salomonis)*, 124.

189 Lévi, *The Mysteries of the Qabalah or Occult Agreement of the Two Testaments*, 48.

Lévi associates Nisroch[190] with Yesod ('Instead of celestial marriage the impure lingam'[191]), as he associates Azima with Gedulah or Chesed ('instead of divine mercy Obscure love – The Goat'[192]). Yesod is often related to the sexual function and Chesed a crowned and throned king (i.e. the Kingly Power). Crowley would later write, 'Capricornus is indigo. The connection is with the colour of Yesod, implying the sexual symbolism of the Goat.'[193]

Returning to Lévi's teachings regarding the Universal Agent, in a similar way (highlighting the reconciliation of opposites) he writes, 'The final word of Egyptian initiation was: "Osiris is a Black God". Reverse the proposition and you will naturally find that "the black God is Osiris"...I affirm that God is white, and I am right: you affirm that he is black and you are not wrong. Which of us two is most in the right? It is whosoever can comprehend how a third person can be equally in the right by affirming that God is neither white nor black.'[194] This is further clarified when Lévi writes, 'It is for this reason that Osiris is neither a man, nor a God, but an image, a shadow... Between divinity and humanity, one alliance is possible. It is the hypostatic[195] union of the true God with the real man.'[196]

---

190 A demon described as "chief cook of Hell" in the *Pseudomonarchia Daemonum* in 1577, but originally considered an Assyrian god, and the name is possibly a scribal error for Nimrod.

191 Lévi, *The Mysteries of the Qabalah or Occult Agreement of the Two Testaments*, 50.

192 Lévi, 50.

193 Crowley, *777 and Other Qabalistic Writings of Aleister Crowley*, 70.

194 Levi, *The Kabalistic and Occult Philosophy of Eliphas Levi*, 1:255.

195 In Theology this pertains to or constitutes a distinct personal being or substance. It also refers to a doctrine of the Trinity that Jesus is both fully divine and fully human.

196 Levi, *The Kabalistic and Occult Philosophy of Eliphas Levi*, 1:116.

This raised the questions of what is a "true God" and what is "the real man"?

If the Universal Agent is, as described by Lévi, a "mediating fire", between what does it mediate? Between what does it bring about a reconciliation? This is the 'Greeting of Earth and Heaven.' It is the 'spiritual made one with the material.'[197] It is the kiss of the finite with the infinite, and that which is within us with that which is external to us. We should also consider the role that Crowley describes of V.V.V.V.V., 'the sole mediator between God and Man', but equally may be 'a Mr. Smith of Clapham'.[198] To the Brothers of the A∴A∴ there is not necessarily a distinction between these two ideas; that there is no separation between the spiritual and the material. V.V.V.V.V. can be both Man and Messiah at the same time. Similarly, we are all both divine and human simultaneously – *Deus est homo*[199] – 'There is no part of me that is not of the Gods.'[200] The work of initiation is to unveil the god that constitutes us, to find that stillness and silence, that space between contenting forces where the voice of God can be heard, and from where the Word of that god can be made flesh.

> For while all things were in quiet silence, and that night was in the midst of her swift course, Thine Almighty word leaped down from heaven out of thy royal throne, as a fierce man of war into the midst of a land of destruction, And brought thine unfeigned commandment as a sharp sword, and standing up filled all things with death; and it touched the heaven, but it stood upon the earth.
>
> *Wisdom of Solomon 18:14*

---

197 Crowley, *The Equinox of the Gods*, 134.

198 Crowley, 87.

199 God is Man

200 Crowley, Desti, and Waddell, *Magick. Liber ABA. Book Four. Parts I-IV*, 597.

Lévi also clearly highlights that Baphomet 'is also the hieroglyphic figure of the great divine Tetragrammaton.'[201] Noting the previous exploration of the Tetragrammaton and the Ark in Lévi's writings. The hieroglyph is also the 'dark side of the divine face',[202] which Lévi taught explained the kissing of the "hind-face" of Baphomet in initiation, because 'the hind-face of the Devil is the hieroglyphic face of God.'[203]

Lévi highlights again the dual nature of "The Great Magical Agent", which he calls 'the double current of light, the living and astral fire of the earth [...] represented by the serpent with the head of an ox, goat or dog, in ancient theogonies. It is the dual serpent of the Caduceus, the old serpent in genesis, but it is also the brazen serpent of Moses, twined about the TAU, that is the generating lingam. It is moreover the Goat of the Sabbath and the Baphomet of the Templars...'[204]

Further, not just describing what the Magical Agent is, Lévi teaches us what is required to properly control this force: 'The Great Work is, before all things, the creation of man by himself, that is to say, the full and entire conquest of his faculties and his future; it is especially the perfect emancipation of his will, assuring him universal dominion over Azoth and the domain of Magnesia, in other words, full power over the Universal Magical Agent.'[205] As discussed above this "perfect emancipation of his will" is the Baphomet consciousness. For only when the initiate is emancipated can the pure will become manifest.

On Lévi's pentagram in *Transcendental Magic* (page 240), as with Baphomet, the Caduceus is placed as a phallus, with an

---

201 Levi, *The Book of Splendours*, 118.

202 Levi, 119.

203 Levi, 119.

204 Lévi, *Transcendental Magic*, 242.

205 Lévi, 113.

even more obvious indication of its Mercurial nature; but also seemingly combined with the astrological symbol for Venus (♀) again highlighting the combination of Male and Female as seen in his Baphomet (although androgynous Mercury is primarily male). This lower symbol (the circle surmounted by a cross) could also be seen as a symbol of the *prima materia*, the material basis of the Great Work conjoined with the Messenger of the Gods, from above the Abyss, as previously introduced.

> ...and is thus the influence of the supernals descending through the Veil of Water (which is blood) upon the energy of man, and so inspires it.[206]

It could also be both these symbols, with the formula of "love under will" vital to the process of the marriage of Earth and Heaven. It is interesting to note the darkened right-hand side of the Pentagram, as also seen in the image of Baphomet – an indication of the 'upright and the averse'- the 'bright and the dark'.

> I who comprehend in myself all the vast and the minute, all the bright and the dark, have mitigated the brilliance of mine unutterable splendour, sending forth V.V.V.V.V. as a ray of my light, as a messenger unto that small dark orb.[207]
>
> *Liber X*, 2

The symbols for the Sun and the Moon are also present in the Pentagram (Male and Female)[208] as are the words ADM

---

206 Crowley, *The Book of Thoth*, 85.

207 Crowley, *The Holy Books of Thelema*, 39.

208 "Note that Sol and Luna are direct images of the masculine and feminine principles, and much more complete Macrocosms than any other planets.

(אדם) and EVE (חוה), the first Man and Woman in the Book of Genesis. If we write Adam and Eve (Hava) in Hebrew (וחוה אדם) we get 70, which (as we have seen) is the value of the Hebrew (an Eye), assigned to Atu XV of the Tarot, *The Devil*, with its clear reference to Baphomet (Crowley's Tarot developed in line with Thelema from that of the Golden Dawn, as the Golden Dawn Tarot developed from Lévi). Crowley would state the following in one of his last and mature works, *The Book of Thoth*, in relation to Levi's attributions in *Dogma et Ritual*, 'Here we come to a slight complication. The chapters correspond, but they correspond wrongly; and this is only to be explained by the fact that Levi felt himself bound by his original oath of secrecy to the Order of Initiates which had given him the secrets of the Tarot.'[209]

This union of female and male, core to Lévi's Baphomet as amply shown, was also an element of his vision for society ("association universelle") and his belief that the liberation of women was core to this progress: 'Mary, redeemed humanity by her Christ-like suffering and would eventually rehabilitate Lucifer, heralding the final universal synthesis. Quite remarkably, this synthesis would bring forth a union not only of humanity and God but also of man and woman: "The two sexes will be one, according to the word of Christ; the great androgyne will be created, humanity will be woman and man."'[210]

Lévi left a key for future generations to pick up (even if

This is explained by their symbols in the Yi King, ☷ and ☳. Note also that Yesod appears openly, this being the Queen Scale, in the violet robes of the spiritual-erotic vibrations referred to above." (Crowley, *777 and other Qabalistic Writings of Aleister Crowley*, 81.)

209 Crowley, *The Book of Thoth*, 6.

210 Strube, 'The "Baphomet" of Eliphas Lévi: Its Meaning and Historical Context', 63.

his intent was for his generation to be the ones to revolution-ise society), and his occultism was synthesised in the form of Baphomet, a symbol that would 'offer the key to everybody who will take it: and this one will be a doctor of nations and a liberator of the world.'[211]

If we want to encapsulate the key element to Lévi's teaching and his vision for the future of humanity and society, in 1862 he wrote:

> One day, the Christ [upon being] asked about the time [when] his kingdom [would come], replied with these mysterious words: "When two shall be one, when that which is interior shall be exterior and when man with woman shall no longer be neither man nor woman." This oracle of the master is not found in the Gospels: but is quoted by one of the apostolic writers: the pope saint Clement.[212]

Thus, harmony in the binary wherein the creative realisa-tion of universal equilibrium, the manifestation of the whole idea in its whole form, and the identification of the sexes in a marriage [is] truly one an indissoluble, such must be, in fact, the Messianism, or the reign of Christ as the Messiah: this reign is what we ask for everyday in our prayers: *Adveniat regnum tuum!*[213] Messianism is Christianity accomplished, and it is this which will cause the antagonism of the binary to cease.'[214]

---

211 Strube, 'Socialist Religion and the Emergence of Occultism: A Genealog-ical Approach to Socialism and Secularization in 19th-Century France', 378.

212 This is referencing the Second Epistle of Clement. Modern scholars do not believe this was penned by Clement and that it may be a sermon written around 95–140 CE.

213 Thy kingdom come.

214 Levi, *The Kabalistic and Occult Philosophy of Eliphas Levi*, 1:132.

The final state for Lévi is intimately connected to the concept of a messiah, whose coming would bring us to wholeness.

> In V.V.V.V.V. is the Great Work perfect.
> Therefore none is that pertaineth not to V.V.V.V.V.[215]

Eliphas Lévi's key was indeed taken up and continued to influence generations of occultists. Most notably, this influence can be seen in the writings of Aleister Crowley. This key pertained to mysteries that cross all planes. From the personal to the interpersonal. From the individual to the societal. From day-to-day life, to the subtle mysteries of existence – of life, death and continuity. These mysteries can only be properly apprehended and appreciated if one has experience of the state of consciousness implied by these glyphs and teachings. One needs to be open and shining. One needs to have transcended duality and have come to a third state in which all these contradictions are resolved – one needs to have achieved the Baphomet consciousness.

> The highest expression of the binary (in the divine sense) is the mystery of the incarnation...God revealing himself in man so that man [will] elevate himself to the divine life...The first of the perfect men, the Christ, the priest and king par excellence, will forever give us all his blood and all his life. We will be him, [just] as he is God![216]

---

215 Crowley, *The Book of Lies*, 92.
216 Levi, *The Kabalistic and Occult Philosophy of Eliphas Levi*, 1:34.

Therefore, as hath already been said, Establish thyself firmly in the equilibrium of forces, in the centre of the Cross of the Elements, that Cross from whose centre the Creative Word[217] issued in the birth of the dawning Universe.[218]

Eliphas Lévi on his deathbed

217 'The Magus is pre-eminently the Master of Magick…His work is to create a new Universe in accordance with His Will.' (Crowley et al., *Commentaries of the Holy Books and Other Papers*, 4:13.)

218 Crowley, 'Liber Librae Sub Figura XXX'.

ALEISTER CROWLEY

He has been able to philosophize about nature from the standpoint of a complete human being; certain phenomena will always be unintelligible to men as such, others, to women as such. He, by being both at once, has been able to formulate a view of existence which combines the positive and the negative, the active and the passive, in a single identical equation.[1]

---

1   Crowley, *The Confessions of Aleister Crowley*, 45.

Male-Female, Quintessential, One...[2]

This is the creation of the world, that the pain of division is as nothing, and the joy of dissolution all.

Liber AL, I:30

For the purposes of this work, Edward Alexander Crowley requires very little introduction. There are a number of very good studies that cover his life in general and in relation to specific elements, periods of time or locations. I would direct you specifically to the books by Richard Kaczynski and Tobias Churton.

Significant to this work is that when Crowley became Grand Master General X° of the British section of the OTO (Mysteria Mystica Maxima or M∴M∴M∴) he took on the name of this mysterious idol that the Knights Templar were accused of worshipping, and prior to him, as we have seen, this figure was revealed by Eliphas Lévi as a storehouse of his magical and sociopolitical teachings.

Crowley would be reviled by the "yellow press", and these sensationalist and baseless accusations and characterisations have continued to be attached to his name, even to this day when there is no shortage of reliable and well researched literature about his life and art. Like Baphomet, Crowley's name has carried associations that are not grounded in fact and have become caricature – a comic book villain to be recycled ad nauseam. Hugh Urban makes the point that Crowley, along with Paschal Beverly Randolph and Pierre Bernard, should be 'understood not as subversive enemies of modern society but,

---

2   Crowley, Desti, and Waddell, *Magick. Liber ABA. Book Four. Parts I-IV*, 395.

rather, as *reflecting some of the deepest ideas, tensions, and contradictions at the heart of modern society itself.*[3] In many ways people like Crowley hold up a mirror to us and our society, and challenge us to look honestly and critically. People, individually and collectively, do not like what they see, or are unable to see (in the same way Baphomet stares out at us, demanding reconciliation).

In the opinion of Australian writer, publisher, political activist, and establisher of the Mandrake Press, Percy Reginald Stephenson (1901-1965), Crowley was 'one of the greatest prose-writers England has ever produced; and a good poet, too...'[4] Louis Wilkinson (1881–1966) writing under the name Louis Marlow also commented in his book *Seven Friends*, 'I do not intend to be able to profess to be able to solve the enigma of his character and his actions. I am glad he was himself and that I knew him. My chief feeling about him is one of personal gratitude, for I have known very few who, as persons, have impressed me more or rewarded me more than he did.'[5] This stands in stark contrast to the portrayals of the man that are still lazily dragged out to this day, and helps to cut through the miasma.

In the previous chapter we explored Eliphas Lévi, and his rendering of Baphomet that has become such a powerful and enduring symbol. Moving now to Crowley, and his absorption of Baphomet, is to trace its growth, development and incorporation into the doctrines of Thelema, but also acknowledge the great influence that Lévi had on Crowley, and the deep connection between these two men.

———————————

3   Urban, *Magia Sexualis: Sex, Magic, and Liberation in Modern Western Esotericism* , 697.

4   Stephensen and Crowley, *The Legend of Aleister Crowley*, 3.

5   Marlow, *Seven Friends*, 63.

The influence of Lévi on Crowley extends to the point where Crowley wrote that Lévi was one of his previous incarnations. In *Magick Without Tears*, a collection of letters written by Crowley in response to questions, he writes about reincarnation in his usual, somewhat pragmatic way:

What do I mean when I say that I think I was Éliphas Lévi? No more than that I possess some of his most essential characteristics, and that some of the incidents in his life are remembered by me as my own. There doesn't seem any impossibility about these bundles of *Sankhara* being shared by two or more persons.[6]

Sankhara (संस्कार) is a complex term used differently in different contexts. This is sometimes referred to as Tendencies. Gunther describes this as, 'the Illusory sheath of thought',[7] equating it with the Hindu *Manomaya ko a*, or mental sheath. There is a similar concept in Buddhism, *manomaya kaya*, or mental body.

In addition, Crowley writes about death and reincarnation in one of his commentaries to *The Book of the Law* - 'When death is as complete as it should be, the individual expands and fulfils himself in all directions; it is an omniform *sam dhi*. This is of course "eternal ecstasy" in the sense already explained. But in the time-world *karma* re-concentrates the elements, and a new incarnation occurs.'[8] Here Crowley points to a Mystery of the "individual" existing both outside of and within time (simultaneously infinite and finite).

He makes this view even clearer (from a Qabbalistic per-

---

6   Crowley, *Magick Without Tears*, 246.

7   Gunther, *The Angel and the Abyss*, 217.

8   Crowley, *The Law Is for All*, 125.

spective) in *Magic Without Tears*: 'Now when a man spends his life (a) building up and developing the six Sephiroth of the Ruach so that they cohere closely in proper balance and relation, (b) in forging, developing and maintaining a link of steel between this solid Ruach and that Triad [the Supernals], Death merely means the dropping off of the Nephesch (Malkuth) so that the man takes over his instrument of Mind (Ruach) with him to his next suitably chosen vehicle.'[9]

Another of Crowley's teachings, that is particularly relevant to those who have sworn Oaths within the A∴A∴, which shows how service, in its broadest and most honourable sense, was a key to his vision for himself and later Adepts: 'There is one Oath more important than all the rest put together, from the point of view of the A∴A∴. You swear to refuse all the "rewards," to acquire your new vehicle without a moment's delay, so that you may carry on your work of helping Mankind with the minimum of interruption. Like all true Magical Oaths, it is certain of success.'[10] Crowley saw himself carrying on the work and teachings of Eliphas Lévi, to instigate a new age of personal and social reformation based on a principle of wholeness. As Gunther writes, 'Levi once again demonstrates the motif of wholeness with his famous illustration of Baphomet...'[11] It is this concept of reincarnation that is particularly interesting in terms of the initiatory system of the A∴A∴. Having reached its highest grades, and developed an impersonal, universal perspective and an understanding of the transitory nature of all things, you would assume that the Adept would develop an indifference to humanity, its problems, and its very existence. Yet the Adept is sworn to continue to reincarnate for the ben-

---

9   Crowley, *Magick Without Tears*, 244–5.

10   Crowley, 245.

11   Gunther, *The Angel and the Abyss*, 278.

efit and progress of humanity. Their initiation is balanced by their Oath and Task, and an understanding of the continuity of existence in its fullest sense. They are bound by obligation and compassion.

Along a similar vein, we can read in Joseph Campbell's *The Inner Reaches of Outer Space*, '...the figure represents [...] the willing participation in the sorrows of space-time of one who, through the knowledge of himself as of the nature of immortal bliss, yet voluntarily, as an avatar [...] joyfully engages in the fragmentation of life in Time. There is a form of the crucifix known as "Christ Triumphant," where the figure of the Savior is shown not broken, bleeding, naked and with head dropped to the side, but with head erect, eyes open, body clothed, arm outstretched as though willingly "thus come" (*tathagata*), as the very image of a Bodhisattva in whom the agony of time and the rapture of eternity are disclosed as one and the same.'[12]

Crowley wrote that, '...Levi was a philosopher and an artist, besides being a supreme literary stylist and a practical joker of the variety called *"Pince sans rire"*;[13] and, being an artist and a profound symbolist, he was immensely attracted by the Tarot. While in England, he proposed to Kenneth Mackenzie,[14] a famous occult scholar and high-grade Freemason, to reconstitute and issue a scientifically-designed pack.'

In his works are new presentations by him of the trumps called The Chariot and The Devil. He seems to have understood that the Tarot was actually a pictorial form of the Qa-

---

12   Campbell, *The Inner Reaches of Outer Space*, 72.

13   This is a French expression that translates as "pinch without laughing" and refers to someone with a deadpan or dry sense of humour.

14   It is reported that Mackenzie referred to himself as 'Baphometus, Astrologer and Spiritist.' (Cavendish, *The Tarot*, 33.)

balistic Tree of Life, which is the basis of the whole Qabalah, so much so that he composed his works on this basis. He wished to write a complete treatise on Magick. He divided his subject into two parts—Theory and Practice which he called *Dogma* and *Ritual*. Each part has twenty-two chapters, one for each of the twenty-two trumps; and each chapter deals with the subject represented by the picture displayed by the trump. The importance of the accuracy of the correspondence will appear in due course.[15]

This is significant, as Crowley also (with artist Lady Frieda Harris (1877–1962)) created a Tarot deck. This shows Crowley expanding on (and perhaps completing) the work commenced by Lévi.

Crowley went further than just considering Baphomet a creation of the Abbé, stating in a diary entry from June 1920, 'When I was Levi I drew myself as Ayin or Baphomet...'.[16] This indicates that he saw Baphomet as not just an encapsulation of Lévi's esoteric thought, but also as a representation of Lévi himself (or Lévi's magical persona). This was a representation and obligation that Crowley took on and developed. Both Lévi and Crowley were Baphomet, and they both wanted to change the world. Crowley even undertook a translation of Lévi's *La Clef Des Grands Mysteres* (titled in English *The Key of the Mysteries*), which was first published as a supplement to *The Equinox I (10)*. In his introduction to this translation Crowley writes that, 'It may be regarded as written by him as his Thesis for the Grade of Exempt Adept, just as his Ritual and Dogma was his Thesis for the grade of Major Adept.'[17] Crowley be-

---

15   Crowley, *The Book of Thoth*, 5–6.

16   Crowley, *The Magical Record of the Beast 666*, 198.

17   Levi, *The Key of the Mysteries*, vii. It is interesting to note that this quote

lieved that he met this requirement himself, referring to his past reincarnation, through his translation of the text (although, as pointed out by others, he more than met this requirement with the publication of Book 4, which could be seen as Crowley's own *Dogma and Ritual*).

Crowley, like Lévi, had a clear political and social element to his teachings, and his vision for the OTO. It could be argued that he took this a step further than Lévi, with the OTO as a vehicle and template, which has been handed to his 'successors and heirs' to continue – a weighty obligation.

Another interesting hint into the nature of Baphomet that was left to us by Crowley is in a new Pentagrammaton - אדדני.

Crowley writes regarding this, 'What letter, then significant of Nuit, will transmute אדני as *shin* does יהוה? The usual letter is *he*, "The Star," Atu XVII, ♒. We thus obtain a Pentagrammaton whose value is 70, ע, the Eye, Set[18] or Saturn, Atu XV "The Devil."'[19]

Here Crowley shows the transformation or development of the name Adonai, with the indwelling of the Hebrew letter *he* (as *shin* indwells the Tetragrammaton). *Shin* is the spirit, and a parallel could be drawn here between spirit and breath;

---

was edited out (for reasons unknown) from the edition published by Rider in 1959, along with the "Translators Note", with its criticisms of A.E. Waite. It should also be noted that the *Key of the Mysteries* was preceded in this volume of the Equinox by an article titled "Dead Weight". I have no doubt that this is not coincidental, with Waite being the main translator of the works of Lévi.

18   Crowley comments that 'Set is the Goat in the south...' (Crowley, *The Magical Record of the Beast 666*, 90.)

19   Crowley et al., *Commentaries of the Holy Books and Other Papers*, 4:219.

breath[20] represented by *he* (refer to Crowley's commentary to Chapter 86 of *The Book of Lies*).

Crowley provides this new Pentagrammaton in his commentary to verse 65 of Chapter V of *Liber LXV*, which reads:

> So also is the end of the book, and the Lord Adonai is about it on all sides like a Thunderbolt, and a Pylon, and a Snake, and a Phallus, and in the midst thereof He is like the Woman that jetteth out the milk of the stars from her paps; yea, the milk of the stars from her paps.[21]

This seems to me to be in reference to the mysteries of both the Holy Guardian Angel, and the Master of the Temple - "He" is like "the Woman". The Angel is primarily male, or functions as male in relation to the Aspirant, whereas the Masters of the Temple are Women (Scarlet Women). What is the milk of the stars? I tentatively put forward, light – a stellar radiance that is a source of nourishment.

> But I have burnt within thee as a pure flame without oil. In the midnight I was brighter than the moon; in the daytime I exceeded utterly the sun, in the byways of thy being I inflamed, and dispelled the illusion.
>
> *Liber LXV, V:9*[22]

Gunther refers to the above Pentagrammaton, and the 'transformative power of the New Light.'[23] This relates to The

---

20   It is also interesting that some Jewish teachers believe that the Tetragrammaton represents inhalation and exhalation (life), and that the sound of the in and out breath in the way the "unpronounceable name" is pronounced.

21   Crowley, *The Holy Books of Thelema*, 83.

22   Crowley, 77.

23   Gunther, *Initiation In the Aeon of the Child*, 152.

Four Gates, which are in Malkuth ("Gate of the Daughter of the Mighty One"). The final represents Adonai surrounded by the Gates, the gates that 'must, in some fashion, be entered by all mankind eventually, in order to partake fully of the material life.'[24] The path of the Candidate, the Aspirant to the A∴A∴ is illuminated by the LVX of Adonai, and this Light also 'opens the way.'[25] So in the above quote from *Liber LXV* it could be read that "He" is both a reference to the male pronoun, but also the Hebrew letter. It could also be seen as in its two positions on the Tree of Life, Malkuth and Binah. The Neophyte and the Master of the Temple, and how both of these relate to the mysteries of Adonai. And if we return to Crowley's comment regarding the new Pentagrammaton, to Baphomet.

It is interesting that if we add the values of *Liber LXV*, and *Liber VII*,[26] we get 72. By Hebrew Gematria this is the value of Adonai as transliterated in the *Lemegeton*, and other sources (אדונאי). It is also the value of "plenitude, fullness" (טלא), as well as "and they are excellent, finished" (ויבללו). It is also "a dove" (ינרה), the descent of which we see represented on the Lamen of the OTO. The dove is sacred to Venus and a symbol of the Holy Ghost, 'the Phallus in its most sublimated form'.[27] In discussing this symbolism, and this mix of "masculine" and "feminine" concepts in relation to the formula of Tetragrammaton (in the context of The Fool), Crowley writes, 'The deep-

---

24   Gunther, 152.

25   Gunther, 152.

26   'This book [Liber LXV] is given to Probationers, as the attainment of the Knowledge and Conversation of the Holy Guardian angel is the Crown of the Outer College. Similarly Liber VII is given to Neophytes, as the grade of Master of the Temple is the next resting-place…' (Crowley, *The Holy Books of Thelema*, xxix.)

27   Crowley, *The Book of Thoth*, 56.

er one goes into the formula, the closer becomes the identification of opposites…There is therefore no reason for surprise in observing the identification of the father with the mother.'[28] When considering the OTO Lamen, one way I view its import, and that of the dove, this sublimated phallus, is something that is radiating out. The Eye in the Triangle being that interior light or Sun that never ceases to shine, and the dove, this light radiating out from ourselves, to be received in the Grail, which is the world, and the reflection of this shows us our own true interior state, a state that is within our power to transform. In one sense, this is a Eucharist.

In *The Vision and the Voice*, again finding a connection with the Eye, it is recorded in the 8th Aethyr, 'For I am not only appointed to guard thee, but we are of the blood royal, the guardians of the Treasure-house of Wisdom. Therefore I am called the Minister of Ra-Hoor-Khuit; and yet he is but a Viceroy of the unknown King. For my name is called Aiwass, that is eight and seventy. And I am the influence of the Concealed One, and the wheel that hath eight and seventy parts, yet in all is equivalent to the Gate that is the name of my Lord when it is spelt fully. And that Gate is the Path that joineth the Wisdom with the Understanding.'[29]

Commenting on the above, Crowley writes, 'This conceals a mystery. I have been fooled myself with my איואס = 78.[30] For 8 + 70 = ח and ע. Cheth is 418, the formula of the New Aeon; and ע or Capricorn is Set or Hadit, the Eye; and He is that Hadit who is manifested as 418.'

---

28 Crowley, 56.

29 Crowley, Neuburg, and Desti, *The Vision & the Voice with Commentary and Other Papers: The Collected Diaries of Aleister Crowley, 1909-1914 E.V.*, 182.

30 Aiwass

One of the fascinating things about the 8th Aethyr is that it is intimately linked with the process and experience of the Knowledge and Conversation of the Holy Guardian Angel, and it is also intimately linked to Aiwass, from whom Crowley received *The Book of the Law* (directly referenced above) – 'Note that the Holy Guardian Angel of the Seer claims to be Aiwass...'[31] Aiwass, in the Aethyr, also makes a connection between himself, the seer and royalty or kingship – 'we are of the blood royal, the guardians of the Treasure-house of Wisdom'. Wisdom of course is one of the titles of Chokmah, the second Sephiroth, whose symbols include the Phallus, and the Inner Robe of Glory (however it is Chesed, Chokmah of a lower arch, that is a "mighty crowned and throned king", representing this energy, this phallic energy, the kingly power, on a lower arch.

Another clear influence on Crowley was Richard Payne Knight (1751–1824). Knight was an 'English antiquarian, philologist, numismatist, free-thinking Deist philosopher, expert on Greek literature, member of the Radical (Whig) Party of Parliament and the Society of Dilletanti, friend of Lord Byron, patron of art and learning, and country gentleman.'[32] This influence can be seen in the use of the seal that appears on OTO pledge forms for the Frater Superior or Outer Head of the Order. This seal can be found in Knight's book *A Discourse on the Worship of Priapus*. Knight describes this "gem"[33] in the

---

31   Crowley, Neuburg, and Desti, *The Vision & the Voice with Commentary and Other Papers: The Collected Diaries of Aleister Crowley, 1909-1914 E.V.*, 182.

32   'Sir Richard Payne Knight | The Invisible Basilica of Sabazius | Essays, Speeches, Commentary, and Rituals by the National Grand Master of OTO USA'.

33   This seal is a 'gryllus in the form of a cock with addorsed griffin's wings. The body is composed of a Seilenos-mask and a ram's head, and a serpent issues from the chin of the mask. In the field is a star.' ('Drawing | British

following way, which shows why it became of significance to the OTO, and Baphomet:

> In a gem in the Museum of Charles Townley, Esq., the head of the Greek Pan is joined to that of a ram, on the body of a cock, over whose head is the asterisk of the sun, and below it the head of an aquatic fowl, attached to the same body." The cock is the symbol of the sun, probably from proclaiming his approach in the morning; and the aquatic fowl is the emblem of water; so that this composition, apparently so whimsical, represents the universe between the two great prolific elements, the one the active, and the other the passive cause of all things.[34]

Crowley thought so highly of Knight that he was included in the list of Saints in the Gnostic Mass, and *Two Essays on the Worship of Priapus* was included in the general reading

---

Museum'.) Silenus was companion and tutor to the wine god Dionysus.

34 Payne Knight, *Book A Discourse on the Worship of Priapus and Its Connection to the Mystic Theology of the Ancients*, 39.

('Books for Serious Study') section of the A∴A∴ curriculum. The writings of Knight would have also been known to the early founders of the OTO, such as Carl Kellner (1850–1905) and 'literature on the sexual basis of religion flourished from 1865 through the 1930s.'[35]

So, we see here in the contemporary literature that would have had an influence on the founders of the OTO, solar symbolism, and also the 'the active, and the other the passive cause of all things.' The creative interplay of Baphomet.

In *The Confessions of Aleister Crowley* he discusses the name Baphomet, stating that 'for six years and more I had tried to discover the proper way to spell this name. I knew that it must have eight letters, and also that the numerical and literal correspondences must be such as to express the meaning of the name in such a way as to confirm what scholarship had found out about it, and also to clear up those problems which archaeologists had so far failed to solve.'[36]

So why did Crowley think that the name Baphomet should correctly have 8 letters? Because this is what had been revealed to him in *Liber A'ash*[37] in 1911. The Amalantrah Working, that would reveal the correct spelling, took place in 1918, and I will explore this working in more detail later.[38]

The Fool

In *The Book of Thoth*, Crowley draws clear links between two cards in the Tarot; The Fool and The Devil, both of which

---

35   Kaczynski, *Forgotten Templars*, 246.

36   Crowley, *The Confessions of Aleister Crowley*, 832.

37   *Liber A'ash vel Capricorni Pneumatici. sub figurâ CCCLXX*

38   It is interesting that Plato taught that the original man was an androgyne with two faces, and that the body was binary with 8 limbs.

represent, I would argue, Baphomet in different phases of operation.

Crowley writes, 'But at this time archaeological research had not gone very far; the nature of Baphomet was not fully understood. (See Atu 0, above.) At least he succeeded in identifying the goat portrayed upon the card with Pan.'[39] In this

____

39 Crowley, *The Book of Thoth*, 105.

quote, Crowley is referring to the work of Lévi, and we can see from it that he is pointing us to Atu 0, "The Fool" in order to understand the nature of The Devil, of Baphomet. It is also worth noting the large number of pages that were dedicated to The Fool in *The Book of Thoth* (like Crowley is setting the foundations for the rest of the main Atu). The fool represents the original state that the aspirant is seeking to return to, via the key shown by Baphomet. They are different phases of the same experience.

'The really important feature of this card is that its number should be 0. It represents therefore the Negative above the Tree of Life, the source of all things. It is the Qabalistic Zero. It is the equation of the Universe, the initial and final balancing of the opposites...'[40] It is also worth noting that the Hebrew letter associated with Atu 0 is Aleph (א),[41] which is sometimes referred to as a silent letter, as is Ayin (ע) – they have no sound by themselves but depend on an accompanying vowel.[42]

> In the silence of a dewdrop is every tendency of his
> soul, and of his mind, and of his body; it is the
> Quintessence and the Elixir of his being. Therein
> are the forces that made him and his father and his
> father's father before him.
> This is the Dew of Immortality.[43]

---

40 Crowley, 53.

41 Lévi wrote that Aleph 'indicates the balance of universal equilibrium...' (Levi, *The Kabalistic and Occult Philosophy of Eliphas Levi*, 1:285.)

42 Aleph can act as a consonant and here it can be heard, but as a "mother of reading" it is silent.

43 Crowley, *The Book of Lies*, 46.

Crowley writes further about silence[44] and its significance to Baphomet in *The Book of Thoth*, 'For Silence is the Equilibrium of Perfection; so that Harpocrates is the omniform, the universal Key to every Mystery soever. The Sphinx is the "Puzzle or Pucelle", the Feminine Idea to which there is only one complement, always different in form, and always identical in essence. This is the signification of the Picture of the God; it is shown more clearly in His adult form as the Fool of the Tarot and as Bacchus Diphues, and without equivocation when He appears as Baphomet.'[45] Now "puzzle" refers to a harlot, and "pucelle" refers to a maid or virgin, showing two phases of the "Feminine Idea", and this is the complementary principle to Baphomet. These could also be seen as complimentary phases or aspects of the same entity, noting the connections highlighted between Baphomet and the Sphinx made by Lévi.

There are some distinct visual keys that link these two cards. If we look behind the image of The Fool depicted in Atu 0 we see a circular pattern, sitting like a halo, that appears to have similarities to the circular shape the phallus is piercing in Atu XV ("The Devil"). Over the left-hand shoulder of The Fool is also grapes and a vine leaf, which can be seen on the head of the goat in The Devil. Both figures are also horned (the Fool less exaggerated). The Fool is also depicting the balance of opposites. In one hand he holds a depiction of a cup or grail, in the other the fire (the elements that are seen to be mixed in Atu XIV, ("Art"), but these elements are not contained within a cauldron, but released into the air; unbounded). They are also both smiling (somewhat sinister, like The Hierophant), as are

---

44 'Te appears as Chockmah-Binah, Benevolence as Chesed, Justice as Geburah, Convention as Tiphareth. Thus Kether alone is "safe"; even Chockmah-Binah risks fall unless it keeps Silence.' (Crowley, *Tao Te King*, 55.)

45 Crowley, *The Book of Thoth*, 120.

the dual figures in Atu XIV ("Art"). The caduceus is also present in The Fool and The Devil. In The Devil, the wand is very much grounded and erect; in The Fool it is free and flowing in circles around the central figure along with the dove and the vulture.

> But they have the half: unite by thine art so that all disappear
> My prophet is a fool with his one, one, one; are they not the Ox, and none by the Book?
>
> *Liber AL,* 1:47-48

In The Devil, the figures contained within the testes are shown as adults seeking unity, whereas The Fool shows two infants (two innocents) in an embrace.

The Fool is, 'a glyph of the creative light',[46] whereas The Devil is, 'creative energy in its most material form.'[47] Along with The Hermit, these three cards 'offer a threefold explanation of the male creative energy.'[48] If we add the numbers of these cards, we get 24, a number explored elsewhere in this book. Twenty-four also reduces to 6, Tiphareth and $\odot$. The radiating sun replacing (or concealing) the genitals of The Fool (arguably completely externalised the representation of The Devil), and serving as a lamp for The Hermit, who represents 'Fertility in its most exalted sense.'[49]

The Devil represents the more material operation of the kingly power, whereas The Fool shows us that exulted state of consciousness, that state of silence or innocence from which that power can be directed. In The Fool are all possibilities, in

---

46 Crowley, 69.

47 Crowley, 105.

48 Crowley, 106.

49 Crowley, 89.

The Devil is the manifestation of these possibilities. The Fool sees all things and does not differentiate. The Devil, Baphomet provides the structure of material existence – he specialises.

* * *

In his personal diary, Crowley shares further insights into the nature of, and his relationship with, Baphomet (introduced earlier in this work):

When I was Levi I drew myself as Ayin or Baphomet, 'The Devil', with Beast's Head. This is the Beast throned, crowned, exalted; the leaper, the erect, the butter-in. Her womb is my city, Babel. This Ayin is therefore my Phallic Will, My Holy Guardian Angel, Aiwaz, who was afterwards called Satan. Distinguish their Ayin-Baphomet crowned from the Teth-Therion ridden. I am Ayin-King in Her city, Pe, Baphomet of Babalon; and she is also Babalon, Whore astride Therion in Teth. Her name seems the same both ways; perhaps always 7 whether I am 6 or 8.[50]

Baphomet is crowned, the Beast is ridden. Baphomet is the King[51] in Her city, whereas the Beast is ridden by Her.

---

50   Crowley, *The Magical Record of the Beast 666*, 198.

51   The number 8 is also connected with the Hebrew letter Cheth, and is connected to The Chariot in the Tarot. The card in its more traditional form shows a crowned king. 'The meaning of this card and its connection with the sign of Cancer are quite obvious. The Sun enters Cancer at the summer solstice, that is, at the period of his greatest triumph.' (Crowley and Adams, *The General Principles of Astrology*, 37.) The figure in The Chariot bears the Grail, something that is also closely associated with Babalon, who 'holds aloft the cup, the Holy Grail aflame with love and death.' (Crowley, *The Book of Thoth*, 94.). So here we see another connection between the 7 and the 8 (Baba-

It is clear here that Crowley is identifying himself directly with Baphomet and connecting it with his past incarnation as Eliphas Lévi. It is also worth noting the connection of Babalon with Pe (ﬦ). This is 'her city', in which Crowley sees himself as Ayin-King (remembering what Philo states about "the kingly power" and that concept explored throughout this book). In *The Book of Thoth*, Crowley writes of Atu XVI (The Tower or War assigned to the letter which is a mouth, the vehicle of speech), 'This suggests another (and totally different) interpretation of the card…The destruction of the garrison may therefore be taken to mean their emancipation from the prisons of organized life, which was confining them. It was their unwisdom to cling to it.'[52] Unwisdom. '…the doctrine is that the ultimate reality (which is Perfection) is Nothingness. Hence all manifestations, however glorious, however delightful, are stains. To obtain perfection, all existing things must be annihilated.'[53]

This seems to indicate a certain union and identity between the figures of The Beast and that of Baphomet. She remains unchanged as 7, whereas Crowley identified two separate functions, and how this union is accomplished. One is ridden, controlled, the other is within the City of Babalon – they are both "conjoined" with her, but in different ways. The union of Babalon and Baphomet, in one sense, is a marriage of Heaven and Earth. We can again see this connection between Baphomet and earth or matter in *The Book of Lies*, Chapter 77.

---

lon and Baphomet), and both bear the Holy Grail.

52   Crowley, *The Book of Thoth*, 108.

53   Crowley, 108.

7, the septenary; 11, the magical number; 77, the manifestation,[54] therefore, of the septenary. Through matter, because
77 is written in Hebrew Ayin Zayin (OZ),[55] and He-Goat,
the symbol of matter, Capricornus, the Devil of the Tarot;
which is the picture of the Goat of the Sabbath upon an altar,
worshipped by two other devils, male and female.[56]

Here also Crowley connects the number 77 to the concept
of redemption, also showing us a connection between this and
Laylah (LAILAH),[57] to whom Chapter 77 is dedicated.

Now, the Devil of the tarot is the Phallus, the Redeemer, and
Laylah, symbolises redemption to Frater P. The number 77,
also, interpreted as in the title, is the redeeming force.[58]

---

54   Just as 49 (associated with Babalon) is 7 squared. A square number is the
result of a number being multiplied by itself.

55   We can also see the connection to earth in Crowley's *Liber Oz*, or the
Rights of Man. In a letter to G.J. York Crowley called this 'the "O.T.O. plan
in words of one syllable"', and it is divided up in five sections 'moral, bodily,
mental, sexual freedom and the safeguard of tyrannicide...' This document
gives us all our rights upon the earth, in incarnation.

56   Crowley, *The Book of Lies*, 165.

57   Laylah refers to Australian violinist Leila Ida Nerissa Bathurst Waddell,
(1880-1932), and one time lover and student of Crowley's. She is shown as
both a normal woman, and also a far more exalted feminine concept that
Crowley 'exalts above God' (Crowley, 143.) – 'The title of the chapter suggests
the two in one, since the ornithorhynchus is both bird and beast; it is also an
Australian animal, like Laylah herself, and was doubtless chosen for this reason.' (Crowley, 125.). Laylah, Crowley explains, is the Arabic for night. 'L +A
+ I + L + A + H = 77, which is also MZL, the Influence of the Highest, OZ, a
goat...' (Crowley, 143.) – 'O ye who dwell in the City of the Pyramids beneath
the Night of PAN, remember that ye shall see no more light but That of the
great fire that shall consume your dust to ashes! (Crowley, 144.)

58   Crowley, *The Book of Lies*, 165.

Crowley describes Laylah (in one way) as 'N.O.X. the night of Pan; and Laylah, the night before His threshold!'.[59] This is from the chapter in *The Book of Lies* called "The Southern Cross." Crowley dismisses this title as just referring to Laylah being an Australian; however there is clearly more to this. The Southern Cross has been used historically in navigation because its two bright stars (Acrux and Gacrux), point to the southern celestial pole. A still point around which everything else revolves. If we turn back a chapter in *The Book of Lies*, we find Chapter 28, "The Pole Star".

> Love destroyeth self, uniting self with that which is
> not-self, so that Love breedeth All and None in
> One.[60]

This "All" and "None" could be seen as The Fool and The Devil, the conjunction of the All and the None (or the undifferentiated and the differentiated).

From this, if we conjoin Babalon (7) with Baphomet (8), we again are taken back to 15, which resolves back to 6 (1+5), the Sun-Therion, and the Mystic Number of the Masters of the Temple - "the idea pertains to a faculty of the mind which is "above the Abyss".

Here we see Crowley associating Baphomet with his Office of The Beast and its relationship with Babalon and the dual nature of the Beast, as 6 or 8 – as the Sun or as Mercury – Therion or Baphomet. Also, very interestingly, we see here Crowley making a connection between Baphomet and his Holy Guardian Angel – defined as Aiwaz. In an earlier diary entry Crowley recorded: 'Later – I invoked Aiwaz, was shown a phantasm

---

59   Crowley, 68.

60   Crowley, 66.

of Baphomet, and suddenly determined to recognise this for Him! I was instantly rewarded by the Word and Oath of an Ipsissimus.'[61] An Ipsissimus represents the highest grade in the A∴A∴. 'The Ipsissimus is wholly free from all limitations soever, existing in the Nature of all things without discrimination of quantity or quality between them.'[62] As discussed earlier, perhaps this state of 'existing in the Nature of all things' is that state represented by The Fool.

When I read this entry the image of Atu V ("The Hierophant") enters my mind, as I personally see this card as a depiction of Aiwaz – who Crowley identified with his Holy guardian Angel (V being ו, the "Prince").

> He seemed to be a tall, dark man in his thirties, well-knit, active and strong, with the face of a savage king, and eyes veiled lest their gaze should destroy what they saw. The dress was not Arab; it suggested Assyria or Persia, but very vaguely.[63]

---

61 Crowley, *The Magical Record of the Beast 666*, 140.

62 Crowley et al., *Commentaries of the Holy Books and Other Papers*, 4:13.

63 Crowley, *The Holy Books of Thelema*, Viii.

Further, Gunther makes clearer the connection between the Hierophant and the Masters of the Temple, making reference to the downward pointing V, formed by the Hierophant's left hand forming the Greek Λ, showing a connection to Atu VIII ("Adjustment"). '[R]ather than the Roman V, he is forming the Greek Λ, which equates to the Hebrew ל, attributed to Atu VIII, Adjustment, and Libra ♎ in the Zodiac. M.A.A.T.'[64]

These two letters together, however (the upright and the

____

64   Gunther, *The Angel and the Abyss*, 280.

averse) form the vesica in which M.A.A.T. stands as a guardian of the gate through which the aspirant must pass in order to enter the Supernal Triad (as one who has passed that gate and stands in balance); where the heart is weighed against the feather of truth.

Also the lady Maat with her feather and her sword abode to judge the righteous.

For Fate was already established.

Liber CCXXXI, 11

It is also worth recalling that Crowley identified Aiwas with The Devil, 'that AIWAZ – the solar-phallic-hermetic "Lucifer" – is His own Holy Guardian Angel, and "The Devil" SATAN or HADIT...This serpent SATAN, is not the enemy of Man, but he who made Gods of our race...He is "The Devil" of the Book of Thoth, and his emblem is BAPHOMET, the Androgyne who is the hieroglyph of arcane perfection.'[65]

If we trace this somewhat frantic train of thought and interrelationships, we can see, perhaps, a deeper indication of why Crowley assumed the name of the Templar idol. Baphomet is a symbolic representation of Aiwaz. Baphomet shows to us Crowley's own Holy Guardian Angel in symbolic form ('he who made Gods of our race'), and the state of equilibrated consciousness this "emblem" represents – a state of "arcane perfection" – Baphomet consciousness.

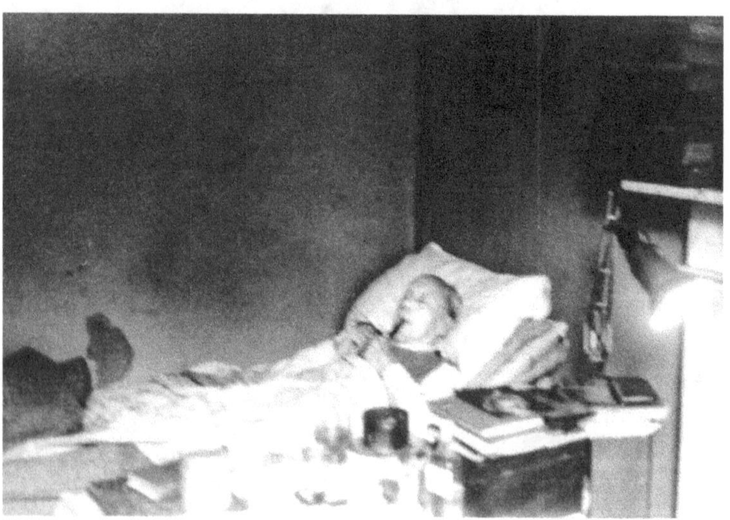

---

65   Crowley, Desti, and Waddell, *Magick. Liber ABA. Book Four. Parts I-IV*, 277.

J.F.C. Fuller

It is interesting to examine the work of J.F.C. Fuller to gain an understanding of the teachings about Baphomet to early initiates of the A∴A∴, in a time before Crowley's involvement with the OTO.

Major-General John Frederick Charles "Boney" Fuller CB CBE DSO (1 September 1878–10 February 1966) was not an uncontroversial character.

Fuller has been described as, 'a small man with a neatly trimmed moustache and a hairline that had retreated over his crown and was beginning to march down the back of his head. He could have passed for a butler in a costume drama, but his appearance belied an inner radicalism. (He had been friends — and then enemies — with the occultist Aleister Crowley.)'[1]

He was one of the early, and influential, theorists on armoured warfare and was involved in Oswald Mosley's British Union of Fascists in the 1930's. Fuller was also sympathetic to Hitler and the Nazis.

When Adolf Hitler came to power in 1933 and began to expand the German army and invest in tanks, he encountered a German military that had been watching, thinking and experimenting for 14 years. On his 50th birthday in 1939, Hitler celebrated with a parade of Germany's newly reconstructed army through Berlin. "For three hours," wrote one witness, "a completely mechanised and motorised army roared past the Führer." This witness was a guest of honour at the celebrations. His name: J F C Fuller.[2]

---

1   Harford, 'Why Big Companies Squander Good Ideas'.

2   Harford.

Fuller has a connection to Baphomet through his relationship with Crowley, and his rendering of Baphomet from 1911, which must have been influenced by his instruction under Crowley and the active relationship between the two men. Fuller would discover Crowley's writings when he was stationed in India, and he penned a book on Crowley's writings called *The Star in the West: A Critical Essay Upon the Works of Aleister Crowley*. Fuller would go on to become the founding Chancellor of the A∴A∴, co-editor of *The Equinox*, and its principal illustrator. His skill as an illustrator can be seen in his rendering of Baphomet, as well as many other works painted for the Temple of A∴A∴.

It is this rendering of Baphomet that will be the main focus of this chapter, and we can only assume that (although it is an original work by Fuller that would capture some of his personal insights) this work includes ideas that would have been taught to him during his time receiving instruction under Crowley, and as an early student of the A∴A∴. Similar to the alchemical image of a mountain in the previous chapter, this shows Baphomet as a glyph of initiation, and, unsurprisingly, a reconciliation of opposites.

I will attempt an analysis as best I can; however, in all available resolutions of the image, some elements are difficult to decipher,[3] and, as far as I am aware, Fuller never provided a written description of the painting, nor have I encountered any contemporary analysis of it.

The painting is dated to 1911 in the collection of the Mary Evans Picture Library, and looks like at some stage it has been in some kind of frame, which has damaged some of the board surrounding the central image. It is uncertain if the additional glyphs are original or have been added later. But their more "rough" appearance would indicate a later addition, or something possibly not designed to be viewed in the same way the central image was.

The circular border that frames and surrounds the image of Baphomet is flaming, and appears to be a representation of the Sun. In the next layer we see an arrow, also forming a circular shape, and within this is a scroll featuring the formula INRI, and the number DCLXVI (666) is shown on the shaft. The analysis of INRI is a well-known teaching within the Golden

---

3   I would like to thank the band White Orange whose LP release (limited edition picture disk) of their album "…and this is why I speak to you in parables" featured a large rendering of Fuller's Baphomet that made this analysis more possible.

Dawn, with one possible interpretation being the Latin *Igne Natura Renovatur Integra* ("The Whole of Nature is Renewed by Fire"). Within the tip of the shaft appears to be a buddha in meditation, seated in a flower.

Also appearing around the shaft of the arrow, but also on one of the points of the inverted pentagram, are various figures. On one we have a lunar goddess, possibly Artemis, who appears to be blowing on a horn in the shape of a lunar crescent. This is a cornucopia, a symbol of abundance or plenty. She seems to represent nature or life. On the opposite point appears Death holding a candle and bell. At the same point as the lunar goddess is the Greek Ω, whereas with Death is the Greek A – the beginning and the end – 'Death begins the Operation by a knock, to which Life answers.'[4]

At another point in the image is the Lion and the Serpent, a glyph known to be associated with Baphomet.[5] The serpent is coiled 3 ½ times to represent kundalini. Opposite and above this seems to be a representation of a Phoenix, or possibly that of a form of Horus.

---

4   Crowley, *Aleister Crowley and the Practice of the Magical Diary*, 27.

5   Liber XV: The Gnostic Mass, Creed.

Cloisonne breastplate of the God Horus, from the Tomb of Tutankhamun

On the shaft of the circular arrow two numbers are shown CCVI (206) and CCVII (207). This is somewhat obscure to me, but a tentative interpretation is that CCVI is the number of 'DBR, Speech, "the Word of Power"', and 207, AVR, Light. Contrast with AVB, 9, the Astral Light, and AVD, 11, the Magical Light. Aub is an illusory thing of witchcraft ("cf." Obi, Obeah); Aud is almost equal to the Kundalini force ("Odic" force). This illustrates well the difference between the sluggish, viscous 9, and the keen, ecstatic 11.'[6] Both, in a sense (Word

---

6   Crowley, *777 and Other Qabalistic Writings of Aleister Crowley*, 33.

and Light), 206 and 207), an externalisation of the internal, a moving towards manifestation.

Within an inner circle are the Kabbalistic images of the Sword and the Serpent, the descent down the Tree of Life, and the ascent up the Tree of Life, with the serpent's heads meeting at the upright pentagram.

Fuller's rendering of Baphomet does share some elements of the image produced by Lady Frieda Harris many years later for the Thoth tarot. Sitting like a halo behind the head of Baphomet is a series of coloured rings, like the one that the tree pierces in Atu XV. Interestingly, there is no representation of the caduceus or Wand of the Chief Adept – instead Fuller places, within the vesica, the Tau. This image first appeared in a supplement to The Equinox I(3), in Fuller's *The Treasure House of Images*. This shows the Tau within three diamonds – 'Within their triangles of Yonis is the Lingam touching and filling it.'[7] There may, however, be a reference to the caduceus at the bottom of the painting, where there seems to be a twin image of a unicorn and a goat (white and black), with their serpentine tails joining, and between them, pointing upwards, is another representation of an arrow, like a phallus. This sits at the lowest point of the inverted pentagram, above which seems to be a tri-coloured bar, or veil.

The upward pointing hand of Baphomet shows serpents in the form of arrows flying upwards towards the Phoenix, whereas from the downward pointing hand (with a dagger) doves fly down towards the Lion and Serpent.

The throne of Baphomet is a three-dimensional circle, square and pyramid, in general alignment with Lévi's description.[8]

---

7   Fuller, 'Liber DCCCCLXIII: The Treasure House of Images', 3.

8   'This Pantheistic figure should be seated on a cube, and its footstool should be a single ball, or a ball and a triangular stool.' (Lévi, *Transcendental*

However, the pyramid as rendered by Fuller points downwards.

Around the body of Baphomet is again 'The girdle of the Starry One!', the wheel of the zodiac.

Here again we can see Baphomet in Fuller's rendering, motionless amongst the multiplicity of existence and contending forces. Simultaneously depicting the sword and the serpent, the emanation of creation and the return to divine unity. The dove and the serpent.

If the pyramid, as Gunther writes, is 'the triad of godhead',[9] then Fuller shows this triad inverted. God has descended into 'the quaternary of man'.[10] God is made flesh – or more the realisation that God was flesh from the start.

> I am clothed with the body of flesh; I am one with the Eternal and Omnipotent God.
>
> *Liber LXV, I:53–54*

Magic, XV.)

9   Gunther, *Initiation In the Aeon of the Child*, 54.

10   Gunther, 54.

THE AMALANTRAH WORKING

A full exploration of the Amalantrah Working would (and should) warrant a book in its own right, and most of the communication is obscure to me. However, there are some important elements of the Working that are relevant for this present study that I will tentatively introduce.

During the communication, the wizard provided an interesting clue into the secret of the Templars – 'a complete formula of the Gnostic and Templar mysteries.'[1] Additionally, it was via this working that the proper spelling of Baphomet was communicated (or a spelling that would convey certain meaning to Crowley). The Amalantrah Working is also linked with the concept and significance of kingship.

At the start of the Amalantrah working, the seer had a vision of herself as a candlestick with 13 candles:

> Over each flame was the opening of a tube which could hold water as a fountain. These tubes met the flame in a throbbing vibration which became almost excruciating when suddenly the part of the candlestick above the stem or staff, broke off and became a crown. The crown floated in the air tilted at a slight angle and a circle which was a halo came down from heaven and dropped into the crown. In the center a wand came and then it all hovered above the candlestick with a veil round it.[2] The veil in some ways appeared as rays of light.[3]

---

1   Crowley and Minor, 'Liber DCCXXIX : The Amalantrah Working'.

2   These elements may have a connection to the interactions between the Emperor, the Empress and the Hierophant discussed later – Crown, halo and wand.

3   Crowley and Minor, 'Liber DCCXXIX : The Amalantrah Working'.

Here the seer sees herself as a symbol of light that becomes crowned. This is also associated with the halo (a symbol used to represent holy or sacred figures, as well as rulers and heroes). There is also a clear connection to a veil, which is also rays of light.

Later the seer had a vision of a king, who was connected to 'an egg in which were many, many tiny convolutions of some flesh-like substance which would form something. The egg was placed in an oblong as in a picture... He was certainly not a king belonging to any kingdom limited by a country's borders, but was a king of men, or a king of the world. I asked his name and the word "Ham" appeared between the egg in the oblong and the soldiers around the king. <<i.e. King of Egypt?>>'[4] Ham is a bija (seed) mantra that is connected to the Vishudda Chakra, where Ether is represented. Ether's quality is dimensionless, all-pervading space. Ether gives rise to all other elements, and its symbol is a black oval or egg.

The King and the Wizard, as they appear in the working, are linked, and therefore could be seen as aspects of the same entity. The seer reports, 'The king went out to one side and a wizard linked his arm in the king's as they disappeared. The wizard looked at me significantly as they left. It was a sort of look as if one would almost wink.'[5]

Tantalisingly, on the 20th of April, 1918, the following is recorded:

Wizard is there looking across Water. All there. A Donkey is grazing near base of mountain. Serpent is there. Mountain Goat on mountain. Chinese doll-head. White cliff. Priest in black with shining smooth satin gown. Chinese Lantern.

---

4   Crowley and Minor.

5   Crowley and Minor.

Here we see a Donkey (ass), a mountain, a Serpent, a Mountain Goat, and indications of a Chinese presence (Chinese doll-head and a Chinese Lantern). All these speak to Baphomet, and it is during these communications, as mentioned, Crowley was delivered the correct spelling of Baphomet (the significance of Donkeys and Serpents will be explored later).

On January 20, 1918 Soror Achitha (The Seer) had the following communication with the Wizard:

> I asked how to spell (Bafometh) <<[Baphomet]>> and a man like the Gods of the Mountains answered my questions about this. Finally I was told B-a-f-o-m-e-t-h. I begged for more information about the message but got none. Many questions were asked about the letters of the spelling as to whether they were Hebrew etc., etc. They were Hebrew.

> I then said Good Bye, noting the boy's beautiful dark eyes, and we went away by a little path to the pool of the spring. We bathed in this and then sank through the bottom and came out directly over Manhattan. We came back into our bodies.[6]

Here I see a connection between mountains ('a man like the Gods of the Mountains'), and at the conclusion of the vision the bathing in 'the pool of the spring', like a baptism. It is also worth noting that during this early (and somewhat difficult) communication with the Wizard, when he was asked "who I was" (Soror Achitha), the answer was "Part of the Tao."[7] The man is associated with high places, mountains, which are connected with the wilderness, which will be a recurring theme in this work.

---

6   Crowley and Minor.

7   Crowley and Minor, 'The Amalantrah Working – Liber XCVII'.

If we wanted any clearer indication of Amalantrah's connection with the Tao as indicated above, then we need not look any further than Crowley's introduction to his *Tao Te Ching*.

> During my Great Magical Retirement on Aesopus Island in the Hudson River during the summer of 1918, I set myself to work, but I discovered immediately that I was totally incompetent. I therefore appealed to an Adept named Amalantrah, with whom I was at that time in almost daily communion. He came readily to my aid, and exhibited to me a codex of the original, which conveyed to me with absolute certitude the exact significance of the text.[8]

Mountains also have significance in Taoism. 'They are one of the elemental Taoist symbols... In the Taoist imagination, the high mountain peak is where the Taoist "mountain man" absorbs the bright yang air of heaven, and meets the constellations face to face.'[9] Mountains hold a fascination and power across different religions and races. They are 'privileged places for experiencing the sacred, either as "hierophanies" (manifestations of the sacred) or "kratophanies" (manifestations of power)... Mountains intervene between godly space, which is at a level above all else, and mortal space. Also, they symbolize the ultimacy of the godhead and facilitate nearness to the divine canopy.'[10] This gives a perspective of the power of mountains representing or giving us access to something external to or above ourselves. But as I. W. Mabbett comments when writing about Mount Meru, 'This is evident in the many layers of symbolism that exchange Meru for the cosmic man, for the temple at the center of the universe, for the office of

---

8   Crowley, *Tao Te King*, 10.

9   Li, 'Gu Xiong'.

10   Michael, 'Mountains and Early Daoism in the Writings of Ge Hong', 23.

kingship, for the stupa, for the mandala, and for the internal ascent undertaken by the tantric mystic. Meru is not, we must recognize, a place, "out there," so to speak. It is "in here.""[11] In this way, mountains are maps of ourselves, when we go out into the wilderness; when we ascend the mountain, this is, in reality, an inward journey.

In East Asia, mountains are gateways to alternate realms and places to communicate with the divine. We can also see the significance of mountains in the stories of Moses (Mount Horeb and Mount Sinai). Jesus was crucified on Golgotha (admittedly considered a hill more than a mountain, but still raised ground) and Muhammad received his divine revelation on Mount Hira.

In China, the use of mountains and caves as places of worship was common, especially amongst the Taoist practitioners. They 'are archetypal chambers of reflection and the classical homes of immortals, where miraculous, inexplicable phenomena abound—such as lush growth despite droughts, or discovery of an ancient scroll within an uninhabited cave.'[12] The founders of new Taoist lineages were also often associated in some way with mountains. Going to the mountains was considered to be beneficial in cultivating the Tao. 'Mountains were where the qi energy of the universe was particularly rarefied.'[13]

As could be easily said of the world today, with its cacophony of voices, 'Those who achieve [long life] are exceedingly rare and hidden, while those who fail are extremely numerous and conspicuous. It is very difficult for worldly people to be aware of those who are hidden because they only see those who are conspicuous...'[14]

---

11 Michael, 24.

12 Michael, 29.

13 Michael, 33.

14 Michael, 34.

Let my servants be few & secret: they shall rule the many &
the known.

Liber AL, I:10[15]

It should be noted that, although they were hidden, the
Taoist hermits who concealed themselves in the mountains and
forests were not necessarily hiding themselves from society.[16]
However, as Ge Hong writes, 'The Dao does not exist exclu-
sively in mountains and forests, but those who cultivate the
Dao must enter mountains and forests because they sincerely
desire to distance themselves from the stench of society and go
into places of purity and quietude.'[17] Ge Hong also makes it
clear that life on the mountains was a dangerous undertaking,
and gave instructions about how the practitioner should approach the mountain, and how to exist on the mountain. 'The
Neipian and Shenxian zhuan name and discuss dozens upon
dozens of Daoists who not only survived but flourished in the
mountains. They were able to do so, according to Ge's thinking, only because they mastered the dangers of mountain dwelling by having mastered the strategies to confront and overcome
them.'[18]

In a similar way that the Commandments were received by
Moses on a mountain, mountains are also associated in Taoism
with the reception of scriptures. 'A standard feature of the early alchemical Daoists (as opposed to early yangsheng Daoists)
in the Shenxian zhuan is that, after entering the mountains,

---

15   Crowley, *The Holy Books of Thelema,* 107.

16   There are examples, such as Li Babai 李八伯, 'who sometimes was hidden
in the mountains and forests, and sometimes appeared in the markets' (Michael, 'Mountains and Early Daoism in the Writings of Ge Hong', 39.)

17   Michael, 34.

18   Michael, 37.

they receive "scriptures" (jing 經) revealed to them by spirits... such scriptures were the original writings of neither humans nor spirits; rather, they were the essential backbone of the cosmic structure of reality, perennially existing in the primordial heavens'[19] If we return again to the concept that mountains are not symbols of an external reality, but an internal one, then we can see these scriptures as emanating from the Taoist adept as a token of, or an outpouring of, their attainment.[20] 'A decisive event in the careers of alchemical Daoists is their reception of revealed scriptures, and this invariably occurs in the mountains.'[21]

Mountains in Taoism are also seen as maps of the human body, and its inner alchemy. 'In Daoist rituals the altar is visualized as a mountain that is symbolically climbed by the officiating priest. In Daoist meditation and inner alchemy, the inside of the body is visualized as a mountainous landscape that reflects the forces of Heaven and Earth that are manifest in human beings.'[22]

---

19 Michael, 44.

20 In *Neipian* 19 we can read, 'When those Daoists who merit these writings go into the mountains with sincere hearts and concentrated minds, the spirit of the mountain will spontaneously open up the mountain to reveal these writings to them.' (Michael, 48.)

21 Michael, 48.

22 'Monks, Meditation, and Mountains: The Body as a Sacred Landscape in Daoism: Part 1'.

*Image from the Duren shangpin miaojing neiyi (Inner Meaning of the
Wondrous Scripture of the Upper Chapters on Salvation)*

In *The Book of Thoth*, Crowley writes of mountains in
connection with the Yi Ching. He explains that 'the earthy
part of Earth is represented by the 52nd hexagram, Kan. The
meaning is "a mountain"; of how sublime a significance is this
Chinese doctrine of Balance, and how closely congruous with
that of the Holy Qabalah! The mountain is the most sacred
of all terrestrial symbols, stark, rugged, and immoveable in its
aspiration to the Highest, thrust up as it is by the Titan energy

of Hidden Fire. It is no less a hieroglyph of the Inmost Godhead than the Phallus itself, even as Capricornus, the sign of the New Year, is exalted in the Zodiac, its deity autochthonous[23] no less than the Most Holy Ancient One[24] himself.'[25]

Mountains also appear in the West in a similar fashion, most notably in the glyph of *Abiegnus*, the '"Mountain of Initiation" of the Brethren of the Rosy Cross, the "Mystic Mountain of the Caverns".[26][27]

---

23   This means "of an inhabitant of a place"- indigenous rather than descended from migrants or colonists.

24   'Furthermore, the Most Holy Ancient One is symbolized and concealed under the conception of the Unity, for He himself is One, and all things are One. And thus all the other Lights are sanctified, are restricted, and are bound together in the Unity or Monad, and are One; and all things are HVA, *Hoa*, Himself. (MacGregor Mathers, *The Kabbalah Unveiled*, 268.) ' Note that the descriptions of the Most Holy Ancient One are complex, and He is also symbolised by the triad and the duad.

25   Crowley, *The Book of Thoth*.

26   'In modernity, the meaning of the world is subjectivized; "objective reality" out there simply follows natural laws; and it is only we, humans, who project meanings onto it. However, this was not necessarily so in the past, as we archaeologists already know. "Reality" could be experienced as permeated by spiritual powers, and even natural phenomena can be perceived as the bearers of hidden meaning, the cosmos appearing to be controlled by a supreme intelligence. Caves could be imagined as a projection of subterranean architectural power that created the landscape... But abject is also ambiguous. Kristeva emphasizes the attraction of the abject, a lure of the return of pre-symbolic oneness with the world. A descent into the cave, katábasis offers the brave access to superior knowledge, possession of extraordinary objects, and contact with the dead and gods, if he or she can survive the encounter as a subject.' (Vrhovnik, 'Approaching Weird', 2.)

27   Gunther, *Initiation In the Aeon of the Child*, 193.

Yet shall this perfect wine be the quintessence, and the elixir, and by the draught thereof shall he renew his youth; and so shall it be eternally, as age by age the worlds do dissolve and change, and the universe unfoldeth itself as a Rose, and shutteth itself up as the Cross that is bent into the cube.

And this is the comedy of Pan, that is played at night in the thick forest. And this is the mystery of Dionysus Zagreus, that is celebrated upon the holy mountain of Kithairon. And this is the secret of the brothers of the Rosy Cross; and this is the heart of the ritual that is accomplished in the Vault of the Adepts that is hidden in the Mountain of the Caverns, even the Holy Mountain Abiegnus.[28]

---

28 Crowley, Neuburg, and Desti, *The Vision & the Voice with Commentary and Other Papers: The Collected Diaries of Aleister Crowley, 1909-1914 E.V.,* 151.

From Cabala, Spiegel der Kunst und Natur by S. Michelspacher (1616)

In myth, mountains are used to symbolise the centre of the earth. The 'peak of the cosmic mountain is not only the high-est point on earth, it is also the earth's navel, the point where creation had its beginning. "This mystic sense of the mountain," writes J. E. Cirlot, 'also comes from the fact that it is the point of contact between heaven and earth, or the center through which the world-axis passes.'[29] Mountains were also used in alchemical imagery to represent the completion of the Great Work, as we can see from the above engraving from a 17th century alchemical text, where a blindfolded man stands before the Mountain of Initiation, which is loaded with symbols that indicate the union of opposites (Sun and Moon, King and Queen), and is surrounded by the wheel of the zodiac – 'The girdle of the Starry One!'[30] From the top of the mountain, Mercury appears to stand, emerging from a fountain,[31] with the caduceus in one hand and a star in the other.

Charles Cicero explains, in *The Rosicrucian Vault*, that:

In the Adeptus Minor Ceremony of the Golden Dawn, the officer known as the Chief Adept[32] represents an Initiate who has undergone this alchemical process of self-transmutation and spiritual evolution. The Chief Adept, representing Christian Rosencreutz at one point in the ritual, tells the Aspirant: "Buried with that Light in a mystical death, rising again in a mystical resurrection, cleansed and purified through Him our Master, O Brother of Cross and the Rose. Like Him, O Adepts of all ages, have ye toiled. Like Him have ye suffered tribulation. Poverty, torture and death have ye passed through. They have been but the purification of the Gold. In the alem-

---

29 Cicero, 'The Rosicrucian Vault'.

30 Crowley, 'Liber Pyramidos Sub Figurâ DCLXXI – Technical Libers of Thelema – The Libri of Aleister Crowley – Hermetic Library'.

31 Fountains appear throughout the Amalantrah Working.

32 Remembering that the Wand of the Chief Adept features prominently in Atu XV, "veiling" his creative energy.

bic of thine heart, through the athanor of affliction, seek thou the true stone of the Wise."[33]

Another name for Christian Rosencreutz in the Adeptus Minor ritual is "Osiris Onnophris, the Justified One".

In the system of the A∴A∴ the Candidate is Osiris, and 'begins the process of the inward journey[34] as ΝΕΚΡΟΣ, the "dead one".[35] Gunther, further highlights that 'The first practical introduction to the formulae of Death in the New Aeon is given to the Neophyte 1°=10□ of the A∴A∴ through experience of the Initiation Ritual DCLXXI vel תרעא, wherein the death of Asar is celebrated in the Pyramid.'[36] Additionally, as explained by Cicero, 'reaching the top of a pyramid has often been compared to climbing to the summit of a mountain, which is a common metaphor for achieving spiritual enlightenment.'[37]

However, Thelemites should note that there have been changes to the formula of initiation in the New Aeon. 'The aspirant in the New Aeon sings a new song, looking toward the West (♏) wherein is Amente, the place of death, he prays for Light upon the ways of his Ka, by which We mean The Holy

---

33 Cicero, 'The Rosicrucian Vault'.

34 'While this kind of psychological openness to the surrounding environment may sound suspiciously akin to the superstitious associations that are rife in magical thinking, there is a significant difference, one that is reflected in the difference between primitive forms of pattern divination and the ethical reflectiveness that is so central to the oracular function of the *I Ching*. This also accords with the goals and aims of Jung's depth psychology, in which synchronicities are viewed as markers in the process of individuation, which represents the inward journey towards the integration of the psyche.' (Browne, 'Examining Coincidences', 25.)

35 Gunther, *The Angel and the Abyss*, 17.

36 Gunther, 59.

37 Cicero, 'The Rosicrucian Vault'.

Guardian for he is no longer Asar the Lord of the Dead, but one who identifies himself with the Self-slain Ankh-af-na-Khonsu, whose Sarcophagus has replaced the Vault of the Shepherd...'[38]

Returning to the Amalantrah working, on April 20, the following exchange occurs,

'T: What are present instructions?

11.55 Arcteon 2 cc.

A: Crocodile—unformed man. Shelf, place walled in—on shelf skeleton. White flag. Skeleton's hand holds white flag. Large wall around place like butterfly net.

T: Give Hebrew word to illustrate.

A: He-Tzaddi-Yod-Vau. (= 111.) <<N.B. The elixir must die in the Cucurbite and the 111 means this exactly. This recalls my dream and vision in N.Y. about killing the lion very dead indeed. It also explains the first answer to the question about the foetus becoming Harpocrates, cf. Jesus "Except a corn of wheat... down to fruit." He-Tzaddi-Yod-Vau is the tetragrammaton of the magical officers. He (Hebrew) is the Emperor, and the Tzaddi the Empress, or High Priestess, vide secret attributions indicated in Liber CCXX. Yod is the Hermit and Vau the Hierophant who unites either with the High Priestess yet without destroying her virginity[39] or with the more natural correlate. This word is therefore, a complete formula of the Gnostic and Templar mysteries, in one of its aspects.>> Daleth crowned with flowers.'[40]

---

38   Gunther, *The Angel and the Abyss*, 58.

39   In his comment to Chapter XLV of the Tao Te Ching (The Overflowing of Te), Crowley explains 'To be pure' by making reference to 'Chastity in the secret Parsifal-O.T.O. sense'. He relates this to *Brahmacharya*, when a person controls their body and mind through aestheticism.

40   Crowley and Minor, 'Liber DCCXXIX : The Amalantrah Working'.

Here we are given another Tetragrammaton, 'a complete formula of the Templar mysteries' (the Baphomet mysteries)- 'the tetragrammaton of the magical officers':

$$\text{הצירן} = 111$$

These attributions are based on the previous Tarot attributions as taught in the Golden Dawn. If we used the current Hebrew attributions for the same cards, we would get צדירן, with a value of 110 (the 2 becoming 1, or the 2 becoming 0).

> Write, & find ecstasy in writing! Work, & be our bed in working! Thrill with the joy of life & death! Ah! thy death shall be lovely: whososeeth it shall be glad. Thy death shall be the seal of the promise of our age long love. Come! lift up thine heart & rejoice! We are one; we are none.
>
> *Liber AL,* II:66

If we focus on the titles on the cards, a key to the above is the dual title of The Empress as the High Priestess, and in the form of the High Priestess may the Hierophant join with her. This becomes even clearer when we find that another title for The Hierophant in Golden Dawn literature is the "High Priest".[41]

The term High Priest only occurs once in *The Book of Thoth*, and it is in relation to the Hexagram Kwan – Sol in Scorpio – which is part of Crowley's Commentary on the Six of Cups.

---

41 Torrens, *The Golden Dawn: The Inner Teachings*, 158.

Kwan, ䷁, which is also "Big Earth", being the Earth Trigram ☷ [42] with doubled lines. Kwan means "manifesting", but also "contemplating". The Thwan[43] refers directly to a High Priest, ceremonially purified, about to present his offerings. The idea of Pleasure-Putrefaction as a Sacrament is therefore implicit in this Hexagram as in this card; while the comments on the separate lines by the Duke of Chau indicate the analytical value of this Eucharist. It is one of the master-keys to the Gate of Initiation. To realize and to enjoy this fully it is necessary to know, to understand, and to experience, the Secret of the Ninth Degree of the O.T.O.[44]

It is interesting to note in the above, in reference to that with which the Hierophant can also unite with - 'the more natural correlate.' Although this is (probably deliberately) obscure, I can only conjecture that it relates to mysteries discussed elsewhere in the working. On February 3rd the following was recorded:

Q: "Will the work of the 9th degree be better carried out by one than two?"
A: "Two."

---

42   It is interesting to note that here in The Book of Thoth Crowley does not give the trigram for Earth (☷), but the trigram Chen or Gen, which is Mountain. In the "Correspondences" section of The Book of Thoth, Crowley assigns this Trigram to Netzach on the Tree of Life, with the attributions of Earth and Hands (which is a traditional attribution, as is its phase, which is earth). Its attribute is resting, or to stand still. Hands are associated with the Hebrew י, and Virgo, the Virgin, associated with wheat – 'the Hierophant who unites either with the High Priestess yet without destroying her virginity...'

43   The "Thwan" is a commentary on the basic text for each hexagram.

44   Crowley, The Book of Thoth, 199.

Q: "Is it better to work in a circle or vesica?"
A: "Circle."[45]

This may be in reference to the allegation levelled at the Templars that they lay with each other – a crime 'against nature and against the law of Our Lord.'[46] Here The Hierophant, the High Priest, joins with The Emperor. In a similar manner as Horus and Set, the Emperor represents Kingship (but divine kingship) whereas the Hierophant represents an interior, spiritual or religious power, a power needed by the king to rule his kingdom.[47]

We should also note the depiction of the Tree behind the figure of Baphomet in Atu XV – 'the trunk of the Tree pierces the heavens; about it is indicated the ring of the body of Nuith. Similarly, the shaft of the Wand goes down indefinitely to the centre of earth.'[48] The Wand and the Tree are really one, and we are reminded of the Mountain that rises to the heavens, while also symbolising a secret interiority. Baphomet, as 'the Himalayan Goat with an eye in the centre of his forehead, [represents] the god Pan, upon the highest and most secret mountains of earth.'[49]

The Emperor represents the 'red tincture of the alchemists',[50] while the Empress the 'White Eagle of the Alchemist. The are

---

45   Crowley and Minor, 'Liber DCCXXIX : The Amalantrah Working'.

46   Read, *The Templars*.

47   In his commentary on The Devil Crowley writes, 'The formula of this card is then the complete appreciation of all existing things. He rejoices in the rugged and the barren no less than in the smooth and the fertile.' (Crowley, *The Book of Thoth*, 106.)

48   Crowley, 106.

49   Crowley, 105.

50   Crowley, 78.

Sun and Moon, she is Salt, and this Salt 'must be energised by Sulphur',[51] one of the elements associated with The Emperor. The Hierophant, however, is connected to mysteries particular to the Aeon of Horus – 'It is impossible at the present time to explain this card thoroughly, for only the course of events can show how the new current of initiation will work out.'[52] One cannot help but notice, connected to the communication above from the Amalantrah Working, the round oriel behind the Hierophant. It is fixed by nine nails and shown to be connected to the mysteries of the dove and the serpent.

Crowley was always very careful with his words. The word oriel comes from the Middle English, which is from the Old French *oriol*, which means a gallery or corridor. It is also connected with the Late Latin *oriolum* (a portico or hall). This may be connected to the Latin *aureoles*, with the meaning of "gilded".

As Crowley wrote for Frater Achad (a participant in the Amalantrah working),

Now the Tao absorbeth all without Reproduction; so then let the Yang turn thereto, and not unto the Yin. And that thou mayst understand this, I say: It is a Mystery of O.T.O. For the Sun ariseth not and entereth to strike upon the High Altar of the Minister by the Great Western Gates, but by the Rose Oriel doth he make Way and Progress in His Pageant. O my Son, the Doors of Silver are wide open, and they tempt thee with their Beauty: but by the narrow Portal of Pure Gold shalt thou come nobly to thy Sanctuary.[53]

---

51 Crowley, 75.

52 Crowley, 79.

53 Crowley, *Liber Aleph Vel CXI: The Book of Wisdom or Folly*, 82.

Crowley goes on further to explain the magical and mystical significance of this in an instruction On The Eye of Hoor:

I say furthermore that this Path is of the Circle, and of the Eye of Horus that sleepeth not, but is vigilant. The Circle is all-perfect, equal every Way, but the Vesica hath bitter Need, and seeketh thy Medicine, that is of right compounded for High Purpose, to ease her Infirmity. Thus is thy Will frustrated, and thy Mind distracted, and thy Work lamed, if it be not brought to Naught. Also thy Puissance in thine Art is minished, by a full Moiety, as I do esteem it. But the Eye of Horus hath no Need, and is free in his Will, not seeking a Level, or requiring a Medicine, and is fit and worthy to be the Companion and the Ally of thee in thy Work, as a Friend to thee, not Mistress and not Slave, that seek ever with Slyness and Deceit to encompass their own Ends. There is moreover a Reason in Physics for my Word; study thou this matter in the Laws of the Changes of Nature. For Things Unlike do in their Marriage produce a Child which is relatively Stable, and resisteth Change; but Things like increase mutually the Potential of their particular Natures. Howbeit, each Path hath his own Use; and thou, being instructed in all Ways, choose thine with Discretion.'[54] The relationship with this method may have also been hinted at by Crowley in a diary entry regarding an Opus undertaken on 21 June, An XVI (1920), where he writes 'used 729's formula[55] (*i.e. Baphomet's formula*).

The final magical officer not yet mentioned is The Hermit (Atu IX), who like the trigram ☶ is connected to the Hand

---

54 Crowley, 175.

55 Crowley, *The Magical Record of the Beast 666*, 179.

(ר), 'the tool or instrument par excellence.'[56] The cloak of The Hermit is the colour of Binah, associated with Zion, 'The Holy City of God', which is also a mountain or hill (Mount Zion), and can represent Jerusalem or the Land of Israel. Binah is 'in whom he [The Hermit] gestates.'[57] Present also is the Orphic egg, surrounded by the snake that is 'many-coloured to signify the iridescence of Mercury. For he is not only creative, but is the fluidic essence of Light, which is the life of the Universe.'[58] The card shows us 'Fertility in its most exalted sense'[59] (i.e. something beyond just physical reproduction). This card also helps us further understand the concept of virginity discussed above. The card is assigned to Virgo (an earthy sign) connected to corn and to the wheat shown in the card. Virgo is ruled by Mercury, and Mercury is exalted in Virgo (The Hermit itself is also considered a form of Mercury and also appears in Atu VI ("The Lovers" or "Brothers").[60] 'Concealed within Mercury is a light which pervades all parts of the Universe equally…' and therefore Mercury acts as a Psychopompos 'the guide of the soul through the lower regions.'[61] The Hermit holds in his

---

56 Crowley, *The Book of Thoth*, 88.

57 Crowley, 89.

58 Crowley, 89.

59 Crowley, 89.

60 'He is himself a form of the god Mercury, described in Atu I; he is closely shrouded, as if to signify that the ultimate reason of things lies in a realm beyond manifestation and intellect. (As elsewhere explained, only two operations are ultimately possible—analysis and synthesis). He is standing in the Sign of the Enterer, as if projecting the mysterious forces of creation. About his arms is a scroll, indicative of the Word which is alike his essence and his message. But the Sign of the Enterer is also the Sign of Benediction and of Consecration; thus his action in this card is the Celebration of the Hermetic Marriage.' (Crowley, 82.)

61 Crowley, 89.

left hand the solar lamp, which is radiating light. The wand in the card, which is also the spermatozoon, is 'growing out of the Abyss'. This spermatozoon is also a poison,[62] 'manifesting the foetus.' This card, then, speaks to mysteries of the Abyss (something beyond my current understanding), and its connection to virginity or purity. 'There is a perfect Identity, not merely Equivalence, of the Extremes, the Manifestation, and the Method.'[63]

Yod ≡ Phallus ≡ Spermatozoon ≡ Hand ≡ Logos ≡ Virgin[64]

Only above the Abyss, can the adept be truly considered pure – The Master of the Temple has attained 'the perfect annihilation of that personality which limits and oppresses the Self...His understanding is entirely free from internal contradiction or external obscurity.'[65] In this state of purity the Master of the Temple becomes an unobstructed conduit for the Self, for the True Will. 'Truth, a state of perfect balance, the unwavering course of a star which we call the True Will, abides within and not without. The bindings of the corpse of Osiris are the fetters of restriction.'[66]

So here in the Amalantrah Working, we see communicated certain secrets that relate to the Templars and to Baphomet, and a new formula of working, a new Tetragrammaton which is malleable in its application. This is resonant with the exploration of Baphomet already covered and throws some more

---

62 'Wolf's bane is not so sharp as steel; yet it pierceth the body more subtly.' LXV, I:13 (Crowley, *The Holy Books of Thelema*, 54.)

63 Crowley, *The Book of Thoth*, 89.

64 Crowley, 89.

65 Crowley et al., *Commentaries of the Holy Books and Other Papers*, 4:13.

66 Gunther, *The Angel and the Abyss*, 116.

light on the connection between the way of the Tao and the IX°. Mysteries as taught within the Sovereign Sanctuary (from what I am able to glean from the outside).

> Wizard now looks like an enormous god, Sphinx head, stalwart, bearded-Assyrian god type. Abdometh is his god name. <<Abdometh = 463, the Middle Pillar and Almond Rod. Equals Servant of the Dragon or of Mithras (? A.C.) or of the Tables, i.e. of Thoth.>> He is sceptered with a kind of battle axe and a knob-kerry in the other hand. He stood against a great dark mountain behind which the sun was rising. The light and effect was one of the most beautiful pictures I ever saw.[67]

---

67 Crowley and Minor, 'Liber DCCXXIX : The Amalantrah Working'.

THE RAINBOW BODY AND THE SHROUD

If our consciousness is realised as unborn, one is no longer subject to death.[1]

A Chö

O Holy Exalted One, O Self beyond self, O Self-Luminous Image of the Unimaginable Naught, O my darling, my beautiful, come Thou forth and follow me.

Liber LXV, V: 42[2]

" The rainbow body" (Tibetan: 'ja' lus) is a phenomenon described in connection to Indo-Tibetan Buddhist Dzogchen practice ("Great Perfection" or "Great Completion"). The rainbow body is a body of light, and is considered a form of the *sambhogakaya*, the "body of enjoyment". At the time of death, an advanced practitioner is said to transform their physical body into this rainbow body, either leaving behind nothing, or only hair and nails. In Chan (Zen) Buddhism, this phenomenon is generally considered in a more metaphorical way.

Catholic priest and scholar Father Francis V. Tiso, who has an interest in inter-religious dialogue and Tibetan Buddhism, has produced a fascinating study on the phenomenon of the rainbow body, and a possible connection between the practic-

---

1   Tiso, *Rainbow Body and Resurrection*, 30.

2   Crowley, *The Holy Books of Thelema*, 80.

es of Dzogchen and contemplative Christianity, specifically the influence of the Syro-Oriental church and the Christian doctrine of the resurrection. He believes this is 'sustained by claims made by Christian mystics of the Syriac tradition about light mysticism and its effects on the human body-mind complex.'[3] These form part of the conversations and exchanges that occurred along the silk road, which would have included Manicheans, yogis, Daoists, Buddhists, Zoroastrians, Muslims and shamans – a vibrant exchange of ideas and practices. Contemplative Christianity travelled across Central Asia and came into contact with other religions, including Buddhism, around the 8th century. The resurrection of Jesus, as taught within Christianity, has commonalities with the phenomena of the Tibetan rainbow body.

In the practice of Dzogchen, compassion (a concept deeply associated with Baphomet, which will be explored shortly) again appears as a core principle, and its connection to the Bodhisattva vow:

> There is nothing beyond *rigpa*.[4] Keep in mind that the motivation is, at the basis, compassion. Within the fact of practice is compassion. Without realisation, our help for others is only temporary, mere palliatives...the perfection of giving is attained in the perfect non-attachment that arises in the realisation of the natural state...the stable realisation of which leads to action, not because of attachment or preference but in relation to the perception of others.[5]

One does not attain to Buddhahood, it is something already present, and associated with *shunyata*, which is interpreted as

---

3   Tiso, *Rainbow Body and Resurrection*, 19.

4   Rigpa is "knowledge", primordial awareness.

5   Tiso, *Rainbow Body and Resurrection*, 79.

"voidness", but as Tiso points out this is better translated as "openness", and that existing in a state of *rigpa* is to abide 'continually in the state of awareness...of that openness.'[6] This openness is Compassion.[7]

The concepts of openness and Compassion described above could be, in a Thelemic context, aligned to the teachings transmitted in *The Book of the Law*. 'The word of Sin is Restriction' (AL, I:41)[8] – the only real sin we can commit as Thelemites is to not be open, to not possess the state of consciousness that is Compassion, remembering that 'Nothing is a secret key of this law...' (AL, I:46)[9] - Love is the law, love under will.

When a practitioner attains to the rainbow body, they are, in essence, reversing the process of creation, or differentiation from the great perfection – the uncreated basis. This basis is immaterial, but from it all phenomena arise. These become "light" of various colours associated with the five classical elements. 'When this process is reversed the gross matter dissolves into its own subtle nature of light and the light returns into the primordial basis...'[10] 'The basis possesses all-pervading compassion.'[11]

Tiso also informs us that there needs to be a clear understanding that the disappearance of the body at death, is not *truly* a rainbow body, or a physical body, but '...is the absence

---

6   Tiso, 92.

7   Compare this to the concept in Crowley's writings of the "Black Brothers", who 'restricting themselves, and being divided in Will, are indeed the Servants of Sin...' (Crowley, *Liber Aleph Vel CXI: The Book of Wisdom or Folly*, 139.)

8   Crowley, *The Holy Books of Thelema*, 110.

9   Crowley, 110.

10   Tiso, *Rainbow Body and Resurrection*, 93.

11   Tiso, 97.

of a body.' However, 'Buddhahood can in fact manifest in any form: as a subtle body of light, gross physical body, human, animal, demon, titan, deity, bridge, raft, flower, etc.'[12] The thing that differentiates the rainbow body is that it is the result of the great perfection leap-over *sadhana*. In the attainment of the body of light, or rainbow body, the 'personal body is not discarded, but transformed.'[13] I think this is a significant point, related to the process of the transubstantiation of the Eucharist, and the process of transfiguration. The physical body returns to its true state.

Alongside the concept of the rainbow body—where a practitioner's physical form either gradually diminishes until it vanishes or transforms into light and dissolves into space through the practices of *trekchö* and *tögal*—is the more rarefied notion of the "Rainbow Body of Great Transference." In this case, the practitioner's body becomes light, yet the master remains in the world for centuries, continuing to serve others.

This idea finds a parallel in Christian tradition. Following his execution and resurrection, the Bible recounts that Jesus appeared to his disciples on several occasions. Christians believe he remains present in their lives today, particularly through the sacrament of the Eucharist and other expressions of faith.

Then the same day at evening, being the first *day* of the week , when the doors were shut where the disciples were assembled for fear of the Jews, came Jesus and stood in the midst, and saith unto them, Peace be unto you.

> And when he had so said, he shewed unto them his hands and his side. Then were the disciples glad, when they saw the Lord.

---

12   Tiso, 119.

13   Tiso, 120.

Then said Jesus to them again, Peace be unto you: as *my* father hath sent me, even so send I you.

And when he had said this, he breathed on them, and saith unto them, Receive ye the Holy Ghost:

John 20:19-22

Most, if not all, readers would be familiar with the famous (and controversial) Shroud of Turin, that some Christians believe was the cloth in which Jesus of Nazareth was wrapped after his crucifixion. It has been kept in the *Duomo di Torino* (Cathedral of Turin) since 1578.

And he stooping down, and looking in, saw the linen clothes lying; yet went he not in.

Then cometh Simon Peter following him, and went into the sepulchre, and seeth the linen clothes lie, And the napkin, that was about his head, not lying with the linen clothes, but wrapped together in a place by itself.

John 20: 5-7

Scientific analysis has been undertaken on the shroud, which indicated that the cloth may be a forgery from the 1300s, but there is also disagreement on this finding. The Catholic Church neither confirms nor denies the authenticity of the relic. For the purposes of this study, the authenticity of the shroud is not of relevance. What is relevant is what the shroud meant to the people who believed it to be the burial shroud of Christ, and those contemporary Christians who accept it as legitimate, and how the practices and reported events associated with the rainbow body may be connected with this fascinating object of worship and study (and its connection to the Templars, and therefore Baphomet).

Tiso proposes that the shroud was at one time in the safe keeping of the Syriac Christians, before being transferred to the Byzantines in the ninth century to safeguard it from Muslim authorities in Mesopotamia. Due to the Muslim expansion, the Christians looked East to spread the doctrines of their church. Tiso believes the teachings around the rainbow body were a response from the Dzogchen lineages following encounters with Christians and Muslims. In the cultural exchange that occurred along the silk road that reached the religious milieu of Tibet, the Christians of Central Asia made resurrection central to their teachings and beliefs. He sees a clear connection between the teaching of the Syro-Christian church and the rainbow body.

Tracing the history of the shroud is far from straightforward, but an historian of the Vatican secret archives, Barbara Frale, proposes there was a period in which the shroud was in the safekeeping of the Templars, and it is from the shroud that some of the confessions that emerged during the trial of the Templars originate. The idea of the worship of a head emerges from the practice of the shroud being displayed inside a wooden case and textile covering so that only the face was visible to most viewers. Frale connects the shroud with an object called the "Mandylion" or "Image of Edessa", a piece of cloth on which the face of Jesus had been imprinted. This is considered by some to be the first icon. Frale believes that the reason that the shroud only displayed the head of Jesus (making it appear as if it was a square or rectangular cloth) was due to the Monophysite[14] ideas present in Edessa that considered Jesus as only a divine figure. Displaying the tortured and wounded body of Jesus 'would have seemed disgraceful.'[15]

To the text of a sermon attributed to Pope Stephen III (768-772), was later added (in the 11th century) the following related to a revised telling of the legend of Abgar:[16]

So, fully to please the sovereign, the mediator between God and men lay the full length of his body over a sheet of snow-white linen; and upon this linen, wonderful to relate or to hear, the most noble form of his face and of his whole body

---

14   In Christianity, this is the belief that Christ's nature remained divine, not divine and human.

15   Frale, *The Templars and the Shroud of Christ*, 136.

16   This legend is a set of letters that appeared in the fourth century and claimed to be between Jesus and King Abgar V Ukkāmā of Osroene. In the Syriac liturgies the letters are commemorated during Lent, and Abgar is considered a saint in the Syrian Church.

was divinely transfigured, so that to be able to see the transfiguration impressed upon that linen should be enough even for those who had not been able to see the Lord in the flesh.[17]

It is unknown when the shroud came into the possession of the Templars, or when it left their safekeeping, but the relic 'left ineffaceable traces on the Templars' spirituality and liturgical uses...'[18]

The shroud has an interesting visual property – the image is only visible when the viewer is standing approximately two to nine meters from the sheet. Moving in and out of this range would have had the effect of the image disappearing and reappearing, which may have seemed otherworldly to the viewers of the relic. The image on the shroud also holds three-dimensional information. 'It is a kind of optical projection, reminiscent of holography in some ways.'[19] One possible cause of an image of this kind has been proposed as a burst of radiation that left the impression and caused the oxidisation of the fibres without burning.[20]

Besides the image of a man on the cloth, there are also traces of writing in Greek, Latin and Hebrew. It is the presence of Hebrew characters on the shroud that Frale believes may have been the reason it was kept secret by the Templars. During the Middle Ages, Europe saw waves of antisemitism and extreme violence against Jewish communities. If outsiders were able to closely view the shroud, and observe the writing imprinted on it, then this could have put the important relic (and possibly the Templars themselves) at risk.

---

17   Frale, *The Templars and the Shroud of Christ*, 141.

18   Frale, 187.

19   Frale, 192.

20   It should be noted that this is generally considered a fringe theory.

Another piece of text that seems to have been transferred to the cloth reads *Iesu sanctissime Miserere nostri* – "Most Holy Jesus have mercy on us". Frale tentatively proposes that due to the style and age of this text, and the known practice of placing written notes onto relics, that this imprint may have been the result of Templar practice. Other examples of text on the shroud may be traceable to the early Christian age (first to third centuries A.D.), perhaps to clarify the identity of the man on the cloth,[21] and the Hebraic writing might suggest an origin in Syria-Palestine, and possibly Qumran.

As with other relics, there is a belief in the power of contact with the object. The Templars had a practice of wearing a strand of linen on their person. Confessions during the Templar trials indicate this strand was considered, in some way, sacred, and this sacredness resulted from contact with the mysterious "idol" 'regarded as so sacred and mighty that someone…had thought it best to make sure that his charisma should reach and protect Templars physically throughout their lives.'[22]

Originally it was thought that these strands were made into relics themselves by contact with places of special power in the Holy Land (such as the Basilica of Nazareth). Once the Holy Land was lost, and the ability to come into physical contact with these sacred sites removed, the Templars started to create relics that they could carry on their person. '[W]hen Jerusalem and the Holy Sepulchre had been guarded by Christians, the Templars would go to the great basilica to celebrate particular nocturnal liturgies of which the sources tell us nothing: probably they consecrated their linen strands, the symbol of the religious vows of the Temple, resting them on that very stone

---

21   Such as the Greek text that seems to indicate "Jesus of Nazareth".

22   Frale, *The Templars and the Shroud of Christ*, 105.

where the corpse of Jesus had been placed...'[23] One can imagine that with the contact with the Holy Sepulchre lost, having possession of what they believed was the burial shroud of Jesus must have seemed like the next best thing, and enabled them to continue the practices established in the Holy Land in some form, even if kept secret from the majority of the Templars.

Interestingly, when the Sultan Baibars took the tower of Saphed in 1266 he found in the mansion's grand hall a bas-relief of a man's face. This was where the Templars would hold chapter. At this time these images could also be found in the mansions of southern France, where the cult around this image arrived sooner and spread faster than in other areas. Eventually they could be found in most countries with a Templar presence.

When in the proposed possession of the Templars, the shroud was never exhibited and they never sought alms or indulgences in relation to it. Indeed, it was even hidden for the most part from its own members. Frale argues that with the loss of Jerusalem, separated from the Holy Land, the shroud became for the Templars a "new Sepulchre", and even compared to the Holy Sepulchre 'it had a much greater power over the imagination.'[24] The Templars, by wearing the consecrated strand, consecrated by contact with the shroud, would 'perpetuate his protection...' If this holds true, then the image the Templars were accused of worshipping as a heresy was actually an image of Jesus (and could be considered the ultimate image of Jesus – an impression of his face and body after his crucifixion), and in some ways could have been a guardian against gnostic heresies by graphically showing a very human Christ, his body broken and deceased.

In the context of this book, which is centred around the glyph of Baphomet and the mysteries that surround this enduring and enigmatic figure, the question we should ask, as did Lévi: 'What was actually this secret and potent association

---

23   Frale, 107.
24   Frale, 243.

which imperilled Church and State, and was thus destroyed unheard?'[25] The Abbé hints at his opinion when he states, 'Judge nothing lightly; they are guilty of a great crime; they have allowed the sanctuary of antique initiation to be entered by the profane.'[26] It seems that Lévi held what he saw as the secret of the Templars in high esteem, but not necessarily the Templars themselves. One cannot help but note, however, that the supposed revelation of these secrets by the Templars that led to their downfall, are the same secrets that Lévi himself presented to the world. However, it cannot convincingly argue that the practices and theories described by Lévi would have been practiced, or even understood, by the Templars; but regardless they have become a vehicle used to carry and transmit mysteries as understood by Lévi and his successors to the present day.

In looking for a connection between the concepts of the rainbow body and the resurrection of Jesus, seemingly captured graphically on the Shroud of Turin, what can we find in the writings of Lévi that might point to the secret that he believed the Templars held?

In a letter written in May 1862 he writes, 'It is certain that neither Enoch, nor Elias, nor Moses, not even Jesus Christ, could have ever raised themselves above the atmosphere and directed themselves towards the Sun with bodies like our own. This is what the Scripture makes us understand by telling us that Moses died, but that an angel concealed his body from men and from demons. And how so? by an immediate and 'lightning-like dissolution of the exterior envelope...'[27] Lévi makes a point of differentiating between the Old Testament figures and Jesus, by stating that 'Jesus Christ alone had the power to

---

25 Lévi, *Transcendental Magic*, 7.

26 Lévi, 8.

27 Levi, *The Kabalistic and Occult Philosophy of Eliphas Levi*, 1:211.

render his glorious body visible and palpable to the corporeal senses, by reason of his power over the equilibrating forces/ strengths...'[28] Lévi believed that it was only Jesus who could appear in his "glorious body" after death. As it was outlined previously the common theme in Lévi's writing and art - that of the equilibration of opposites. 'The binary is also, then, the manifested light, the splendour of the *Zohar*,[29] the radiation of Shekinah [שכינה] (Shekinah means "light of glory"[30]).'[31]

> 0. Learn first — Oh thou who aspirest unto our ancient Order! — that Equilibrium is the basis of the Work. If thou thyself hast not a sure foundation, whereon wilt thou stand to direct the forces of Nature?

Liber Librae Sub Figurâ XXX

In what seems like a similar vein of thought, Crowley writing about the Eucharist in *Book 4* states that 'The magician becomes filled with God, fed upon God, intoxicated with God. Little by little his body will become purified by the internal lustration of God; day by day his mortal frame, shedding its earthly elements, will become in very truth the Temple of the Holy Ghost. Day by day matter is replaced by spirit, the human by the divine; ultimately the change will be complete; God manifested in flesh will be his name.'[32]

Although the above describes a more gradual process that the 'lightning-like dissolution' of Lévi, it does show a continui-

---

28   Levi, 1:212.

29   Hebrew: זֹהַר, Zōhar ("Splendor" or "Radiance")

30   This is a very liberal interpretation of the meaning of Shekinah.

31   Levi, *The Kabalistic and Occult Philosophy of Eliphas Levi*, 1:128.

32   Crowley, Desti, and Waddell, *Magick. Liber ABA. Book Four. Parts I-IV*, 269.

ty of thought regarding the subtle body, and the dissolution of the material body, the 'shedding of [...] earthly elements' until man, through his own efforts, may become 'God manifested in flesh'.

So, what do we make of this? The evidence to support a literal "rainbow body", the phenomena of a person's body disappearing at the time of death, appears weak (despite emic[33] accounts), and as Tiso rightly points out, 'In the end, nature dissolves the body in any case...'[34] Tiso does however think 'that there is now sufficient anthropological evidence to justify further research on this phenomenon.'[35] He also proposes that there may be further avenues of research in the study of biophotons and their relation to light phenomenon experienced by meditators, synaesthesia and cell biochemistry and genetics. '[I]t might be possible to explore whether or not the energy emissions (i.e. biophotons) emanating from living cells can be altered by meditation on light.'[36] Can advanced meditation practices increase the emission of biophotons, and could this provide (even preliminary) evidence for the phenomena of the rainbow body? Should we also 'consider the possibility of quantum interactions in neuron function'?[37] This is noting that some claims around the rainbow body include an effect at the atomic level. This becomes even more fascinating if we consider the research that the DNA helix may be held in place by quantum mechanical effects. There is also 'persistent debate

---

33 "an approach to the study or description of a particular language or culture in terms of its internal elements" [ed]

34 Tiso, *Rainbow Body and Resurrection*, 310.

35 Tiso, 'Taking the next Step in Rainbow Body Research: Anthropological and Neurophysiological Objectives', 1.

36 Tiso, 3.

37 Tiso, 6.

about the fundamental nature of consciousness, the way it interfaces with physical reality and the powerful tools it might place at our disposal.'[38]

If there is a quantum element to the experiences of the rainbow body, could this also indicate a connection to the astral light posited by Levi and others, whose function is revealed in the figure of Baphomet? The 'invisible all-pervading fluid or medium on which thoughts can be imprinted and through which phenomena can be influenced.'[39] Could the ability to act at a distance – to act through the medium of the astral light – be aligned with the emerging research around non-locality and quantum biology?[40] '[P]hotobiology[41] may be part of a much larger picture of cellular and inter-organism entanglement/ quantum communication, perhaps representing an evolutionary pathway from the simplest biological structures to ever increasing levels of cooperation and complexity, which may ultimately span the entire biosphere.'[42]

It has also potentially been shown that visualisation and meditation practices (like those seen in Dzogchen and some early contemplative Christianity) can produce biophoton emissions. Studies have also shown that 'biophoton emissions of remote organisms mentally targeted by a healer, sibling or partner... fluctuate to a statistically significant degree during the

---

38   Bajpai, 'Tinkering with the Unbearable Lightness of Being', 3.

39   McIntosh, *Eliphas Levi and the French Occult Revival*, 8.

40   Quantum biology is the study of applications of quantum mechanics and theoretical chemistry to biological objects and problems. The study of these effects is difficult and the field is commonly speculative.

41   Photobiology is the study of the beneficial and harmful interactions of light (technically, non-ionizing radiation) in living organisms.

42   Bajpai, 'Tinkering with the Unbearable Lightness of Being', 5.

windows of intent transmission.'[43] Much of this is inconclusive at this time, but does offer much food for thought when considering the concepts of the rainbow body, the astral light, the possible theoretical basis for its functioning, and how these ideas may be represented in the Baphomet glyph.

I would encourage the reader not to fall into the New Age trap of overextending the connection between some scientific discoveries and occult or esoteric phenomena. We should seek to bridge this gap, but with intelligence and discipline. I also refer to J. Daniel Gunther, echoing the Dalai Lama, who when lecturing highlights that if our beliefs conflict with science we should revisit our beliefs,[44] and also to directly reference the Dalai Lama, 'What science finds to be nonexistent we should all accept as nonexistent, but what science merely does not find is a completely different matter.'[45]

Crowley points out that it is the physical body that is the cause of our suffering, so why does the fear of losing it through the process of death exist? 'Then I knew also this: all these poor dead men that lay about me had been slain by their own fear, their fault of faith in deeming that the Sun – or any Star – could die.'[46]

So here we have a connection between a phenomenon of light, dissolution and returning to, or having the consciousness of, an unborn state, seen in the practices of Dzogchen and contemplative Christianity. By existing in an undifferentiated field of consciousness, which could be argued, provides the ability to

---

43 Bajpai, 8–9.

44 'I have often said that if science proves facts that conflict with Buddhist understanding, Buddhism must change accordingly' (Popova, 'The Dalai Lama on Science and Spirituality'.)

45 Popova. 'The Dalai Lama on Science and Spirituality'.

46 Crowley, *The Heart of the Master & Other Papers by Aleister Crowley*, 35.

better manipulate the fluctuations of the material world for the benefit of humanity. If it is true that the Templars possessed the Shroud of Turin, then this connection can be traced historically and may reflect a worldview and set of practices that ultimately point toward a form of *Baphomet consciousness*, enabling the Adept to wield kingly power. I believe similar practices are progressively taught in both the OTO and A∴A∴.. - this is the magick of light.

THE SCAPEGOAT AND THE DAY OF ATONEMENT

Yom Kippur (יוֹם כִּיפּוּר) is the holiest day in the Jewish religious calendar, and is observed with fasting, prayer and confession. In the Midrashic tradition, it commemorates the day Moses received the second set of the 10 Commandments, following a second period of 40 days during which he received instruction from God. The Israelites were also at this time granted atonement for "the sin of the calf" (חֵטְא הָעֵגֶל). This is an incident described in Exodus 32, where the Israelites, after Moses failed to return, gave Aaron their golden earrings and, 'he received *them* at their hand, and fashioned it with a graving tool, after he had made it a molten calf...' (Exodus 32:4). In Exodus it is stated that, 'These *be* thy gods, O Israel, which brought thee out of the land of Egypt.' (Exodus 32:4). Before this new idol the people burnt offerings, and brought peace offerings[1] on what Aaron called 'a feast to the Lord.' (Exodus 32:4). This betrayal stirred the wrath of the Lord,[2] but Moses interceded and 'the Lord repented of the evil which he thought to do unto his people.' (Exodus 32:4). When Moses returned and saw the worship of the calf, he broke the tablets that '*were*

---

1   Peace offerings are a slaughter offering or zevakh (זֶבַח). In Hebrew, the concept of the peace offering also encompasses concepts such as harmony, health, and prosperity. It is interesting to note that the value of zevakh ("sacrifice") by gematria is 17, which is the same value as (גדי), the Hebrew for Capricornus (♑). The word used for peace offering is zevah shelamim (שלמים זבח). This literally means "a whole, or complete offering".

2   The Israelites are often referred to as "stiffnecked", meaning that they were difficult to lead and obstinate.

the work of God...' (Exodus 32:16). Following this the sons of Levi, who answered Moses' call to affirm that they were on the Lord's side, slaughtered approximately three thousand Israelites – 'slay every man his brother, and every man his companion, and every man his neighbour.' (Exodus 32:27). The Lord sent more suffering unto the people who had transgressed and sinned against him. Moses then 'took the tabernacle, and pitched it without the camp, afar off from the camp, and called it the Tabernacle of the congregation. And it came to pass, *that* every one which sought the Lord went out unto the tabernacle of the congregation, which *was* without the camp.' (Exodus 33:7).

It was in this tabernacle, outside of the camp, that the Lord appeared as a 'cloudy pillar' at the tabernacle door, and 'the Lord talked with Moses.' (Exodus 33:9). The Lord did not only speak with Moses, but spoke to him 'face to face, as a man speaketh unto his friend.' (Exodus 33:11). This seems to be in opposition to Exodus 33:18-23 where Moses asks the Lord to show him his "glory". In response to this the Lord responded with, 'thou canst not see my face: for there shall no man see me, and live.' (Exodus 33:20). However, the Lord tells Moses, '*there* is a place by me, and thou shalt stand upon a rock...' (Exodus 33:21). The Lord then explains to Moses that when he passes by, he will conceal him in this rock, and 'cover thee with my hand while I pass by...'[3] Moses is not permitted to see the face of the Lord, but only his 'back parts'.[4] The face of the Lord 'shall not be seen.' (Exodus 33:21). Following this Moses is instructed to make new tablets and return to Mount Sinai, and a covenant is made. Exodus highlights the contradic-

---

3   *The KJV Study Bible*, 99.

4   A connection here could perhaps be drawn with Lévi's descriptions of the "hind-face" of Baphomet during initiation.

tory nature of the God of Israel. On one hand we have a God that is 'merciful and gracious, longsuffering, and abundant in goodness and truth.' (Exodus 34:6). On the other hand, he is shown as 'a jealous God' – not just jealous, but the *name* of the Lord is 'Jealous' (Exodus 34:14). This is a God who will readily punish and slaughter his people for transgressions, and also order that for those of other faiths that the Israelites encounter, 'ye shall destroy their altars, break their images, and cut down their groves.' (Exodus 34:13). This is a God who will look after you if you are on his side and do exactly what you are told.

Connected with the holy day of Yom Kippur is the concept of the scapegoat, which is the most important sacrifice (or sacrifices) associated with this Day of Atonement. The term scapegoat has become embedded in the popular vernacular, but in reality, this part of the ritual of Yom Kippur involves the sacrifice of two goats, one goat 'for Azazel' the other 'for the Lord.' I also think there is a connection between the scapegoat, and the above from Exodus, where following the transgressions of the Israelites Moses pitches the tabernacle outside of the camp. It is outside the camp, to this tabernacle, where those who sought the Lord went. Similarly, the scapegoat is sent away into the wilderness. One goat is taken outside of the camp, while the other remains inside.

'On the annual Day of Atonement, the priest would send the scapegoat out of the camp. This goat was, of course, sinless, but it carried with it all the transgressions for all the Israelites for that entire year. The goat would be sent out into the wilderness, as Jesus would be crucified outside of Jerusalem.'[5] Christians believe that the sacrifice of Jesus now makes this annual atonement of sin redundant. Their sins taken 'upon Himself,

---

5   *The KJV Study Bible*, 128.

and away from us, once and for all.'[6] Like the scapegoat, Christ was taken outside the city to suffer and die for the sins of His people. Where does the Lord abide? Within, or without the Camp? Or both within and without? Moses, in one way, could be seen as a prototypical Christ; interceding between God and the Israelites when they had sinned. In order to communicate with God he would leave the camp, either to ascend Mt. Sinai or to enter the tabernacle – he would go out into the wilderness. Go to a place that was unbounded.

Explicit in the rituals surrounding Yom Kippur is the concept of harmony, of balance and reconciliation. I agree with José R. Luna that it is possibly an error to read into the sacrifice of the goats an antithetical dualism – that one goat is for God and the other for Satan (the adversary of God), and that Satan 'must pay for the all the sins that he has instigated people to commit.'[7] Rabbi Raymond Apple makes the point that, 'In English, *Yom Kippur* is the "Day of Atonement" — a name that (perhaps surprisingly) does not mean expiating guilt, but comes from the Middle English *onement* (that is, harmony). In Hebrew, it is from a root that means to cover. The English and Hebrew are thus not entirely equivalent. The idea of at-one-ment invests the day with three aspects: being at one with Jewish identity; being at one with God; and being at one with other people. Each element is both a confirmation and a challenge.'[8] Where is there space for Satan, during this time to reconcile, and be in harmony with God through the atonement of sins? If God is truly God, where is there space for Satan at all? If both goats are 'without blemish' (Leviticus 1:10), and both presented 'before the Lord at the door of the tabernacle

---

6   *The KJV Study Bible*, 128.

7   Luna, 'Pairs and Pluralism in Yom Kippur: A Perspective', 2.

8   Apple, 'The Challenge of Yom Kippur'.

of the congregation' (Leviticus 16:7), it seems unlikely that one of these goats would be seen as Satan. If Jesus, the Son of God, is to be seen as the final scapegoat, then there is even less room for an interpretation that includes Satan. The two goats must be seen as complimentary, not antithetical.

Lévi also seems to tackle this when he writes, 'If God may be defined as He Who exists of necessity, may we not define His antagonist and enemy as necessarily he who does not exist at all? The absolute affirmation of good implies an absolute negation of evil; so also in the light, shadow itself is luminous.'[9]

Much information about Yom Kippur is found in Leviticus, a book from the Old Testament, traditionally said to be authored by Moses, that is a guide for the priests and people; the priests 'put in place after the institution of the Mosaic Covenant at mount Sinai.'[10] This includes instructions regarding worship, but also 'practical ways to live out holiness in everyday life.'[11]

Leviticus 16 contains many things that need to be undertaken in pairs. Luna points out that a recognisable pattern in the instructions are things that are presented in pairs, complimentary actions or principles needed for the atonement of sin. It opens with a reference to the 'two sons of Aaron' (Leviticus 16:1), Nadab and Abihu, who offered 'strange fire before the Lord', which caused a 'fire from the Lord', which 'devoured them, and they died before the Lord.' (Leviticus 10:1-2). The animal sacrifices are also described as paired; a 'young bullock'[12] for a sin offering, and a 'ram for a burnt offering.' (Le-

---

9   Lévi, *Transcendental Magic*, 310.

10   *The KJV Study Bible*, 109.

11   *The KJV Study Bible*, 109.

12   This bullock offering was only for Aaron himself and his house (Leviticus 16:6)

viticus 16:3). There is the pair of goats that Aaron took to 'present them before the Lord at the door of the tabernacle of the congregation.' (Leviticus 16:7). It could also be interpreted that two lots were also 'cast upon the two goats…' as there are two goats presented, and the plural is used. There are also two sources for the animal sacrifices, the congregation (Leviticus 16:5), and the priests represented by Aaron. (Leviticus 16:7). The blood of the goat and the calf were spread in two places, 'upon the mercy seat and before the mercy seat.' (Leviticus 16:15). During the confession two hands were laid 'upon the head of the live goat' (Leviticus 16:21) and two people took part in the confession, Aaron (the priest), and 'a fit man' who would take the scapegoat into the wilderness. (Leviticus 16:21). The priest who was to make the atonement was anointed and consecrated. (Leviticus 16:32).

There are other examples, but the above should be ample to give consideration to this pattern. The only other pairing that is of interest, that has been mentioned previously, is the 'the camp' (Leviticus 16:27) and 'the wilderness' (Leviticus 16:22), or desolate place. In the Bible Commentaries edited by Charles John Ellicott it states that the translation is 'Unto a land not inhabited—Literally, *unto a land cut off*, that is, a place the ground of which is separated from all around it, hence a summit, a peak standing out by itself, a precipice.'[13] The distinction between what was in and what was away from the camp seems significant. This also returns to the theme of mountains, of summits in religions around the world, and their relationship to the Great Work.

Lévi addresses directly what he saw as the connection between Baphomet and the scapegoat in Chapter XV of *Tran-*

---

13   Ellicott, *A Bible Commentary for English Readers by Various Writers*, 1:410.

scendental Magic, 'The Sabbath of the Sorcerers' when he writes about 'the three symbolical animals of hermetic magic'[14] (the bull, the dog and the goat). The goat, writes Lévi, is fire, and 'the symbol of generation'.[15]

'Two goats, one pure and one impure,[16] were consecrated in Judea; the first was sacrificed in expiation for sins; the other, loaded with those sins by imprecation,[17] was set at liberty in the desert – a strange ordinance, but one of deep symbolism, signifying reconciliation by sacrifice and expiation by liberty!'[18] This is an interesting concept, "expiation by liberty", the reconciliation, the making amends of the sins of the people was through an act of liberty, of freedom. Lévi also makes reference to the mysteries of the wilderness. He writes of a 'Magic of the Sanctuary and that of the wilderness…'[19] He then differentiates between the White and the Black Church; the White being 'the priesthood of public assemblies', the Black 'the Sanhedrim of the Sabbath.'[20] I don't read into this a simple reference to black and white magic, or good and evil practices, but to the public face of religious worship and practices, and the deeper mysteries, the secret practices, the Magic of the Wilderness. It is in the wilderness that freedom is found. Beyond the structures of the camp or city – the structures of the mind. These must be understood and torn down, transcended, so one can appreciate the unbounded view to the horizon and beyond. Our apparent

---

14 Lévi, *Transcendental Magic*, 308.

15 Lévi, 308.

16 I do not necessarily agree with Lévi that one goat is pure and the other impure. In my opinion both are pure, but in this context Lévi is using this as a vehicle for other concepts.

17 A spoken curse

18 Lévi, *Transcendental Magic*, 308.

19 Lévi, 308.

20 Lévi, 308.

sins,[21] our apparent vices, our nature, are the vehicle of our liberty. This unbounded environment, this wilderness, these high places could be another metaphor for that field of consciousness associated with Baphomet consciousness.

> I am not come to rebuke you, or to enslave you.
> I bid you not turn from your voluptuous ways, from your idleness, from your follies.
> But I bring you joy to your pleasure, peace to your languor, wisdom to your folly.
> All that ye do is right, if so be that ye enjoy it.
>
> *Liber XC,* 6-9[22]

Azazel

Another entity connected to the scapegoat is the "demon" Azazel. An enigmatic and mysterious force that has engendered numerous interpretations in both Jewish and Christian theology, as well as occult speculations. However, there are additional elements associated with the myths surrounding Azazel that are suggestive of the Baphomet mysteries.

In an article on Azazel, Rabbi Lord Jonathan Sacks makes mention of a meaning of Azazel given by Ibn Ezra (c.1089–1092–c.1164–1167) and Nachmanides (1194–1270):

> Azazel was the name of a spirit or demon, one of the fallen angels referred to in Genesis 6:2, similar to the goat-spirit called Pan in Greek mythology, Faunus in Latin. This is a

---

21 Noting that, as pointed out by Gunther, the English word "sin" originates from an archery term that means "to miss the mark."

22 Crowley, *The Holy Books of Thelema,* 95.

difficult idea, which is why Ibn Ezra alluded to it, as he did in similar cases, by way of a riddle, a puzzle, that only the wise would be able to decipher. He writes: "I will reveal to you part of the secret by hint: when you reach thirty-three you will know it." Nachmanides reveals the secret. Thirty three verses later on, the Torah commands: "They must no longer offer any of their sacrifices to the goat idols [seirim] after whom they go astray" (Lev. 17: 7).[23]

The above shows another connection between the ritual of the scapegoat, and concepts associated with Baphomet – the goat and Pan.[24] It was to this mysterious entity, Azazel, that the scapegoat was sent. 'The original name for Azazel has the prepositional prefix ל (*la* in la'aza'zel) appended to it which is usually directional (to, toward, for).'[25]

There has been further confusion caused about the identity of Azazel due to the King James version of the Bible translating Azazel as "scapegoat" and 'the development of this theology has often made the two synonymous.'[26] This identity between the scapegoat and Azazel has obvious problems for some Christian theology, where Christ is considered a type of scapegoat, and Azazel interpreted as Satan (such as in Adventist theology). For Christians there is difficulty with this shared identity.

Barker writes that, 'The ancient ritual of the scapegoat required that a goat be sent into the wilderness to Azazel. The

---

23 Sacks, 'Covenant & Conversation', 1.

24 This connection with Pan may also be seen in the fact that 'Azazel also holds grapes in his hands. In view of such correspondences, it is possible that the text attempts to envision the antagonist as an embodiment of the infamous arboreal symbol [The Tree of Knowledge].' (Orlov, 'Azazel as the Serpent and the Tree of Knowledge', 119.)

25 Beckworth, 'Are We Wrong: The Symbolic Identity of the Goat for Azazel (the Scapegoat)', 2–3

26 Beckworth, 2

goat carries all the transgressions and sins of Israel into the wilderness, to Azazel (Leviticus 16:20-22). The Old Testament tells us nothing more about Azazel, or why he was in the wilderness. He must have been important, as he is the only one apart from God to whom a sacrifice is to be offered, and it was thought appropriate to send sins to him in the wilderness.'[27]

Further, 'In Enoch we find that Asael, the fallen leader of the angels, is imprisoned in the wilderness. Enoch tells us how he got there, and who he really was.'[28] Asael was an angel who knew the secrets of creation and chose to teach some of those to the people of earth.

We can also read in *The Book of Enoch* Azazel's connection to sin, and to the desert:

And again the Lord said to Raphael, "Bind Azazel hand and foot, and cast him into the darkness: and make an opening in the desert, which is in Dudael, and cast him therein. And place upon him rough and jagged rocks, and cover him with darkness, and let him abide there for ever, and cover his face that he may not see light. And on the day of the great judgement he shall be cast into the fire.

And heal the earth which the angels have corrupted, and proclaim the healing of the earth, that they may heal the plague, and that all the children of men may not perish through all the secret things that the Watchers have disclosed and have taught their sons. And the whole earth has been corrupted through the works that were taught by Azazel, to him ascribe all sin."[29]

---

27   Barker, *The Lost Prophet: The Book of Enoch and Its Influence on Christianity*, 23.

28   Barker, 23.

29   Winter, *The Complete Book of Enoch: Standard English Version*, 11.

A possible link between this "sin" and sex or sexuality can be found in the *Apocalypse of Abraham*, Chapter Twenty Three:

> And they were standing under a tree of Eden, and the fruit of the tree was like the appearance of a bunch of grapes of vine. And behind the tree was standing, as it were, a serpent in form, but having hands and feet like a man, and wings on its shoulders: six on the right side and six on the left. And he was holding in his hands the grapes of the tree and feeding the two whom I saw entwined with each other. And I said, "Who are these two entwined with each other, or who is this between them, or what is the fruit which they are eating, Mighty Eternal One?" And he said, "This is the reason of men, this is Adam, and this is their desire on earth, this is Eve. And he who is between them is the Impiety of their pursuits for destruction, Azazel himself.[30]

The above forms a fascinating image of a three in one (male, female and serpent/Azazel). 'In thinking about this Edenic portrayal, which depicts a bizarre intertwining of Adam, Eve, and Azazel, Daniel Harlow suggests that 'the three of them appear in a ménage à trois, the man and woman entwined in an erotic embrace, the fallen angel in serpentine guise feeding[31] them grapes.'[32]

Another element of significance to this work in the questions raised by Andrei A. Orlov is 'whether the sexual union of Azazel and the primordial couple intends to create a race of demonic creatures, as in the case of the conjugal encounters between the fallen angels and women in *the Book of the*

---

30   Orlov, 'Azazel as the Serpent and the Tree of Knowledge', 117.

31   'Scholars have noted that in rabbinic culture food and feeding often become metaphors for sexual activity.' (Orlov, 120.)

32   Orlov, 117.

Watchers... In *the Book of the Watchers*, the aetiology of demons is tied to the peculiar anthropology of the Giants who were born from a union of the celestial and earthly creatures. Archie Wright states that "by procreating through the women, the Watchers have created an unauthorized new being, one that is a mix of the heavenly nature of angels and the body and flesh of humans: 'they will be called evil spirits' and they will dwell among humans (15:8)."[33]

Archie Wright highlights that 'the Giants, like their human counterparts, were composed of two elements; they each had a fleshly body, which could die, and they each had an immortal spirit (in the sense that its existence continued following a physical death). The spiritual element of the Giants, however, had a slightly different nature to that of the human spirit. The Giants' spirits, unlike the human spirit, were able to roam the earth unseen (1 Enoch 15:11), a trait inherited from their fathers.'[34] Here, it seems, that the giants, these 'unauthorised new beings' are in most ways quite human, except for a special inheritance, and I speculate whether this is some kind of initiated knowledge, a knowledge of the union of the celestial and the earthly.

The Servant

And he sat down, and called the twelve, and said unto them, If any man desire to be the first, *the same* shall be the last of all, and servant[35] of all.

Mark 9:35

---

33   Orlov, 118.

34   Orlov, 119.

35   'They are all, however, bound by the original and fundamental Oath of the Order, to devote their energy to assisting the Progress of their Inferiors in the Order. Those who accept the rewards of their emancipation for them-

In her book *Temple Mysticism*, Barker explores her interpretation of a figure called "the Servant", which is connected to Jesus,[36] the second Adam[37] who regained his loss. The Adam of Genesis being, initially, male-and-female.[38]

'Here the mystery is impenetrable, although the earliest Christians understood it, or, at the very least, knew about it. The Servant had the roles of *both* goats on the day of atonement: he poured himself out, like the goat whose blood was taken into the Holy of Holies, and he bore the sins, like the second goat who was driven away. The Mishnah emphasised that both goats were identical in every way, and maybe this is why; both represented a single figure.'[39] The Servant, the scapegoat (two in one), has a dual function, one that draws inward, that takes on the sins of the people, and the other that pours itself outward, represented by the sacrificial blood. Barker also notes that it is the sacrifice that must proceed enthronement, the pouring out is intimately linked to the exultation – 'sprin-

---

selves are no longer within the Order.' (Crowley et al., *Commentaries of the Holy Books and Other Papers*, 4:11.)

36 It should be noted that Gunther in his Commentary to Liber LXV, Chapter I questions this association between the Messiah and the "servant", stating that, 'The "servant" described in these verses represented *all the people* of Israel, not the Messiah...' (Gunther and Gunther, *I Am the Heart: A Commentary on Liber LXV Chapter I, Ever the Heart: An Essay on the Symbolism of The Heart of Blood*, 150.)

37 Adam the original High Priest in Jewish tradition.

38 Barker also describes Ezekiel's telling of the Adam story where a *cherub* is cast from Eden (Ezekiel 28:12-19). In some texts the *cherub* was clothed as a high priest. The *cherub* was cast down to earth due to his sanctuaries being made unholy; he became mortal. The *cherub* was 'presumably the one who sealed the eternal covenant; he was full of wisdom and perfect beauty... the *cherub* was described with a mixture of masculine and feminine forms...' (Barker, *Temple Mysticism: An Introduction*, 136.)

39 Barker, 160.

kling blood on the mercy seat/throne (Leviticus 16:15) was the enthronement.'[40] Here we see the concept of enthronement, of becoming a king connected to the pouring out of blood, which is the life.

Barker also makes the point that what is now known as gemination,[41] was a concept that would have been understood at the time of First-Isaiah – that a double form was sometimes used to represent great people. For example, 'The crown prince of Ugarit…had been called the Morning Star and the Evening Star, two aspects or functions of Venus.'[42]

Through the ritual sacrifices the high priest took the blood into the Holy of Holies, which was heaven, but then came out again, returned to earth to remove from it the effects of sin. This was the renewal of the creation, and the restoration of the bonds of the eternal covenant.

It was during this ritual, that the priest, having taken on the sins of the people, transferred them to the scapegoat. This was the only time the high priest called out the Name, 'not using some substitute such as Adonai, but actually pronouncing the Name.'[43] This is the same name Lévi connected intimately with the Ark of the Covenant in the Holy of Holies.

---

40 Barker, 151.

41 A doubling; duplication; repetition.

42 Barker, *Temple Mysticism: An Introduction*, 160.

43 Barker, 145.

Tetragrammaton by Francisco Goya: "The Name of God", YHWH in triangle, detail from fresco Adoration of the Name of God, 1772

The connection between the marriage of heaven and earth is also posited by Barker in relation to the other sacrifice made on the Day of Atonement, that of the bull. Although any clear evidence of the meaning has been lost, it is possible the blood of the bull represented the high priest as human, as mortal. The goat's blood was the 'heavenly life of the Lord.'[44] These two bloods, the earthly and the heavenly, were mixed and then

---

44   Barker, 148.

sprinkled around the outer temple. The heavenly life and the earthly were joined.

> Between the being which is indivisible and remains always the same and the being which is transient and divisible into bodies, he mixed in the middle a third form of being...
>
> *Plato's Timaeus*[45]

So here again is an association between the sacrifice of the goats as part of the celebration of Yom Kippur, and Christ as the goat, as heaven, whose blood is mixed with the earthly life, the blood of a bull, in a state of reconciliation and balance. Harmony has returned to the creation, the high priest has carried the blood, the life, to a place outside of time and space (the Inner Sanctuary). The second identical goat is driven out into the wilderness – the same in a different manner. The unpronounceable name of God is pronounced, which is a name of creation and of life.

> The Many is as adorable to the One as the One is to the Many. This is the Love of These; creation parturition is the Bliss of the One; coition-dissolution is the Bliss of the Many.[46]

---

45 Barker, 148.

46 Crowley, *The Book of Lies*, 16.

Parsifal

The blessed end of all eternal,
do you know how I attained it?
Grieving love's deepest compassion
opened the gates to me:
Those who above all,
value this life,
turn your eyes from me.
On those who with compassion,
gaze after the departing one,
there dawns from afar
the redemption that I attained.
So greeting the world, I depart![47]

I will now take another, perhaps unexpected, side road, and explore what could also be seen to be a connection between the scapegoat and The Fool (the pure fool, Parsifal),[48] who unburdened by complex thought is free to act naturally, although 'the wantonness of innocence'[49] eventually matures after Parsifal seizes the lance. '[T]o reconsecrate[50] the temple, he has only to plunge the lance into the Holy Grail',[51] the Temple returned

---

47   Everett, 'Parsifal under the Bodhi Tree', 3.

48   'The name Parsifal may have had a Celtic origin. Or Chrétien de Troyes may have made it up around 1180 for his Story of the Grail. Some say it means 'pierce the vale' in Old French, some 'having to go all through life's experience', or 'the Persians may fall'. Wagner thought it was Persian for 'pure fool'.'(Middenway, 'Parsifal, Kundry and the Dance of the Seven Veils', 3.)

49   Crowley, *The Book of Thoth*, 59.

50   Wagner called Parsifal a "Bühnenweihfestspiel", which roughly translates 'stage-consecrating festival play'.

51   Crowley, *The Book of Thoth*, 59.

of its virtue, and reconsecrated – The Fool becomes The Devil – the Temple requires a sacrifice.

Much of the influence of Parsifal on Crowley stems from Richard Wagner's opera of the same name. 'The main theme of the *Parsifal* drama is Compassion,[52] the highest aspect of that Love which was the keynote of Wagner's own life, and whose sacred power is contained in the chalice of the Grail.'[53]

As Frater Achad explains in *The Chalice of Ecstasy*, the lance or spear represents Wisdom: 'And this WISDOM Parzival does in due course secure, but not until he has undergone many trials. For WISDOM is the HOLY SPEAR itself, long lost to the Knights of the Grail but eventually recovered by The Pure Fool.'[54] Achad also equates Wisdom with the Will, '[f]or the CUP is the UNDERSTANDING, though in this instance it is divorced from WILL or WISDOM, the Holy Spear which alone is capable of enlightening it perfectly.'[55] 'Understanding without Wisdom is Pure Darkness…'[56] I will deal with Wisdom in more detail in another place, but it is interesting that Achad also draws a comparison with the way of the Tao, and that Parsifal also, after claiming the lance, disappears into the wilderness, 'set out alone upon his Holy Quest.'[57] It is also of note that in the figure of Parsifal, Wagner blended the char-

---

52   'Only the Lance which caused the wound can heal that wound, and that only the "Pure Fool" *(der reine Tor),* made wise through compassion, can regain the Lance and heal the wounded king.' (Sabazius, 'Parzival'.)

53   Leighton Cleather and Crump, *Parsifal Lohengrin and the Legend of the Holy Grail*, 103.

54   Frater Achad, *The Chalice of Ecstasy Being the Inmost Secret of Parzival*, 16.

55   Frater Achad, 16.

56   Frater Achad, 18.

57   Frater Achad, 19.

acteristics of Jesus and the Buddha, Western Christianity and Eastern Buddhism.[58] Parsifal 'learns the cause of the World's pain through Sympathy, or Compassion, which is the highest aspect of the Will. It then becomes the power to redeem, and its weapon is the sacred Lance, which should never be separated from the Grail: for Will needs Wisdom[59] to control and guide it.'[60]

Although Wagner at times writes of compassion in the more "human" sense, he also seems to consider it in a more transcendent manner: 'Under the highest and most favourable conditions we attain to a sympathy with all things living...In this perfect unison with all that has been kept apart from us by the illusion of individuation lies the root of all virtue, the true secret of redemption.'[61] I do, however, think that Thelemites turn their back on the more human nature of compassion at their own risk. If there is no compassion; no sympathy with other life, then organisations such as the two Great Orders, and the Bodhisattva vow become meaningless. Compassion, however, needs to be tempered and understood within its plane of operation. But, 'as above, so below', this compassion can open a door to Compassion. It can broaden our limited horizon and open the door to an understanding of Self beyond self. We must, however, consider the initiated meaning of Compassion, as taught by Crowley in response to Wagner. Not long after I began writing this section, a fascinating paper appeared in

---

58   Wagner once signed off a letter to a friend as 'Your grateful Buddhist'. (Leighton Cleather and Crump, *Parsifal Lohengrin and the Legend of the Holy Grail*, 178.)

59   Perhaps the creative and kingly powers described by Philo.

60   Leighton Cleather and Crump, *Parsifal Lohengrin and the Legend of the Holy Grail*, 106.

61   Leighton Cleather and Crump, 110.

Ora et Labora Vol 3, written by Percy A. Mindnich titled *That I May Follow and Dispel the Night*, in which the concept of Compassion is explored in the context of Wagner's Parsifal. Mindnich beautifully puts it that 'redeemer is a function, a function that can be fulfilled by anyone who is capable of feeling compassion, thus overcoming duality. Consequently, the blood in the Grail is the blood of every enlightened person, that which Crowley calls the Blood of the Saints.'[62]

This side-road discussing Wagner's Parsifal may seem out of place, but I see in the narrative of the Grail Knights elements that speak to the mysteries of the Day of Atonement, and the scapegoat. Parsifal is sent out, like the goat, into the wilderness, and when he returns with the spear Gurnemanz performs a rite, folding his hands on Parsifal's head, saying, 'So was it promised to us...so do I bless thy head, - and hail thee as king. Thou – pure one – compassionate sufferer, enlightened deliverer [the Thoren motive is heard]. As thou hast borne the sufferings of the redeemed one, so now take the last burden from his head.'[63] Parsifal, like the scapegoat, and as a form of Christ, has taken on the burden of the redeemer. Just like Parsifal, the scapegoat is innocent and unknowing, yet still takes on the burden of the sin of the people of Israel (and it is perhaps this innocence that allows the scapegoat to take on such a burden). This part of the opera also takes place on Good Friday, the day commemorating Jesus' death at Calvary – the day he became the final scapegoat in the Christian tradition.

---

62   Mindnich, 'That I May Follow and Dispel the Night: Wagner's Parsifal and Liber XV', 229.

63   Leighton Cleather and Crump, *Parsifal Lohengrin and the Legend of the Holy Grail*, 154.

We can clearly see Wagner's influence on Crowley from *The Book of Wisdom or Folly*, written in 1918 (Achad's *The Chalice of Ecstasy* would be published in 1923), in Chapter 44, *De Sapientia in re Sexuali* (On the Wisdom of Sexual Affairs):

Therefore thine Uncle Richard Wagner made of our Doctrine a Musical Fable...[64]

In this chapter Crowley warns of the dangers of Love, 'yet without Love Man were not a Man.'[65] Here we can draw a parallel with Crowley's use of the term Love, with that of Compassion (the highest aspect of Will). This Compassion is not weakness, it is an act of great courage.

Derrick Everett argues that the theme of redemption that appears in Parsifal has its origin in Wagner's interest in and respect for Mahayana Buddhism, and that these Buddhist elements are not incidental. Parsifal 'was written around the archetype of a *Bodhisattva*... As the *Bodhisattva* grows in wisdom and compassion, each of these balances and enhances the other.'[66]

Parsifal can be seen as 'the *Bodhisattva* awakens (from the life-dream) to Buddhahood and becomes a fountain of karma (merit). Then instead of entering into nirvana he chooses to pause on the threshold out of his great compassion (Sanskrit: *mahákaruná*) for those sentient beings who are still trapped in samsara, the cycle of rebirth, suffering and death; to which in Buddhist doctrine even gods are subject.'[67] In this way, could the scapegoat also have a link to this concept of the Bodhi-

---

64 Crowley, *Liber Aleph Vel CXI: The Book of Wisdom or Folly*, 44.

65 Crowley, 44.

66 Everett, 'Parsifal under the Bodhi Tree', 2.

67 Everett, 2.

sattva? One goat sacrificed as a blood offering, entering into the infinite, entering the Holy of Holies, whereas the scapegoat returns to the wilderness for the sins of the people.

Parsifal demonstrates, through the healing of Amfortas, that he possesses the Kingly Power and therefore relieves Amfortas of his duty and takes this upon himself.

Crowley describes the hero of Wagner as 'not merely a king, but a holy king. He was the custodian of a sacred treasure; he wielded magic weapons, and wore armour consecrated and invulnerable.'[68] In *The Book of Thoth*, when describing various archetypes featured on the cards, always pays attention to the nature of the armour worn, in relation to the type of energy, or manifestation represented.

This seems to indicate a connection between the concepts of the "knight in shining armour", the wandering hero, and an Adept of the secrets of the OTO (something that cannot be conferred but earned through thorough application of the secret).

Crowley writes similarly of the Robe in Book Four:

> The Robe is that which conceals, and which protects the Magician from the elements; it is the silence and secrecy with which he works, the hiding of himself in the occult life of Magick and Meditation. This is the "going away into the wilderness" which we find in the lives of all men of the highest types of greatness. And it is also the withdrawing of one's self from life as such.[69]

---

68   Stephensen and Crowley, *The Legend of Aleister Crowley*, 115.

69   Crowley, Desti, and Waddell, *Magick. Liber ABA. Book Four. Parts I-IV*, 106.

The robe is the armour of the magician, his "aura", 'shining elastic and impenetrable'.[70] This armour, however, must allow the light to pass, so that it can 'illumine them that sit in darkness and the shadow of death'.[71] This speaks directly, again, to the obligation of the initiates of the IX° of the OTO, who are direct representatives of the Supreme and Most Holy King. They must radiate 'his light upon the world', yet they are concealed, armoured. They 'veil their glory in a cloud of darkness…unseen and unrecognised'. They are to lead the brethren 'into the holy ineffable mysteries of the True Light'.[72]

Aspirants to the A∴A∴ are similarly obligated; they are to accept no attainment for themselves, but work for the benefit of those who are placed within their charge. They serve as a conduit for the Order, as to guide them inwards.

These concepts above could be applicable to teachings regarding transmigration – 'The labour and heroism of incarnation'[73] - and eastern traditions such as the Tibetan "Rainbow Body" (*jalu*) - a body both individual and universal. We should note that we accomplish the "Miracle of Incarnation" through the "Baptism of Wisdom" – through Baphomet.[74]

This interacts with the teachings of the admirable Soror Hilarion, as interpreted by Crowley, regarding the practice recovered and explored by Frater Shiva X° called "Living in the Sunlight", and the "Kingly Power". Crowley wrote in a private correspondence that 'The main point seems to be the

---

70   Crowley, Desti, and Waddell, 106.

71   Crowley, Desti, and Waddell, 106.

72   Crowley, 'Liber CXCIV, An Intimation with Reference to the Constitution of the Order', 177.

73   Crowley, Desti, and Waddell, *Magick. Liber ABA. Book Four. Parts I-IV*, 356.

74   Crowley, Desti, and Waddell, 585.

conception of yourself as a King – Vide Liber CCXX Cap 2'. Additionally, he expands, 'I ought to add that it involves making everybody in your sphere reflect your radiance. This is the measure of your success.' This seems very close to the concept above of the IX° who 'illumine them that sit in darkness and the shadow of death'. The IX° radiates the light[75] from themselves, from the Sovereign Sanctuary, for the benefit of the brethren, and this is 'the way of the Tao.'[76]

> The Tao is one, and the Te but a phase thereof. The abyss of this Mystery is the Portal of Serpent Wonder.[77]

Interestingly, Crowley references Chapter 2 of *Liber CCXX* (*Liber AL vel Legis*, "The Book of the Law") above, which deals with the teaching regarding kings. This also seems cognate to concepts of the Rainbow Body and the radiance of the Sun:

> Think not, o king, upon that lie: That Thou Must Die: verily thou shalt not die, but live. Now let it be understood: If the body of the King dissolve, he shall remain in pure ecstasy

---

75   In a similar way Masaaki Hatsumi, the head of the Bujinkan organisation, of which I am a member, states, 'A person who lights the way is called a Saint in Christianity. Light is a symbol of important things…While that light is shining it is an expression of the next life and contains a vital "Ki"…A person who is a "Denshosha" (伝照者 [noting the standard reading of 伝書者]) knows the essence of this light and values it…With that meaning, the most important thing for a person who is a guardian of a tradition is to value things that radiate light…consistently having "Fūbō" (a person's features [風貌]) is important for the creation of good people for the next generation after you have passed on.' (*Masaaki Hatsumi: Kuden Vol. 1.*)

76   Shiva X°, 'Australia: The Land of Sun Worshippers – Part IV: The OTO Living in the Sunlight Meditation', 3.

77   Crowley, *Tao Te King*, 16.

for ever. Nuit! Hadit! Ra-Hoor-Khuit! The Sun, Strength &
Sight, Light; these are for the servants of the Star & the Snake.

Liber AL, II:21

This chapter also links with the concept above regarding
the Robe of the magician; going into the wilderness and with-
drawing oneself:

I am alone: there is no God where I am.

Behold! these be grave mysteries; for there are also of my
friends who be hermits. Now think not to find them in the
forest or on the mountain; but in beds of purple, caressed by
magnificent beasts of women with large limbs, and fire and
light in their eyes, and masses of flaming hair about them;
there shall ye find them. Ye shall see them at rule, at victorious armies, at all the joy; and there shall be in them a joy a
million times greater than this.

Liber AL, II:23-24

Here, The Book of the Law seems to provide a different
perspective of the nature of the wilderness. The wilderness is an
internal state, regardless of the physical location and physical
activity of the Adept.

In a similar way to the duties of the members of the Sovereign Sanctuary, the death of the father in Parsifal occurs when
duty or obligation is not followed – when the grail is not revealed to the brethren. When the king fails[78] in his duty and the
light of the grail is not revealed does the old king die.

---

78 'Without the Tao, Heaven would dissolve, Earth disrupt, Spirits become
impotent, Vehicles empty; living things would perish, and rulers lose their
power.' (Crowley, 57.)

Behold the Sacred Spear

Parsifal, or the Legend of the Holy Grail Retold from Antient Sources with Acknowledgement to the "Parsifal" of Richard Wagner - 1912

The other character in Parsifal that draws attention to these mysteries, is Klingsor, who had sought to join the grail knights, but, because he was unable to control his thoughts, castrated himself. This caused him to be expelled from the Order, after which he set up his own domain in the valley, where he placed the Flower Maidens to tempt and seduce the Grail Knights, and this was where Amfortas himself failed and was wounded by the Spear that should have been within his control. Following this Amfortas has a vision in which he is told that he should await a "pure fool, enlightened by compassion". Crowley makes the point that the hero (Parsifal) must make Kundry his servant so he can heal the king (which leads him to become the king), but 'he must cease to depend on her, earning his lance...'[79] If we take Kundry as physical existence then it shows us that the king does not reject the world and its realities, but he is master of them, and also independent of them. We are called to 'enjoy all things of sense and rapture' and told that 'The exposure of innocence is a lie' (AL II:22). At the same time 'there is that which remains' (AL II:9). It is also in this part of *The Book of the Law* that certain sexual mysteries are being imparted by Aiwass; instructions about kundalini and instruction about these 'grave mysteries' (AL II:24) that are connected to the wilderness, spiritual solitude, and dual phases of heaven and earth.[80] In *Book Four* Crowley writes of Parsifal in connection with The Hermit and the Hebrew Yod, 'The youth setting out on his adventures after receiving the Wand – Parsifal in the desert.'[81]

---

79 Crowley, Desti, and Waddell, *Magick. Liber ABA. Book Four. Parts I-IV*, 162.

80 'I am the secret Serpent coiled about to spring: in my coiling there is joy. If I lift up my head, I and my Nuit are one. If I droop down my head, and shoot forth venom, then is rapture of the earth, and I and the earth are one.' (AL II:26)

81 Crowley, Desti, and Waddell, *Magick. Liber ABA. Book Four. Parts I-IV*, 161.

Parsifal in the Forest

Parsifal, or the Legend of the Holy Grail Retold from Antient Sources with Acknowledgement to the "Parsifal" of Richard Wagner - 1912

I hope this brief exploration has highlighted the connection between the concepts behind Yom Kippur and the scapegoat, and the interpretation used by Crowley (through the filter of Wagner). In this context Parsifal can be seen as another scapegoat, another Christ, another king who is redeemed by the Universal Agent – the Agent that is represented by the glyph of Baphomet gifted to us by Eliphas Lévi.

The First Temple and the Woman Clothed with the Sun

Doth not wisdom cry? and understanding put forth her voice?

She standeth in the top of high places, by the way in the places of the paths.

She crieth at the gates, at the entry of the city, at the coming in at the doors.

Unto you, O men, I call; and my voice is to the sons of man.

Proverbs 8:1-4

The deity Wisdom appears numerous times in this book, and is important in our consideration of Baphomet, the "baptism of wisdom", and to the new perspective that was born with the advent of the New Aeon.

The 'Temple played a prominent role in the life of Israel in the post-exilic, pre-Hellenistic period. It was not only the centre of the religious, but also of the national life. It was not only an edifice but an institution as well. The religious personnel were responsible for the correct cultic activity and for the regular conduct of community life. Collecting taxes and judging "personal problems" were included in the everyday activities.'[82]

---

82 Zsengellér, 'Does Wisdom Come from the Temple?', 137.

It may seem strange to describe Wisdom as a deity. Below I will quote from Barker at length, where she discusses the nature of Wisdom, and Her role and requirement in the process of creation.

Wisdom describes herself in the Holy of Holies in Proverbs 8. In the temple, this had been constructed as a perfect cube and lined with gold to represent the light and fire of the divine presence (2 Chron., 3.8); here in Proverbs 8 it is the state beyond the visible and temporal creation. Wisdom was herself begotten and brought forth in this state (Proverbs 8.24-25), and she was beside the Creator as he established the heavens and marked out the foundations of the earth. She witnessed the creation. She was also the *Amon*,[83] a rare Hebrew word which probably means craftsman; in the Greek it became *harmozousa*, the woman who joins together, or the woman who maintains the harmony (Prov., 8.30). This Wisdom poem does not describe the visible creation – trees, birds, animals – but only the structures which were established in the invisible state, the 'engraved things'. She was there when the Creator engraved the circle on the face of the deep, set the engraved mark for the sea which it could not pass, engraved the foundations of the earth (Prov., 8.27-29). She was the Creator's delight, and she danced and played before him. The male and female Creator is familiar from Genesis 1.26-27: 'Then God (a plural word in Hebrew) said 'Let us make the human in our image, after our likeness... So God created the human in his image, male and female he created them.' The female figure also appears in Genesis 1.2: '...the Spirit of God was moving over the face of the waters' 'Moving' here is a feminine form: *she* was hovering, fluttering over the face of the

---

83   'Amon is Wisdom who assisted at the creation and later appeared in the gnostic texts as the Demiurge, the agent of the creation. (Barker, *The Great Angel: A Study of Israel's Second God*, 202.)

waters. When Genesis was translated into Aramaic, a version used in Palestine, and so one the first Christians would have known, gave the first verse of Genesis as 'In the beginning with Wisdom the LORD created...' People remembered that Wisdom had been present at the creation, and that she was also known as the Spirit.[84]

From the above we can see that Wisdom is that which binds together, and brings into harmony; a marriage of heaven and earth. Wisdom is further associated with a "perfect cube", her dwelling place; the Holy of Holies – this being the throne of Baphomet. The cube is also lined with gold, associated with the Sun – 'the light and fire of the divine presence...'.[85] There is a connection here between the word "Amon" and its association with craftsmen and freemasonry, the "joining together" that builds the temple. Harmozousa is "the bringer into harmony".

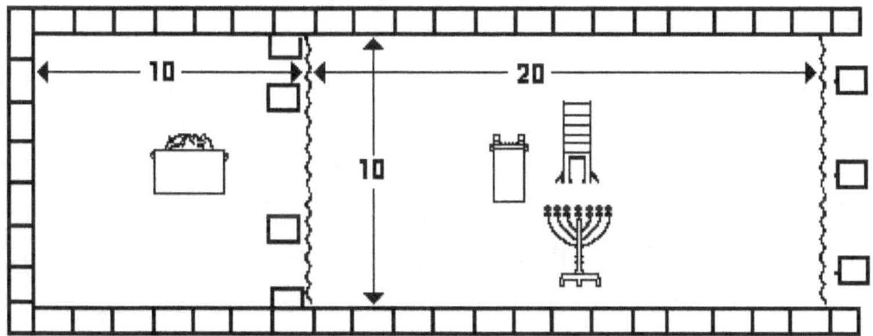

Tabernacle with the holy and Holy of Holies (inner sanctuary)

Barker clearly identifies Wisdom as the female counterpart, or female aspect of God, who was present at, or was required to be present at the creation. She also describes Wisdom as

---

84 Barker, 'Where Shall Wisdom be Found? (Job 28:12)'.

85 Barker, *Temple Theology: An Introduction*, 81.

'one of the names of the female aspect of God. She illuminates the human mind and helps us to better understand creation.'[86]

As Benjamin Blech explains, 'Judaism long ago acknowledged the validity of this feminine dimension of the Deity. The two names of God differ grammatically with regard to sexual connotation. The feminine ending in Hebrew is usually produced by appending the letter *Heh* and the vowel *qamaz*...The Tetragrammaton (YHVH) similarly ends in this manner. The Word for the Lord is feminine; it refers to God as if "He" were in fact "She." Yet, as we have frequently noted, the Lord is also called ELoHiYM. That name ends with the *Yod* and *Mem* which in Hebrew form the masculine plural... If human beings are created in God's image, and the single most important thing we know about God is that He is One – why did God create two kinds of people, male and female, after His likeness? ...God chose to create two different kinds of people on this earth, not in spite of the fact that He is One, but precisely because God in the deepest sense of the word is really two. Of course we do not suggest any kind of dualism implying separate identities. Rather, as the very names of God imply, there are two distinct aspects to the Deity. God is both masculine and feminine. This gender difference is not one of physical attributes but one of emotion and typology.'[87] God's presence, the *Shekhinah* (שְׁכִינָה),[88] is feminine grammatically and associated with the Holy Spirit.

We can find further connections between this Woman and Baphomet. Both, as seen, could be associated with creations and therefore fertility, as feminine Wisdom could also be said

---

86   Barker, *An Extraordinary Gathering of Angels*, 422.

87   Blech, 'Understanding Judaism : The Basics of Deed and Creed', 273.

88   By gematria this is 385, the same value as Assiah, the World of Matter. It is perhaps no surprise then that the work *Shekhinah* translates as "dwelling" or "settling".

to have breasts (as does Baphomet), and additionally there is a connection between both and desolate place, wilderness. 'And to the Woman were given two wings of a great eagle that she might fly into the wilderness...' (Revelation 12:14).

Theosophist James M. Pryse (1859–1942) interprets the wings of Wisdom as 'being sushumna, the two wings of the Eagle are ida and pingala. The winged Woman represents the objective, or substantial, working of the kundalini...'[89]

Pryse also alludes to the dual nature of the Woman (as with Baphomet), the harmozousa, when he writes, 'As the Word-Mother, the White Virgin of the Skies, whether called Diana, Aphrodite, or Mary, she is the pure ether, the Logos-Light, or primordial force-substance; and as the Fallen Woman, the Queen of the Abyss, she is the parturient energy of nature, the basis of physical life...'[90] She shares both the subtle "pure ether" and the more earthly "parturient energy of nature". She is as much of the earth as she is of heaven.

If we move forward into a Thelemic perspective, we can refer to Crowley's comments in the 23rd Aethyr of *The Vision and the Voice* that the Lion-Serpent, identified with the Beast 666, has for a father '♄, Set or Pan; his mother, the Woman Clothed with the Sun, as in Atu XIV.'[91] Atu XIV, of course, being Art, an alchemical image showing a fusion of the male and the female. He goes on further to state that 'He is the burden of the Moon, sanctified by 418 Atu XI (a partial form) with Atu XX

---

89 Pryse, *The Apocalypse Unsealed: Being an Interpretation of the Initiation of Ioannes*, 160.

90 Ibid., 155.

91 Crowley, Neuburg, and Desti, *The Vision & the Voice with Commentary and Other Papers: The Collected Diaries of Aleister Crowley, 1909-1914 E.V.*, 62.

(XI + XX = XXXI) gives the Key to the New Aeon.'[92] The two cards that equal 31 are Lust (attributed to the fiery Leo and the Hebrew letter Teth, a serpent) and The Aeon.

In one reading of Lust we see the act of union which brings forth the child:

> ...the Woman in the card may be regarded as a form of the Moon, very fully illuminated by the Sun, and intimately united with him in such wise as to produce, incarnate in human form, the representative or representatives of the Lord of the Aeon.[93]

Crowley explains that the above is due to the path of the moon, connecting Kether to Tiphareth, crossing the Path attributed to Teth and Leo; Leo being the 'house of the Sun'.[94] As opposed to the representation in Atu VI, Atu XIV represents nature, with 'no attempt to direct the course of the operation.'[95] This act is 'independent of the criticism of reason...the will of the Aeon.[96]

Lust represents both the destruction and the creation of the world.

> For he is ever a sun, and she a moon. But to him is the winged secret flame, and to her the stooping starlight.
>
> *Liber AL,* I:16

---

92   Crowley, Neuburg, and Desti, 62.

93   Crowley, *The Book of Thoth*, 94.

94   Crowley, 94.

95   Crowley, 93.

96   Crowley, 95.

The child shown in the second card, in Atu XX, is Horus or Heru-ra-ha. He is a dual god representing both extroversion and introversion (Ra-hoor-khuit and Hoor-pa-kraat). The child is solar, 'shown coming forth in golden light.'[97] Like Baphomet the child Horus is a symbol of balance and integration – a symbol of wholeness, the child of The Woman Clothed with the Sun, and the god of kingship.

Here we see the archetypal roots of the Templar idol stretching back to the first temple in Jerusalem, and the lost Woman of the Temple, enthroned once again in the New Aeon.

Wisdom says: be strong! Then canst thou bear more joy. Be not animal; refine thy rapture! If thou drink, drink by the eight and ninety rules of art: if thou love, exceed by delicacy; and if thou do aught joyous, let there be subtlety therein!

Liber AL, II:70[98]

---

97 Crowley, 115.

98 Crowley, *The Holy Books of Thelema*, 119.

Woman Clothed with the Sun
From a copy of the Commentary on the Apocalypse

Mithras

As presented earlier, Crowley associated Baphomet with the Roman-Iranian deity Mithras, calling him "Father Mithras". Much has been written about Mithras in terms of its connection to, and influence on, Christianity, and on proposed links between its practice and beliefs and those of the Masonic fraternity (and I will also further explore Mithras in connection to the *farr-e Izadi*[1]). All this must, to a certain extent, be taken with a grain of salt. As a friend of mine wrote to me, 'Also a tendency I see in a bit of occult writing (although not confined to such writing) is to try to make sweeping historical connections, which is such a fraught business.'[2] This seems especially fraught when dealing with something like Mithraism (and many other elements in this book), which offers relatively scant documentary evidence. However, these connections, not always with reliable historical evidence, unmask some of the archetypal links between the historical ideas and practices, and those of contemporary writers and thinkers. Sometimes it is what the human imagination makes of these connections, as opposed to the accuracy of the historical connections themselves that speaks to us. They show that in the current of human mentation there is a creative element that seeks to explore the foundations of our being. Although not always logical, this points to broader truths about ourselves, both individually and collectively.

---

1 'A special grace bestowed upon kings enabling them to overcome the forces of evil. Without Farr-e-Izadi there is no true kingship, only mere power...' (Guppy, 'A Paean to Kingship'.)

2 Tyson Wils, Personal correspondence, 25 March 2021.

Mithraism is thought to have its origins in Persia and was an 'outgrowth of Zoroastrian culture, though not of Zoroaster's teachings.'[3] There are, however, differences between the form of worship undertaken in Persia and the form of Mithraism that took root in and developed within Roman culture. DeFrancisco posits that a possible link between the Persian and Roman forms of Mithras are the kingdoms of Parthia and Pontus in Asia Minor, where the kings were called *Mithradates* ('given by Mithra'). In the 2nd century BCE, Pergamum Greek sculptors created images of *Mithra Taurocthonos* ('Mithra the bull-slayer').

Mithraism is considered to have arrived in Rome from the east with its legions as a mature religion in the first century BCE. The first contact with Mithraism may have been 'with the conquest of then Zoroastrian Armenia.'[4] The first mention of Mithras in Latin is seen in *the Thebaid of Statius*, 'Mithras who twists the unruly horns beneath the rocks of a Persian cave'.[5] It is not until 102 CE that we find the first sculpture of 'Mithras sacrificing the bull, consecrated by Alcimus, slave of a prefect of Trajan.'[6]

In Mithraism, man had a duty to 'worship the four simple elements' (water and fire, air and earth). The seven planets, like the elements, were seen as beneficent. 'The souls of men, which were all created together from the beginning and which at birth had but to descend from the empyrean heaven to the bodies prepared for them, received from the seven planets their passions and characteristics.'[7] The days of the week have their

---

3   DeFrancisco, 'Mithraism and Blood Sacrifice in Christian Belief and Practice and Its Relationship to Christianity', 12.

4   DeFrancisco, 13."Original Sin and Its Relationship to Sacrifice", and 2

5   Simeoni, 'From Mithraism to Freemasonry. A History of Ideas', 1.

6   Simeoni, 1.

7   DeFrancisco, 'Mithraism and Blood Sacrifice in Christian Belief and Practice and Its Relationship to Christianity', 6.

roots in this association with Mithraism and the planets. Mithras was seen as the *Mesites;*[8] like Christ, he was the mediator between God and man. '[A]s the light-god he is supposed to float midway between the upper heaven and the earth.'[9] Also, as a representation of the Sun, Mithras had his place in the centre of the other planets.

The followers of Mithras worshipped in caves (or buildings imitating caves).[10] in which a fire was kept perpetually burning (As Jung also points out, 'the Mithraic liturgy is full of fire related attributes, and that the god comes from the north, the quarter from which Ezekiel's vision of God came despite the fact that it is the birthplace of all evil.'[11]). The practitioners of Mithraism prayed to the Sun three times a day in the east, south and west. Sunday was kept to honour Mithras, and his birthday was celebrated on the 25th of December – *natalis invicti* – the winter-sun reborn. 'A Mithraic community was not merely a religious congregation; it was a social and legal body with its *decemprimi, magistri, curatores, defensores,* and *patroni.*'[12]

Central to Mithraism is the motif of the sacrifice of the Celestial Bull, attended by a raven, a scorpion, a dog and a snake. This sacrifice allowed for nature to be regenerated. An important concept found in the writings of Porphyry (c.234– c.305 AD) describes one of the principal doctrines of Mithraism to be the descent of souls from heaven, and the ascent of souls from

---

8   One who intervenes between two, either in order to make or restore peace and friendship, or form a compact, or for ratifying a covenant ('Mesites Meaning - Greek Lexicon | New Testament (NAS)'.)

9   DeFrancisco, 'Mithraism and Blood Sacrifice in Christian Belief and Practice and Its Relationship to Christianity', 7.

10   Mithraea

11   Jung, *Aion*, 124.

12   DeFrancisco, 'Mithraism and Blood Sacrifice in Christian Belief and Practice and Its Relationship to Christianity', 8.

the earth. One can see a clear reflection of the formula of *Solve et Coagula* that is associated with Lévi's depiction of Baphomet here. This process Porphyry associates with the winds. '...that Boreas befits souls descending into generation because it freezes them. Notus is convenient for the souls that go back because it dissolves... The souls, which are created by the bull like bees in a sort of bougonia,[13] and which are animated by his blood, descend into the cycle of generation and incarnation and are dragged down by Boreas, the cold wind that keeps them cool in the place of earthly generation. After successive reincarnations...the warm wind of Notus dissolves the carnal vestments that imprison them and returns them to the heat of the divine, in other words, to the Sun.'[14] Also interestingly we see this process connected with both the Sun and the Moon in the writings of Porphyry - 'The Theologians make the Sun and Moon gates for souls, and say that they ascend through the Sun and descend through the Moon.'[15] In Transcendental Magic Lévi writes 'that the sun dries up and the moon moistens...in the *Zohar*... "the magical serpent, the son of the Sun, was about to devour the world, when the Sea, daughter of the moon, set her foot upon his head and subdued him."'[16]

Lévi connected Mithras with fertility concepts written about elsewhere in this work related to Baphomet. He connected the element earth with 'the sword of Mithras, who each year immolates the sacred bull, and, together with its blood, pours forth that sap which gives increase to all fruits of earth.'[17] It should be noted that much of Lévi's understanding of Mithras would have

---

13   The idea that bees are spontaneously generated from a cow's carcass.

14   Albanese, 'Porphyry, the Cave of the Nymphs, and the Mysteries of Mithras', 685–86.

15   Albanese, 686.

16   Lévi, *Transcendental Magic*, 151.

17   Lévi, 378.

been influenced by the theories published by Franz Cumont (1868–1947) in 1896 and 1899, which remained unchallenged until the early 1970s. His theories leant on a more direct connection to the Iranian Mithraic traditions (it has been argued that he over invested in this connection). His writing about the slaying of the bull that Lévi may be referencing above is based on a contrivance in Cumont's writing; referencing the *Bundahishn,*[18] where it is Ahriman, not Mithra, who slays the bull.[19]

Crowley associated Mithras with one of the Cherubs, and the powers of the Sphinx:

> ...this is thy Will, constant and unwearied, whose Letter is Vau, which is 6, the Number of the Sun. He is therefore the Forces and the Substance of thy Being; but, besides this, he is the Hierophant in the Taro, as if this were said: that thy Will leadeth thee unto the Shrine of Light. And in the Rites of Mithras the Bull is slain, and the Blood poured upon the Initiate, to endow him with that Will and that Power of Work.[20]

Crowley further associates the Will with the Phallus, '...for this Will operateth through Love...'[21]

It might also be worth considering Crowley's commentary to Chapter 79 of *The Book of Lies* (The Bal Bullier): 'The Buddhist analysis may be true, but not for men of courage. The plea that love is sorrow, because its ecstasies are only transitory, is contemptible.'[22]

Lévi also explicitly associates Mithras with the Bull, and

---

18 This translates as "Primal Creation" and is the title of a collection of Zoroastrian cosmogony and cosmology.

19 Ulansey, *The Origins of the Mithraic Mysteries*, 9.

20 Crowley, *Liber Aleph Vel CXI: The Book of Wisdom or Folly*, 153.

21 Crowley, 153.

22 Crowley, *The Book of Lies*, 169.

again the Cherubs, calling the cherub, the "symbolic bull, which Moses placed at the gate of the Edenic world, bearing a fiery sword...a sphinx, having a bull's body and a human head; it is the antique Assyrian sphinx, and the combat and victory of Mithras were its hieroglyphic analysis.'[23] Lévi also states that this "Mosaic cherub" represented the Great Magical Mystery, and further draws a link between this and the number 7, and the word Ararita, which forms a word of 7 letters 'by means of a triple and double repetition...'[24] This expresses 'the triplicity of the secondary principle, the dualism of means, the equal unity of the first and final principle, the alliance between the triad and the tetrad...'[25]

Although Lévi and Crowley both draw links between the iconography and practices of Mithraism and the glyph of Baphomet, we also need to consider this in light of the New Aeonic perspective, regarding the blood sacrifice. As Crowley clearly writes, '...the actual God worshipped (☉ in the North) has progressed from ♉, the laborious slain Bull of Mithras, to ♊, the Children Ra-Hoor-Khuit and Hoor-paar-kraat.'[26] The North, the place of the Sun at its zenith (in the Northern Hemisphere), the "birthplace of all evil" has been replaced with a new solar perspective and consciousness. '...the twin children who (in one form or another) have so frequently recurred in this whole symbolism. They represent the male and female, eternally young, shameless and innocent. They are dancing in the light, and yet they dwell upon the earth. They represent the next stage which is to be attained by mankind, in which complete freedom is alike the cause and the result of the new

---

23   Lévi, *Transcendental Magic*, 81–82.

24   Lévi, 82.

25   Lévi, 82.

26   Crowley et al., *Commentaries of the Holy Books and Other Papers*, 4:219.

access of solar energy upon the earth.'[27] We have moved from the subterranean caves of Mithraism to be living in the sunlight. However, as Thelemites who seek wholeness, we partake of both of these aspects – we still need to follow the formula of V.I.T.R.I.O.L.[28] It is from the interior world that our light shines. Crowley points out that the "hidden stone" referred to in this formula 'is also called the Universal Medicine. It is sometimes described as a stone, sometimes as a powder, sometimes as a tincture. It divides again into two forms, the gold and the silver, the red and the white; but its essence is always the same…The important word in the injunction is the central word RECTIFICANDO; it implies the right leading of the new living substance in the path of the True Will.'[29]

So in the myths of Mithraism we have elements of a mediator between heaven and earth, *solve et coagula*, creation and dissolution and that 'Will and Power of Work', which exists between these two phases of manifestation.

> So far, the Wizard had shown great qualities! He had cleared up the etymological problem and shown why the Templars should have given the name Baphomet to their so-called idol. Baphomet was Father Mithras, the cubical stone which was the corner of the Temple.[30]

Remembering the connections made between the cubical shape and the inner sanctum of the first temple, the Kaaba in

---

27 Crowley, *The Book of Thoth*, 113–14.

28 VISTA INTERIORA TERRAE RECTIFICANDO INVENIES OCCULTUM LAPIDEM ("Visit the interior parts of the earth: by rectification thou shalt find the hidden stone"). In The *Book of Thoth* Crowley points out that this equals 726, which further reduces to 15, and to 6, the number of the Sun.

29 Crowley, *The Book of Thoth*, 104.

30 Crowley, *The Confessions of Aleister Crowley*, 833.

Mecca and the throne of Baphomet, noting here that Crowley makes an even closer association with Baphomet and the cubical stone. Baphomet is the stone, 'the corner of the Temple'. Although in contemporary buildings the cornerstone has come to serve a more ceremonial function, historically, the cornerstone was the first to be set in the construction of a masonry foundation. All other stones were set in relation to the cornerstone. The cornerstone, therefore, determined the position of the entire structure.

Although we will move onto Freemasonry in relation to Mithras, it is worth making reference to some of the writing of Albert Mackey (1807–1881) regarding the cornerstone. 'As, for instance, in Psalm cxviii. 22, "The stone which the builders refused is become the head-stone of the corner," which, Clarke says, "seems to have been originally spoken of David, who was at first rejected by the Jewish rulers, but was afterwards chosen by the Lord to be the great ruler of His people in Israel"; and in Isaiah xxviii. 16, "Behold, I lay in Zion, for a foundation, a stone, a tried stone, a precious corner-stone, a sure foundation," which clearly refers to the promised Messiah.'[31] So, here, the cornerstone also has a messianic interpretation, and concept of 'the stone that the builders rejected'.

Mackey further explores the symbolism of the cornerstone in relation to the Masonic First Degree, which is positioned in the north-east corner of the Lodge. 'He is an Apprentice, with some of the ignorance of the world cleaving to him, and some of the light of the Order beaming upon him. Hence this divided allegiance — this double character — this mingling of the departing darkness of the north with the approaching brightness of the east —is well expressed, in our symbolism, by the appro-

---

31   Mackey and Clegg, *Mackey's Symbolism of Freemasonry: Its Science, Philosophy, Legends, Myths and Symbols*, 160.

priate position of the spiritual corner-stone in the north-east corner of the Lodge. One surface of the stone faces the north, and the other surface faces the east. It is neither wholly in the one part nor wholly in the other, and in so far it is a symbol of initiation not fully developed — that which is incomplete and imperfect, and is, therefore, fitly represented by the recipient of the first degree, at the very moment of his initiation.'[32] Although incomplete in terms of full Blue Lodge Masonry, the Apprentice stands at a point of balance between the light and the dark – a unity of North and East, gifted in his way to becoming a Master.

The above is a strong indication that we should meditate deeply on the mysteries of "Father Mithras", and Baphomet, for they are our very foundation and touchstone.

Mithraism and Freemasonry

[In the name of God, who has separated] earth from heaven,
[Light from darkness,] the day from night,
[The cosmos from chaos], life from death,
[And generation] from corruption, I swear
[Indeed and in sincere good faith] to preserve
[As secrets] the mysteries transmitted to me...[33]

From Cumont's Restored Obligation

There is speculation that there is a link between the ancient practices of Mithraism (as much as they are known), and those of the Freemasons. J.R. Russell admits that 'the lines of historical continuity are extremely difficult to trace...' but goes on to

---

32 Mackey and Clegg, 160.

33 Russell, *Heredom*, 4:271.

state that 'it is possible that some aspects of the ancient fraternity were transmitted to and survive in the Craft of today.'[34]

This proposed connection between Mithraism and freemasonry can be seen in their common aspects, despite the twelve centuries that passed before documented evidence of craft Freemasonry in the 16th century. In arguing for a connection between Mithraism and the Masonic fraternity Gaby Simeoni states that 'Knowledge, ideas, wisdom and culture in general are a strange matter. Like energy — perhaps that is what it is all about — ideas do not arise out of nothing and are never completely destroyed, they are simply transformed...Perhaps this is so because ideas are as eternal as existence itself, or because they are made of the same essence as archetypes, which are the raw material from which both mythology and the most banal dreams are nourished.'[35]

Both Freemasonry and Mithraism included oaths or obligations as well as catechisms. An obligation for the degree of Leo in Mithraism, in which one was made a full member of the order, referenced "sharp goads" (perhaps similar to the dagger or poniard on which Freemasons are received). In a Mithraic catechism presented by William Brashear we also find possible references to a sharp instrument used during initiation. There is also evidence that the candidates are given a new name, which is also seen in some Masonic jurisdictions after the First Degree.

> ... did not your own kinsman Gracchus whose name betokens his patrician origin, when a few years back he held the prefecture of the City, overthrow, break in pieces, and shake to pieces the grotto of Mithras and all the dreadful images therein? Those I mean by which the worshippers were initiated as

---

34 Russell, *Heredom*.

35 Simeoni, 'From Mithraism to Freemasonry. A History of Ideas', 2.

Raven, Bridegroom, Soldier, Lion, Perseus, Sun, Crab, and Father? Did he not, I repeat, destroy these and then, sending them before him as hostages, obtain for himself Christian baptism?

> Jerome (ca. 400 CE) Letter 107, ch.2 "To Laeta"[36]

As we can see from the above written by Jerome, the practitioners of Mithraism were reported to have a series of degrees of initiation, like Freemasonry.

---

36 Pearse, 'Mithras: All the Passages in Graeco-Roman Literature'.

Grade	Name	Planet or Deity
1st	*Corax, Corux, or Corvex* (raven or crow)	Mercury
2nd	*Nymphus, Nymphobus* (bridegroom)	Venus
3rd	*Miles* (soldier)	Mars
4th	*Leo* (lion)	Jupiter
5th	*Perses* (Persian)	Luna
6th	*Heliodromus* (sun-runner)	Sol
7th	*Pater* (father)	Saturn

Mithraism, despite its series of degrees, like Freemasonry, taught an equality among its members regardless of status in the external world. In Mithraism we see evidence of emperors[37] and slaves amongst its initiates. This is perhaps an old aeonic reflection of the Thelemic concept of equality ('Every man and every woman is a star', AL I:3) that has now been brought into wholeness.

The two figures of *Cautopates* and *Cautes* depicted on frescoes flanking the entrance to the Mithraeum appear (according to Russell) to be acting in the roles of conducting and receiving a candidate. These two are torchbearers, with one holding his torch upright (*Cautes*), the other pointing downward (*Cautopates*). They represent the rising and the setting sun, and therefore could be seen as symbols of light (or light emerging in and out of darkness). This may also be seen as representing life and death (or alternatively the Spring and Autumn Equinoxes). Mithraic frescoes also show candidates hoodwinked and bound as we see today in Freemasonry, and other rites that have stemmed directly or indirectly from Masonic initiation. The Mithraic temple was commonly rectangular in shape, like a Masonic lodge, with a ceiling decorated with stars, 'and its other parts frequently adorned with representations of the zodiac and of the orbits of the seven planets, each equated with a degree of initiation.'[38] Both temples are a representation of the cosmos through which the candidate goes through a process of life and death (reincarnation or evolution). This process is explored in Porphyry's *The Cave of the Nymphs*, in which 'the cave of the Nymphs is the place in which the worshippers were initiated into the platonic mystery of the descent and ascent of

---

37 It should be noted that the claims that the emperors Nero, Commodus, Septimius Severus, Caracalla, and the Tetrarchs were initiates is met with suspicion by scholars.

38 Russell, *Heredom*, 4:273.

souls. Mithras, assimilated to the Demiurge of the *Timaeus*, generates souls by killing the bull he has caught, ridden and dragged into the cave which symbolises the cosmos. The souls, which are created by the bull/moon like bees in a sort of *bougonia*,[39] and which are animated by his blood, descend into the cycle of generation and incarnation and are dragged down by Boreas, the cold wind that keeps them cool in the place of earthly generation. After successive reincarnations the warm wind of Notus dissolves the carnal vestments that imprison them and returns them to the heat of the Sun.'[40]

---

39   In the ancient Mediterranean this is a ritual based on the belief (or poetic trope) that bees were spontaneously generated from a cow's carcass. This also seems to be mirrored in "Samson's Riddle" found in Judges 14 – '...behold there was a swarm of bees and honey in the carcass of the lion. And he took thereof in his hands, and went on eating, and came to his father and mother and he gave them, and they did eat; but he told them not that he had taken the honey out of the carcass of the lion.' (*The KJV Study Bible*, 275–76). James L. Crenshaw also posits that 'on another level, the riddle suggests copulation... Similarly, "food" and "sweetness" signify semen, which is sweet to the bride who "eats" the sperm. From man proceeds sperm which nourishes woman; from a strong man goes semen that is pleasant to a wife.' (Crenshaw, *Samson*, 115.) We should also note Crowley writing about The Cup in *Book 4*, 'Yet the sprinkling of its water not only purifies the Temple, but blesseth them that are without: freely it must be poured! But let no one know your real purpose, and let no one know the secret of your strength. Remember Samson!' (Crowley, Desti, and Waddell, *Magick. Liber ABA. Book Four. Parts I-IV*, 77.)

40   Albanese, 'Porphyry, the Cave of the Nymphs, and the Mysteries of Mithras', 681.

Antiochus shakes hands with Mithras

The practitioners of Mithraism were also called *syndex-ios* (Greek), which means 'one who has exchanged the hand-shake',[41] which also brings to mind Freemasonry, and its successor in the New Aeon, the OTO. Handshakes are also often

---

41 Russell, *Heredom*, 4:273.

used to symbolise an agreement or promise, and Mithras is "the guarantor of the promises".

> 'Not aloud shall they praise thee; but in the night watch one shall steal close, and grip thee with the secret grip...'
>
> *Liber LXV* I:23

A number of the elements of the catechism from Brashear's text are centred around death and new life, indicating the candidate is 'reborn to light'.[42] This is a common phrase found in graffiti in relation to the birthdays of members. There has also been discovered in some *spelaea* depressions in the floor where it was thought a sarcophagus was placed, and in which was placed also 'the body of the symbolically deceased brother.' There is some evidence that associated with this process of initiation through death to new life is "the Ahrimanic god" or *leontocephalus*. Somehow this 'lion of wrath and destruction by fire was an obstacle'[43] and represented the power of death. 'The old man had to confront and be slain by this creature for the new man to be born to light, in the degree that bears the Lion's name.'[44]

---

42 Russell, 4:273.

43 Russell, 4:275.

44 Russell, 4:275.

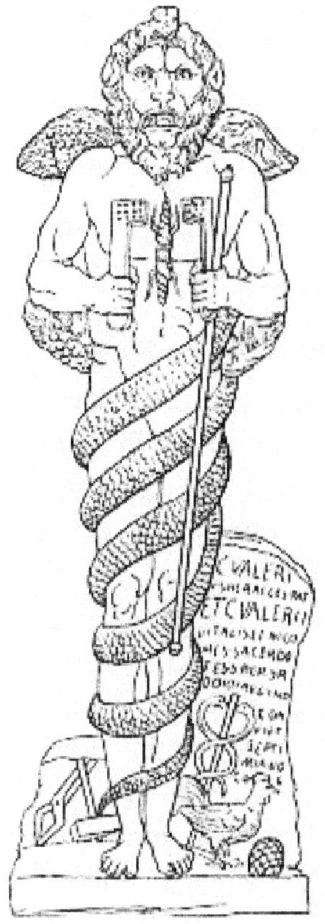

There are in Iran, and other Ancient Near Eastern countries, depictions of combat between lions, as the king of beasts,
and kings.

Blessed…is the lion which the man eats and the lion will become man; and cursed is the man whom the lion eats and the
lion will become man.[45]

The Gospel According to Thomas (Log. 5-8, 24-28)

---

45 Guillaumont et al., *The Gospel According to Thomas*, 5.

The Freemasons use a different calendar (as we do as Thelemites), which is baselined from what is titled *Anno Lucis*, the "Year of Light". This is the year in which they teach that God created the world (approximately 4,000 years before the beginning of the Common Era). The motifs that are found in the Mithraic Tauroctony show the intersection at the celestial equator of the constellation Taurus together with those of Canis Minor, Hydra, Corvus and Scorpius – the Age of Taurus. This last intersection occurred between 4000 and 2000 B.C. 'This age is marked by the peak of the Sumerian civilisation, the creation of the first city states in Mesopotamia and the birth of writing.'[46] This period, interestingly, coincides with the Masonic *Anno Lucis* – the year of creation.

Additionally, 'Mithraism was emphatically a soldier religion: Mithra, its hero, was especially a divinity of fidelity, manliness, and bravery; the stress it laid on good fellowship and brotherliness, its exclusion of women, and the secret bond amongst its members have suggested the idea that Mithraism was Masonry amongst the Roman soldiery.'[47] We can also see this in the way (similar to in Roman times) Freemasonry has been popular with men involved in the military, especially after the world wars. A place where there is a sense of military discipline, comradeship, but also possibly a philosophy of life to help manage the unavoidable trauma of war.

Freemasonry also shares with Mithraism the practice of a formal banquet. In Mithraism this reflects a mythological episode where Mithras and Sol share a meal on the skin of the bull and are assisted by Cautes and Cautopates. 'The roles of Mithras and Sol are assumed by the Pater and Heliodromus. The whole community participates in this banquet, those of lower

---

46   Simeoni, 'From Mithraism to Freemasonry. A History of Ideas', 3.

47   DeFrancisco, 'Mithraism and Blood Sacrifice in Christian Belief and Practice and Its Relationship to Christianity', 6.

degree, such as the Masonic apprentices, will be responsible for assisting their brethren.'[48]

The connection between Baphomet, Mithraism and Freemasonry is significant within the context of this work, due to the historical connections between Freemasonry, the OTO, and Crowley's choice of the name Baphomet within the Order. We should also note that the Priest in the Gnostic Mass, having parted the veil to our mysteries, calls on a number of deities or forms of God, one of which is "Lord Meithras".[49] In this moment the priest, as aspirant, invokes the names of powerful male deities, and becomes himself fully male, and fully himself. In this moment instead of shutting himself up, he radiates his light, he parts the veil with his lance and there is confronted with, and has the opportunity to join with, unbounded space – unbounded experience. His consciousness has symbolically altered, and he is no longer constrained by his ego and complexes – the path is opened unto him. This is the essence of phallic consciousness, beyond mere biological constraints.

> Whoever has ears let him hear. Within a man of light there is light and he lights the whole world. When he does not shine, there is darkness.
>
> *The Gospel of Thomas,* 6-10[50]

---

48 Simeoni, 'From Mithraism to Freemasonry. A History of Ideas', 4.

49 Meithras (Μειθρας), like Abrasax, adds to 365. This is also the value by Hebrew gematria of פריעה, *an uncovering, exposing.*

50 Guillaumont et al., *The Gospel According to Thomas,* 19.

Christianity

Some scholars and historians believe that Mithraism had a clear influence on Christianity, especially in relation to sacrifice. 'When exploring the idea of sacrifice in Christianity a special emphasis must be placed on the influence that Mithraism played on religion within the Roman Empire. As we have discussed, Mithraism is a pagan religion consisting mainly of the cult of the ancient Indo-Iranian Sun-god Mithra.'[51] We can see from the previous pages, some obvious connections to the worship of Mithras and later Christian worship, but we also need to acknowledge that the information we have about Mithraism is limited. It had no scripture, and its teachings were passed on from initiate to initiate, so our main source of information about Mithras are the images of him that have survived. It is also possible that some elements of Mithraism were borrowed from Christianity (not the other way round), and some of the similarities may be superficial. As DeFrancisco points out, 'During these centuries Christianity was coining its own technical terms, and naturally took names, terms, and expressions current in that day; and so did Mithraism.'[52] He also highlights that, 'During the 3rd century CE, Mithraism and Christianity were the main competitors for the religious affiliation of the citizens of Romans.'[53] This competition between the religions may have caused conceptual overlap within Roman culture and thought, between the teachings and practice of Mithraism and those of the emerging Christianity.

It should be noted that it is commonly referenced (even

---

51   DeFrancisco, 'Mithraism and Blood Sacrifice in Christian Belief and Practice and Its Relationship to Christianity', 5.

52   DeFrancisco, 9. "Original Sin and Its Relationship to Sacrifice", and 2

53   DeFrancisco, 16. "Original Sin and Its Relationship to Sacrifice", and 2

quoted by DeFrancisco) that there is an inscription to Mithras that is translated as, 'He who will not eat of my body and drink of my blood, so that he will be made one with me and I with him, the same shall not know salvation.' The similarity is noted between this and John 6:53-54. Andrew Criddle and Roger Pearce of The Tertullian Project have compiled evidence that they think shows that 'the "quote" is wrong, and has nothing whatever to do with Mithras. The connection to Mithras is merely an imaginative hypothesis of Cumont's (discussed earlier), without any actual evidence for it. In fact the quote is a mistranslation of something attributing a saying of Jesus to Zoroaster, not to Mithras.'[54]

Pearce further states, 'Now part of the proof of the Christian gospel in the middle ages was that Jewish writers predicted the coming of Christ. During this period, however, a second line of prophecy develops, from pagan philosophers. Consequently there are collections of sayings, specifically for this purpose. Sadly the "quotations" are all bogus. But naturally these find their way into contemporary literature, and this seems to be exactly what has happened here.'[55]

Despite this, there are many similarities between Mithraism and Christianity that are worth exploring. In the West, Christianity has been a dominant religious, moral and cultural force, and its influence can be seen in both mainstream Churches, and in the occult world.

Many early Christians celebrated the birth of Jesus on January 6th, which was also the date on which the birth of Aion was celebrated in Alexandria (now Egypt). This celebration eventually moved to December 25th for both Christians and pa-

---

54 Criddle and Pearse, 'The "Body and Blood of Mithras" Myth'.

55 Pearse, 'Did Mithras Say "He Who Will Not Eat of My Body and Drink of My Blood…"?'

gans. Both Christians and the followers of Mithras practiced baptism, this was done naked, after they would put on white clothing and a crown. The Christians would carry candles in procession, whereas the followers of Mithras carried torches. Both also partook in a form of the Eucharist, where bread and wine symbolised the body and blood of the "god-man". It has also been noted that Jesus was crucified between two criminals, whereas Mithras was flanked by two torchbearers with one torch up, the other down, as already discussed.

In his work *Ego and Archetype* Edward Edinger makes the observation that the 'Bible records that Jesus was crucified between two thieves. One went to heaven and the other to hell. In the Mithras mysteries, a common image showed Mithras flanked by two torchbearers, one on either side. One held a torch pointed upwards, the other downwards. This symbolized ascent to heaven or descent to hell.'[56] Edward Edinger writes further of these two torchbearers in relation to depth psychology, 'The theme of "the middle way," in which a third middle course emerges out of the dialectic of opposites is another expression of triadic symbolism. In this connection, one thinks of the saying of Lao Tse, "The one engenders the two, the two engenders the three and the three engenders all things."'[57]

There are other similarities between Christianity and Mithraism, but for the sake of this work the above sample will suffice.

Along a similar vein, it is worth exploring Crowley's revelation about Mercury during The Paris Working, which also touch on the mysteries of Christ and his crucifixion, and by extension to Mithras:

---

56   DeFrancisco, 'Mithraism and Blood Sacrifice in Christian Belief and Practice and Its Relationship to Christianity', 17.

57   Edinger, *Ego and Archetype*, 187.

In the beginning was the Word, the Logos, who is Mercury; and is therefore to be identified with Christ. Both are messengers; their birth-mysteries are similar; the pranks of their childhood are similar. In the Vision of the Universal Mercury, Hermes is seen descending upon the sea, which refers to Mary. The Crucifixion represents the Caduceus; the two thieves, the two serpents; the cliff in the Vision of the Universal Mercury is Golgotha; Maria is simply Maia with the solar R in her womb. The controversy about Christ between the Synoptics and John was really a contention between the priests of Bacchus, Sol, and Osiris, also, perhaps, of Adonis and Attis, on the one hand, and those of Hermes on the other, at that period when initiates all over the world found it necessary, owing to the growth of the Roman Empire and the opening up of means of communication, to replace conflicting Polytheisms by a synthetic Faith. (This is absolutely new to me,[58] this conception of Christ as Mercury.)[59]

The concept of the "solar R" was also central to Crowley's understanding of Baphomet and Mithras (and by extension Christ). He writes in *Rex de Arte Regia*, 'Then I saw the justification, Baphomet being traditionally Mithraic. It now means, therefore, quite simply, FATHER MITHRA. The R has been suppressed as a blind – it blinded me all right! – and because the Sun has been concealed (in the Aeon of Osiris, I suppose). Looking in *Liber D* for further confirmation, I find 729 = שמך

---

58 In relation to the connection between Christ and Mercury, it is interesting that Crowley commented that, 'this is absolutely new to me, this conception of Christ as Mercury.' Crowley should have been familiar with this connection through the Golden Dawn's 'The Vision of the Universal Mercury'.

59 Crowley, Neuburg, and Desti, *The Vision & the Voice with Commentary and Other Papers: The Collected Diaries of Aleister Crowley, 1909-1914 E.V.*, 359.

קוץ, the curse of Satan. Of course! Look at the frontispiece to my *Ritual de la haute Magie*, where I have figured the Devil of the Tarot as Baphomet. This is a great and wonderful Arcanum, and I doubt not will lead to many further mysteries of the holy Kingdom. (P.S. It did).'[60] It is curious that in this same diary entry Crowley also contemplates the concept of the combination of the 8 and 3 – 'I then asked…for a geometrical figure of equivalent Magical Value. She got a "queer triangle" (apparently equilateral with an H at two angles, nothing at the third) and then a "solid" figure 4. These together do of course indicate a cube of 3 or 3 squared in a way; but the Wizard, getting a clearer idea of her question, broke right away and said, "The segment of an octagonal column". That is, the combination of the figure 8 and the Phallus. Now, this pointed straight to BAPHOMET. Could this word be, after all, the combination of the 8 and the 3, as it should be?'[61]

The above is most likely in reference to Verse 18 from *Liber A'Ash* – 'I am Baphomet, that is the Eightfold Word that shall be equilibrated with the Three.'[62] There are also considerations here for initiates of the OTO, as well as a possible relationship to the 8°=3□ grade of the A∴A∴.. – 'as it should be'.

Just prior to this, in Verse 17, the voice of *Liber A'Ash* declares, 'Now shalt thou adore me who am the Eye and the Tooth, the Goat of the Spirit, the Lord of Creation. I am the Eye in the Triangle, the Silver Star that ye adore'.

Here we can see similar symbolism repeating from *Rex de Arte Regia*. The Tooth is Shin (שׁ) which can also be seen as a triangle, so the Eye and the Tooth could also be read (as Frater Achad did), as The Eye in the Triangle, equated with the Silver

60 Crowley, *The Magical Record of the Beast 666*, 68.

61 Crowley, 68.

62 Crowley, *The Holy Books of Thelema*, 208.

Star, which could be seen as a reference to the Third Order of the A∴A∴, the Order of the S.S..

I hope this relatively brief exploration of Mithras, and the connection to both Freemasonry, Christianity and Thelema will help to orient you to Crowley's positioning and understanding of Baphomet within Thelemic doctrine – mysteries of the holy Kingdom – a kingdom of the flesh and of the spirit. Some aspects related to Mithras will be explored in the next section related to the Kingly Power.

KINGLY POWER

As introduced earlier, Baphomet was associated with the Cherubs of the Ark of the Covenant by Lévi, and with the Holy of Holies, and that Philo connected Cherubs with God and what he called the "kingly power".[1]

As stated by Lévi in *The Book of Splendours*, 'error must be left to the profane and the truth should be rendered impenetrable to everyone, except priests and kings.'[2] Thelemites will also see this reflected in the Gnostic Mass, where the priest is not just a priest; he is a Priest and King, whose ambience is the 'flame of the Sun.'[3] This could, again, reflect the creative and kingly powers described by Philo.

This concept of kingly power is also present in the iconography and mythology related to Mithras, associated with Baphomet. The connection between kingly power and Mithras is through the concepts and iconography associated with the *farr-e Izadi*, the teaching that the king received power from God. Divine light was transmitted to the king, who became a source of spiritual guidance.

I am aware that there is debate about the continuity between the Iranian (Zoroastrian) and Roman Mithraic worship and practice, but here I assume there is a strong enough continuity for the sake of the following discussion. As Roger Beck argues, 'That Roman Mithras was a Persian god in more than just the perception and self-definition of his Roman initiates

---

1   Sacks, 'Covenant & Conversation', 1.

2   Levi, *The Book of Splendours*, 120.

3   Crowley, Desti, and Waddell, *Magick. Liber ABA. Book Four. Parts I-IV*, 587.

is indisputable. To say that he was "the same" god, or that he "came from" Iran is equally true, though it begs as many questions as it appears to answer.'[4]

Soudavar also argues that there is evidence for a connection between these traditions in the *Historia Augusta*, depicting Roman Emperor Aurelian visiting the Sasanians:[5]

> ... when he (Aurelian prior to his ascent to the throne) had gone as an envoy to the Persians, he was presented with a sacrificial saucer, of the kind that the king of the Persians is wont to present to the emperor, on which was engraved the Sun god in the same attire in which he was worshipped in the very temple where the mother of Aurelian had been a priestess.[6]

This shows Aurelian recognising the iconography shown to him; the god in similar attire to those worn in the mithraeums of the Roman rites. It is further argued that this was the 'attire that Mithrā was still depicted with in Iran',[7] as opposed to mirroring the Roman iconography, and therefore showing continuity, to a certain extent.

An additional sign of continuity between the two traditions argued by Soudavar is the icon of the scorpion above a pair of wings (a symbol of the *farr*) on a Sasanian seal, stemming from the banned aspects of Mithraism. The scorpion was abhorred by the Zoroastrians, but elements of this can be seen in Western Mithraism, in which both the scorpion and the serpent are present in the iconography of Mithra attacking the bull.

---

4   Beck, 'Mithraism'.

5   This refers to the Empire of Iranians or Neo-Persian Empire, and was the last Persian imperial dynasty prior to the Muslim conquest in the mid seventh century AD.

6   Soudavar, *The Aura of Kings*, 112.

7   Soudavar, 113.

This may indicate that under Sasanian rule the scorpion has shifted from being an auspicious symbol to a reviled "noxious creature" (*khrafstar*) in the eyes of the Zoroastrians. But for some Iranians the scorpion,[8] combined with falcon wings, still projected the *khvarenah*.[9] Following the Zoroastrian reforms, Mithrā was still worshipped by those who did not accept them.[10]

---

8   It is of note that the Yezidi's also had reverence for the scorpion, and the scorpion and the serpent were revered animals.

9   An Avestan term for a Zoroastrian concept denoting "glory" or "splendour". This is understood as a divine mystical force.

10   Soudavar, *The Aura of Kings*, 29–30.

The theories that Crowley would also have been familiar with during his lifetime would have been those based on the writings of Franz Cumont (discussed earlier), which were founded on an Iranian origin of the Roman Mithraism. It is also worth noting in relation to the origins of Mithraism, the description of the Hierophant in *The Book of Thoth* as "Persian", as well as the inclusion of the symbolism of the bull, associated with the Roman or Western Mithras. This also points to the intermingling of kingly and hierophantic functions; with kings often basing their power of divine descent, and therefore, it could be argued, also serving a hierophantic function. It is also interesting that David Ulansey links the figure of the Roman Mithras with the procession of the equinox; the procession upending the sense of a stable and fixed universe. 'By killing the bull—causing the procession of the equinoxes—Mithras was in effect moving the entire universe. A god capable of performing such a tremendous deed would be eminently deserving of worship.'[11] In line with the procession of the equinox, Crowley writes of the Hierophant, 'The rhythm of the Hierophant is such that he moves only at intervals of 2,000 years.'[12] It is perhaps the mystery inherent in this upending of the perceived order of things that constitutes the 'something mysterious, even sinister' discernible in the 'expression of the initiator.' [13]

In his book *The Aura of Kings*, Abolala Soudavar discusses the symbolism of the "Divine Glory"; known as the *khvarenah*, *kharra*, *farreh* or *farr*. He points out that, although this symbolism is associated with royal authority (which I associate with the concept of the kingly power), and can be held by every-

---

11   Ulansey, 'David Ulansey, "The Mithraic Mysteries," Scientific American, December 1989'.

12   Crowley, *The Book of Thoth*, 80.

13   Crowley, 79.

one: 'Ahura-Mazdā informs Zoroaster that mortals must seek *khvarenah* in order to obtain advantages and success.'[14] This was sometimes symbolised by a winged disk.[15] However, 'the possession of *khvarenah* could not be perceived as permanent. For the *khvarenah* could be increased in victory, decreased in defeat, or ultimately lost...'[16]

Turco-Mongol Muslim ruler emperor Akbar or Akbar the Great (1556–1605), seeking to legitimise his rule over various peoples, and failing to find suitable justification under the principles of Islam, sought something of a more universal nature that would appeal to both Muslims and Indians.[17] 'The result was the *Din-e Elāhi* (Divine Religion) and *Solh-e koll* (Universal Peace) formulated by Akbar's vizier, confidant, and chief-ideologue, Abol-Fazl-e `Allāmi who justified kingly authority in the following terms:

> Kingship is a light emanating from God, and a ray from the sun, the illuminator of the universe; it is the argument of the book of perfection, the receptacle of all virtues. Modern language calls this light *Farr-e Izadi* [Divine Glory] and the tongue of antiquity called *it Kayān Kharra* [Kayānid Glory]. It is communicated by God to kings without the intermediate assistance of anyone, and men in the presence of it bend the forehead of praise toward the ground of submission.[18]

---

14 Soudavar, *The Aura of Kings*, 2.

15 Margaret Barker argues that the one of the symbols of the Woman Clothed with the Sun, 'the heavenly mother of the priest-kings', is that of the winged sun. This was the royal seal of the Jerusalem kings (Barker, 'Jesus the Nazorean', 3.)

16 Soudavar, *The Aura of Kings*, 14.

17 During his rule Akbar had enlarged the Mughal Empire to include much of the Indian subcontinent.

18 Soudavar, *The Aura of Kings*, 23.

The above from Abol-Fazl-e ʿAllāmi (1551- 1602) was based on the Philosophy of Sheh b-od-din Yahy -ye Sohravardi (1154-1191), who in turn has was influenced by the 'Illumination on the light symbolism of the *khvarenah*.'[19] Abol-Fazl, possibly influenced by Zoroastrian beliefs, chose the sunburst (*shamseh*) as the symbol of the *khvarenah*.[20] Abol-Fazl wrote that the *shamseh* was not just an ornament, but 'the Divine Glory itself.'[21] The *shamseh*, the divine light of the Sun, radiated from the king.

> The shadow of his turban (*dastār*) is to kingly sunshine, a parasol of victory, while [its] front and back herald victory and triumph.
>
> Suzani-ye Samarqandi (d. 1174)[22]

As shown above, Soudavar argues that another symbol of the *khvarenah* was the turban. The symbolism of the *dastār* is closely associated with victory, and the meaning of *dast* is victory, and therefore *dast-ār* is a "purveyor of dast" (an agent for conveying victory). This is seen as 'an angel offering a flying ribbon' in the Tāq-e Bostān composition.[23] With each victory a new ribbon is added and *khvarenah* increased. Arab Bedouins were known to keep loose ends on their turbans to act as face covers, and these became associated with the above flying ribbons, and therefore *khvarenah*; 'the victorious Arabs were surely perceived to possess the *khvarenah* and to merit the

---

19   Soudavar, 8.

20   Shamseh means "little sun" and represents the unity of God – His transcendent, indivisible and infinite nature.

21   Soudavar, *The Aura of Kings*, 8.

22   Soudavar, 15.

23   Soudavar, 13.

dastār…. the hanging turban tail-ends (as in fig. 7), which, like flying ribbons, were perceived as agents of victory and the symbol of "kingly sunshine" (i.e., *khvarenah*).'[24]

Although this seems like somewhat of a detour, as indicated at the beginning of this chapter, there is an association between the concept of the *khvarenah* and Mithrā.

Other symbols identified by Soudavar as associated with the *khvarenah* radiance are a pair of wings,[25] and the head of a ram. 'In the well-known episode of the *Kārnāmag-i Ardashir-i Pāpakān*, when the last of the Parthians, Ardavān, inquires about the ram that was following Ardashir, the *dastur* (*dast-var*) replies that it represents Kingly Glory.'[26] This story also demonstrates a connection between the symbolism of the ram, the wings and the *khvarenah* - 'it represents his farr, and his wings of kingship and good fortune.'[27] Later images combined the image of the ram and the turban (*dastār*), where the flying ribbons are tied as a turban around the horns of a ram.

In Zoroastrianism it is the deity Verethragna[28] who is often associated with *khvarenah*. Soudavar, however, shows that Verethragna only possessed it, whereas Mithrā bestows this power, and can also take it away – Verethragna is subordinate to Mithrā as a receiver of the *khvarenah*. The connection with

---

24 Soudavar, 15.

25 This is associated with the Arabic word *azfun*, which has the meaning of "arise up" or nurturing / growing. 'The afzun monogram transformed into a symmetrically balanced composition, in which each letter is doubled with a mirror image, and placed on top of a pair of wings.'(Soudavar, 20.). It is also worth noting that the wings are considered those of a falcon, as is the head of the Egyptian god of kingship, Horus.

26 Soudavar, 20–21.

27 Soudavar, 21.

28 Verethragna was a god of victory ("miting of resistance"). Some parallels have been drawn between Verethragna and the Egyptian Horus.

falcons, the *khvarenah* and Mithrā is shown in iconography such as the Elymaic bas-relief in which falcons are shown to carry rings to a standing ruler and a mounted king. In the story of Jamshid 'He drifts toward falsehood and loses his *khvaren-ah*, which turns into a falcon (varegna) and goes to Mithrā...'[29] Jamshid is worthy of mention himself in this context, due to his connection with the "Cup of Jamshid".

Jamshid was considered among the greatest rulers in the *Shāhnāmeh*, until he was deposed by Zahhak, an evil ruler depicted with two snakes on his shoulders. The Cup of Jamshid, like the Holy Grail, bestowed immortality, and 'has the property of displaying the whole world'.[30] It has been argued that this cup may have had an influence on the European grail myths. One of the interpretations of the Cup of Jamshid in literature is 'the pure spirit's ability to see the truth.'[31] In the end Jamshid became '"ungrateful, proud, forgetful of God's name" ... and consequently he loses God's farr.'[32]

> Turn thy face from the deceitful Turkestan of nature towards the Iran of the Holy Law, Guide thee to the Kay Khosrow of the soul and then place in thy hand the goblet of Jamshid, In order that in that goblet thou mayst see for ever with thy own eyes every single atom as clear as the sun.[33]

---

29 Soudavar, *The Aura of Kings*, 23.

30 Nematollahi, 'The True Meaning of the Cup of Jamshid: Medieval and Pre-Modern Symbolic Readings of the Shāhnāmeh', 5.

31 Nematollahi, 7.

32 Nematollahi, 8.

33 Nematollahi, 6.

In the *Shāhnāmeh*[34] we read in relation to the cup:

He sought to see the cup itself in order for a moment to see
the whole world at once
But though he saw the whole world he could not see in the
cup of Jamshid the cup itself
He puzzled much over that mystery, but no veil was raised
from before it.
Finally he described a piece of writing: "How canst thou see
me in myself?

Since I have quite vanished from myself who shall see any
mark of me in this world of dust? Since both body and soul
have vanished from me, there remains neither name nor trace
of me...

If thou wouldst be like me, become like me, bid farewell to
thyself, vanish into annihilation. Thou must build a castle of
annihilation, otherwise blows will rain down on thee from
every side."[35]

Nematollahi interprets the true meaning of the cup as 'the
heart of a mystic who is vanished from himself, and thereby is
capable of realizing the truth.'[36] Jamshid serves as an example
of one who did not achieve this and succumbed to the power
the cup offered. 'The most fundamental tenet of Iranian kingship, as related by the story of Jamshid and the later "mirror

---

34   An epic poem written by the Persian poet Ferdowsi

35   Nematollahi, 'The True Meaning of the Cup of Jamshid: Medieval and
Pre-Modern Symbolic Readings of the Shāhnāmeh', 9.

36   Nematollahi, 11.

for princes" literature, is that this trait is temporary and can be lost when kings stray from the path of righteousness.'[37]

The above should serve as a warning to anyone who treads the mystical or magical paths – every step must be earnt (and preserved), and every step must be for the benefit of others, lest you stray from the path of righteousness.

Returning from the lessons of Jamshid to Mithrā and Verethragna, in the iconography and myths surrounding Verethragna, although he is shown with the attributes of the *khvarenah* through his avatars (wind, ram and falcon), he does not possess the solar radiance (as discussed), the main attribute of the *khvarenah*, which is, 'the quintessential symbol of Mithrā.[38] Therefore it is Mithrā who is called on in the representation of kings over Verethragna.

The *khvarenah* is also represented in Mithraic iconography associated with a tradition based in astrology, when the Sun entered the Constellation of the Ram at the start of spring. This was associated with festivities into the Islamic period. In connection with this is the image of a lion mask, with ram's horns[39] and wings. Soudavar puts forward that 'we may envision that all three (i.e., ram-horns, sun-mask, and wings) represent the *khvarenah*.'[40]

---

37   Soudavar, *The Aura of Kings*, 43.

38   Soudavar, 25.

39   The ram's head is also a symbol of the *farr*, and could indicate a king's increased glory.

40   Soudavar, *The Aura of Kings*, 36.

Fig. 30 - Lion masks with ram-horns
and wings

There are indications of the Mithraic iconography appearing in other religious contexts, such as a Bāmiyān fresco, where the Buddha is seen in the place of Mithrā.

The Buddha is seen surrounded by a nimbus and radiant disk, showing the Buddha with similar symbols as the solar radiance of Mithrā. There are also 'angels at the top corners of the fresco as well as flowing behind Buddha's head, a previously discussed symbol, namely the *dastār*.'[41]

---

41   Soudavar, 27.

Some of the iconography of the *khvarenah* also appears in Egyptian images serving a similar role in the second millennium BC. The Ram is used to represent Amon and the solar disk depicts Re-Harakhty, the Sun god. Eventually the symbols were fused, and we find the 'ram with a solar disk on its head represented the combined deity, Amon-Re.'[42] Over time the ram-head was to an extent interchangeable, with the solar disk (representing the sky-god). We see the ram-head 'inserted into the symbol of the sky-god in lieu of the disk.'[43] The god of the sky is Horus (also god of kingship), who was also seen to contain the Sun and Moon.

The flying ribbons also appear in depictions of Akhenaton. They are the '"breath of Life" that came with the solar rays of Aton and blew past the faces of Akhenaton (r. 1354-34 BC) and his family.'[44]

---

42 Soudavar, 81.

43 Soudavar, 81.

44 Soudavar, 81–82.

Akhenaton was a pharaoh who revolutionised Egyptian religious worship and practice during his reign with the introduction of Atenism. Because of this, he was 'rejected into oblivion
by his direct successors.'[45] The temples dedicated to the Aten
were open roofed so that the rays of the Sun would lighten the
sanctuary unimpeded. Soudavar stresses that the above sharing
of iconography does not show that the 'Mithrāic symbols of the
khvarenah were directly derived from Egyptian mythology—
although they may have been affected by it—but that the Achaemenid conquest of Egypt reopened the door to a rich symbolism that could be adopted and/or adapted to Iranian needs.'[46]

---

45   Laboury, *Akhénaton.*
46   Soudavar, *The Aura of Kings,* 82.

With the advent of Zoroastrianism, elements of Mithraism were banned, and became associated with "demonic creatures". Speaking of Mithrā could result in death. 'There was an *omerta*[47] to be observed in esoteric Mithrāism, the same that perhaps led to a secretive organizational structure for Western Mithrāism.'[48]

Another element of the Mithraic iconography, that speaks to the element of opposites and their reconciliation in Baphomet, is his pairing with another deity called Apam-Napāt. This deity took Jamshid's *khvarenah* after he lost it and hid it under the sea to protect it. Apam-Napāt is designated *ahura* (imperial or regal), and his name means "Son of Waters." Stretching back to the pre-Zoroastrian period Apam-Napāt was seen as equal to Mithrā, and both were connected to the division of the day – 'the morning was set under the "protection of Mithrā and the afternoon under that of Apam-Napāt...they were the two sides of the same coin, or more precisely the representatives of the two halves of the same cycle: the rise of the sun to the skies followed by its dive into the sea."'[49] Both these deities were in a sense interchangeable; one protected the *khvarenah*, the other projected it. In one sense, this could be seen as representing the internal and external processes associated with the "divine glory", or "kingly power"- its internal cultivation, and its external use to illuminate the external world. These two deities were represented by the Lotus (Apam-Napāt) and the Sunflower (Mithrā). The sunflower, the solar radiance; and the lotus, the waters. In the Achaemenid period these two icons became combined, which showed the sunflower emerging from the lotus.

---

47 A code of obedience and silence, contemporarily associated with the Mafia. One etymology gives the sanskrit ksam ("earth") as opposed to "sky".

48 Soudavar, *The Aura of Kings*, 28.

49 Soudavar, 52–53.

In Egyptian iconography the Lotus is also solar and associated with rebirth. In an image of lotus fields found in Persepolis the lotus and sunflower are combined to represent a dual *khvarenah*, with the representation of the lotus, and the stacking design borrowed from Egypt, 'projecting the rise of the *khvarenah* from the depth of waters to the height of the skies.'[50]

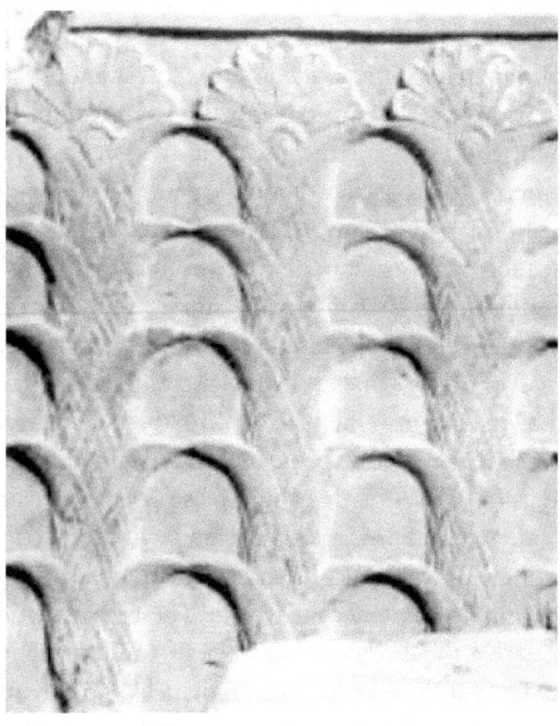

In another depiction at the Eastern stairway of Apadana, we see a *Khvarenah* frieze displayed above Persian and Mede guards. This shows the winged disk with the vertical stacking

---

50 Soudavar, 83.

of lotus, showing that that the winged-disk rose from the waters and carried the seed of the *khvarenah* that Jamshid had lost and Apam-Napāt had guarded.'[51]

Soudavar also points out that the term "winged-disk" is incorrect, and that the representation is really that of a sphere and therefore it should be "winged-sphere" or "winged-pearl", with pearls connected to the waters, and therefore Apam-Napāt.

In Mithraism, the bull is also seen as a giver of the *farr*. In the *Bondahesh* where it tells of the beginning of creation, the Primordial Bull's seeds are taken to the Moon so that the seeds of other animals can be obtained, and fours bulls are sometimes shown pulling the chariot of the Moon. The bull is a symbol of the Moon and the seas, like Apam-Napāt, whereas Mithra is symbolised by the lion. 'The lion-bull icon...must

---

51 Soudavar, 100.

therefore represent the day and night cycle, which reflects the ancient Iranian division of daily hours between Mithrā and Apam-Napāt.'[52] Soudavar argues that in these images the lion is not killing the bull, but overcoming it, and the bull is shown as a majestic animal springing back up, at the other end. It's a metaphor for the sun that overwhelms the night at dawn but looses its grip at dusk.'[53]

The word *khvarenah* itself is connected to the Sun, and has been linked to the Indo-European root which means "brilliance" and also "shine". This also developed into the English word "splendour".[54] The Avestan speakers played on the similarity between the word *khvar* (sun), and *khvarenah*, linking it with the Sun. 'Consequently, the universal symbol of holiness that the aura has become, and which appears as a halo and nimbus behind the head of Buddha, Jesus, prophets, saints, and kings, was in effect the result of just one more effort to emphasize the power of the *khvarenah*.'[55]

Another interesting indication of the nature of the kingly power is in the concept of the Melchizedek priests, which has been argued was the order, or tradition, Jesus belonged to. The Melchizedek priests were eternal because they had already been resurrected. They could not die. The Aaron[56] priests were

---

52   Soudavar, 116.

53   Soudavar, 117.

54   The word splendour appears 7 times in Liber AL, for example 'Hoor in his secret name and splendour is the Lord initiating' (AL I:49) and 'There is a splendour in my name hidden and glorious, as the sun of midnight is ever the son.' (AL III:74) and 'Now rejoice! now come in our splendour & rapture! Come in our passionate peace, & write sweet words for the Kings.' (AL II:64), with some indication of a link between kingship and the Sun.

55   Soudavar, *The Aura of Kings*, 123.

56   I will deal with John the Baptist in more detail later, but it is worth noting that John was from the line of Aaron (the temporal line), as opposed to the

a temporal line, passed on from father to son. Barker evidences the continuity between Jesus and the Melchizedek priests in the story of the miracle at Cana, where Jesus turns the water into wine. This is a reflection of the story where 'Melchizedek offered wine to Abraham when he was expecting water.'[57] The act of the transformation of the water 'manifested forth his glory;[58] and his disciples believed in him' (John 2:1-11) Melchizedek was both a priest and a king, his name meaning "king of righteousness" (מַלְכִּי־צֶדֶק). He was a priest of Elyon (עליון) and king of Salem.

> And they remembered that God ['Ēlōhīm] was their rock, and
> the high God ['Ēl 'Elyōn] their redeemer.
>
> *Psalms* 78:35

The word Salem in Hebrew (שָׁלֵם) means "whole", "entire" or "complete". By gematria this is also equal to Creation (עש), a foundation or basis (עקר) and to rend, cut, blame or curse (קרע). All three include the Hebrew ayin (ע). This number is 370, which is also the number of the Holy Book titled *Liber A'ash vel Capricorni Pneumatici*.[59] This Liber 'Analyses the nature of the creative magical force in man, explains how to awaken it, how to use it and indicates the general as well as

---

"eternal" Melchizedek line of Jesus indicated here. This is shown in the Gospel of Luke, where it states of John's mother that she 'was of the daughters of Aaron...' (Luke 1:5).

57 Barker, 'Jesus the Nazorean', 5.

58 The word glory 'was used in Biblical writing to translate a Hebrew word which had a sense of "brightness, splendor, magnificence, majesty of outward appearance."' ('Glory | Origin and Meaning of Glory by Online Etymology Dictionary'.)

59 The book of Creation or the Goat of the Spirit

the particular objects to be gained thereby.'[60] In the "Syllabus of the Official Instructions of the A∴A∴" it is stated that the text 'contains the true secret of all practical magick'.[61] We will return to this Holy Book later.

Another symbol associated with kings, the Pharaohs of Egypt, is the Uraeus. It is thought that the word uraeus comes from the Egyptian 'She who rears up'[62] The deity, associated with the common cobra, is Wadjet. Her 'name may mean 'the green or fresh one,' or 'she of the papyrus.' According to one of the Pyramid Texts, she was responsible for creating the papyrus swamps. This shows a connection between the images of snakes, power, and fertility.[63]

As a final word on this kingly power (although the theme is present throughout this book), I would refer again to Steve King's essential instructional book *Living in the Sunlight*.[64] In King's book, he quotes a letter from Crowley to Charles Stansfield Jones, where Crowley describes this practice as 'making everybody in your sphere reflect your radiance.'[65] A king is

---

60   'O.T.O. and A∴A∴ Libri by Class'.

61   Crowley, Desti, and Waddell, *Magick. Liber ABA. Book Four. Parts I-IV*, 471.

62   Lansberry, 'Egyptian Serpent Power', 1.

63   'The triple uraeus (serpent band of gold worn by Egyptian royalty) of three coiled snakes, was often associated with the Egyptian crown, symbolising both the threefold wisdom of the three divine aspects and the three currents – positive, negative and neutral – of the creative Serpent fire, occultly aroused and sublimated to the head of the initiate and Pharaoh.' (Hodson, *At The Sign of the Square and Compass*, 271.)

64   When contemplating verses 16 of *Liber B vel Magi* Crowley speculates - 'Can this have been the IX° OTO Mystery? Or the Way of the Tao, called "Living in the Sunlight" by Soror Hilarion?' He concludes, however, 'No: it's the regular Analysis-Method…' (Crowley et al., *Commentaries of the Holy Books and Other Papers*, 4:340.)

65   King, *Living in the Sunlight*, 9.

gifted "divine light", but he cannot function as a king unless he radiates this light, this power. If he is a good king, a radiant king, this will be reflected in his Kingdom, which will become an outward manifestation of his inner divine will. Crowley also passes on, in relation to Sister Hilarion's teaching, that 'The main point seems to be the conception of yourself as a King – Vide Liber CCXX Cap II.'[66]

> A King may choose his garment as he will...
> If he be a King, thou canst not hurt him.
> There is a light before thine eyes, o prophet, a light unde
> sired, most desirable.
>
> *Liber AL*, II 58-61

It should also be noted that one of the titles given to Tiphareth, the Sun (Shemesh), the source of light and life is "the King".

As expressed by the respected writer on the occult and associate of Crowley in later life, Dion Fortune (1890–1946), 'The sun is the central point of our existence. Without the sun there would be no solar system. Sunlight plays a very important part in the metabolism, the life-process, of living creatures...We see, therefore, that the sun-light is a very important factor in our well-being; we might go even further to say that it is essential to our very existence and that our association with the sun is far more intimate than we realise.'[67]

---

66 King, 8.

67 Fortune, *The Mystical Qabalah*, 199.

Muhammad and the First Three Imams Crowned with Light

Crowley further links Baphomet to the concepts of Satan and The Devil (making it clear that in his opinion that the Devil does not exist), and light. 'He is "The Devil" of The Book of Thoth, and His emblem is BAPHOMET, the Androgyne who is the hieroglyph of arcane perfection... He is therefore Life, and Love. But moreover his letter is *ayin*, the Eye, so that he is Light; and his Zodiacal image is Capricornus, that leaping goat whose attribute is Liberty.'[68]

---

68   Crowley, Desti, and Waddell, *Magick. Liber ABA. Book Four. Parts I-IV*, 277.

Therefore in this "emblem", in Baphomet, we see encapsulated Light, Life, Love and Liberty. The Law proclaimed by the Deacon at the opening of the Gnostic Mass in the name of IAO.[69]

> By Light shall ye look upon yourselves, and behold All Things that are in Truth One Thing only, whose name hath been called No Thing for a cause which later shall be declared unto you. But the substance of Light is Life, since without Existence and Energy it were naught. By Life therefore are you made yourselves, eternal and incorruptible, flaming forth as suns, self-created and self-supported, each the sole centre of the Universe.[70]

---

69 There is another interesting mystery in relation to IAO and the Eightfold Word equilibrated with the Three. The Wizards spelling of Baphomet in Hebrew not only gives the eightfold word, but also conceals the threefold IAO. In Hebrew Baphomet is באועמיתר, which also contains אעי, IAO, with a value of 81. 81 is also the value of כםא (Throne) and is also 9^2. This is Yesod (foundation) to the power of 2. Crowley notes of these three letters; "The three vowel-consonants of the Hebrew alphabet, Aleph, Yod, Ayin, these three form the sacred name of God, I.A.O. These three Atu, IX, 0 and XV, thus offer a threefold explanation of male creative energy." (Crowley, *The Book of Thoth*, 106.)

70 Crowley, 'De Lege Libellum'.

THE EMPEROR

Another interesting hint that Crowley gives regarding the nature of Baphomet is in *The General Principles of Astrology*, where he states that, 'We must then regard this Devil as the Emperor in disguise, beneath a veil...'[1] Further, in *The Book of Thoth*, Crowley writes of The Emperor, 'The sign is thus a combination of energy in its most material form with the idea of authority.'[2] We can compare this to the description of The Devil already given, which is '...creative energy in its most material form.'[3] If we combine the value of these two cards we get 19, the same value as Chavvah (חוה), which means "to manifest", "to shew forth", as well as Eve (חוה). Here, perhaps, the wild impulse of The Devil takes form or is controlled and directed in the figure of The Emperor. But there is also a hint in this numeration at the female element of this process – kundalini or shakti – the serpent power. If we further add 1 and 9 we get 10, Malkuth, the Kingdom (Bride of Microprosopos).

Crowley, referring to the older forms of the card, explains that the torch and the cup depicted are the same as the sceptre and Orb as held by The Emperor. It is not hard to see the connection in the Thoth Deck re-imagining of the image with the two rams staring over the Emperor's shoulders. He also draws a parallel between the pentagram (or pentacle) and the "Pope" card, which is another earthy sign – Taurus. Both of these are sovereigns in their own right (One temporal, the other spiritu-

---

1   Crowley and Adams, *The General Principles of Astrology*, 41.

2   Crowley, *The Book of Thoth*, 77.

3   Crowley, 105.

al). In older versions of The Emperor, he is shown throned on a cube, as is Baphomet in the rendering by Lévi.

Although the Emperor card shows depictions of rams, and the Devil is a goat, both are described as Himalayan in *The Book of Thoth* (a mountain range, a symbol of "high places").[4] Also noting the references to the ram in the earlier discussion of the *farr* and the kingly power. The horns on the depiction of the Devil spiral up, whereas the horns of the rams spiral down. We also read in the 15th Aethyr of *The Vision and the Voice*, 'Above the altar is a veiled Figure, whose name is Pan. Those in the outer tier adore him as a Man; and in the next tier they adore him as a Goat; and in the next tier they adore him as a Ram; and in the next tier they adore him as a Crab; and in the next tier they adore him as an Ibis; and in the next tier they adore him as a Golden Hawk; and in the next tier they adore him not.'[5]

In his commentary, Crowley associates the Goat with Geburah (which he calls Mendes Khem), the Ram with Chesed (which he associates with Amoun) and the Man with Tiphareth.

Crowley further points us to a connection between The Emperor and The Devil (and therefore the kingly power) when he highlights that '"The Devil" is standing upon the cubic stone, and this fact is not unrelated to that upon which we have animadverted in our discussion of "The Emperor".[6]

---

4   This conflation of rams and goats is also noted by Maspero, who writes in a footnote related to Osiris, 'The ram of Mendes is sometimes Osiris, and sometimes the soul of Osiris. The ancients took it for a he-goat, and to them we are indebted for the record of its exploits...' (Maspero, *The Dawn of Civilisation*, 131.) Some have also noted the connection between Osiris and herding, through the crook and flail, tools used by shepherds.

5   Crowley, Neuburg, and Desti, *The Vision & the Voice with Commentary and Other Papers: The Collected Diaries of Aleister Crowley, 1909-1914 E.V.*, 132.

6   Crowley and Adams, *The General Principles of Astrology*, 41.

Further Crowley states that, 'the whole will become clear when we recall what festival has replaced Saturnalia, what was the principal event in the world's history that occurred at the entry of the Sun into Capricornus. It is the birth of the Babe who shall redeem the world.'[7] A redeemer – a messiah.

We also read in Crowley's commentary to Chapter 61 of *The Book of Lies*:

In Hebrew, the letter which follows O is P; it therefore follows Ayin, the Devil of the Tarot.

AYIN is spelt O I N, thus replacing the A in A I N by an O, the letter of the Devil, or Pan, the phallic God.

Now AIN means nothing, and thus the replacing of AIN by OIN means the completion of the Yoni by the Lingam, which is followed by the complete dissolution symbolised in the letter P.

These letters, O P, are then seen to be the root of opus, the Latin word for "work", in this case, the Great Work. And they also begin the word "opening". In Hindu philosophy, it is said that Shiva, the Destroyer, is asleep, and that when he opens his eye the universe is destroyed – another synonym, therefore, for the accomplishment of the Great Work. But the "eye" of Shiva is also his Lingam. Shiva is himself the Mahalingam, which unites these symbolisms. The opening of the eye, the ejaculation of the lingam, the destruction of the universe, the accomplishment of the Great Work – all these are different ways of saying the same thing.

---

7   Crowley and Adams, 41.

The doctrine is that the Great Work should be accomplished without creating new Karma, for the letter N, the fish, the vesica, the womb, breeds, whereas the Eye of Horus does not; or, if it does so, breeds, according to Turkish tradition, *a Messiah*. [my emphasis][8]

OP-us, the Work! The OP-ening of THE EYE![9]

To consider this more, we can turn to another chapter in *The Book of Lies*, Chapter 42, Dust Devils, and the relationship between the Angel, and the Masters of the Temple.

The Masters of the Temple are now introduced; they are inhabitants, not of this desert; their abode is not this universe. They come from the Great Sea, Binah, the City of the Pyramids. V.V.V.V.V. is indicated as one of these travellers; He is described as a camel, not because of the connotation of the French form of this word, but because "camel" is in Hebrew Gimel, and Gimel is the path leading from Tiphareth to Kether, uniting Microprosopus and Macroprosopus, i.e. performing the Great Work. The card Gimel in the Tarot is the High Priestess, the Lady of Initiation; one might even say, the Holy Guardian Angel.[10]

V.V.V.V.V. is one of these Masters, but also an Angel, and in one sense, the Angel is one, both Universal and personal. Each Master of the Temple, having achieved 'perfect annihilation of that personality which limits and oppresses the Self',[11] is

---

8   Crowley, *The Book of Lies*, 133.

9   Crowley, 132.

10   Crowley, 95.

11   Crowley et al., *Commentaries of the Holy Books and Other Papers*, 4:13.

then 'cast forth' – they are reborn. After this it is 'His principle business [...] to tend his 'garden[12] of disciples...'[13] He is reborn as a Messiah. He does not "breed" as do the Black Brothers – 'Now, if there is any difference at all between the White and the Black Adept in similar case, it is that the one, working by "love under will" achieves a marriage with the new idea, while the other, merely grabbing, adds a concubine to his harem of slaves.'[14]

In the 13th Aethyr, Crowley experienced a vision set in a garden that is instructive in relation to the mysteries of Baphomet:

And an Angel cometh forth, of pure pale gold, walking upon the water.[15] Above his head is a rainbow,[16] and the water foams beneath his feet. And he saith: Before his face am I come that hath the thirty-three thunders of increase in his hand. From the golden water shalt thou gather corn...And now waves of light roll through the Aethyr, as if they were

---

12 'Every branch in me that beareth not fruit be taketh away: and every branch that beareth fruit, he purgeth it, that it may bring forth more fruit.' - John 15:2 (*The KJV Study Bible*, 1062.). The Hebrew for garden is (גן). This is also the value of stone, rock, also secret foundation, and a border, also running waters (נוגלים).

13 Crowley et al., *Commentaries of the Holy Books and Other Papers*, 4:10.

14 Crowley, *Magick Without Tears*, 110.

15 'So when they had rowed about five and twenty or thirty furlongs, they saw Jesus walking on the sea, and drawing nigh unto the ship: and they were afraid.' – John 6:19 (*The KJV Study Bible*, 1050.)

16 'And God said, "This is the token of the covenant which I make between Me and you and every living creature that is with you, for perpetual generations: I do set My rainbow in the cloud, and it shall be for a token of a covenant between Me and the earth.' – Genesis 9:12-13 (*The KJV Study Bible*, 10.) 'And I saw another mighty angel come down from heaven, clothed with a cloud; and a rainbow was upon his head, and his face was as it were the sun, and his feet as pillars of fire.' - Revelation 10:1 (*The KJV Study Bible*, 1245.)

playing. Therefore suddenly I am in a garden, upon a terrace of a great castle, that is upon a rocky mountain. In the garden are fountains and many flowers…A voice comes: This water which thou seest is called the water of death.[17] But NEMO hath filled therefrom our springs.

And I said: Who is NEMO?

And the voice answered: A dolphin's tooth, and a ram's horns, and the hand of a man that is hanged, and the phallus of a goat. (By this I understand that nun is explained by shin, and he by resh, and mem by yod, and ayin by tau. NEMO is therefore called 165 = 11×15; and is in himself 910 = 91 Amen x 10; and 13×70 = The One Eye, *Achad Ayin*.)

And now there cometh an Angel into the garden, but he hath not any of the attributes of the former Angels, for he is like a young man, dressed in white linen robes.

And he saith: No man hath beheld the face of my Father. Therefore he that hath beheld it is called NEMO. And know thou that every man that is called NEMO hath a garden that he tendeth. And every garden that is and flourisheth hath been prepared from the desert by NEMO, watered with the waters that were called death.

---

17   We can see this in contrast to the "living water" of the New Testament – 'If any man thirst, let him come unto me, and drink. He that believeth on me, as the scripture hath said, out of his belly shall flow rivers of living water. (But this spake he of the Spirit, which they that believe on him should receive: for the Holy Ghost was not yet given; because that Jesus was not yet glorified.)' – John 7:37-39 (*The KJV Study Bible*, 1053.)

Instead of the living waters, waters of life, here we have the waters of death as central to the experience of the Masters of the Temple. As explained by Gunther, 'the central theme of the new book is the opening of the Fifty Gates of Death and the Birth of the Master of the Temple.'[18]

In relation to Dionysus Zagreus and Bacchus Diphues Crowley writes, 'It is convenient to treat the two gods as one. Zagreus is only important to the present purpose because he possesses horns, and because (in the Eleusinian Mysteries) it is said that he was torn to pieces by the Titans. But Athena rescued his heart and carried it to his father, Zeus. His mother was Demeter; he is thus the fruit of the marriage of Heaven and Earth. This identifies him as the Vau of Tetragrammaton, but the legends of his "death" refer to initiation, which accords with the doctrine of the Devourer.'[19]

Paradoxically, as you would have come to expect, this "death" is a birth,[20] the birth of a Master of the Temple; this "death" creates a new life.[21]

---

18   Gunther, *The Angel and the Abyss*, 10.

19   Crowley, *The Book of Thoth*, 65.

20   'The woman in the Holy of Holies, clothed with the sun and giving birth to the Messiah, must have prompted the early Church to tell the story of Mary as the story of Wisdom…The memory of the Holy Spirit as the Mother of Jesus is preserved in the writings of the Hebrew Christians.' (Barker, 'Where Shall Wisdom Be Found? (Job 28.12)', 4.)

21   'Here is another parable. Peter, the Stone of the Philosophers, cuts off the ear of Malchus, the servant of the High Priest (the ear is the organ of Spirit). In analysis the spiritual part of Malkuth must be separated from it by the philosophical stone, and then Christus, the Anointed One, makes it whole once more. "Solve et coagula!"' *Liber ABA*, Ch VIII – The Sword.

Kuan Yin
觀音

Kuan Yin is 'Popularly known in the West in the present feminine form as the "Goddess of Mercy" or the "Buddhist Madonna," and hailed by Henry Adams as the sexless 'merciful guardian of the human race.'[1] It is said that every house has a Kuan-Yin.

Kuan Yin is the Chinese translation of the bodhisattva known as Avalokiteśvara, who embodies the compassion of all Buddhas. The name is sometimes translated as "lord who gazes down (at the world)".

John Blofeld (who was a friend of Gerald Yorke) argues that the transformation of Avalokiteśvara to the feminine Kwan Yin, was due to a merging of the bodhisattva with that of the Buddhist figure Tara, due to the more bizarre depictions of Avalokite vara being not as appealing to the humanistic inclinations of the Chinese; creating iconography more sympathetic with the ideas of compassion seen in the depictions of Tara. Blofeld also believes some of the characteristics of Kwan Yin were assimilated from those of the legendary Princess Miao Shan.

There is also a theory that Kuan Yin as seen in China has been influenced by Zoroastrianism following the Arab conquest of Persia, and that there are correspondences between Kuan Yin and Sraoša[2] known in the 1st and 2nd centuries AD.

---

1   Tay, 'Kuan-Yin: The Cult of Half Asia', 147.

2   An epithet of Saroša is 'whose body is the sacred word', and Zoroastrian scriptures emphasise a link with Mithra. Saroša is also seen as a mediator

It has also been proposed that Kuan Yin was introduced into China by Zoroastrians via the Silk Road.[3]

'While Amita[4] (Japanese, Amida) vows to take the sentient beings after death into a world where the retribution of karma is no more effective, Kuan-yin caters to the human desire to rise above our own karma even while in this life.'[5] In this way, Kuan Yin could be seen as a redeemer.

C.N. Tay further writes that, 'In popular religion Kuan-Yin is an object for worship and devotion; but the illumined may find in him an ideal and tangible aid for concentration and mental tranquilisation, through which they may identify themselves with the universal mind.'[6]

In line with this universality of the deity:

If needed as a Buddha or a Hinayana teacher, he appears as such; if as Brahma, or Indra, or Isvara, or a deva, a king, an elder, a citizen, an official, a brahman, a monk, nun, or male or female disciple, then he appears as such. If needed in the form of a wife or an elder, citizen, official or brahman, he appears as such; or if as youth or maiden, he appears as such. If needed as a god, or a demon, he so appears.'[7] Yet, 'Although Kuan-Yin appears in many forms, reality is one. Although Kuan-yin traverses the worlds, he remains unmoved.[8]

In popular religious practice (in Japan, Korea and especially

---

between the corporeal and incorporeal worlds.

3   Abreu, *Zoroastrianism in China*, 9.

4   The principle Buddha in Pure Land Buddhism.

5   Tay, 'Kuan-Yin: The Cult of Half Asia', 147–48.

6   Tay, 148.

7   Tay, 154.

8   Tay, 156.

China) Kuan Yin has been revered as a goddess, despite the fact that in Buddhism she is not one, but a celestial Bodhisattva.

Another interesting aspect of Kuan Yin that appears in a story told by Blofeld regarding his early introduction to the bodhisattva is that the "goddess" does not need to be bargained with. She does not demand a sacrifice. A woman who had come to a shrine to pray for a son and when he asked what the woman would do after, the response was that 'Kuan Yin, being compassionate, would naturally be happy to grant such a wish.'[9]

> I give unimaginable joys on earth: certainty, not faith, while in life, upon death; peace unutterable, rest, ecstasy; nor do I demand aught in sacrifice.
>
> *Liber AL, I:58*

It may seem out of place to discuss a popular Buddhist deity when discussing Baphomet, but in *Liber 58* we read this fascinating statement:

> In Daath is said to be the Head of the great Serpent Nechesh or Leviathan, called Evil to conceal its Holiness (נחש = 358 = משיה, the Messiah or Redeemer, and לויתך =496 = מלכות, the Bride.) It is identical with the Kundalini of the Hindu Philosophy, the Kwan-se-on of the Mongolian Peoples, and means the magical Force in Man, which is the sexual Force applied to the Brain, Heart, and other Organs, and redeemeth him.[10]

---

9   Blofeld, *Bodhisattva of Compassion: The Mystical Tradition of Kuan Yin*, 19.

10   Crowley, *777 and Other Qabalistic Writings of Aleister Crowley*, 19.

Although in the above Crowley refers to Kwan-se-on as "Mongolian", we can see Crowley making reference to his rendering of Kuan Yin being of Japanese origin in his *Alice: An Adultery*.

> She was too young to know that shrine
> the son's;
> Or see the Virgin's House in Kwan-se-on's:

In a footnote to this section he writes, 'The Dai-Butsu,[11] a vast statue of Buddha.'[12]

The introductory quote above uses the term "mercy" as an attribute of Kuan Yin, but Kuan-Yin is commonly associated in English with compassion - 'maternal love and infinite compassion.'[13]

Crowley's association of Baphomet with Kwan Yin may also seem obscure until you work backwards to the writings of Blavatsky and Theosophy, where we find familiar themes that have been explored in this book. Blavatsky, however, differentiates between "Kwan-Shi-Yin" (觀世音) and "Kwan-Yin", even though in Chinese this refers to the same entity, with

---

11   The famous Dai-Butsu at Kamakura is a representation of Amida (Buddha of Infinite Light), not Kwan-se-on (Kannon). When in Japan Crowley was considering "settling down" in a monastery, but it was here that he knew his destiny was pushing him in a different direction – '...I turned then sadly from Daibutsu, as I had turned from love, ambition and ease, my spirit silently acquiescing in the arcane arbitrament of the mysterious daimon who drove me darkly onward; how I knew not, wither I knew not, but only this, that he was irresistible as inscrutable..." (Crowley, *The Confessions of Aleister Crowley*, 228.). This moment in Crowley's life is one of great significance that should not be overlooked.

12   Crowley, *Collected Works of Aleister Crowley*, II:80.

13   Tay, 'Kuan-Yin: The Cult of Half Asia', 151.

Kwan Shi Yin being the proper form. Blavatsky associates these two as male and female, nature and man, Divine Wisdom and intelligence, "Christos-Sophia", Logos and shakti. In Theosophy Kwan-Yin refers to the female principle, and Kwan-Shi-Yin the male principle. It is also taught that it was Blavatsky and the "Mahatmas" who had instructed that this was not a single entity, but two.

The doctrine regarding Kwan-Shi-Yin has its origins in the *Stanzas of Dzyan*, found in the first volume of *The Secret Doctrine*. These are purported to be of Tibetan origin and part of the Book of Dyzan.

7. BEHOLD, OH LANOO! THE RADIANT CHILD OF THE TWO, THE UNPARALLELED REFULGENT GLORY: BRIGHT SPACE SON OF DARK SPACE, WHICH EMERGES FROM THE DEPTHS OF THE GREAT DARK WATERS. IT IS OEAOHOO THE YOUNGER, THE * * * HE SHINES FORTH AS THE SUN;[14] HE IS THE BLAZING DIVINE DRAGON OF WISDOM; THE ONE IS FOUR, AND FOUR TAKES TO ITSELF THREE,** AND THE UNION PRODUCES THE SAPTA, IN WHOM ARE THE SEVEN WHICH BECOME THE TRIDASA (OR THE HOSTS AND THE MULTITUDES). BEHOLD HIM LIFTING THE VEIL AND UNFURLING IT FROM EAST TO WEST. HE SHUTS OUT THE ABOVE, AND LEAVES THE BELOW TO BE SEEN AS THE GREAT ILLUSION. HE MARKS THE PLACES FOR THE SHINING ONES, AND TURNS THE UPPER INTO A SHORELESS SEA OF FIRE, AND THE ONE MANIFESTED INTO THE GREAT WATERS.[15]

---

14 In different sources I have seen this given as both "Sun" and "Son", but I believe "Sun" to be correct.

15 Blavatsky, *The Secret Doctrine*, 1:100.

In a commentary to the above, Blavatsky writes of OEAO-HOO, 'whom thou knowest now as Kwan-Shai-Yin.'[16] OEAO-HOO 'SHINES FORTH AS THE SUN ... THE BLAZING DIVINE DRAGON OF WISDOM...' It should be noted that some sources associate Leviathan (quoted by Crowley above) with a dragon. For example, 'Isaiah 27:1 listed Leviathan as one figure that would face judgement and was clearly subordinate, as well as easily defeated. The figure is described in the prophetic work as a "twisting serpent," "fleeing serpent," and "dragon who lives in the sea."'[17]

In her writings Blavatsky connects the symbolism of the Dragon, and that of unity - "One" (wholeness). She taught that 'Jehova – esoterically Elohim – is also the Serpent or Dragon that tempted Eve; and the Dragon is an old glyph for the Astral Light (Primordial Principal), "which is the Wisdom of Chaos."'[18] In theosophy 'Chaos is space filled with darkness, which is primordial matter in its pre-cosmic state. It contains in itself all the Elements in their rudimentary, undifferentiated State.'[19] Chaos is, in one sense, the *prima materia*.

Blavatsky also connects the symbolism of the serpent with that of Hermes, 'The primitive symbol of the serpent symbolised divine Wisdom and Perfection, and had always stood for psychical Regeneration and Immortality. Hence—Hermes, calling the serpent the most spiritual of all beings.'[20] Blavatsky further reminds us that Jesus told his disciples "Be ye wise as ser-

---

16   Blavatsky, 1:71.

17   McPeters, 'The Demiurge and the Primeval Serpent Motif within Classical Thought and Its Culmination within Gnosticism and Early Christianity', 31.

18   Blavatsky, *The Secret Doctrine*, 1:102.

19   Blavatsky, 'Chaos – Theosophy Wiki'.

20   Blavatsky, *The Secret Doctrine*, 1:73.

pents" (Matthew 10:16). It is worth noting that Matthew also tells us that Jesus gave the apostles 'power against unclean spirits, to cast them out, and to heal all manner of sickness and all manner of disease.' (Matthew 10:1). Jesus gave to his apostles the power to perform miracles. This seems to be in alignment with Crowley's conception of Kwan Yin – Baphomet; that it is 'the magical Force in Man, which is the sexual Force applied to the Brain, Heart, and other Organs, and redeemeth him.' Redemption, Regeneration and immortality.

OEAOHOO is Kwan-Shai-Yin, the Dragon, the Serpent and the Sun – a glyph of the Astral Light. This is '"the Incorporeal man who contains in himself the divine Idea,"—the generator of Light and Life... He is called the "Blazing Dragon of Wisdom,", 'He who bathes in the light of Oeaohoo will never be deceived by the veil of Mâyâ.'[21]

Blavatsky also emphasises the androgynous nature of Kwan-Shi-Yin, and the similarity with the Tetragrammaton and "Logoi". The Logoi in Christianity being the creative Word of God, that was made incarnate in Christ – 'St. John's vision in Revelation, that of the Logos, who is now connected with Jesus—is hermaphrodite, for he is described as having female breasts.'[22]

> ...the first Light of the primordial Elohim—the Adam, "male and female"—or (scientifically) electricity and life.[23]

Blavatsky calls Kwan-Shi-Yin the seventh Universal Principle, and in Theosophy this seventh Principle is active and male. 'Atma when spoken of in connection with an individual and

---

21 Blavatsky, *The Secret Doctrine*, 1:71.

22 Blavatsky, 1:72.

23 Blavatsky, 1:76.

Purush when applied in its relation to the Universe.' It is 'the active male, for it is the CENTRE OF ENERGY acting through and upon its female vehicle, the sixth principle.'[24] This sixth principle is Kuan-Yin, which Theosophy teaches is cosmically *ālaya,*[25] while in humans it is *buddhi.*[26]

There is a further clue to the connection between Kuan Yin and Baphomet in *The Voice of the Silence* (Liber 71).

Verse 94 of part 3 states:

The more thou dost become at one with it, thy being melted in its BEING, the more thy Soul unites with that which IS, the more thou wilt become COMPASSION ABSOLUTE.[27]

To this, Crowley as Frater O.M. comments:

This verse throws a little further light upon its predecessor. COMPASSION is really a certain Chinese figure whose names are numerous. One of them is BAPHOMET.[28]

So here we see Crowley, in commentary to a work by Blavatsky, connecting the concept of Compassion, a "Chinese figure" and Baphomet.

In the preceding verse, Compassion also appears as a core concept:

---

24 'Seventh Principle – Theosophy Wiki'.

25 Universal soul and the basis of all.

26 This is the female form of Buddha, and the vehicle of ātman (the seventh principle).

27 Crowley et al., *Commentaries of the Holy Books and Other Papers*, 4:333.

28 Crowley et al., 4:334.

There Kleśa is destroyed for ever, Tanhâ's roots torn out. But stay, Disciple . . . Yet, one word. Canst thou destroy divine compassion? Compassion is no attribute. It is the LAW of laws—eternal Harmony,[29] Alaya's SELF; a shoreless universal essence, the light of everlasting Right, and fitness of all things, the law of love eternal.[30]

To which Crowley comments:

It would be improper here to disclose what is presumably the true meaning of this verse. One can only commend it to the earnest consideration of members of the Sanctuary of the Gnosis, the IX° of the O.T.O.[31]

Crowley also points out the paradoxical and misleading way in which Blavatsky states that 'Compassion is no attribute', and therefore 'defines it in a peculiar way...'[32] This begs the question as to why she would be "misleading" on this point. In his commentary Crowley identifies *kleśa* with, 'Love of worldly enjoyment', and *tanhâ* as 'the creative force.[33]

So, above, we can see Crowley linking Kuan Yin, the concept of Compassion, worldly enjoyment, the creative force, Baphomet and the mysteries of the IX° of the OTO.

Further, Blavatsky states, 'It is the Buddha of Compassion only that can transcend this third macrocosmic plane.'[34] Planes

---

29 Harmozousa

30 Crowley et al., *Commentaries of the Holy Books and Other Papers*, 4:333.

31 Crowley et al., 4:333.

32 Crowley et al., 4:333.

33 Crowley et al., 4:333.

34 Blavatsky, *The Inner Group Teachings of H.P. Blavatsky*, 35.

form part of the teachings in Theosophy that the universe is sevenfold. Choosing not to explain the universe as a whole (or "*Kosmos*"), which she felt was beyond explanation, she explained the sevenfold principles in the solar system (macrocosmos) that have a reflection in humanity (*microcosmos*).

This "third macrocosmic plane" (or solar plane) is called *Jiva* (the Universal Life)[35] and was part of Blavatsky's seven-fold description of the manifested universe.

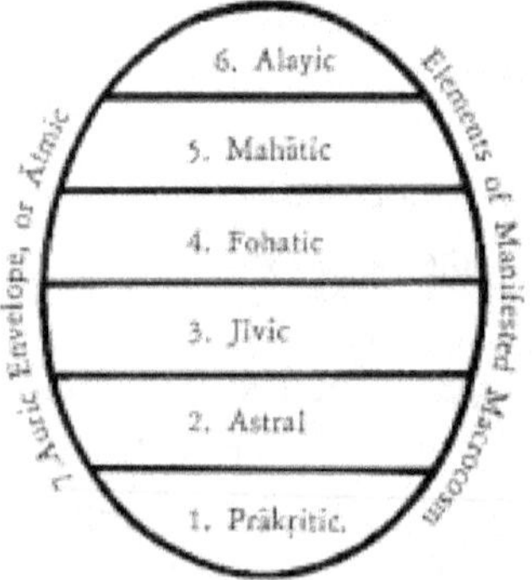

It is a Sanskrit word that means "soul, life, vital breath". In Hinduism and Jainism, a *jiva* is a living being; the immortal essence of a living organism. The word is derived from the Sanskrit verb-root *jīv*, which means "to breathe or to live".

Despite the love of divisions in Theosophy (and occultism in general), Blavatsky makes it clear that *Jiva*, like *Prakriti*, are indivisible (indivisible abstractions). These are 'to be divided only out of condescension for the weakness of our human intellect.'[36]

---

35 'Thou shalt mingle thy life with the universal life. Thou shalt keep not back one drop.' (*Liber Cheth Vel Vallum Abiegni sub Figura CLVI*)

36 Blavatsky, 'Life Principle – Blavatsky.Net'.

More than any other, the life principle in man is one with which we are most familiar, and yet are so hopelessly ignorant as to its nature. Matter and force are ever found allied. Matter without force, and force without matter, are inconceivable. In the mineral kingdom the universal life energy is one and unindividualized...[37]

In another of the "inner group" teachings Blavatsky is recorded to have said, 'The Pratyeka Buddhas do not go beyond the 3rd Cosmic Plane. They have conquered all their material desires, but have not yet freed themselves from their mental and spiritual desires.'[38]

Pratyeka Buddhas are sometimes called "solitary" and refer to someone who has attained Buddhahood without a teacher. They also do not accept students and do not work for others to attain. They accept their attainment for themselves. This is counter to one of the core principles of the A∴A∴, that 'those who accept the rewards of emancipation for themselves are no longer within the Order.'[39] The Pratyeka Buddhas lack Compassion.

We can also gain some insights into Crowley's understanding and adoption of these principles, and its connection to the concepts of Aud, Aub and Aour (Od, Ob, Aour) as taught by Lévi (the active, passive and balanced forces).

In *Liber LVIII* ("An Essay upon Number"), when writing about the number 207, Crowley states that, 'AVR, Light. Contrast with AVB, 9, the astral light, and AVD, 11, the Magical Light. Aub is an illusory thing of witchcraft (*cf.*'Obi, Obeah);

---

37 Blavatsky.

38 Blavatsky, *The Inner Group Teachings of H.P. Blavatsky*, 34.

39 Crowley et al., *Commentaries of the Holy Books and Other Papers*, 4:11.

Aud is almost = the Kundalini force ("Ŏdic" force[40]). This illustrates well the difference between the sluggish, viscous 9, and the keen, ecstatic 11.'[41] Here Crowley is connecting the concept of Aud, the active force, with the magick of the New Aeon. 11 is the number of ABRAHADABRA, 'the Word of the Aeon, which signifieth "The Great Work accomplished."'.[42] The Word of the Aeon is a 'Word of Double Power',[43] through which the 'Adept becomes one with God'[44] It 'represents the establishment of the pillar or phallus of the Macrocosm of 6 positive ideas in the void of the Microcosm of *5 alephs*. *Aleph* is a void or *kteis*, being the Atu marked 0.'[45] ABRAHADABRA is 'the interpenetrating Spirit, within and without.'[46]

Beauty and strength, leaping laughter and delicious languor, force and fire, are of us.

Liber AL, II:20[47]

The above quotation from *The Book of the Law* seems to provide instruction or an insight into these dual elements from

---

40   "Odic Force" is a term given by Carl Ludwig von Reichenbach (1788 -1869) to a hypothetical force (life force or vital energy), and was named after the god Odin. This force was also called Od [ŏd]. Od is a term (as already seen) employed by Lévi to describe the igneous or active agent (igneous related to volcanic processes).

41   Crowley, 'The Temple of Solomon the King', 103.

42   Crowley, Desti, and Waddell, *Magick. Liber ABA. Book Four. Parts I-IV,* 539.

43   Crowley et al., *Commentaries of the Holy Books and Other Papers,* 4:358.

44   Crowley et al., 4:358.

45   Crowley et al., 4:185.

46   Crowley, *The Book of Lies,* 86.

47   Crowley, *The Holy Books of Thelema,* 115.

the perspective of the New Aeon. Showing that a state of "languor" (a pleasurable inactivity), and "leaping laughter, force and fire", are equally of "us". To this verse Crowley comments that 'one must be a flaming harlot – one must let oneself go, whether one's star be twin with that of Shelley, or of Blake, or of Titian, or of Beethoven. Beauty and strength come from doing one's Will; you only have to look at anyone who is doing it to recognize the glory of it.'[48] Our rest and our activity, our active and passive natures, our speech and our silence are equally tools for the accomplishment of our Wills.

Further, in *Liber Aleph*, Crowley provides instruction regarding the Lion, which shows the complexity and interchangeability between these active and passive elements (perhaps a sign that they are different manifestations of the same thing). He writes that,

His letter is Teth, whose Implication is a Serpent, and the Number thereof Nine, whereof is Aub, the secret Fire of Obeah. Also Nine is of Jesod, uniting Change with Stability. But in the Book of Thoth He is the Atu called Strength, whose Number is eleven which is Aud, the Light Odic of Magick. And therein is figured the Lion, even the Beast, and Our Lady Babalon with Her Hands upon His Mouth, that She may master Him. Here I would have thee to mark well how these our Symbols are cognate, and flow forth the one into the other, because each Soul partaketh in proper Measure of the Mystery of Holiness, and is kin with his Fellow. But now let me show how this Lion of Courage is more especially the Light in thee, as Leo is the House of the Sun that is the Father of Light. And it is thus: that thy Light, conscious of itself, is the Source and Instigator of thy Will, enforcing it to spring

---

48 Crowley, *The Law Is for All*, 102.

forth and conquer. Therefore also is his Nature strong with Hardihood and Lust of Battle, else shouldst thou fear that which is unlike thee, and avoid it, so that thy Separateness should increase upon thee. For this Cause he that is defective in Courage becometh a Black Brother, and to Dare is the Crown of all thy Virtue, the Root of the Tree of Magick.[49]

This Magick of Light, as indicated above, is intimately linked to the formula of the New Aeon - 'Now therefore understand thou the Formula of Horus, the Lion God, the Child crowned and conquering that cometh forth in Force and Fire! For thy Changes are not Phases of thee, but of the Phantoms which thou mistakest for thy Self.'[50]

Horus also encompasses these dual aspects in harmonious interaction. The Aeons of the Mother and the Dying God having been fulfilled, i.e. they have become conjoined, we have 'the appearance of Horus (Heru-Ra-Ha in his twin aspects (a) Force and Fire, and (b) Silence).'[51] The adept must know when to embody or manifest these twin forces. When to question and when to wait for an answer, when to act and when to be patient and endure. Knowing how to petition the gods, but also leaving space in which they can manifest themselves. One needs to know when to increase, and when to decrease – 'If thou thyself hast not a sure foundation, whereon wilt thou stand to direct the forces of Nature?'[52]

---

49   Crowley, *Liber Aleph Vel CXI: The Book of Wisdom or Folly*, 154.

50   Crowley, 99.

51   Crowley et al., *Commentaries of the Holy Books and Other Papers*, 4:185.

52   Crowley, 'Liber Librae Sub Figura XXX', 83.

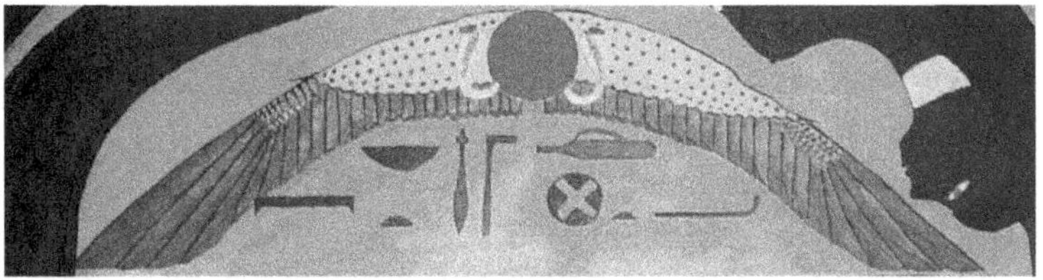

We can see that this interplay between the active and the passive, and the interchangeability between these things is one of the Keys to Crowley's teachings about magick and mysticism, but to wield these, one needs to have come to a conscious understanding and integration with their Will. The adept becomes Hadit or can observe the Universe from this perspective. 'As soon as one realizes one's self as Hadit, one obtains all His qualities. It is all a question of doing one's Will.'[53] This is the Baphomet consciousness – this moving from a still point, being open and compassionate (so that the Will is not restricted). These aspects are also seen in the nature of Kuan Yin as a cognate representation of Baphomet. The kundalini. The serpent power. The redeemer.

Infant Buddha

天上天下唯我独尊

Some iconographies of the Buddha show him after his birth, and this is often associated with the phrase 天上天下唯我独尊 ("I am the only one in heaven and earth" or "I alone am honoured in heaven and on earth" or "I am the most noble in heaven and earth"). In the legends surrounding the birth, Buddha was said to have been born near the ancient city of Ka-

---

53 Crowley, *The Law Is for All*, 101.

pilavatthu, coming forth from his mother's side, which emitted a seven-coloured light. The child then took seven steps forward (seven lotus blossoms bloomed from where the child's feet had touched the earth) while pointing his right hand to the heavens and left hand to earth. Images representing the infant Buddha in this position are primarily seen in Korea and Japan, and associated with rituals in which the infant Buddha is washed. Such a ritual is conducted during Hana Matsuri (flower festival) at Sensoji in Asakusa, Tokyo on April 8th, where people place flowers in front of a statue of the infant buddha (誕生仏像) and pour amacha (甘茶), a sweet tea made from hydrangeas, over the statue. This symbolises Shakyamuni's first bath, when he was was purified by sweet rain. This rain was triggered by eight great dragon kings (or the 9-headed dragon Kuzuryu (九頭竜), depending on variations in the mythology).

An example of this icon from the Ming Dynasty was even found in Western Australia (WA). 'The most exciting possible explanation for the object's presence in WA is that it came on the 1421 Ming treasure voyage, when the Chinese emperor sent the great explorer Zheng He to travel the world... A less potentially geopolitically sensitive explanation is that it arrived in the 150 or so years since the 1870s, when the Chinese are first known to have come to the north-west coast.'54

The statement uttered by the newly born Buddha as it is used in China and Japan is different from the original Pali in the Mahāpādāna Sutta, which is 'Aggo 'ham asmi lokassa, jettho 'ham asmi lokassa, settho 'ham asmi lokassa, ayam antim jāti, natthi dāni punabbhavo' ("I am the highest in this world; I am foremost in this world; I am the best in this world; this is the last birth; there is no further becoming here.").55 It is also written

____

54 Young, 'West Australian-Found Buddha Is a Ming Dynasty Treasure'.

55 'Buddha'.

that this was uttered with the 'fearless voice, the lion's roar'.[56]

In Japanese, there is a term called connected to the Lion's Roar called Shakubuku (折伏), which means "break and subdue". This is the Buddhist practice of challenging or breaking down others' false views. It is to bring another to truth. In one sense this is considered an act of courage and compassion.

Following his birth, in alignment to similar concepts presented in this work of stepping outside a bounded environment, *Siddhārtha* was protected from the outside world within palaces so that he would not follow a spiritual path and remain attached to the material world. However, as is well known, he eventually ventured beyond these confines and witnessed old age and illness, and the path of asceticism. Eventually he 'put on the saffron robe of an ascetic and wandered off into the wilderness.'[57]

As with the glyph of Baphomet created by Lévi, the infant Buddha is depicted with one hand pointing to the heavens, the other pointing to the earth. This gesture symbolises the unity of the world. The Buddha at his birth becomes a bridge between heaven and earth, the spiritual and the material – a representation of the potential of all people.

The meaning behind the Lion's Roar and the previous chapter on Kuan Yin is connected through figures where Avalokiteshvara is depicted seated on a lion. In The Metropolitan Museum of art in New York, there is a figure titled "Bodhisattva Avalokiteshvara of the Lion's Roar, or Simhanada Avalokiteshvara (Shi Hou Guanyin)" from the Ming dynasty (1368–1644).

---

56 獅子吼

57 'Background Story: The Life of the Buddha, Path to the Present'.

獅吼觀音菩薩 – *Bodhisattva Avalokiteshvara of the Lion's Roar, or Simhanada Avalokiteshvara (Shi Hou Guanyin)*

The Lion's Roar is also connected to the concept of silence: 'Among the hordes of animals that roam the wild, whether the jungle, the mountains or the plain, the lion is universally recognised to be their chief. The living embodiment of self-possessed power, he is the most regal in manner and deportment; the mightiest, the foremost with respect to speed, courage and dominion. The expression of the lion's supremacy is its roar—a roar which reduces to silence the cries, howls, bellows, shrieks, barks and growls of lesser creatures. When the lion steps forth from his den and sounds his roar, all the other animals stop and listen. On such an occasion none dares even to sound its own cry, let alone to come into the open and challenge the fearless, unsurpassable roar of the golden-maned king of beasts.'[58] It is a sound that subdues and silences.[59]

> Mightier than God or man, I am in them, and pervade them.
> Follow out these my words.
> Fear nothing.
> Fear nothing.
> Fear nothing.
> For I am nothing, and me thou shalt fear, O my virgin, my
> prophet within whose bowels I rejoice.
> Thou shalt fear with the fear of love: I will overcome thee.
> Thou shalt be very nigh to death.
>
> But I will overcome thee; the New Life shall illumine thee
> with the Light that is beyond the Stars.

---

58 Bodhi, *The Lion's Roar: Two Discourses of the Buddha from the Majjhima Nikāya*, 6.

59 It is also worth noting that in Egypt, 'Just as the warring king is often compared with violent gods like Sekhmet and Seth, he is frequently compared to aggressive animals, such as lions, in royal inscriptions... However, this line demonstrates that it was not simply the power or ferociousness of the lion that was relevant. The sound of the lion was also important, and the king was understood to share the lion's loud roar.' (Prakash, 'Emotions and the Manifestation of Ancient Egyptian Royal Power', 8.)

Thinkest thou? I, the force that have created all, am not to be despised.

And I will slay thee in my lust.

Thou shalt scream with the joy and the pain and the fear and the love – so that the ΛΟΓΟΣ of a new God leaps out among the Stars.

There shall be no sound heard but this thy lion-roar of rapture; yea, this thy lion-roar of rapture.

Liber LXVI, 56–66[60]

---

60 Crowley, *The Holy Books of Thelema*, 91.

Tanjobutsu (the historical Buddha Sakyamuni as infant).
Japan, Edo period, 17th- 18th century

THE HEAD

As previously discussed, one of the objects described by the Templars as representing Baphomet during their trials was a skull or a head with three faces. It should, however, be noted that in the confessions of the Templars the name Baphomet is not used to describe the idol used in worship. The Templar Gaucerant de Montpezat instead refers to a '*tête baphométique*' – a baphometic head[1] – a description that has been elusive for scholars. In *Les Grandes Chroniques de France*, a vernacular compilation (1270 and 1461) regarding the reigns of the French kings, is described 'the worship of an idol, which ... was an ancient embalmed head with "hollow, carbuncled eyes, glowing like the light of the sky".'[2]

Authors such as Keith Laidler go as far as to claim that the Templar head is, 'the embalmed head of Christ' (obviously buried under Rosslyn chapel in Scotland according to conspiracy and rumour). I do not wish to add to the misinformation and abuse of history,[3] but these views do point to an interesting archetypal connection between the worship of heads, beheading, Baphomet, and the state of consciousness that this signifies. Even though the testimony of the Templars under torture cannot be seen as reliable, it must be assumed that the various descriptions of Baphomet have had some source – they must have stemmed from something that the Templars were familiar with, either from within or without the walls of their order.

---

1   Marvell, 71.

2   Barber, *The Trial of the Templars*, 182.

3   For those interested in these kinds of books, I would direct them to Italian writer and philosopher, Umberto Eco's novel *Foucault's Pendulum*.

Heads in some traditions are seen as power objects. In tantric iconography (especially those associated with the *Mahāvidyās*), heads and skulls are prominent. *Tārā* and *Kālī* are often depicted with garlands of heads or skulls, and *Kālī* is known for her fierce iconography where she holds a severed head in one hand. This iconography is relevant to the study of Baphomet, even though the severing of heads represents death and destruction, they 'are said to represent the letters of the alphabet, particularly when the heads number fifty[4] or fifty-two and are threaded as a garland around the goddess's neck. As sounds or letters they are sometimes referred to as *Matrkās*, "mothers." They give birth to the creation in the form of sound...'[5] The heads that hang from the neck of *Kālī* represent death and destruction, as well as birth and creation.

> Death from the universal force
> > Means to the forceless universe
> Birth, I accept the furious course,
> > Invoke the all-embracing curse.
> Blessing and peace beyond may lie
> When I annihilate the "I."[6]

Kali by Aleister Crowley

---

4   Just as there are "50 Gates of Understanding" (Nun Sha'arei Binah).

5   Kinsley, *Tantric Visions of the Divine Feminine*, 153.

6   Crowley, *Olla: An Anthology of Sixty Years of Song*, 66.

Veneration of heads is also linked to humanities movement from societies of hunter-gatherers, to agropastoral. In this new phase, this "Neolithic Revolution", the veneration of ancestors became prominent. Here 'selected individuals (i.e., probably spiritual leaders) became ideological references who... were materially transformed into a physical presence of ancestral power in the earthly world. In this process, the skulls of these individuals were displaced from their bodies, followed by the decoration of the skull's surface with plaster and pigments, while shells were inlaid into the eye sockets. These reconstructed heads – the material embodiment of the spiritual essence of the deceased's soul – were placed within ritual houses in order to be visible to members of the community seeking to connect with the spiritual power of their ancestors in a form of animistic religiosity.[7]

Figurines of male heads from the ninth and tenth centuries B.C.E. have also been discovered in *Khirbet Qeiyafa* and *Moza* originating from the earlier period of the kingdom of Judah. 'The combination of archaeological contexts, time periods, geographic distribution, iconography, Ugaritic texts, and the biblical tradition indicates that these figurines represent a male god...'[8] These pottery heads were also found with representations of horses, and Garfinkel argues for a connection between these heads and the Canaanite god Baal being described as a "rider of the clouds". 'In the biblical tradition there are several descriptions, or metaphors, of the male god Yahweh as a rider.'[9]

---

7   Laneri, 'Why Ancient Mesopotamians Buried Their Dead beneath the Floor | Psyche Ideas'.

8   Garfinkel, 'The Face of Yahweh?'

9   Garfinkel.

There is none like unto the God of Jeshurun, *who* rideth upon
the heaven in thy help; and in his excellency on the sky.

Deuteronomy 33:26

Additionally, the emphasis of the facial elements Garfinkel
argues 'can be explained in light of the biblical expression "before the Lord," which in Hebrew can literally be read "face of
Yahweh," a term commonly associated with pilgrimage to cult
centres such as Shiloh (1 Samuel 1:22-23) and Jerusalem.'[10]

But Hannah went not up; for she said unto her husband, *I
will not go up* until the child be weaned, and *then* I will bring
him, that he may appear before the LORD, and there abide
for ever.

1 Samuel 1:22-23 4

Importantly, connection between the head and acts of worship are through the face and eyes. 'Another aspect of seeing
the face of a god during pilgrimage to a cult centre should be
noted. As the believer sees the face of the idol, in that very
moment the idol also looks at the believer. This is a metaphysical moment, a contact between earth and heaven, the core of
the religious experience. This moment is also described in the
Priestly Blessing in Numbers 6:24-26: "The Lord bless you and
keep you; the Lord make his face to shine upon you, and be
gracious to you; the Lord lift up his countenance upon you,
and give you peace."'[11] Here, prior to the banning of idolatry
within the Jewish tradition (Garfinkel argues this was in the
eighth century B.C.E.), it is possible that pilgrims could, in a
very real way, come face to face with God, through the medium

---

10   Garfinkel, 'The Face of Yahweh?'.
11   Garfinkel, 'The Face of Yahweh?'.

of a clay image. What remains uncertain is whether these heads were once attached to something else (either bodies or pottery vessels), but it does point to a form of ancient use of idols in the Jewish tradition, associated with male heads.

Jaime Paul Lamb argues (referencing an article by Tracy Twyman) that Sufi author Indries Shah claims that the Baphomet head is actually that of Mansur Al-Hallaj (Abū 'l-Mugīth Al-Husayn bin Mansūr al-Hallāj).[12] Al-Hallaj was a Persian poet and mystic, who was martyred in 922 when he was either decapitated or hanged. Shah (to my reading) does not make such a direct link between the head worshipped as Baphomet, and Al-Hallaj as Lamb states, but you could draw this conclusion by reading his chapter in *The Sufis* called 'The Head of Wisdom', and then the section titled 'Templars' in his "Annotations" at the end of this work. *The Sufis* was an attempt to 'highlight the sober and practical purpose of genuine mysticism, and to provide a sense of Sufism's universality, which, according to Shah, went far beyond its role in Islam.'[13] I will state, however, that I approach Shah with some trepidation, and I am aware that he has a number of detractors. Although some of his claims are of interest in relation to this work, I find his pages of unsubstantiated claims something to approach with a level of scepticism; rather, I take his work (hopefully as it was meant) as a mystical/magical text, whose purpose is to convey certain ideas and teachings to the reader, and I consider those teachings as important. In this way Shah and Lévi are similar.

Shah was also a friend of Gerald Gardner, and wrote on magic and witchcraft, so I can only assume he had some familiarity with Crowley's writings, and that this may have had an

---

12 Lamb, 'The Mystery of Baphomet', 7.

13 Zada, 'On Contemporary Sufism and the Works of Idries Shah'.

influence on his exploration of themes such as the Templars and Baphomet.

I also wonder if Shah was influenced by the writings of Adam Alfred Rudolf Glauer (1875–1945). Glauer was a German occultist and the founder of the Thule Society.[14] He was also a Sufi of the Bektashi order, and wrote a book called *Secret Practices of the Sufi Freemasons*. The foundations of his esoteric teaching have not been deeply explored, mainly due to the controversy surrounding him. Stephen Flowers warns of *Secret Practices of the Sufi Freemasons*, 'You have been warned that you are embarking on a strange adventure... Part of its content is well organized, clear, and concise; while other features of it are mixed with elements of a confusing and chaotic nature.'[15] Like Lévi, Glauer also had strong socialist leanings. As Flowers points out, 'Despite its outsider status the realm of the occult often becomes the breeding ground for revolutionary ideas.'[16] One of the keys to his work is 'the idea of the perfectibility of the individual. This is the root concept behind the exercises belonging to the science of the key,[17] as the ancient practice of Freemasonry is sometimes known.'[18] Glauer, however, believed that this extended beyond the individual, but 'The fruits of this

---

14   It is also of note that Glauer spent time in Australia prospecting for gold. He was also connected to the German Intelligence Service in Istanbul.

15   von Sebottendorff, *Secret Practices of the Sufi Freemasons*, 11.

16   von Sebottendorff, 22.

17   In a similar way Lévi described Baphomet as 'the guardian of the key to the temple.' Glauer states that Masons call themselves 'sons of the key' (Beni el Mim). I have not been able to find any reference to this in any Masonic literature, however, Freemasons have been referred to as 'Sons of Light'; with the science of Freemasonry called "Lux" or "Light" (Mackey, *Encyclopedia of Freemasonry and Its Kindred Sciences Comprising the Whole Range of Arts, Sciences and Literature as Connected with the Institution*, 829.)

18   von Sebottendorff, *Secret Practices of the Sufi Freemasons*, 22.

labor should [...] be transferred to the larger society in which the individual lives and this doctrine of perfectibility spread throughout the country... The individual can, in a manner of speaking, become something akin to a philosopher's stone.'[19]

With this the work of the Oriental Mason is finished—the work upon oneself. A raw, uneven stone has become a cubical one.[20]

Glauer describes the teachings and practices he is conveying regarding Freemasonry in the following way: 'These exercises are characterized by the use of the three signs of recognition employed by modern Freemasons: sign, grip, and word. However, they are not signs of recognition, not mere symbols in any case, but rather magical operations designed to induct the finer radiation of primordial power—to incorporate them into the body and thereby make the body more spiritual; to give the balance of power to the spirit over the body.'[21] It is also of note that as part of the practices he describes (the more coherent part of the book) is connected with the vowels I, A and O. He also states that 'the little gold[22] that is necessary is rarefied solar power.'[23] When undertaking the practices he describes, Glauer also warns, 'This can be done without injury, but care should be taken not to influence the head—it must remain free...we consciously block entrance to the head by means of the neck grip.'[24] Here Glauer makes a connection to the teachings of the

____

19   von Sebottendorff, 22.

20   von Sebottendorff, 59.

21   von Sebottendorff, 54.

22   Rarified gold

23   von Sebottendorff, *Secret Practices of the Sufi Freemasons*, 72.

24   von Sebottendorff, 79.

Sufi Freemasons and the concept of the head – the head must remain free.

Shah provides an alternative to Baphomet (Bafomet) being a variation of Muhammad, but states that it 'could well be a corruption of the Arabic *abufihamat*…The word means "father of understanding."[25] He goes on to write that a related term '*rasel-fhmat* (head of knowledge) means the mentation of man after undergoing refinement – the transmuted consciousness.'[26] Shah explains that knowledge and understanding are from the Arabic root FHM, and this also stands for derivatives that are associated with black.

> Baphomet is none other than the symbol of the completed man. The black head,[27] negro head, or Turks head which appears in heraldry and in English country-inn signs is a crusader substitute word (cant word[28]) for this kind of knowledge.[29]

Shah taught that the Templars thought in a Sufi way rather than Solomonic, and that the Temple Churches were modelled on 'the octagonal Dome of the Rock, built in the seventh centu-

---

25   Shah, *The Sufis*, 274.

26   Shah, 275.

27   In connection to this it is worth considering Crowley's comment in his notes for a New Commentary for The Book of the Law – 'Our work is therefore historically authentic, the rediscovery of the Sumerian tradition.' (Bogdan and Starr, *Aleister Crowley and Western Esotericism*, 182.). Black-headed is a description associated with the Sumerians. 'The people of ancient Sumer are sometimes referred to as 'black-headed people'…' (Karlsson, 'From Sumer to Assyria', 127.)

28   A "cant" is a word that has become jargon for a particular group. It can also refer to language used so often and mechanically that it becomes void of meaning.

29   Shah, *The Sufis*, 275.

ry on a Sufi mathematical design…The Sufi legend of the building of the Temple accords with the alleged Masonic version. As an example we may note that the "Solomon" of the Sufi Builders legend is not King Solomon but the Sufi "King" Maaruf Karkhi (died 815),[30] disciple of David (Daud of Tai, died 781), and hence by extension considered of David, and referred to cryptically as Solomon – who was the son of David. The great murder commemorated by the Sufi Builders is not that of the person supposed by Masonic tradition to have been killed. The martyr of the Sufi Builders is Mansur el-Hallaj (858-922), juridically murdered because of the Sufi secret, which he spoke in a manner which could not be understood, and thus was dismembered as a heretic.'[31]

أنا الحق

Here we can see Shah associating the Templars, and the worship of a head with a transmuted consciousness; a refined consciousness that is associated with blackness, head symbolism and the Sufi Saint, Mansur el-Hallaj.

---

30 'Sirri al-Saqti (ra) says, "I dreamt that Ma'ruf Al-Karkhi(ra) was seated totally absorbed in the love of God, under the throne and Almighty God said, 'O Angels! Who is this?' the Angels said, O God You are All Knowing. There is nothing hidden from you.' Almighty God said, 'This is Ma'ruf Al-Karkhi(ra) who is drowned in My love and closeness and until he does not see me, he will not regain his consciousness and neither will he gain contentment without his sight upon me.'"' ('Maruf Al-Karkhi – Sufiwiki'.)

31 Shah, *The Sufis*, 481.

*The burning and crucifixion of Mansur al-Hallaj (A leaf from an
illustrated manuscript on poetry, Kashmir, 19th century)*

There is additionally a claim made by Shah that the
shield carried by Hughes de Payen (c. 1070–24 May 1136),
the co-founder and first Grand Master of the Knights Templar, had an insignia featuring three black heads ('the heads of
knowledge'), but I have been unable to confirm the accuracy of
this, as all sources seem to return, uncritically, to Shah. Shah
goes on to mention other uses of heads in religious or magi-

cal contexts, such as Pope Gerbert's "brazen head", Albertus Magnus' "brass head", and, his pupil, Thomas Aquinas' 'head, which "talked too much."'[32]

There is also a link to Crowley, and the "brazen head" from a diary entry from January 12, 1923, which records a ritual undertaken to communicate with the spirit Belial.

> Belial entered into an Image of Brass and gave answers unto them that did sacrifice unto Him, and did worship the Image as their God.'[33]

I will discuss the brazen head in more detail later.

Another association that is often made with heads, is that of John the Baptist, and St. Paul, who in some accounts was executed by beheading, with imagery of both featuring a head on a platter or disk (although this is more commonly associated with John). John the Baptist is also discussed more fully elsewhere in this work.

In his writing on alchemy, Carl Jung discusses the head in relation to the Tao. He writes that the character for Tao (道) is composed of the characters of both "head" and "going", "walk" or "proceed" (辶 and 首).[34] Tao has been translated in

---

32　Shah, 275.

33　Beta and A.E.N., 'The Magical Link', 5.

34　Tao has also been rendered with the character 導, which "lead", "guide" or "conduct", and includes the character for hand, showing the dynamic nature of the Tao, and can also be connected to the concepts of "load stone" and "load star" - a magnetic stone and a guiding star, especially the Pole Star. As stated by Peter A. Boodberg, 'To sum up, we feel that the traditional translation of Tao as "the Way" does little justice to the wealth of the Chinese term's semantic connotations. What word should be substituted for "way" is a matter of choice and taste.' (Boodberg, 'Philological Notes on Chapter One of the Lao Tzu', 602.)

different ways (even as God by the Jesuits). Jung writes that "head" may be seen as consciousness and "going" as travelling a way - 'the idea would then be: to go consciously, or the conscious way. This is borne out by the fact that the "light of heaven" which "dwells between the eyes" as the "heart of heaven" is used synonymously with Tao. Human nature and life are contained in the "light of heaven" and, according to the Hui Ming Ching, are the most important secrets of the Tao. "Light" is the symbolical equivalent of consciousness, and the nature of consciousness is expressed by analogies with light.'[35] Jung writes further, which is of relevance to our exploration of Baphomet as a state of consciousness, 'If we take the Tao to be the method or conscious way by which to unite what is separated, we have probably come close to the psychological meaning of the concept. At all events, the separation of consciousness and life[36] cannot very well be understood as anything else than what I described earlier as an aberration or uprooting of consciousness. There can be no doubt, either, that the realization of the opposite hidden in the unconscious—the process of "reversal"—signifies reunion with the unconscious laws of our being, and the purpose of this reunion is the attainment of conscious life or, expressed in Chinese terms, the realization of the Tao.'[37]

The internal alchemical process as explored by Jung and connected to the attainment of the "diamond body" is a unification of (or bridging of) consciousness and life for which a

---

35   Jung, *Alchemical Studies*, 13:20.

36   The place in which consciousness and life are in unity is the "germinal vesicle", biologically the nucleus of an oocyte (a female germ cell in the process of development or immature ovum). '[F]rom the depths below, fire penetrates the seed and makes it grow, causing a great golden flower to unfold from the germinal vesicle.' (Jung, 13:24.)

37   Jung, 13:21.

"heating" is necessary. '[T]here must be an intensification of consciousness in order that light may be kindled in the dwelling place of the true self. Not only consciousness, but life itself must be intensified: the union of these two produces conscious life.'[38] Jung emphases that this process, this heating, or intensification is not a rational process (due to the partisan nature of consciousness) or the result solely of the exertion of will, but 'it is a process of psychic development that expresses itself in symbols.'[39] The central symbol that is expressed is the circle, the mandala[40] - the magic circle. These types of expressions are found in both the east and the west, such as representations of Christ with the four evangelists. 'Horus and his four sons were represented in the same way by the Egyptians. It is known that Horus with his four sons has close connections with Christ and the four evangelists.'[41] Jung describes the birth of light from darkness; the making conscious that which is unconscious – 'out of the "lead of the water region" grows the noble gold',[42] which is analogous to the processes of Kundalini yoga. The Unity of life and consciousness is the Tao, the "central white light". 'This light dwells in the "square inch" or in the "face," that is, between the eyes[43]... It is a visualization of the "creative point," of that which has intensity without extension,[44] in conjunction with the

---

38 Jung, 13:21.

39 Jung, 13:21.

40 Mandalas both being an expression, but also a vehicle to cause an effect in the viewer.

41 Jung, *Alchemical Studies*, 13:22.

42 Jung, 13:24.

43 I.e. in the head.

44 'Jung considered the creativity displayed in synchronistic events to be part of a *creatio continua* born out of, borrowing from scholastic philosophy, what he called the *unus mundus*, a realm both transcendent and immanent "where

"field of the square inch," the symbol for that which has extension.'[45] Jung's thinking was partially influenced by The Secret of the Golden Flower (太乙金華宗旨), a Chinese Taoist text on inner alchemical meditation. Jung provided an introduction to the Richard Wilhelm translation.

> As for the field of a square inch on the face, what can it be other than the heavenly heart? In the middle of the square inch dwells the splendour. In the purple hall of the City of Jade dwells the God of Utmost Emptiness and Life.[46]

---

there is no incommensurability between so-called matter and so-called psyche" (in von Franz 1992, p. 217). The *unus mundus*, like the tao, is the 'background of existence' and a 'potential matrix' (pp. 159-60) which gives rise to the idea of a continual creation, or *creatio continua*, which, as von Franz explains, "should be seen not only as a successive series of creative acts but equally as the eternal presence of the one creative act" (p. 48); in addition: "Synchronistic events are 'singularities' in which the oneness of psyche and matter, the *unus mundus*, becomes sporadically manifest" (Browne, 'Examining Coincidences', 14.). Additionally, Jung became particularly enthusiastic about Gerard Dorn, a sixteenth century alchemist who wrote extensively about the stages of the alchemical 'work' and its final fruition or consummation, which could "be expected only when the unity of spirit, soul, and body is made one with the original *unus mundus*"' (Browne, 34.)

45 Jung, *Alchemical Studies*, 13:25.

46 Wilhelm, *The Secret of the Golden Flower: A Chinese Book of Life*, 24. I have retained this translation by Wilhelm to reflect its influence on the thoughts of Jung in relation to it. It should be noted that it is now considered incorrect and misleading. 'In the first section of this text, for example, Wilhelm translates *zhixu zhiling zhi shen*, which means a spirit (i.e., mind) that is completely open and completely effective, as "God of Utmost Emptiness and Life." Based on this sort of translation, Jung thought that the Chinese had no idea that they were discussing psychological phenomena.' (Cleary, *The Secret of the Golden Flower: The Classic Chinese Book of Life*, 82.)

Reflecting, in some ways, the fifth power of the Sphinx (IRE, to Go), Jung writes that 'The "circular course" is not merely motion in a circle, but means, on the one side, the marking off of the sacred precinct, and, on the other, fixation and concentration. The sun-wheel begins to run; that is to say, the sun is activated, and begins to take its course, or, in other words, Tao begins to be effective and to take the leadership. Action is reversed into non-action; all that is peripheral is subjected to the command of the centre. Therefore it is said: Movement is only another name for mastery. Psychologically, this circular course would be the "turning in a circle about oneself by means of which, apparently, all sides of the personality become implicated. The poles of Light and Darkness are made to rotate; there comes a change from day to night."[47]

---

47 Wilhelm, 101.

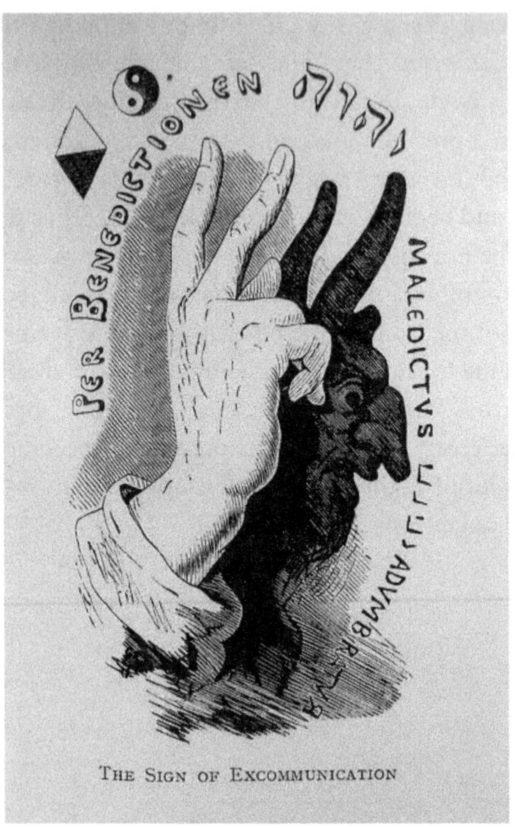

The Sign of Excommunication from Transcendental Magic

So here we have the head, one of the descriptions of Baphomet, as part of an expression of the Tao, seen as a union of opposites, of darkness and light. The state of equilibrium discovered is one of both stillness and of movement, of speech and of silence, whose primary symbol is the circle. This is connected with the "creative point", something that represents movement in all directions, expanded, undifferentiated consciousness, with Jung identifying consciousness itself with the Tao.

Absence of a Head

When I was born I had no head
My eye was single and my body was filled with light[48]
And the light that I was, was the light that I saw by
And the light that I saw by was the light that I was
     Douglas Traherne Harding – *The Incredible String Band*

Let us, by meditation and by all the true mystical practices, learn that the light of the body is the spiritual eye, and that the eye must be single, devoid of every thought of duality, to the end that the body and mind and soul shall be full of light.[49]

Since one of the representations of Baphomet, as confessed during the Templar trials, was a head, it is not such a step to consider that some of the mysteries surrounding the figure are therefore connected to decapitation – the removal of the head (or "headlessness").

In his book *On Having No Head: Zen and the rediscovery of the obvious*, D.E. Harding[50] describes the following state, supposedly first encountered during his "Himalayan" experience:

---

48 'The light of the body is the eye: if therefore thine eye be single, thy whole body shall be full of light. But if thine eye be evil, thy whole body shall be full of darkness. If therefore the light that is in thee be darkness, how great is that darkness!' Matthew 4:22-23

49 Crowley, 'The Attainment of Happiness | Vanity Fair'.

50 Interestingly Hardy was raised in the strict Exclusive Plymouth Brethren,

In any case, when I start groping around for my lost head, instead of finding it here I only lose my exploring hand as well: it, too, is swallowed up in the abyss at the centre of my being. Apparently this yawning cavern, this unoccupied base of all my operations, this nearest but virtually unknown region, this magical locality where I thought I kept my head, is in fact more like a beacon-fire so fierce that all things approaching it are instantly and utterly consumed, in order that its world-illuminating brilliance and clarity shall never for a moment be obscured.[51]

The head, representing the seat of the ego (of a limited, dual perspective) has been removed. 'The word of sin is Restriction' (AL I:41) - the bounded experience represented by the head is gone and has been replaced with a perception of 'boundless space'; not seeing from eyes (duality), but a single (non-dual) eye, like the unifying eye in the depiction of The Devil in the Book of Thoth.

Caput decollatus amisit, et pretioso nunc lapide coronatus incedit.

"The beheaded let go his head, and now goes forth crowned with precious stone"[52]

Peter Damian

In the figure of Baphomet, the human head is replaced with that of the goat, the animal of sacrifice connected to the Day of Atonement. The ego has been sacrificed, and the boundless has been opened to the Adept, or this boundlessness, this loss of self, is truly a mystery of the Magister. Here we should remem-

---

51   Harding, *On Having No Head*, 8–9.

52   Masciandaro, 'Non Potest Hoc Corpus Decollari', 25.

ber the correlations drawn between the scapegoat, and that of Christ (the goat's head, the scapegoat, on Lévi's rendering of Baphomet).

> Given such a description of the activity of the revivifying (s) word of God, I am tempted to read John's "animas decollatorum propter testimonium Iesu, et propter verbum Dei"[53] not only as an image of the resurrected souls of those who suffered physically for the Truth and thereby "won" eternal life, but as an image of those who were more truly slain by the word of God, who were decapitated in the sense of the surrender and death of the old self, and who thereby gained their true head, which is Christ...[54]

This new head, in a sense, could be seen as a crowning, the making of a king. As Edinger interprets, '"Even if you have to die, keep faithful, and I will give you the crown of life for your prize...for those who prove victorious will come to no harm from the second death" (Rev. 2:10-11). Here the gift for the victorious is a "crown" of eternal life. This crown represents the *solificatio*,[55] being anointed with a sun-like quality; those golden circles surrounding the head, that we often see in art, are halos of sunlight...What is ultimately being referred to is the deification of the recipient, identifying him with the sun, just as the apocalyptic Christ is identified with the sun...'[56]

Solificatio was a term employed by Jung, 'Since sun and

---

53 'The souls of the beheaded because of the testimony of Jesus, and because of the word of God.'

54 Masciandaro, 'John the Baptist and the Symbolism of Decapitation', 9.

55 'Vessel and content and the mother herself, who contains the father, have become the son, who has risen up from "blackest shade" to the pure whiteness of Luna and attained his redness (rubedo) through the *solificatio*. In him all opposites are fused together.' Jung, *Mysterium Coniunctionis*, 441.

56 Edinger, *Archetype of the Apocalypse*, 29.

gold are equivalent concepts in alchemy, the *solificatio* means that the "inwards of the head"—whatever we are to understand by that—are transformed into light, or "Marez," the precious white earth.'

> Thus from a Square, the Bed a Globe is made,
> And Purest Whiteness from the Blackest Shade;
> While from the Bed the Ruddy Son doth spring
> To grasp the Joyful Sceptre of a King.
>
> *Cantilena* by Sir George Ripley (1415-1490)[57]

In the 5th Aethyr of *The Vision and the Voice* ("The reception of the Magister Templi among the Brethren of the A∴A∴") we read, 'For the seer hath no head; it is expanded into the universe, a vast and silent sea, crowned with the stars of night. Yet in the very midst thereof is the arrow.'[58] Regarding the arrow Crowley comments, 'The arrow persists for it is the direction of Energy, the Will that createth all Becoming.'[59]

This state of "headlessness" could be compared to that of the Buddhist anatta, a doctrine of non-self. Although sometimes interpreted as a doctrine that denies the existence of a self, it is more a state of non-attachment. The question of an unchanging essence left unaddressed – the Buddha's answers to these questions 'seems to be No with a hidden Yes... This question was one he explicitly put aside.'[60] From a Thelemic

---

57   Jung and Jung, *Mysterium Coniunctionis*, 440.

58   Crowley, Neuburg, and Desti, *The Vision & the Voice with Commentary and Other Papers: The Collected Diaries of Aleister Crowley, 1909-1914 E.V.*, 205.

59   Crowley, Neuburg, and Desti, 205.

60   Bhikkhu, 'Selves & Not-Self: The Buddhist Teaching on Anatta'.

perspective, however, 'there is that which remains.' [AL II:9][61] As Crowley explains, 'for he can no more be destroyed, or his True Will be thwarted, than matter diminish, or Energy disappear.'[62] The Master of the Temple, the "seer" above that 'hath no head', has undergone a transformation after which he understands the Universe perfectly, and is utterly indifferent to its pressure. The Magister is free of this pressure because he understands; however, it is the Ipsissimus who is 'the Master of the Law of Unsubstantiality (anatta)...He has no Will in any direction,[63] and no Consciousness of any kind involving duality...'[64] In his early essay Science and Buddhism, Crowley succinctly and pragmatically describes anatta as 'absence of an Ego.'[65]

Another fascinating link to the concept of "headlessness" is found in the ritual captured in the Papyri Graecae Magicae V. 96–172 ("Stele of Jeu the Hieroglyphist").

The ritual text begins with:

I summon you, the Headless One,[66] who created earth and heaven, who created night and day, / you, who created light and darkness; you are Osoronnophris whom none has ever seen...you have distinguished the just and the unjust; you have made female and male; / you have revealed seeds and fruits; you have made men love each other and hate each other.[67]

---

61   Crowley, *The Holy Books of Thelema*, 114.

62   Crowley, *The Law Is for All*, 96.

63   Perhaps because it is in all directions.

64   Crowley et al., *Commentaries of the Holy Books and Other Papers*, 4:12.

65   Crowley, *Collected Works of Aleister Crowley*, II:246.

66   Acephalos (Ἀκέφαλος).

67   Dieter Betz, *The Greek Magical Papyri in Translation*, 103.

Crowley would use this ritual as the basis for his ritual titled *Liber Samekh*. This was written for his student Frater Progradior (Frank Bennett) in 1921 for the attainment of the Knowledge and Conversation of the Holy Guardian Angel. Crowley would translate "Headless One" in this ritual as "Bornless One".

This ritual is filled with concepts connected to creation and fertility, as we see commonly in this exploration of Baphomet, along with the balancing of conflicting forces. The Latin subtitle for this ritual is *'Theurgia Goetia Summa (Congress Cum Daemone)'* – Highest Goetic Theurgy (Congress with the Daimon). It was assigned in the A∴A∴ to the Grade of Adeptus Minor.[68] We can, therefore, see Crowley making an additional connection between this concept of being "headless"/"Bornless" and the experience of Holy Guardian Angel. Crowley assigned to *Liber Samekh* the number 800 (DCCC), which is קשת the number for 'a bow; ⟋. The three Paths leading from Malkuth; hence much symbolism of the Rainbow of Promise.'[69] – 'Yet in the very midst thereof is the arrow.'

Crowley also called this ritual "The Ritual of the Heart girt with the serpent", which is in alignment with the original text, in which the Headless One states 'my name is a heart encircled by a serpent; come forth and follow.'[70]

The sexual and related fertility aspect of the ritual is further highlighted in the words, 'I am the one whose sweat is the heavy rain which falls upon the earth that it might be insem-

---

68   The task of the Adeptus Minor (without) is to attain the Knowledge and Conversation of their Holy Guardian Angel. 'This is in truth the sole task; the others are useful only as adjuvants to and preparations for the One Work.' (Crowley et al., *Commentaries of the Holy Books and Other Papers*, 4:37.)

69   Crowley, *777 and Other Qabalistic Writings of Aleister Crowley*, 62.

70   Dieter Betz, *The Greek Magical Papyri in Translation*, 103.

inated...'[71] Crowley translated this more cautiously (and poetically) as 'I am He, from whom is the Shower of the Life of Earth.'[72]

An indication of what may be implied in the use of Headless/Bornless can be found in the words of the saint A Chö – 'If the mind is directed towards the Dharma, everything is easy, even dying. If our consciousness is realised as unborn, one is no longer subject to death.'[73]

Another example of the iconography of headlessness can be found in the Acéphale[74] created by André Masson (1896–1987), in conjunction with philosopher Georges Bataille (1897–1962), who Leon Marvell posits may have come into contact with, and been inspired by the "Stele of Jeu the Hieroglyphist". This relates to the *Akephalos* (Greek aképhalos "without a head") which refer to a headless demon. In ancient times these *Akephaloi* were executed criminals who then roamed without heads. This later developed in Greek-Egyptian magical writings to show a god to whom everything was open.

---

71 Dieter Betz, 103.

72 Crowley, Desti, and Waddell, *Magick. Liber ABA. Book Four. Parts I-IV*, 521.

73 Tiso, *Rainbow Body and Resurrection*, 30.

74 The Acéphale was, in one sense, a reaction against the growth of fascism.

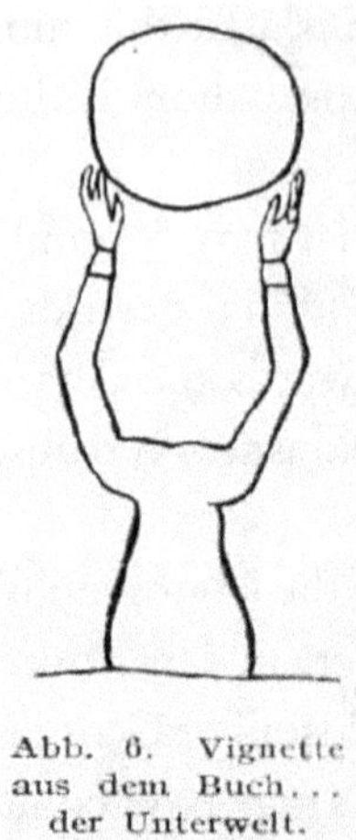

Abb. 6. Vignette
aus dem Buch...
der Unterwelt.

Egyptian drawing of the headless one holding a sun disk

Bataille writes in the *Encyclopaedia Acephalica*, 'The ace-phalic man mythologically expresses sovereignty committed to the destruction and death of God, and in this the identification with the headless man merges and melds with the identification with the superhuman, which is entirely 'the death of God.'[75] By being headless, we become something more than human or other than human, and the 'death of God' is most likely in reference to Nietzsche, with the death of God as a social construct, and absolutism at the core of the Christian faith. For Thelemites this is replaced with the personal deity - *'Deus est Homo'*. In the experience of headlessness we find that, '[a] magician who has invoked a Headless daemon into himself is of course no longer a man and not a god, but something that is neither one nor the other. He is himself but more than himself.'[76]

---

75   Marvell, 63.

76   Marvell, 65.

The human being arrives at the threshold: there he must throw himself headlong [vivant] into that which has no foundation and has no head.[77]

Georges Bataille

'THE OBJECT OF ECSTASY IS THE ABSENCE OF AN OUTSIDE ANSWER. THE INEXPLICABLE PRESENCE OF MAN IS THE ANSWER THE WILL GIVES ITSELF, SUSPENDED IN THE VOID OF UNKNOWABLE NIGHT'[78]

Georges Bataille

Acéphale, André Masson, 1936

---

77   Masciandaro, 'Non Potest Hoc Corpus Decollari', 15.

78   Masciandaro, 36.

In some ways the Acéphale is an image that was designed to instigate the 'apocalyptic annihilation of images…[the] herald of the sacred darkness that would subsume all representations'[79] The figure without a head cannot see, except in a transmuted, impersonal way, represented by the skull, the dead head, now in the position of the genitals.

Marvell sees the *Acéphale*, and the iconography of Baphomet as complementary figures, twins, combined in a chemical marriage to reveal what he calls 'Baphomet Restored'.[80] The headless figure and the figure with the animalistic head – the head of the individual, of the self, replaced with a kind of monster. It is in this impersonal state that one finds real power, or the ability to channel and direct that power that is latent in us all. 'The vacancy of the self is a form of subversion that releases the animal, while simultaneously it founds the community.' This "vacancy" is a destructive and a creative force, and it is both personal and impersonal.

> Without contraries is no progression. Attraction and repulsion, reason and energy, love and hate, are necessary to human existence.[81]
>
> William Blake

Alexandre Roig, shows the erotic substrate of the figure of the *Acéphale*, the skull concealing or subsuming the genitals. 'The little death expresses the paradox of enjoyment even in death, where the being loses itself, where, for an instant, it abandons the consciousness of its discontinuity and finds itself,

---

79 Marvell, 66.

80 Marvell's restored figure also combines elements of the praying mantis – an insect associated with decapitation during sexual congress.

81 Roig, 'The Headless Body', 2.

as in the religious bond, in a sense of "boundless" continuity. It is in this ruin of the subject, finally diluted, that the return to the body is experienced, that sovereignty is expressed for a moment in the continuity. The Energy is then deployed even in death; the body experiences sovereignty.'[82] It is in this "boundless", in this loss of self, that one becomes a king. 'The sovereign is what escapes, for a moment, reason, modernity.'[83]

Masciandaro draws parallels between decapitation and that of negation of the self, but also a death which is a new life – 'The moment of decapitation is here a moment of surrender, renunciation, and self-sacrifice. Bowing his head before God, the lover of God loses the head that was an offence to Him, only to find that such loss is not annihilation, but the birth of a new head, a new life.'[84] He also highlights that there are two aspects to the descriptions of decapitation in biblical literature. One represents the above humility and acceptance of death, the other is decapitation for being "stiffnecked" – prideful. One is to resist the loss of self, the other is to accept it. 'To lose one's head in this sense, to be killed by that sword, is to die to oneself and live in God.'[85]

I am a Traitor!–die the traitor's death![86]

Nor by memory, nor by imagination, nor by prayer, nor by fasting, nor by scourging, nor by drugs, nor by ritual, nor by meditation; only by passive love shall he avail.

---

82 Roig, 3.

83 Roig, 3.

84 Masciandaro, 'John the Baptist and the Symbolism of Decapitation', 2.

85 Masciandaro, 1.

86 Crowley, 'Liber Pyramidos Sub Figurâ DCLXXI – Technical Libers of Thelema – The Libri of Aleister Crowley – Hermetic Library'.

He shall await the sword of the Beloved and bare his throat for the stroke.

Then shall his blood leap out and write me runes in the sky; yea, write me runes in the sky.

Liber VII, V:46-48[87]

This presence of an underlying eroticism, sainthood and decapitation can be read in the description of the martyrdom of St. Agnes (circa 291).[88] In addressing her executioner, described as 'a fierce man with a naked sword', she states 'I rejoice that there comes a man like this [...] This lover, this one at last, I confess it, pleases me. I shall meet his eager steps half-way and not put off his hot desires.'[89]

Bernard Marillier, Marvell shows, also linked these themes of decapitation to the rites of initiation of the Templars. He thought the Templars were heirs to a 'mythico-initiatic' tradition, and that Baphomet symbolised the "rite of the severed head". 'The rite of decapitation is linked to a double initiation: by cutting off the head of an enemy – the initiate as conqueror – the neophyte receives both the mana contained in the head and spiritual power, and abandons his envelope of flesh for the Spirit.'[90] He further explained that, 'For the rite of symbolic decapitation, the Templars... captured the spirit and spiritual power, aligned themselves with the divine, and prepared to defeat both their visible and invisible enemies, the most formidable of which reside in the very depths of their being... The

---

87   Crowley, *The Holy Books of Thelema*, 28.

88   A saint who devoted her virginity to Jesus and rejected marriage. An unsuccessful attempt to burn her at the stake led to her execution by beheading.

89   Masciandaro, 'Non Potest Hoc Corpus Decollari', 32.

90   Marvell, 69.

neophyte, by reciting formulas and participating in dramatized scenes, identifies with the deity, allowing him to make his spiritual rebirth in intimate communion with the divine'[91] Whether this conception of the rites of the Templars is true or not, it provides a powerful insight into some of the ideas that have been woven around their mysterious idol.

When thou seest in the pathway a severed head, Which is rolling towards our field, Ask of it, ask of it, the secrets of the heart: For of it thou wilt learn of our hidden mystery.

Diwani Shams-i-Tabriz II.3[92]

In union with Thee, like the candle found the order that one, Who, beneath Thy sword, momently another head hath.

Divan-i-Hafiz 164.3[93]

Decapitation, and symbols and narratives that explore the absence of a head, or the replacement of the head with something new – a new life – reflect a state of consciousness freed from the fetters, the bonds of the self. It is only by yielding, by giving up oneself, that the aspirant may have the opportunity to come into contact with that 'Self beyond self'. Having died they are reborn, and perhaps gifted a new head, as a token of their Pure Will.

In a Christian context, Masciandaro highlights that it is only God that can be lifted up. Man can only lift his head towards the heavens as Jesus did during his crucifixion. But in the New Aeon and with the change in perspective that comes with

---

91 Marvell, 69.

92 Masciandaro, 'John the Baptist and the Symbolism of Decapitation', 1.

93 Masciandaro, 1.

this, God is now within – not without out. We can all by our own efforts be raised and experience that consciousness that is ourselves, but also beyond ourselves. In this state we may be crowned; not as martyrs, but ones who have given ourselves up to the beloved – the circumference that is nowhere found.

> Therefore lift up thyself as I am lifted up. Hold thyself in as I am master to accomplish. At the end, be the end far distant as the stars that lie in the navel of Nuit, do thou slay thyself as I at the end am slain, in the death that is life, in the peace that is mother of war, in the darkness that holds light in his hand as a harlot that plucks a jewel from her nostrils.'
>
> *Liber A'Ash,* 38[94]

The Light One

> I am like a black eunuch; and Thou art the scimitar. I smite off the head of the light one, the breaker of bread and salt.
>
> *Liber VII,* III:34[95]

Although this verse from *Liber VII* is still obscure to me, I think a doorway to its understanding is through trying to understand the meaning behind the "light one", who goes through the process of decapitation via the scimitar of the black eunuch.

In *The Angel and the Abyss*, Gunther, in connection with the symbolism of death and dismemberment, writes about the deity *Quetzalcoatl*, who he describes as the "light one", and *Tezcatlipoca*, described as the "dark one". This is curious

---

94 Crowley, *The Holy Books of Thelema*, 210.

95 Crowley, 19.

when we refer to Crowley's commentary on this verse, where he very simply states, 'Black and White'.[96]

Gunther writes, in relation to blood sacrifice and dismemberment, 'Another superlative example of this is found in one of the Aztec creation myths, where it was recounted how the earth was created when the "light one" *Quetzalcoatl*, and the "dark one" *Tezcatlipoca* dismembered the ancient great Mother Goddess *Tlaltecuhtli* and formed the earth and sky from her torn body…This is a creation myth with echoes of the birth of the Patriarchal epoch, demonstrating the separated world parents (the light and the dark) dividing the original "round" or womb, prototypical of the Great Mother, onto conscious components no longer dominated by the Matriarchate.'[97] Here then is an act of separation, the tearing of the body of *Tlaltecuhtli* – creating a duality from an original state of wholeness.

Quetzalcoatl is seen as a God of life, light and wisdom, lord of the day and the winds and the ruler of the West.[98] *Tezcatlipoca* is a God of providence, the invisible and darkness – Lord of the Night and the Ruler of the North. *Tlaltecuhtli* was seen as the God of Earth.

It must be noted that there is some ambiguity about the gender of *Tlaltecuhtli*, and the deity may have been seen to have a dual gender (described as both a god and goddess), therefore undifferentiated into male or female.

---

96   Crowley, Neuburg, and Desti, *The Vision & the Voice with Commentary and Other Papers: The Collected Diaries of Aleister Crowley, 1909-1914 E.V.*, 343.

97   Gunther, *The Angel and the Abyss*, 35.

98   Another entity that has been described as the "light one" is the ancient Egyptian Akh. This is an Egyptian term for intelligence, spiritual light, illumination, irradiation. This was associated with an individual who had died, was transfigured and commonly identified with light. 'Akh is the "light one" indeed, but not the light radiated by a kind of ghost is meant here.' (Elshamy, 'Ancient Egypt', 14.)

The "dark one", as featured in *Liber VII*, III:34, who is a eunuch, lacking the power of reproduction, smites off the head of the "light one" with the scimitar, a curved weapon that could be by its shape associated with the Moon. Isis (considered a moon goddess) is also connected to cutting (as pointed out by Gunther) through the "flint knife of Isis". The use of obsidian or flint knives continued after the development of metallurgy, and was used in ritual and mummification. 'More importantly, and more revealing, a flint or obsidian instrument continued to be used in the rite of circumcision. The Matriarchal source of this is further shown by representations of the lunar gods Khonsu and Thoth who also bear the stone knife.'[99] Here, perhaps, the unconscious (the night) slays the conscious (the day). The head of ego driven identification is removed, ahead of a new holistic integration of opposites.

So here we have a reference to a kind of *"separatio"*, but also a way back to unity, to wholeness - *"coniunctio"*. Bread and salt could be seen as a symbol of a covenant between two things, a covenant that had been broken, and the removal of the head part of the action of reunification. Bread and salt in the Hebrew both equal 78 by gematria. Combined they are 156, which is BABALON (please refer to my article titled "Bread and Salt" in *Ora et Labora, Volume III*).[100]

> I shall gain the Pain of the Goat for my prize; and the God that sitteth upon the shoulders of Time shall drowse.
>
> Then shall all this which is written be accomplished; yea, it shall be accomplished.
>
> *Liber VII*, III:59-60[101]

---

99   Gunther, *The Angel and the Abyss*, 36.

100 Walls, *Ora et Labora Vol 3.*, 2022, 119.

101 Crowley, *The Holy Books of Thelema*, 20.

The Brazen Head

In the previous chapter we discussed Crowley's use of the *Papyri Graecae Magicae* in his creation of *Liber Samehk* and its connection to the Knowledge and Conversation of the Holy Guardian Angel. Another ritual that exists in one of Crowley's diaries is a magical working with the spirit Belial. The significance of this becomes clearer when we note that Crowley refers to Belial as 'my own special ΔAIMON', and further that his ritual was entitled "The Brazen Head".[102] I am careful not to read too much into this statement, but it is tempting to link this concept, Crowley's "special ΔAIMON", the Headless/Bornless One and the experiences connected to the Knowledge and Conversation of the Holy Guardian Angel.

Belial is the 68th Spirit in the Goetia and is a 'Mighty and Powerful King' said to have been 'created next after Lucifer'. He is described as taking the form of 'Two Beautiful Angels sitting in a Chariot of Fire...[and] he fell first from among the worthier sort, that were before Michael, and the other Heavenly Angels.'[103] Crowley clarifies this description by writing, 'he was the leader of the "Old Nobility" who resisted the usurpation of the upstart Jehovah.'[104]

---

102 Crowley, *The Goetia: The Lesser Key of Solomon the King – Clavicula Salomonis Regis*, xxvi.

103 Crowley, 64.

104 Beta and A.E.N., 'The Magical Link, Vol. 9, No. 3', 5.

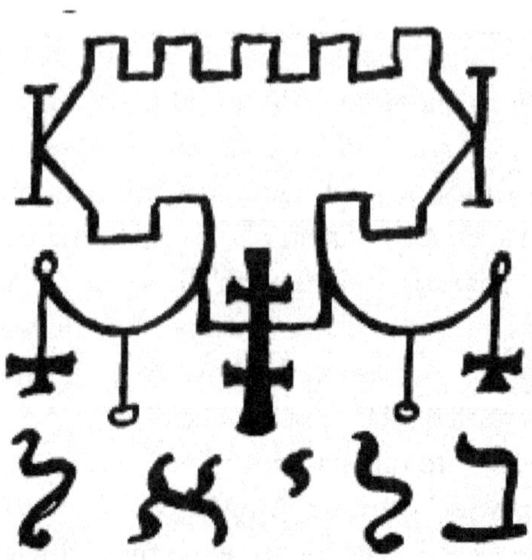

Sigil of Belial as drawn by Aleister Crowley

Crowley describes Belial as the "No-God Belial". The Image of Belial in the temple was to be of 'molten Bronze, after the fashion of the Head of a Man, such as the Magus ΤΟ ΜΕΓΑ ΘHPION shall by His Art devise, design, model, and execute in Red and Yellow Wax.'[105]

The concept of the Brazen Head has historical and literary precedents, and were either mechanical or magical devices that were able to answer questions that were put to them. This was a recurring motif in the medieval period.

The "mechanical" influence can be seen in Crowley's description of the head where 'within the Imago itself shall be contrived by the Art Magick of Reginaldus de Gouraldus an Organ of Speech, so that the Magus or Pontifex may be able to reply to the Postulant, or to direct that which shall be done

---

105 Beta and A.E.N., 5.

before the circle.'[106] Hymenaeus Beta comments that this may have been a two-way radio system.

One of the Saints of the Gnostic Catholic Church, Roger Bacon (1214–1294), is connected to stories about the creation of a Brazen Head. In Robert Greene's romantic comedy *Friar Bacon and Friar Bungay*, Bacon produces a speaking machine, but this is broken after uttering three things to Bacon's bad servant Miles - "Time is", "Time was" and "Time is past".

In Crowley's Belial ritual, the altar is described as being constructed of 'open brass work, but its top a plate of thin Iron.' Crowley comments 'For Iron is of Mars, who marrieth with Brass, Copper or Bronze, or Orichalcum[107] of Venus.'[108] A marriage of Mars and Venus, male and female. It is the active and fiery Mars, and the passive Venus that "yields", that can receive the message from the Brazen Head.

Belial appears in the Hebrew Bible, and later came to represent the Devil in Christian writings, so it is not surprising that Crowley took him on as his special daimon. Belial also appears in some Qumran texts, and appears to represent "otherness" - those who existed outside of the community; a personification of evil. Miryam T. Brand shows that there is a conceptual connection between Belial and Azazel through the shared use of the word *gwrl*[109] or "lot" that appears in both Qumran texts and in Leviticus. The "lot" used to choose the fate of the respective goats was through the action of Aaron. Likewise, 'The curse of the hypocrite in the Community Rule assumes that one's lot in Belial can be "placed" in the same way, as a result

---

106 Beta and A.E.N., 5.

107 A metal mentioned in several ancient writings, considered second in value only to gold.

108 Beta and A.E.N., 'The Magical Link, Vol. 9, No. 3', 5.

109 גּוֹרָל - Lot, portion (thing assigned by casting lots).

of one's actions.'[110] In this way Belial can be seen as a symbolic representation of the free will; one's ability to choose to exist within or without the defined community; beyond the defined borders. The term "lot" in this context might imply "decision" – to join the "lot of God" or the "lot of Belial". The Brazen Head shows where Crowley felt his lot had fallen. Yet in the Qumran texts, Belial was equally a creation of God to carry out his will, as men and women were created both good and evil.

In 1QM XIII, 11-12, (the Qumran "War Scroll"):

> You created Belial for the pit angel of enmity; his [dom]ain is in darkness, his council is for evil and wickedness. All the spirits of his lot angels of destruction walk in the laws of darkness.[111]

Belial was the Angel of Darkness, in opposition to the Angel of Light, sometimes identified with Melchizedek - 'In the very beginning God created two spirits, two angelic beings, one of whom he placed in charge of the Light, and the other in charge of the Darkness, one to be loved and one to be hated. This prince of Darkness is yet another interpretation of the devil. This time though, he has been created by God and given power over all those whom God assigns him, both spirits and men.'[112]

If we wanted to consider a response to the Qumran concepts of boundary, and the demarcation of the group from a perceived external evil personified by Belial, we should consider the 2nd Aethyr from *The Vision and the Voice*, in which is

---

110 Brand, 'Belial, Free Will, and Identity-Building in the Community Rule.', 86.

111 Martone, 'Evil or Devil? Belial Between the Bible and Qumran', 123.

112 Martone, 126.

given 'The understanding of the Curse, that is become a Blessing'. This is the 'Marriage of the Seer with BABALON.'[113]

I cling unto the burning Aethyr like Lucifer that fell through the Abyss, and by the fury of his flight kindled the air.

And I am Belial, for having seen the Rose upon thy breast, I have denied God.

And I am Satan! I am Satan! I am cast out upon a burning crag! And the sea boils about the desolation thereof. And already the vultures gather and feast upon my flesh.

Yea! Before thee all the most holy is profane, O thou desolator of Shrines! O thou falsifier of the oracles of truth! Ever as I went, hath it been thus. The truth of the profane was the falsehood of the Neophyte, and the truth of the Neophyte was the falsehood of the Zelator! Again and again the fortress must be battered down! Again and again the pylon must be overthrown! Again and again the gods must be desecrated![114]

The above vision was received on December 20, 1909, around 13 years before the working with Belial. Here the otherness, that which sits outside the community is embraced. The seer is Belial and the fortress is battered down and the gods desecrated; they must be understood for what they really are.

---

113 Crowley, Neuburg, and Desti, *The Vision & the Voice with Commentary and Other Papers: The Collected Diaries of Aleister Crowley, 1909-1914 E.V.*, 34.
114 Crowley, Neuburg, and Desti, 236.

Break down the fortress of thine Individual Self, that Truth may spring free from the ruins![115]

Ass Headed

Although the central image that has been focused on in this book is the depiction of Baphomet with the head of the goat, in *The Book of Thoth* Crowley described Baphomet as the 'ass-headed idol of the Knights of the Temple'.[116] To this Crowley adds a footnote, noting that 'The Early Christians also were accused of worshipping an Ass, or ass-headed god.'[117] Crowley specifically directs the reader to *The Ring and the Book*, and its chapter titled 'The Pope'. *The Ring and the Book* is a narrative poem by Robert Browning (1812 -1889). The work is based on a Roman murder trial in 1698 and is considered to be a work of genius (Crowley's references to it show his respect for the poem and poet).

I am unsure why Crowley mentions the chapter titled 'The Pope'. The only reference I can find to an 'Ass' in this work is in Chapter XII – 'The Book and the Ring':

Here skulk in safety, lurk, defying law,
" " The devotees to execrable creed,
" " Adoring — with what culture... Jove, avert
" " Thy vengeance from us worshippers of thee!...
" " What rites obscene — their idol-god, an Ass![118]

---

115 Crowley, *The Heart of the Master & Other Papers by Aleister Crowley*, 83.

116 Crowley, *The Book of Thoth*, 105.

117 Crowley, 105.

118 Browning, 'The Ring and the Book'.

I can only assume that Crowley was working from memory and made an error in his reference.

Crowley expands further on the connection with the Christians being accused of worshipping an ass-headed god, stating that, 'this is connected with the wild ass of the wilderness, the god Set, identified with Saturn and Satan.'[119]

A publication that Crowley would have been familiar with, as it published some of his writing and wrote about him, was *The Open Court* – Devoted to the Science of Religion, the Religion of Science, and the Extension of the Religious Parliament of Ideas. In February 1901 it featured an article by "The Editor" (Paul Carus (1852–1919)) titled *Anubis, Seth and Christ: The Significance of the "Spottcrucifix"*. Although this article commences with Anubis, and his role as a 'saviour from death everlasting',[120] it soon points out what Carus believes is an error in interpretation, arguing that the image of the Spott-Crucifix does not depict Anubis, but Seth, referring to the research of philologist Professor Richard Wünsch (1869–1915). The article explains the ass as being sacred to Seth and reads 'though the god is said to be ass-headed, it is only in the later days of Gnostic syncretism that he is plainly pictured as such'.[121] Carus also reminds the reader that in Tacitus, Moses was said to have followed the tracks of asses to discover water in the desert (perhaps explaining the link between Seth and the oasis expanded on later). He also references the story from the genealogy of Mary that tells of the high-priest Zacharias, who beheld 'in the sanctuary of the temple, the deity of the Jews with an ass's

---

119 Crowley, *The Book of Thoth*, 67.

120 Carus, 'Anubis, Seth, and Christ: The Significance of the "Spott-Crucifix"', 70.

121 Carus, 74.

head.'[122] For disclosing this discovery Zacharias was murdered as a blasphemer. Carus further references Plutarch, who wrote that Typhon founded Jerusalem and Judea after he struggled with "Hor" and fled on a donkey.

Carus believed it was probable that after the exodus of the Israelites from Egypt they brought with them some of its customs and institutions, and were 'addicted to the cult of Baal, who is frequently identified with Seth...'[123]

The article further quotes extensively from Mr. W. Pleyte who describes the god Tartak from 2 Kings 17, who was also represented as ass-headed. Pleyte believed that Tartak was worshipped by the Israelites along with the Samaritans. He further cites an interesting reference to the ass from the Talmud, Sanhedrin (fol. 63), where the firstling of an ass, like that of man, 'may be redeemed by another animal',[124] otherwise it would be killed.

> And every firstling of an ass thou shalt redeem with lamb; and if thou wilt not redeem it, thou shalt break his neck: and all the firstborn of man among thy children shalt thou redeem.
>
> *Exodus* 13:13

Ellicott in his commentary to this verse points out the connection between the ass and Seth, and the fact that, although the ass was seen as unclean, it was of great value due to its use as a beast of burden. Therefore "redeeming" it with a lamb would have been seen as a considerable sacrifice – 'There will always be in every nation those who grudge to make any offering to

---

122 Carus, 74.

123 Carus, 76.

124 Carus, 76.

God, and who will seek to evade every requisition for a gift.'[125]

The ass, it further argues, was named Chamor by the Hebrews due to its red colour, and this saw it connected to the red heifer, another sacrificial animal that in the non-canonical Christian tradition was associated with Jesus (Epistle of Barnabas). In the New Testament, this is taught to be connected to the descriptions in Hebrews of "without the gate" (Hebrews 13:12) and "without the camp" (Hebrews 13:12) when describing the suffering of Jesus.

The ass is also seen in the Dionysian Mysteries (where Dionysus who enters on a donkey is called Sabazios) and in the worship of Vesta. The ass was also associated with a Myth where the animal is brought by Silenus, and its braying gives the goddess warning when Priapus was intent on violating her. Because of this, in some iconography, Vesta is depicted with an ass and the animal is sacred to her.

These pagan practices and beliefs, Carus presents, found their way into the Church in the Middle Ages, where festivals dedicated to asses flourished in which an ass 'mounted by a young girl was conducted with great ceremony before the altar, and during the mass chants were sung which terminated with the imitation of the braying of an ass.'[126] The priest also gave the benediction by braying three times.

Carus, again quoting from Pleyte, discusses the accusations of the Israelites having worshipped God in the form of an ass – 'this head, if it ever existed, came originally from the temple of Typhon. If this opinion has any foundation, and if we may assume that this head was preserved in the temple, it is very prob-

---

125 Ellicott, *A Bible Commentary for English Readers by Various Writers*, 1:235.

126 Carus, 'Anubis, Seth, and Christ: The Significance of the "Spott-Crucifix"', 77.

able that the Israelites rendered homage to Seth in this form.'[127] Carus notes the "protests" of Josephus against any accusations of polytheism levelled against the Jews (as had become the case in his time), 'only serves to record the statement made by some Greek authors that a golden ass's head was taken from the sanctuary of Jerusalem by Antiochus.'[128] This association of the Jewish worship of an ass was later transferred to Christianity. Carus, however, believed that this accusation had some historical basis: the worship of Seth may have persisted among Egyptianized Semites, and later scriptural confusion between Seth the god and Seth the patriarch was subsequently transferred to Christ, with Seth being regarded by early Christians as a prototype of Christ.

> But if our tablets do in fact present Sethian doctrine, we have for a Gnostic sect two gods of the same name Seth, the Egyptian god Typhon-Seth, who is essentially like the Jewish Sabaoth, and Seth the son of Adam, who is the Jewish Christ, and the question arises, what the relation is of these two divine beings to each other. And I believe, in view of the widespread tendency of that age to assimilation, that the two beings thus related by name could not possibly have remained separate any length of time; a personal union was inevitable, and thus Typhon-Seth, as ass-headed, and Christ-Seth, the crucified, became one and the same thing.[129]

The Sethians, along with Valentinianism and Basilideanism, were one of the primary gnostic currents, who attributed gnosis to Seth, one of the sons of Adam and Eve. In the Sethian

---

127 Carus, 79.

128 Carus, 79.

129 Carus, 93.

creation myth, aeons emanate from the "unknown God", as a series of male and female beings in pairs.

Seth, the son of Adam, was considered after his father to have been the founder of the human race (Abel was slain, and his brother Cain's seed did not continue) and this may have been the source of a myth that 'Typhon-Seth was the ancestor of mankind, and directly of the Jewish people...'[130] This is transmitted by Plutarch – 'Some say that Typhon, after the quarrel over the ass, fled for seven days, and that, being rescued, he begot sons Jerusolymus and Judaeus, thus evidently involving Jewish matters in the myth.'[131]

Carus goes on further to write, '...when Christianity began its march through the world and even this Gnosticism was forced to take sides with reference to it, it was the phrase "the son of man," used of himself by Christ, that determined the conception of him formed by these Gnostics: Adam means "man", and the son who was called to found a new and pure humanity, is Seth thus Christ, the son of man, and Seth, the son of man, are united, and in case the latter had still preserved one idea of his Egyptian character a god was sure to result to whom belonged equally the symbols of the ass-head and the cross.'[132]

It should be noted that the above proposed links between the biblical Seth (third son of Adam and Eve) with the Egyptian deity are countered by Birger Pearson, who writes 'usually no evidence is given for this assertion, for the very good reason that there is none.'[133] He suggests that, if a connection were to be made with the Gnostic manifestation of Seth, it would be possible – albeit indirectly – by looking instead to Thoth.

---

130 Carus, 93.

131 Carus, 93.

132 Carus, 93.

133 Pearson, 'The Figure of Seth in Gnostic Literature', 80.

However, the ideas presented by Carus are relevant here, as they show ideas that would have been circulating within groups and expressed in publications Crowley would have been familiar with.

In the Spottcrucifix we see an ass-headed, crucified, figure that is most commonly seen to be a mockery of Christianity, or satire. Next to the cross is a man in adoration, curiously with one hand raised and the other lowered as in the Baphomet glyph. The inscription with the image reads 'Alexamenos adores god'. Carus put forward an alternative to the interpretation (referencing Wünsch) that this image may not be intended as a satire, and that it could be an "onolatry"[134] produced by Christians. To support this, Carus references another image from the Palatine, which is also ascribed to 'Alexamenos the faithful', which had not been identified as satire, and postulates that they were produced by the same hand. He argues that this 'cannot be regarded as the ridicule of an enemy.',[135] instead proposing it to be a 'symbol from the speculative sphere of Sethian Gnosticism.'[136] He further argues that this is evidenced by the presence of the Y next to the crucified figure, and posits that this was 'a secret symbol of the faith, known and understood only by the initiated; but a mocker would never have taken the pains to introduce such an isolated sign which would add nothing to the keenness of his ridicule.'[137]

---

134 The worship of donkeys or asses.

135 Carus, 'Anubis, Seth, and Christ: The Significance of the "Spott-Crucifix"', 96.

136 Carus, 96.

137 Carus, 97.

Spottcrucifix

As discussed, although the above theories are disputable, they would represent some of the theories and thoughts that existed when Crowley was formulating some of his concepts around the significance of Baphomet and cognate ideas, and were being explored and promoted by people he was acquainted with.

In *Transcendental Magic*, in the "Explanation of the Figures", the goat head on Baphomet is described as synthetic, uniting 'some characteristics of the dog, bull, and ass', which is further explained to 'represent the exclusive responsibility of matter and the expiation of bodily sins in the body.'[138]

---

138 Lévi, *Transcendental Magic*, xiv.

It has been pointed out that the word for donkey (ass) in Hebrew is (חמור), which sounds similar to the word in Hebrew for material (חומר), linking the symbolism of the ass with that of material substance. This, perhaps, sheds some light on Lévi's meaning above ('sins of the body'), with the goat incorporating the nature of the dog, bull and ass (loyalty, toiling, and bearing). But this head of materiality is marked with the pentagram, the 'symbol of human intelligence'. This sits below the torch, whose flame is 'an image of divine revelation', made so by the presence of the pentagram – matter and spirit are infused, made possible by human intelligence.[139]

I am here reminded of the 23rd Aethyr from *The Vision and the Voice* where it is shown '…a black bull, furiously pawing the ground. The flames from his mouth increase and whirl, and he cries; Behold the mystery of toil, O thou who art taken in the toils of mystery. For I who trample the earth thereby make whirlpools in the air; be comforted, therefore, for thought I be black, in the roof of my mouth is the sign of the Beetle.'[140] Crowley identifies this Bull with Apis,[141] and the beetle with the "Midnight Sun", 'the hope hidden in Earth.'[142]

Within Earth itself, within our very materiality, is the hope of redemption. This redemption, however, must come as a result of our own efforts; our personal toil, in whatever form that

---

139 Intelligence being the ability to not only acquire, but also apply knowledge.

140 Crowley, Neuburg, and Desti, *The Vision & the Voice with Commentary and Other Papers: The Collected Diaries of Aleister Crowley, 1909-1914 E.V.*, 73–74.

141 Apis is associated with the process of sacrifice and rebirth, and served as an intermediary between more powerful gods and humanity (such as Ptah, Osiris and Atum).

142 Crowley, Neuburg, and Desti, *The Vision & the Voice*, 74.

takes. As Lévi points out of Baphomet; 'The hands are human, to exhibit the sanctity of labour...'[143]

> I disport myself in the ruins of Eden, even as Leviathan in the false sea, being whole as the rose at the crown of the cross. Come yea unto me, my children, and be glad. At the end of labour is the power of labour. And in my stability is the concentrated eternal change.[144]

Crowley interprets the bull in the 23rd Aethyr partly as a personal message, 'A warning [...] not to allow himself to ignore or despise the plain facts of life. Mysteries – nay, even The Mysteries Themselves! – are apt to seduce the Aspirant. He becomes *exalté*[145] [...] instead of exulted'.[146]

A vision of a black bull also appears in the *Vision and the Voice* prior to his one, in the 25th Aethyr, where is seen as an 'Angel upon a black bull'. This Angel is preceded by the Angel of the 25th Aire and another 'Angel on a white horse.' Crowley comments that the Angel upon the black bull 'represents Jehovah and Jesus. The pain of Toil',[147] whereas the Angel on the horse is 'The Sorrow of Death'. These represent Old Aeonic points of view which are then swallowed up by a lion, which is the 'symbol of The Beast 666'. These two Angels are consumed and transformed by the lion, the avatar of the Sun,[148]

---

143 Lévi, *Transcendental Magic*, xiv.

144 Crowley, Neuburg, and Desti, *The Vision & the Voice*, 75.

145 In French this word can be directly translated as "exulted" in itself, but can carry the meaning of "excited" and in a pejorative sense, a "fanatic".

146 Crowley, Neuburg, and Desti, *The Vision & the Voice*, 73.

147 Crowley, Neuburg, and Desti, *The Vision & the Voice*, 62.

148 Crowley also identifies the 25th Aethyr as 'Caput Draconis, the head of the Lion-Serpent, the Beast 666...' (Crowley, Neuburg, and Desti, 62.). The

'and his roaring[149] shall enkindle the worlds.'[150] The pain of Toil is transmuted into 'the joy of the Earth!' and the Sorrow of Death is transmuted into 'the life of the Sun!'[151]

Although Lévi incorporates the ass into his description of the head of Baphomet, he does not discuss this animal much further in relation to this in *Transcendental Magic*. He does, however, reference several times the *Golden Ass[152]* of Apuleius, which is the *Metamorphoses of Apuleius*, the only ancient Roman novel written in Latin to still be complete. This is a tale of magic and of transformation (transmutation and metamorphoses), and a cautionary tale of 'love under will.' As Lévi states, 'This allegory contains the most hidden secrets of love.'[153] He taught that these elements (transmutation and metamorphoses) are the essence of Magic.

Lévi contextualises his understanding of the ass by writing, 'The ass has its merit, I agree; it was consecrated to Priapus as was the goat to the god of Mendes. But take it for what it is worth, and decide whether ass or man shall be master. He alone can possess truly the pleasure of love who has conquered the

---

Lion and the Serpent are invoked during the Gnostic Mass 'that destroy the destroyer...' (Crowley, Desti, and Waddell, *Magick. Liber ABA. Book Four. Parts I-IV*, 596.)

149 Remembering the "Lions Roar" associated with the birth of the Budha.

150 Crowley, Neuburg, and Desti, *The Vision & the Voice*, 63.

151 Crowley, Desti, and Waddell, *Magick. Liber ABA. Book Four. Parts I-IV*, 597.

152 'There is a record of as much as was lawful to be told in the Golden Asse, where Apuleius uses the words "I approached to the confines of death and having trod on the threshold of Proserpine, I returned from it, being carried through all the elements. At midnight I saw the sun shining with splendid light and I manifestly drew nearer to the gods above and proximately adored them.' (Torrens, *The Golden Dawn: The Inner Teachings*, 11.)

153 Lévi, *Transcendental Magic*, 133.

love of pleasure.'[154] Although, as is common around this time, women were seen as a kind of demon temptress. The message conveyed, however, for both men and women, is that the physical and emotional aspects of our constitution should not be allowed to overshadow the Will. These elements are important, are what make us human, and are there to be experienced, but they need to be kept in their proper place, and in a proportion that is healthy to the individual. Lévi's clear warning, and guidance, here is 'Love begins magician and ends sorcerer.'[155] There is a parallel in the above with Amfortas in Wagner's Parsifal, where he was given the guardianship of the spear, but while in Klingsor's domain, was seduced by a woman, which enabled Klingsor to take the spear and wound Amfortas, causing his physical suffering as well as shame for his failure.

Lévi says of transformation, 'The life of beings is a progressive transformation, and its forms can be determined, renewed, prolonged further, or destroyed sooner.'[156] It is acceptance of this aspect of existence that has the potential to free one from the dangers Lévi warns the reader about.

In the *Metamorphoses of Apuleius*, the main character, Lucius, after seeing Photis perform magic that transforms her into a bird, begs her to likewise transform him. During this operation, however, she accidentally turns him into an ass. He is told that the only way he can be returned to his human form is to eat a "fresh rose". Lucius is, however, stolen, and goes on a series of adventures, elements of which are connected with human love, lust and emotions, including various inserted tales (such as one about Cupid and Psyche). At the end of the story, Lucius, on a beach, purifies himself by immersing himself sev-

---

154 Lévi, 31.

155 Lévi, 301.

156 Lévi, 302.

en times in the sea, and then prays to the Queen of Heaven to make him human again. His prayers are answered by the eating of a crown of roses during a religious procession. In return for this he is initiated via the *Navigium Isidis* (vessel of Isis)[157] and made a priest of Isis. He is later initiated into the Mysteries of Isis,[158] and initiated further until he is appointed to the College of Pastophori (Shrine-Bearer), and he then serves the mysteries of Osiris and Isis.

> And a garland of flowers was upon my head, with white palm-leaves sprouting out on every side like rays; thus I was adorned like unto the sun, and made in the fashion of an image.[159]

Our hero (if we can call him that), after undergoing many trials, eventually undertakes a process of progressive initiation that opens up to him the true mysteries of life. Lucius' initial error was to seek transformation by the efforts of another. It was not until he took action himself, purifying himself and offering heartfelt prayers, that initiation and transformation was opened to him. This is supported by the description of the head of Baphomet from *Transcendental Magic* given earlier. Because of the presence of the upright pentagram, the sign of the Microcosm and human intelligence, can the flame be considered a symbol of divine revelation.

---

157 This celebrated Isis' influence on the sea and the safety of seafarers. This later transferred to the Roman people themselves and the Roman leadership.

158 The Metamorphoses of Apuleius is the only place that these rites are described. The candidate undergoes purification before descending into the inner sanctum of the temple. There they experience a ritual death and rebirth before having a vision of the gods.

159 Adlington and Apuleius, 'The Project Gutenberg eBook of The Golden Asse, by Lucius Apuleius'.

Let not the priest of Isis uncover the nakedness of Nuit, for every step is a death and a birth. The priest of Isis lifted the veil of Isis, and was slain by the kisses of her mouth. Then was he the priest of Nuit, and drank of the milk of the stars.

Liber LXV, V:50[160]

Crowley also describes Baphomet as "ass headed" in Chapter 33 of *The Book of Lies*, as well as making a direct link between the "ass headed" idol and the Knight Templars, specifically its final Grand Master, Jacobus Burgundus Molensis the martyr. Crowley further (as indicated by the number of the chapter) links Baphomet to the 33° of Freemasonry. Here is described a Black two-headed Eagle[161] bearing a sword and a black triangle as GOD. This is, of course, the well-known symbol of the Ancient and Accepted Scottish Rite of Freemasonry and adorns the cover of Albert Pike's *Morals and Dogma*.

When writing about the alchemists and their symbols, Pike states, 'All the Masters in Alchemy who have written of the Great Work, have employed symbolic and figurative expressions; being constrained to do so, as well to repel the profane from a work that would be dangerous for them, as to be well understood by Adepts, in revealing to them the whole world of analogies governed by the single and sovereign dogma of Hermes. So, in their language, gold and silver are the King and Queen, or the Sun and Moon; Sulphur, the flying Eagle; Mercury, the Man-woman, winged, bearded, mounted on a cube, and crowned with flames; Matter or Salt, the winged Dragon; the

---

160 Crowley, *The Holy Books of Thelema*, 81.

161 It should be noted that the two-headed eagle was also the personal standard of Saladin, considered a model of chivalry. If not always historically accurate, this vision of Saladin has had a lasting impact (especially within fraternal and chivalric orders) in the West.

Metals in ebullition, Lions of different colors; and, finally, the entire work has for its symbols the Pelican and the Phœnix.'[162]

This is striking,[163] and a clear reference to Lévi's Baphomet[164] - 'Mercury, the Man-woman, winged, bearded, mounted on a cube, and crowned with flames...' It is also interesting that this is from the chapter in which Pike is writing about the degree called "Knight of the Sun, or Prince Adept". Additionally, the "flying Eagle" is given as a cognate emblem of these mysteries.

The Knight of the Sun initiation is held in a "Council-Chamber" in which are hung banners representing the 'open country – mountains, plains, forests and fields.'[165] This represents the wilderness, and in this environment is a single Light in the South to represent the Sun. The lecture portion of this initiation speaks of 'one God, uncreated, eternal, infinite, and inaccessible...'[166] The rite further goes on to explain that 'the soul of man is immortal, and his existent life but a point in the centre of eternity: that harmony is in equilibrium, and equilibrium

---

162 Pike, *Morals and Dogma of the Accepted and Ancient Scottish Rite of Freemasonry*, 774.

163 Striking, but not surprising. Pike borrowed extensively from Lévi to the extent that, by contemporary standards, it would be considered plagiarism. Robert L. Uzzel considers that 'Pike was the primary agent for the transmission of Lévi's ideas in nineteenth-century America.' (Uzzel, *Eliphas Levi and the Kabbalah: The Masonic and French Connection of the American Mystery Tradition*, 68.)

164 Uzzel highlights the strong influence Lévi had on Pike – 'Lévi was not the only influence on Pike, but he was certainly one of the major ones.' (Uzzel, 68.)

165 McClenechan, 'AASR – 1884 – 28th Degree: Knight of the Sun (or Prince Adept)'.

166 McClenechan.

subsists by the analogy of contraries:[167] that analogy is the key of all secrets of nature and the sole reason of being of all revelations...'[168] This all sounds very familiar, and the argument further explains that 'Magism was made for kings and priests alone. He who dreads to lose his own ideas, and fears new truths, and is not disposed to doubt everything, rather than admit anything at random, should not seek to learn the teachings of this degree.'[169] The teachings of this degree are for priests and kings; knights of the Sun.

This degree also has resonances with some of the teachings and instructions in *Liber AL*:

Death *is not* for the sage. It is a phantom...

Change is the evidence of movement, and movement reveals *life* alone.

If change should be called death, we die and are born again every day...

What we call death is change.

There is no real death in nature; all is living.

Man is what deity meant he should be – imperfect, feeble, fallible, liable to err, and sensitive to pain, but capable of improvement and progression, and of a heroism that can smile

---

167 The number of this degree in the Scottish Right is 28, and this is also the number of the Hebrew for Union or unity (יחוד), and also power (כה).

168 McClenechan, 'AASR – 1884 – 28th Degree: Knight of the Sun (or Prince Adept)'.

169 McClenechan.

at agony, be content with destitution, persevere and equal
mind under the lash of injustice, and without unmanly fear
await the approach of death and count the pulse of his life.
The man who can do this has attained the equilibrium of faith
and reason, and may claim to be called Magus, Prince, Adept,
and Knight of the Sun.[170]

So, in this degree, with what appears in the writings of Pike,
there is a clear connection to the mysteries of Baphomet, but
in a Masonic context. Also in relation to this, as seen above,
Crowley makes reference to the last Master of the Temple,
Jacobus Burgundus Molensis, who Crowley seems to be connecting (through the symbolism of his death) with these principles.

> This Eagle is burnt up in the Great Fire; yet not a
> feather is scorched. This Eagle is swallowed
> up in the Great Sea; yet not a feather is wetted. So
> flieth He in the air, and lighteth upon the earth at
> His pleasure.

> So spake IACOBUS BURGUNDUS MOLENSIS
> the Grand Master of the Temple; and of the GOD
> that is Ass-headed did he dare not speak.[171]

As the Sun rises and sets with the illusion of death, so does
the Eagle, and the Grand Master, and Knight of the Sun. They
engage with the elements (the Tetragrammaton) in life, but are
untouched by them. They are living among the elements, in the
wilderness, in the desert, in the sunlight.

---

170 McClenechan.

171 Crowley, *The Book of Lies*, 76.

In relation to the Grand Master, Crowley states, 'The secrets of his order were, however, not lost, and are still being communicated to the worthy by his successors, as intimated by the last paragraph, which implies knowledge of a secret worship, of which the Grand Master did not speak.'[172] He did not speak of the 'GOD that is Ass-headed'.[173] Although there is confusion about the dates associated with the publication of *The Book of Lies*, it is clear that Crowley believed that the "successors" were the OTO, and one of its degrees is clearly titled "Illustrious Knights Templar of the Order of Kadosh & Companion of the Holy Grail". Crowley further points to these mysteries, mysteries of generation, by highlighting that the initials of the Grand Master are I.B.M, and that these are the Three Pillars of the Temple. By gematria this is '52, 13X4, BN,[174] the Son.'[175] In one sense implying rebirth or generation. By gematria we have the Hebrew word (ירבא), which equals 13. This is *to enter, go within, penetrate; have sex.*[176] This forms the idea of entering into the four elements. 13 is also Achad (אחד), which means unity.

In another part of *The Book of Lies* Crowley identifies the Son with 'Osiris-Apis the Redeemer, with whom the Master (Fra. P.) identifies himself.'[177] This is from the commentary to Chapter 52, "The Bull Baiting", which touches on the ideas written about elsewhere in this Work, that was emphasised by Lévi in relation to Baphomet, about the importance of work in The Great Work and its connection to the bull; 'learn first what

---

172 Crowley, 77.

173 Crowley, 33.

174 בן

175 Crowley, *The Book of Lies*, 115.

176 Heidrick, 'HEBREW GEMATRIA: Values from 10 – 19'.

177 Crowley, *The Book of Lies*, 115.

is work! and THE GREAT WORK is not so far beyond.'[178] This chapter also indicates the importance of silence in the completion of the Work (stillness in motion and motion in stillness).

If we further examine the elements above as IHVH and spell the Tetragrammaton in full, we get IVD HH VV HH (יודההוודהה), we also find the value of 52 – creation fully manifested is experienced in the son. The son is concealed within the Tetragrammaton, and this expanded Tetragrammaton is its spelling in Assiah,[179] as given in *The Qabbalah Unveiled*. BN is the "Secret Name" or "Secret Nature" of Assiah[180] - the world of action. 52 also reduces to 7, showing the operation of Love in this process. This is reflected again in other gematria related to the number 52; the Supernal Mother (אימא), and Father and Mother (אבא ואמא).

Rita Lucarelli in her research into Graeco-Egyptian Papyri highlights the clear connection between the ass and the god Seth, and from the fifth century BCE the association between Seth and the ass also became connected to Typhon. The ancient Egyptian for Seth[181] 'is determined from the Middle Kingdom with the Seth animal [...] and it appears as a manifestation of Seth in animal form or as a hybrid with human body and donkey head until the Graeco-Roman period...'[182]

Seth (or Set) is a fascinating deity, associated with the strange and frightening (such as thunderstorms, eclipses and earthquakes).[183] He represented the desert, and by extension

---

178 Crowley, 114.

179 The Material World

180 MacGregor Mathers, *The Kabbalah Unveiled*, 32–33.

181 ꜥꜣ,

182 Lucarelli, 'The Donkey in the Graeco-Egyptian Papyri', 89.

183 Seth is also a very ancient god, and was possibly the first "state" god; 'certainly he was closely associated with the kingship in Early Dynastic times

the lands beyond the desert and things that are foreign. You see the hieroglyph for Seth featured in the words for "turmoil", "confusion", "illness", "storm", and "rage". Yet, at the same time, he was seen as a friend of the dead, assisting them to heaven on his ladder. He was also the protector of the oasis of the desert (a source of life in a barren land). He represents the turmoil of change, but also the benefits that come from the embrace of change, and the necessity of destruction and death (transformation) in the working of nature. Although often considered a god of confusion, Turner instead proposes the description of a 'complex god', which I think is far more appropriate given Seth's complex history and ever-changing place in the minds of the Egyptians through the stages of their development and decline, and how the god was considered in different locations. Turner also argues, 'Perhaps within the general populace Seth always held a position of particular affection...'[184] His characteristics would have reminded them of themselves, their families and their communities. 'His quarrelsome nature, his strength and his might and, indeed, his liking for drink and sex were all things that they could readily identify within themselves and their families and friends and may well have contributed to his popularity which probably reached its zenith under the Ramessides.'[185] In Seth, people saw themselves and 'unlike the other deities, Seth always remains something of an enigma to the ancient Egyptians. He exists on the boundary between the transitory and the everlasting, the same boundary that separates order and chaos.'[186] In *Liber A'ash* there is an indication of Seth's nature as a god of the boundary. Seth is the "holy covenant", the 'New Covenant of the Open Way, the Covenant

(Turner, 'Seth: A Misrepresented God in the Egyptian Pantheon?', 28.)

184 Turner, 162.

185 Turner, 161–62.

186 Turner, 14.

of Hoor-Set in the Path of the Great Return.'[187] Seth represents the work of destruction necessary to eventually, if the aspirant perseveres, become Hoor-Set, fulfilling the Covenant between God and Man.[188]

> Set is his holy covenant, that he shall display in the great day of M.A.A.T., that is being interpreted the Master of the Temple of A∴A∴, whose name is Truth.
>
> *Liber A'Ash, 7*[189]

Connected to the above is an inscription on the tomb of Thuthmosis III:

> *This god* (i.e. Ra) *enters through the western gateway of the horizon. Seth stands upon the riverbank.*

Here Seth could be interpreted as a menacing figure; 'murderer of Osiris and as a possible threat to the sun-god himself.'[190] This story is divided into twelve hours, the above is described in the first, whereas in the twelfth a figure is shown, with the heads of both Horus and Seth; a unification and resolution of the dark and the light – a reconciliation of opposites. I see Seth on the riverbank as both the guardian (threat or challenge to the individual) and a gateway (vehicle of transformation that leads to reconciliation and redemption – that which unifies the individual with that which lies beyond it). Seth stands on the riverbank, on the threshold – waiting on the other side.

---

187 Gunther, *The Angel and the Abyss*, 232.

188 Shown in the Ritual Attitudes of *Sa* (Man) and *Neter* (God). This is The Woman Satisfied, shown in the Sign of the Grade Mater Triumphans, which is also called Set Triumphant. This is the Great Work accomplished ($5°=6^{\square}$).

189 Crowley, *The Holy Books of Thelema*, 207.

190 Turner, 'Seth: A Misrepresented God in the Egyptian Pantheon?', 67.

The way has been opened unto the Abodes that are beyond Decay, and it may be ours now, before an hour hath struck upon the bell, and forever more.[191]

In verse 21 of *Liber A'ash* there is listed a number of "sacred animals", which also includes humanity:

These animals are sacred unto me; the goat, and the duck, and the ass, and the gazelle, the man, the woman and the child

The gazelle is an animal mentioned in *The Contendings of Horus and Seth*:

'Now as for Horus, he was lying under a shenusha-tree in the land of the oasis. Seth found him, seized hold of him, threw him down upon his back on the mountain, removed his two eyes from their sockets, and buried them on the mountain so as to illumine the earth. The two balls of his eyes became two bulbs which grew into lotuses. Seth came away and told Re-Harakhti falsely: "I did not find Horus" - although he had found him.

Then Hathor, Mistress of the Southern Sycamore, set out, and she found Horus lying weeping in the desert. She captured a gazelle and milked it. She said to Horus: "Open your eye(s) that I may put this milk in them."

Then he opened his eye(s) and she put the milk in them, putting some in the right one and putting some in the left one. She told him: "Open your eye(s)." And he opened his eye(s). (She) looked at them and found that they were healed.[192]

---

191 Gunther, *The Angel and the Abyss*, 232.

192 Carawan, 'The Contendings of Horus and Set'.

It is the milk of the gazelle that served to make Horus whole again, by restoring his eye and his sight.

A'ash, as is shown in Appendix 2 to *Initiation in the Aeon of the Child* is attributed to the Ritual Attitude that is translated as "summons". This attitude is related to the South, the direction associated with Seth in the Northern Hemisphere. This is also Leo, the Lion Serpent and the Egyptian deity Mau. This sign also connects to the Hebrew Vau, the Son, and AL, God. The South is Hadit, and the North is Nuit (desert and ocean). A'ash is also the Ritual Attitude assumed by Ankh-af-na-khonsu (Ankhefenkhons i) on the Stele of Revealing, as he stands before Re-Harakhty (Ra-Hoor-Khuit).

In the Pyramid Texts, Seth is depicted in positive, negative and neutral ways. In some texts he is not the murderer of Osiris but is shown to assist him in his ascent to heaven by either lifting him up or providing a ladder. 'The dead king is to be feared [...] and has escaped death like Seth.'[193] Seth helps to remove the fetters of Osiris and resurrect him.

> O meal and honey and oil! O beautiful flag on the moon, that she hangs out in the centre of bliss!
>
> These loosen the swathings of the corpse; these unbind the feet of Osiris, so that the flaming God may rage through the firmament with his fantastic spear.[194]
>
> *Liber VII*, VII:2-3[195]

---

193 Turner, 'Seth: A Misrepresented God in the Egyptian Pantheon?', 43.

194 It is worth noting that the spear is commonly associated with Seth in Egyptian mythology and iconography. Here it seems as if, through his liberation, Osiris has taken on some of the characteristics of Seth.

195 Crowley, *The Holy Books of Thelema*, 32.

In both the working of Osiris and Horus, Seth is a power that forever lies underneath. As taught by Gunther, one must first understand Osiris, before one can understand Horus. The candidate needs to embrace and understand their mortality, their humanity, before they can enter the mysteries of their eternal nature.

> Not Isis my mother, nor Osiris my self; but the incestuous Horus given over to Typhon,[196] so may I be.
>
> *Liber VII*, I:30

Most readers would be familiar with the mythological connection between Seth and Horus, and the mediating, or healing, role played by Thoth in this relationship. Thoth heals the eye of Horus,[197] and the testicles of Seth.[198] 'The Eye of Horus, whose graphical form seems to incorporate aspects of the eyes of a human, a hawk, and a leopard or cheetah, is called the wedjat [wḏꜣt], or 'Sound <Eye>', from *w* , meaning healthy, flourishing, or prosperous or, as a verb, to proceed or attain. Its hieroglyph depicts a papyrus stalk, and hence it is also literally 'green', with all of the other meanings seeming to flow from the metaphor of vegetable growth.'[199] Seth's testicles are an obvious symbol of his fertility, and the loss used to explain the barrenness of the desert. The conflict between *Horus and Seth* was a contest of legitimacy. Was the throne to belong to the legitimate successor of Osiris (Horus his son) or was the cosmic sovereignty 'to be accorded to brute force — or more charitably, sheer animal

---

196 Set

197 In some versions of the myth it is Hathoor who heals Horus.

198 Acknowledging the variations in this mythology over time and the position of the deities in the Egyptian pantheon.

199 Butler, 'The Nature and Functions of Thoth in Egyptian Theology', 238–39.

vigour...'[200] Horus, as the son of Osiris, carries Osiris' humanity, his mortality. Seth is acknowledged to be the stronger of the two claimants, but Horus' healing, the restoration of the *wedjat*, forms a bond between him and Thoth, and therefore 'between the functions of *wisdom* and *sovereignty*...'[201] In the end it is not brute force that settles the dispute between Horus and Seth, but knowledge, and the correct application of that knowledge. Seth tries to subjugate Horus through an act of homosexual intercourse, but Horus is able to prevent this with the help of Isis, and is instead able to trick Seth into consuming his seed,[202] which then appears as a disk on top of Seth's head. This is the lunar disk often associated with Thoth, connecting the sovereign seed of Horus with the wisdom of Thoth; the wisdom that had brought the raw power of Seth under control.[203] This knowledge comes from Isis, nature. Horus' power as a sovereign comes from an understanding of the mysteries of the natural world, and natural existence.

We should not, however, understand the victory of Horus over Seth to be seen as negating Seth's role in the power and authority of the Pharaoh; the 'king needed to be an amalgamation of the powers of Horus and Seth.'[204]

---

200 Butler, 240.

201 Butler, 240.

202 This is accomplished by tricking Seth into eating Horus' semen that had been placed on lettuce. Lettuce was considered an aphrodisiac in ancient Egypt, associated with the god Min, a deity associated with fertility. This also shows an interesting contradiction in Seth, his wounding shows a removal of fertility, but he is also associated with virility. This connection is further strengthened in the *Papyrus Chester Beatty I*, where lettuce is said to be the food that Seth eats.

203 Some have contended that this lunar disk might be equated with the eye of Horus (Turner, 'Seth: A Misrepresented God in the Egyptian Pantheon?', 101.)

204 Turner, 28.

As we read on the obelisk of Hatshepsut at the Karnak Temple: 'as I wear the White Crown, as I appear in the Red Crown, as Horus and Seth have united for me their halves, as I rule this land like the son of Isis (i.e. Horus), as I have become strong like the son of Nut (i.e. Seth).'

Additionally from the walls of Karnak, 'Seth giveth victory and might to Horus'.

Here Hatshepsut is showing that she can rule like Horus but, if necessary, can use the force of Seth – 'neither of these two aspects of kingship can be dispensed with and hence Seth cannot be ignored.'[205]

The contending between the gods, and their wounding at each other's hands shows their incompleteness and struggle. Once they are healed, once they are made whole, and understand their place and function amongst the gods, *maat*[206] is restored. The process 'therefore came to symbolise the general process of 'making whole' and healing.'[207] This wholeness, and healing power was symbolised by the Eye of Horus. It should also be noted that the initial disruption caused by Seth, his murder of his brother Osiris, and his challenge to Horus could be interpreted as him undertaking the work of nature. Seth is the brother of Isis, and as Gunther states, perhaps in a similar way that Judas is considered in relation to his betrayal of Jesus; 'he was thus the active hand who ultimately carried out her will.'[208] This can also be seen in the descriptions of The Signs of the Grades, where the Sign for 8°=3□ (Master of the Temple) is called both Isis Rejoicing and Set Triumphant.[209] Crowley in his

---

205 Turner, 64.

206 Order or truth.

207 Turner, 'Seth: A Misrepresented God in the Egyptian Pantheon?', 42.

208 Gunther, *The Angel and the Abyss*, 38.

209 Crowley, Desti, and Waddell, *Magick. Liber ABA. Book Four. Parts I-IV*, 617.

commentary to *Liber V Vel Reguli*[210] describes "Set-Isis" (indicating a combined function) when discussing the *Sh* element of *ShT*. *Sh* is the child of Set-Isis, their 'logos or Word uttered by their "Angel".[211] This is the marriage of Heaven and Earth, 'the Holy Spirit as a "tongue of fire" manifest in triplicity...'[212]

Seth is also seen as a beneficent, protective deity when he, combined with the magic of Isis, wielding his spear protects the Sun god's bark from the threat of Apophis, preventing the course of the Sun from coming to a standstill. 'Force which cannot be legalised is being placed in the service of the law.'[213]

One view of the contradictory nature of Seth is that his character and function have different effects on different planes of action. In the context of Ra, the Sun god,[214] he is necessary to keep the cycle of the Sun continuing, but in the context of Osiris, of humanity, this force needs to be controlled and contained, due to the threat it poses. Seth's "evil" is either positive or negative depending on the plane on which it is functioning.[215] Osiris stands for order, whereas Seth stands for disorder. Osiris was the ruler of the "Black Land" whereas Seth ruled the desert ("red lands"). Horus was the "solar sky falcon", whereas Seth brought clouds and storms.

As explained by Janne Arp-Neumann, 'Osiris was the pro-

---

210 Reguli is the plural of regulus, which can refer to a "petty king" or a prince. A petty king refers to a tribal ruler, or one who exercised more limited local rule.

211 *Crowley, Desti, and Waddell, Magick,* 578.

212 Crowley, Desti, and Waddell, 578.

213 Turner, 'Seth: A Misrepresented God in the Egyptian Pantheon?', 17.

214 'The king himself was supposed to feel luminous, as though he were radiating dazzling light, just like the sun.' (Prakash, 'Emotions and the Manifestation of Ancient Egyptian Royal Power', 9.)

215 Turner, 'Seth: A Misrepresented God in the Egyptian Pantheon?', 17.

totype for the dead, especially the dead king, and Horus the prototype for the rightful living king. Isis was the caregiver, who used special capacities for hiding, finding, defending, healing, etc., and therefore was often referred to in medico-magical texts. Seth's role was that of a destructive power which could be used for evil but also for good.'[216] Seth eventually takes his place on the bark of Ra, where from the prow he defends against Apophis, the enemy of the Sun god. Here Seth's power is utilised rightfully in order to maintain the balance, maintain Maat, and perhaps the balance between life and death ruled by Osiris and Horus, with these two gods (as father and son) aspects of a conjoined entity representing the kingship of life, and the kingship of death. The actions of Seth are necessary to cause the transformation that brings this balance into being – 'Osiris was the god who died, who had to die, to give way to the next generation of the living, but also to pave the way for the future dead.[217]

In one rendering of the mythology, the battle between Seth and Horus that leads to their wounding starts in an oasis in the desert, where Horus had fled after attacking Isis (his mother) and decapitating her in retaliation for defending Seth – he had caused a violation against nature.[218] Horus lost his eye, and Seth one of his testicles. Horus' eye was the Moon, and therefore the cosmic implication of its destruction was the world being cast into darkness.

> May Osiris and Isis be content.
> May Horus be content with his Eye,
> May Set be content with his testicles.

---

216 Arp-Neumann, 'Negating Seth', 163.

217 Arp-Neumann, 166.

218 Thoth also intervenes here by healing Isis.

May Re-Harakhti be content
with vindication, while his enemy is felled for him
daily.

Stela of Amaini MMA 12.182.2[219]

There is a resonance here in the 23rd Aethyr from *The Vision and the Voice*:

And the voice said: Thy fear is known; thine ignorance is known; thy weakness is known; but thou art nothing in this matter. Shall the grain which is cast into the earth by the hand of the sower debate within itself, saying, am I oats or barley? Bondslave of the curse, we give nothing, we take all. Be thou content. That which thou art, thou art. Be content.[220]

We could see the relationship between Seth and Horus as an indication of what Crowley meant by referring to The Emperor as "the Devil in disguise". Seth being the Devil, the source of the Kingly Power, and Horus the Emperor; this power on display, in use and manifest (controlled) in order to maintain balance and order. As stated by Turner, 'The identification of his place in the ancient Egyptian pantheon was also not helped by the attempts of early Egyptologists to fit Egyptian religion into a Christian format. In this scenario a Devil was required and to the early Egyptologists Seth fitted that bill!"[221]

In some depictions Seth and Horus are seen on either side of a Pharaoh. They are the male equivalent of the two female deities shown (Wadjet and Nekhbet), and the Egyptian kings

---

219 Lansberry, 'May Set Possess His Power'.

220 Crowley, Neuburg, and Desti, *The Vision & the Voice with Commentary and Other Papers: The Collected Diaries of Aleister Crowley, 1909-1914 E.V.*, 66.

221 Turner, 'Seth: A Misrepresented God in the Egyptian Pantheon?', 161.

were given the title 'He of the Two Ladies'.[222] There is also a statue in the Cairo Museum depicting the coronation of Ramesses III, where Seth and Horus stand on either side of the Pharaoh performing the crowning.

As can also be seen in the image above, the king wears the Uraeus, a cobra and symbol of the Pharaoh's power.[223]

Related to this, early dynastic queens of Egypt – reflecting the duality of Horus and Seth – held titles such as 'She-who-unites-the Two-Lords' and 'She-who-sees-Horus and Seth',[224] indicating the presence and influence of both deities within the sovereign. The two gods, and the two lands of Egypt were united within the Pharaoh, and possibly also highlighting this connection to the queen.

---

222 Lansberry, 'Egyptian Serpent Power', 3.

223 The Uraeus and the images of snakes is discussed in the chapter on the "Kingly Power".

224 Turner, 'Seth: A Misrepresented God in the Egyptian Pantheon?', 158.

We can see this reflected in a text from the twelfth dynasty, describing the appearance of Amenemhet:[225]

Then a king will come from the South,
Ameny, the justified, by name,
Son of a woman of Ta-Seti, child of Upper Egypt.
He will take the white crown,
He will wear the red crown;
He will join the Two Mighty Ones,
He will please the Two Lords with what they wish.

The 'Two Mighty Ones' are again the vulture goddess *Nekhbet* and the cobra goddess *Wadjet*, whereas the 'Two Lords' are Horus and Seth, showing a connection between these female and male deities, and also the ruler's role in maintaining *maat*. The king was an intermediary between the gods and the people. Maat was as the gods had ordained at the time of creation, and needed to be maintained, otherwise a state of chaos, or *isfet*, would arise.

Utterance 213 of the Unas Pyramid Texts

134: O Unas, you have not gone dead, you have gone alive to sit on the throne of Osiris. Your sceptre is in your hand that you may give orders to the living, the handle of your lotus-shaped sceptre in your hand. Give orders to those of the Mysterious Sites (the dead)!

135: Your arm is that of Atum, your shoulders are those of Atum, your belly is that of Atum, your back is that of Atum,

---

225 Amenemhet was the first ruler of the twelfth dynasty, considered to be a golden age of the Middle Kingdom.

your bottom is that of Atum, your two legs are those of Atum, your face is that of Anubis. The sites of Horus serve you, the sites of Seth serve you.

* * *

In the opening to this section, I quoted from *The Book of Thoth* regarding Crowley's statements about the accusations against the early Christians having worshipped an ass, or a god with an ass head. In this place Crowley further writes '… and this again is connected with the wild ass of the wilderness, the god Set, identified with Saturn and Satan. (See infra, Atu XV.) He is the South, as Nuit is the North: the Egyptians had a Desert and an Ocean in those quarters.'[226] Crowley also makes the connection here between Baphomet and Mithras, specifically pointing out his connection to the bull.

There is clear archaeological evidence that shows a connection between Seth and bull iconography (associated with Mithras, and therefore Baphomet). In addition, Seth is depicted as winged and horned. In the collection of the Glyptotek Museum is a stele which depicts a winged and bull-headed Seth called "Bull of Nebwty". The bull was previously an icon of Seth and is described in the Leyden Papyrus as, "the son of Nwt" (an epithet of Seth) with the title "Bull of the night, Bull of Bull".'

---

226 Crowley, *The Book of Thoth*, 67.

Photo ©NCG: Ny Carlsberg Glyptotek ÆIN 726, Acquired 1890

Seth was also associated by the Hyksos rulers, in the fif-
teenth dynasty, with their god Baal, who was an object of
worship in their original lands, and one of his representations
was the bull as a symbol of fertility and strength. The Hyksos
practiced burial rites that include the internment of equids,[227]

---

227 A mammal of the horse family [ed]

believed to be due to the association in Egypt between Seth and donkeys. This association between Seth and the foreign Hyksos also contributed to Seth's association with things considered foreign (particularly heightened during the Persian and Assyrian conquests). Images of Seth from the Delta regions show him with Asiatic features and dress, associated with Baal.

There are also depictions of Seth in which he is shown with ram's horns, indicating a transformation into Amun – another deity associated with the ram, virility, and fertility. Over time, this association led to Amun becoming fused with the god Min, resulting in the composite deity Amun-Min. This indicates a connection between these deities, their characteristics and Seth. The donkey itself is also associated with virility and fertility, with the phallus sometimes used in the way "donkey" was expressed in Egyptian hieroglyphs. The donkey was regarded for its sexual prowess,[228] connection to lustfulness and the size of their phallus. The glyph for the phallus is also associated with other animals, such as bulls. 'An association with the verb ⳼ '3ʿ 'to conceive, to beget' had been proposed to explain the etymological roots of the word ʿ3 …'[229]

The quasi-exclusivity of the association between the donkey and Seth grew during the Ptolemaic period. The hieroglyphs for donkey would even, at times, show the donkey with Seth's split tail.[230]

---

228 It is also worth noting that in the Qabalah, under The Orders of Qliphoth, Yesod is assigned to 'Gamaliel, the "obscene ass," a perversion of the sphere's sexual function.' (Bonner, *Qabalah: A Magical Primer*, 47.)

229 Vandenbeusch, 'Thinking and Writing "Donkey" in Ancient Egypt: Examples from the Religious Literature', 140.

230 Vandenbeusch, 140.

Vandenbeusch explains that even when Seth is not explicitly named, he is being alluded to when 'his fetish animal is used as a determinative.'[231] Determinatives are glyphs which carry no phonetic significance, but are used to specify meaning and assist in the division of words.

Another fascinating association, that adds another layer of meaning to the complex figure of Seth, is seen in the Middle Kingdom where the donkey (*hiw*) appears in the Coffin Texts. In spell 266 a donkey is depicted lying on its belly – *ḥr ḫt.f*, which refers to animals that crawl. 'The *hiw* creature described here could therefore be a hybrid entity, half donkey, half snake, reminding us of some of the fantastic beings evolving in the netherworld.'[232]

Coffin of Sepi – Cairo, Egyptian Museum CG 28083

---

231 Vandenbeusch, 141.

232 Vandenbeusch, 141.

Here we see a continuity of ideas between the donkey, the snake, and Seth. If we consider the concept of the hybrid representation of the donkey and the snake, Vandenbeusch also puts forward spell 1101 (CT VII, 421), where it states 'the entity *hiw* stands ( ) against you (i.e. guardian of the second door, Ikenti)'[233] represents a donkey on its hind legs, or similarly a cobra rearing up.

So here we see a complex relationship between sovereignty, the ass, Seth, Christ, the snake and other fascinating associations. The ass, as Seth, could be seen as another representation of the "Kingly Power", the transformative energy that needs to be harnessed. The marriage of these symbols, between Horus and Seth, shows the balance between the light and the dark, the equilibrium that maintains *maat*, which is also the state of consciousness, that state of rest between two extremes that we see expressed in the figure of Baphomet.

John the Baptist

Another important figure that speaks to the nature of the mysterious head and its connection to Baphomet is John the Baptist. He is an important, and one could argue underplayed, figure for Christians, and he can be seen as a bridge between the old and the new testaments. John the Baptist prepared the way, and in this role was the first New Testament prophet – he was the 'prophet of the Highest.' (Luke 1:76)

I send a messenger before thy face, which shall prepare the way before thee.

The Voice crying in the wilderness, Prepare ye the way of the Lord, make his paths straight.

Mark 1:2-3

---

233 Vandenbeusch, 141.

John the Baptist could also be seen as a scapegoat figure, like Jesus, and preached 'the baptism of repentance for the remission of sins.' (Mark 1:4). Also, in the Gospel of Matthew, Jesus responds to a question about the prophet Elijah, and states, 'Elijah is come already, and they knew him not, but have done unto him whatsoever they listed. Likewise shall also the Son of man suffer of them.' (Matthew 17:12) The symbolism of the scapegoat prefigured John the Baptist, as the murder of John the Baptist prefigured the passion of Jesus.

The Baptist also has the rare honour among Christian saints for having his birth marked with a liturgical commemoration on June 24th. The only other celebrations of this kind are for the Virgin Mary, and for Jesus himself. June 24th marks the longest day of the year in the Northern hemisphere, with the days slowly becoming shorter until the winter solstice, and the celebration of the birth of Christ on December 25th.

John was called by God using the word *angelon* (ἄγγελόν); a messenger or forerunner. Because of this, in some iconography of the saint, he is depicted, like Levi's Baphomet, with wings[234] - 'an angel-like position is added to the components of his identity.'[235] This winged representation of John connects him with the prophet Elijah, who was taken to heaven before his death, and is in some Qabbalistic literature considered to be an angel who had taken human form.

> ...Behold, I will send you Elijah the prophet before the coming of the great and dreadful day of the LORD
>
> *Malachi 4:5*

---

234 This, and the connection of John as an angel, is only found in Eastern sources and in the Orthodox church.

235 Tinaz, 'The Winged Figure of Saint John the Baptist', 2.

For all the Prophets and the Law prophesied until John. And if ye will receive it, he is Elias [Elijah] who is to come.

Matthew 11: 13-14

Elijah is also connected to the angel Sandalphon (Σανδαλφών). Sandalphon is seen as a protector of unborn children, and his name may derive from the Greek prefix *sym-/syn-* (together) and *adelphos* (brother).[236] Tinaz translates this as "twins-couple" (although this is generally rendered as "co-brothers"), indicating a dual nature. One of these pairings is with another angel, Metatron. It is also said that Sandalphon and Metatron are the "lads" from Genesis 48:16 and Metatron was Enoch, as Sandalphon was Elijah (both of whom were taken to heaven prior to their physical deaths).

The First Pentacle of the Sun

---

236 In contemporary Greek this is used to designate a co-worker.

A tantalising archetype that hints at the nature of the relationship between Sandalphon and Metatron (and its relationship to John) is found in *The Key of Solomon the King*, in connection to "The First Pentacle of the Sun". It states that 'This singular Pentacle contains the head of the great Angel Methraton or Metatron, the vice-regent and representative of Shaddai,[237] who is called Prince of Countenances, and right-hand masculine Cherub of the Ark, as Sandalphon is the feminine.'[238] Here we can recall one of Lévi's descriptions of Baphomet, 'He is a hold-over from the Cherubs of the ark and the Holy of holies.'[239] One also cannot help but note the bearded and horned representation of Shaddai on this Pentacle of the Sun, and whether this could be the source of Lévi's 'bearded devil of the alchemists' and his link between Baphomet and the Cherubs, where he points to the mysteries of the Templars and the completion of the Great Work. Around Shaddai is written in Latin, 'Behold His face and form by Whom all things were made, and whom all creatures obey.'[240] This speaks to the creative[241] element of Baphomet reflected through A'ash[242] (עש), the title of *Liber CCCLXX*.

---

237 It should also be noted that both Metatron and Shaddai have a value of 314 by gematria. In Sepher Sephiroth it is also noted that Metatron when spelt with י after מ denotes Shekinah ("dwelling" or "settling"- the presence of God. In the Kabbalah the Shekinah is considered feminine).

238 MacGregor Mathers, *The Key of Solomon the King (Clavicula Salomonis)*, 72–73.

239 Levi, *The Book of Splendours*, 118–19.

240 MacGregor Mathers, *The Key of Solomon the King (Clavicula Salomonis)*, 73.

241 It has been highlighted that 'all of the passages using El Shaddai in Genesis, with one exception, are fertility blessings… An examination of these texts demonstrates that a tradition, which I believe to have been early, understood El Shaddai as a fertility god.' (Biale, 'The God with Breasts: El Shaddai in the Bible', 247.)

242 Creation (Crowley, *The Holy Books of Thelema*, xxxiii.)

Tinaz also states that in the Talmud Hagiga (13b) Sandalphon 'is described while sitting on the left side of the Ark of the Covenant.'[243] I have not been able to evidence this clearly in the Talmud Hagiga, which states in relation to Sandalphon, 'he stands behind the divine chariot and binds crowns for his Creator.'[244] This is given as an interpretation in Ezekiel 1:15 – 'Now as I beheld the living creatures, behold one wheel upon the earth by the living creatures, with his four faces.' This description is, however, interesting in relation to the kingly power ('binds crowns for his creator'), and the relationship with John who, by Baptising Jesus, confirmed his position as the Son of God, the messiah, and therefore King. Sandalphon stands upon the earth, but his head is with the living creatures (*hayyot*), the highest angelic beings – a link between heaven and earth. Sandalphon is also said to be involved in deciding the gender of children (transforming them from their original undifferentiated state[245]) and also carries prayers to God. Sandalphon is not found in any non-Jewish sources, so the angel is considered to be connected to the 'esoteric lore of the Merkabah.'[246]

> ...and by the Almighty [El Shaddai], who shall bless thee with blessings of heaven above, blessing of the deep that lieth under, blessing of the breasts [*shadayim*] and womb [*rahem*].
>
> *Genesis* 49:25

As Biale points out regarding the above quote from Genesis (with caveats), 'Here we have not only a fertility blessing

---

243 Tinaz, 'The Winged Figure of Saint John the Baptist', 5.

244 Rodkinson, *The Babylonian Talmud*, 1–10:1628.

245 Remembering what was written about previously regarding the "germinal vesicle" and the undifferentiated state in Taoism.

246 Bacher and Blau, 'SANDALFON – JewishEncyclopedia.Com'.

[...], but also a wordplay suggesting a meaning for the name El Shaddai. The author associates Shaddai with *shadayim* (breasts).',[247] further suggesting that the author of the passage may have interpreted the name as "El with breasts" or a similar rendering. This then provides a connection to the breasted figure of Baphomet gifted to us by Lévi.

Additionally in the *Dictionary of Deities and Demons in the Bible*, El Shaddai (Shadday) is translated as "God of the Wilderness".[248] It has also been put forward (although this is not accepted by all) that the association of El Shaddai with breasts came, by association, to be connected with mountains – high places - 'originally conceived as "the one of the mountains."'[249] '[T]he "primitive" meaning of the Akkadian *shadu* is "breast." The root then came to mean "mountain"'.[250] There could also be a source here in Egyptian where there is the phonetically similar "*shdi*", which means "to suckle".[251] It is also possible that the fertility blessings found in Genesis are related to Kings, and in their current form are from the time of David and Solomon[252] – 'the consequence of their fertility will be the

---

247 Biale, 'The God with Breasts: El Shaddai in the Bible', 248.

248 van der Toorn, Becking, and van der Horst, *Dictionary of Deities and Demons in the Bible*, 749.

249 Biale, 'The God with Breasts: El Shaddai in the Bible', 241.

250 Biale, 248–49.

251 Biale, 249.

252 It should also be remembered that the "Throne of Solomon" was another symbol of kingship associated with David and Solomon. In Judaism it was described to have many steps, alongside which were twelve sculptured lions of gold, who had golden sculptures of eagles before them, the right paw of each lion set opposite the left wing of each eagle. As one approached the top of the staircase, there were another six steps directly in front of the semi-circular throne, each step with a pair of sculpted animals, each in gold. Above the throne was a seven-branched candlestick which afforded light, each branch

issue of kings.'[253] This blessing was part of a covenant between God, David[254] and his heirs, and this concept of a fertility god with breasts may have started early in the monarchy.

Some scholars 'believe that the name El Shaddai is extremely ancient and may [...] have been one of the authentic pre-Canaanite epithets for the "god of the fathers" brought along by the patriarchs from their Mesopotamian homeland.'[255] Because of this long history, the images and the idea behind El Shaddai represent an ancient archetype. El Shaddai also has a strong presence in Genesis, with a preference for younger brothers, showing the god intervening to change the "natural" order to benefit the future of the nation. This intervention is a sign of the covenant between God and the patriarchs. The act of circumcision in Jewish tradition may also represent a sacrifice given in thanks for God's "blessing of fertility" and intervention. It 'is both a personal gesture and a sign of a national covenant.'[256] There are even references that show God begetting in Deuteronomy (noting here God being associated with a "Rock"):

Of the Rock *that* beget thee thou art unmindful, and hast forgotten God that formed thee.

Deuteronomy 32:18

---

bearing an image of the seven patriarchs. Here we see a series of symbolical pairings (noting the alchemical usages of the eagle and the lion), which led to a sevenfold light. The throne was also said to have been one of the earliest mechanical devices. When the king stepped onto the throne the device was set in motion.

253 Biale, 'The God with Breasts: El Shaddai in the Bible', 250.

254 מלכות בית דוד‎| - "Kingdom of the House of David", which is considered in Judaism to be the lineage of the Messiah.

255 Biale, 'The God with Breasts: El Shaddai in the Bible', 241.

256 Biale, 252.

There is evidence that these elements had a Canaanite origin with the worship of Asherah, a goddess often represented with prominent breasts, until this was suppressed by the Deuteronomic reforms. Asherah formed part of the Israelites worship, and there was even a statue of her in the temple in Jerusalem. 'When Elijah persecuted the prophets of Baal, he did not take similar action against the prophets of Asherah.'[257] There is even evidence that the 'Hebrew God had a Canaanite consort.'[258] El was transformed into Yahweh, so too Asherah, with a change in gender, became El Shaddai; Yahweh both male and female, in an "androgynous monotheism." As Biale points out, Genesis indicates that the "first man" was androgynous – 'that "God created Adam in the image of himself, in the image of God he created him, male and female he created them." If the first man was androgynous – as the Jewish Midrash thought – so must be the God who created "him."'[259] The god of fertility was eventually transformed into its opposite, a God of war, but it seems that the deep memory of God with both male and female characteristics would persist, if only because a solitary male god, creator of all things, would be an irrational concept, creating a discordance in the psychology of the people.

A further link to the concept of fertility, Shaddai and John can be seen in the story of his conception in the Gospel of Luke. This describes John's mother, Elizabeth, as "barren", and describes both Elizabeth and Zacharias (John's father), as 'well stricken in years.' (Luke 1:7) Zacharias was a priest, and when he was burning incense in the temple the angel Gabriel[260] ap-

---

257 Biale, 'The God with Breasts: El Shaddai in the Bible', 253.

258 Biale, 253.

259 Biale, 254.

260 Gabriel would later appear to Mary to announce that she had 'found favour with God.' (Luke 1:26)

peared to him and informed him that his wife would bear a son, who would be 'filled with the Holy Ghost,[261] even from his mother's womb.' (Luke 1:15). The Psalmists described Gabriel as the Lord's strength, and 'enthroned upon the cherubim…'[262] Further, the prophet Isaiah, in a vision, saw two seraphim in relation to the heavenly throne, the Lord on the right-hand side and the Holy Spirit on the left. In Jewish tradition this is also Michael on the right (the Lord) and Gabriel on the left (Holy Spirit). In Islam, Gabriel was also the angel that gave the magic ring to Solomon.[263] In Syria there is a symbol used which shows the Greek letters *XMΓ*. Barker proposes that this may represent Christ, Michael and Gabriel. Michael and the Holy Spirit also bear Jesus from the tomb in The Ascension of Isaiah, 'like the seraphim supporting the heavenly throne.'[264]

A possible hint at the link between this androgynous God and John the Baptist is explored by Tobias Churton, discussing the image of John painted by Leonardo da Vinci which can be seen in the Louvre in Paris. It shows John 'emerging from blackness' with 'enigmatic eyes and androgynous form', a 'cheeky girl/boy face' and 'all knowing smile'.[265]

The depictions of John as winged, his connection to Elijah and the angel Sandalphon could be seen as a reincarnation, or perhaps an avatar of Elijah. John was 'carrying the soul of Elijah.'[266] According to some Qabbalistic teaching, Elijah was an Angel 'created by the "Life Tree" itself, so that he can come

---

261 'At John's birth, Zechariah is struck dumb. His lost voice passes into the prophetic voice of his son.' (Baert, 'Vox Clamantis in Deserto', 82.)

262 Barker, *An Extraordinary Gathering of Angels*, 90.

263 A hexagram – a symbol of opposites in union.

264 Barker, *An Extraordinary Gathering of Angels*, 90.

265 Churton, *The Mysteries of John the Baptist*, 6.

266 Tinaz, 'The Winged Figure of Saint John the Baptist', 4.

time by time to Earth as a man or woman to call the people to the redemption',[267] just as John also called the people from the wilderness (in the Orthodox Churches John is titled "The Angel of the Wilderness"). Here John could be seen as both a return of Elijah, and as an angel. As commented by Saint Germanus I (c. 634–733 or 740): 'How shall we call you? As an Angel? An Apostle? A Martyr? As an Angel because of your incorporeal nature, as an Apostle because you invited the people to the redemption and as a Martyr because you sacrificed your precious head in the name of Jesus.'[268]

The winged iconography of John has been directly associated with the sacrifice of Jesus. Some images depict the head of John in a liturgical vessel, just as Christ offered his blood in the cup, and the liturgy[269] seen as a way of salvation. This connection is sometimes made more explicit with the infant Jesus shown in the vessel in place of the head. As Ellen Schwartz states, 'This is a direct allusion to the species of the Eucharist as the body and blood of Christ, linking even more closely the Baptist, the Passion, and the liturgy, and the dual themes of sacrifice and salvation.'[270]

---

267 Tinaz, 4.

268 Tinaz, 6.

269 The service of the Eucharist in the Orthodox Church

270 Schwartz, 'Russian Icons and Byzantine Legacy; The Angel of Wilderness', 173.

In the Paschal Chronicle,[271] there is an interesting story recorded regarding the head of the Baptist:

____

271 A 7th-century Greek Christian chronicle of the world.

After the execution of John, Herodias, fearing lest he should rise again should his head be buried with his body, took the head and buried it in Jerusalem, secretly, near the dwelling of Herod. "In the time of Marcian the prince, which was the year of Our Lord three hundred and fifty-three, John showed his head to two monks that were come to Jerusalem. And then they went to the palace which was belonging to Herod and found the head of S. John wrapped in an hair, and as I suppose, they were of the vestments that he ware in the desert. And then they went with the head toward their proper places. And as they went on their way a poor man which was of the city of Emissene came and fellowshipped with them, and they delivered him the bag in which was the holy head. Then this man was warned in the night that he should go his way and flee from them with the head, and so he went with the head, and brought it into the city of Emissene. And there as long as he lived he worshipped the head in a cave, and had always good prosperity.[272]

The above story indicates a precedent for the concept of the worship of the head of John, and that this worship was thought to bring prosperity. A latter part of this story tells of the rediscovery of the head by a monk following a vision of a star. When the monk touched the pot containing the head his hand was burnt onto the pot, and when he withdrew it, he was not whole. John appeared to the monk and said to him that after his head is put in the church, he should touch the pot again. The monk did this and was made whole again.

It should be noted that John is associated with healing and is represented in some places by a single column, such as in the

---

272 Haring, 'The Winged St. John the Baptist Two Examples in American Collections', 38–39.

church of St. John of the Column in Athens (built in the 12th century upon the foundations of a 9th century church). It is thought the column was originally part of a sanctuary dedicated to Asclepius[273] (Greek god of medicine and healing).

In Greece many of the rites of worship originally in honour of Adonis[274] are continued in the veneration of John. 'It may well be that here is another survival of the cult of Adonis and that the Adonic symbol of fertility[275] and health has become the health giving monument to St. John.'[276]

We can also see the association of the wilderness and Jesus. Following his baptism by John he was immediately driven into the wilderness by the Spirit, 'And he was there in the wilderness for forty days, tempted of Satan; and was with the wild beasts; and the angels ministered unto him.' (Mark 1:12) Jesus also departs unto "desert places" after healing a leper, who broke his instruction to 'say nothing to any man'. (Mark 1:44) It was in a desert place that Jesus accomplished the miracles of the loaves and fishes ("The Five Thousand Fed"). It was also in the desert that Aleister Crowley and Victor Neuburg confronted Choronzon and were tempted: 'THERE IS NO BEING in the outermost Abyss, but constant forms come forth from the nothingness of it.'[277] This occurs as part of the working

---

273 The Rod of Asclepius is still used as a symbol for medicine and health, although sometimes confused with the Caduceus.

274 The mortal lover of Aphrodite in Greek mythology, thought to have its origins in Inanna (Ishtar) and Dumuzid (Tammuz).

275 The connection between St. John and fertility in relation to the Baphomet of the Templars might be found in some of their descriptions of the idol they were accused of venerating; 'that it could make the trees flower... that it made the land germinate..' (Lamb, 'The Mystery of Baphomet', 3.)

276 Haring, 'The Winged St. John the Baptist Two Examples in American Collections', 40.

277 Crowley, Neuburg, and Desti, *The Vision & the Voice with Commentary*

of the 10th Aethyr – The Abyss. There is also, perhaps, a reference to the Baptist in Crowley's naming of *Liber DCCCLX* "John St. John". This is a record of one of Crowley's magical retirements. Although in this record Crowley is working very much within the world while undertaking his "retirement", the lesson is still to separate oneself (even psychologically, if not physically) as John took up a life in the wilderness – a life of self-reliance. We read in the Oath that Crowley took at the start of this retirement, '…VIII. That I will work in truth: IX. That I will rely upon myself:…'.[278] St Bede the Venerable, wrote about John stating, 'His persecutor (Herod) had demanded not that he should deny Christ, but only that He should keep silent about the truth. Nevertheless, he died for Christ. Does Christ not say, "I am the truth?" Therefore, because John shed his blood for the truth, he surely died for Christ.'[279]

Crowley writes about the mysteries of John, where he differentiates between the Greater and Lesser Mysteries; 'The legend of the Gospels, dealing with the Greater Mysteries of the Lance and the Cup (those of the god Iacchus Iao) as superior to the Lesser Mysteries (those of the God Ion=Noah, and the N gods in general) in which the Sword slays the god that his head may be offered on a Plate, or Disk…'[280] Crowley does not specifically mention John here, but it seems clear that he is referring to the beheading of the Baptist.

The reference to the Lesser and Greater Mysteries has their origin in the Rites of Eleusis - 'The Lesser Mysteries can best be characterized as a preliminary purification that a candidate

---

and Other Papers: The Collected Diaries of Aleister Crowley, 1909-1914 E.V., 163.

278 Crowley, *Aleister Crowley and the Practice of the Magical Diary,* 7.

279 Moneme, 'John the Baptist'.

280 Crowley, *The Book of Thoth,* 98–99.

must undergo before taking part in the Greater Mysteries.'[281] Of these Socrates commented that before anyone could take part in the Greater Mysteries, they needed to have first been initiated into the Lesser.

The importance of these rites can be seen in a quote from Plato that states, 'Whoever arrives in Hades as an uninitiate and non-participant in the initiation rites will lie in mud, but he or she who has been both purified and has participated in the initiation rites, upon arrival there, will dwell with the gods.'[282] The Lesser Mysteries were rites of purification. They were referred to as *myesis*, "to teach", and "to initiate", whereas the Greater Mysteries were *epopteia*, which means "to witness" and "to be initiated". 'In the Lesser Mysteries, candidates were taught the theology of the two Goddesses, and the meaning of the rites of the Mysteries. However, in the Greater Mysteries, they could experience what they had learned...'[283] The initiates into the Lesser Mysteries were purified with water, air and fire, and there is a reference to a "threefold darkness" – 'the darkness of the veiling, that of the sacred nights in Agrae and Eleusis, and his own inner darkness—that the *mists* find their way back to their own suffering, and conceiving motherliness.'[284]

A snake coils from the *kiste* to Demeter's lap, and the *mystes*, distinguished by his bundle of twigs, is seen touching this snake without fear—having transcended human anxiety, moving free and relaxed in a divine sphere.[285]

---

281 Goodart, 'The Lesser Mysteries of Eleusis', 1.

282 Goodart, 1.

283 Goodart, 22.

284 Goodart, 24.

285 Goodart, 24.

Imagery of the rites show that at the completion of the initiation Demeter still stands between the initiate and Persephone (associated with purity), showing that the Greater Mysteries were still to be experienced.

Gwen Gunther proposes 'that the ritual centered around the natural phenomena of the seed and the plant, with the purpose of imparting the spiritual meaning of death and birth...the earthy dominant Feminine Archetype was represented by...Demeter. She was the Mother whose power of fertility governed plant, mineral, and animal life. She was the embodiment of the fertile earth and the guardian of the secret that transformed seed into grain. She was the guardian of the knowledge of immortality.'[286]

By referring to the Mysteries of Eleusis, and the role of John, we can perhaps catch a glimpse of what Crowley is communicating. As the Lesser Mysteries at Eleusis were a preliminary of the Greater Mysteries, so was John (Elias), who 'cometh first, and restoreth all things', followed by Jesus, the embodiment of The Greater Mysteries. Crowley referred to the crucifixion to explain these Greater Mysteries – 'And a soldier with a spear pierced his side; and there forth there came out blood and water. This Wine, collected by the Beloved Disciple and the Virgin-Mother, waiting beneath the Cross or Tree for that purpose, in a Cup or Chalice; this is the Holy Grail or Sangreal (Sangraal) of Monsalvat, the Mountain of Salvation.'[287] John shows the process 'in which the Sword slays the god that his head may be offered on a Plate, or Disk...'[288] - John is of the

---

286 Gunther and Gunther, *I Am the Heart: A Commentary on Liber LXV Chapter I, Ever the Heart: An Essay on the Symbolism of The Heart of Blood*, 269.

287 Crowley, *The Book of Thoth*, 99.

288 Crowley, 99.

earth; the "wheel upon the earth". The above may be of relevance to initiates of the III° of the OTO, and also speaks to the mysteries of Parsifal, dealt with elsewhere in this book. In order for both of these mysteries to be properly enacted, there is the need (on some level) for the initiate to be sacrificed. They must die in order to live. Perhaps these could be considered the mysteries of generation (the sacrifice of the self to the earth), the path in eternity. The mysteries of Christ are that of the great return; we sacrifice the eternal to manifest on earth, that through this experience we may be reborn in the life that the profane world calls death.

There is still a group of people, practicing today, who venerate John the Baptist as a great prophet (the last great teacher and healer to live on the earth), and continue the ritual practice of Baptism for both the living and the dead – 'We're normally baptised in a river because it's fresh and, as they say, it's flowing — where the life is always flowing...'[289] The Mandaeans ("Knower" or "Gnostic") were a persecuted minority before and after the fall of Saddam Hussein. Most fled Iraq and have settled in Australia, Europe, and the United States.

The Mandaeans teach that the body of John cannot be burnt by fire,[290] and that he 'received his wisdom from the divine "Life" and from "Primal MAN" who is "LIGHT". They see John, like Enoch as a "Son of Man" – "one whose eyes have beheld the Light and looked within it."'[291]

The Mandaeans saw John as one of their own, '...the last

---

289 Hegarty, 'Meet the Mandaeans: Australian Followers of John the Baptist Celebrate New Year'.

290 Noting the differences between the baptisms of John and Jesus – John baptised with water, whereas Jesus' baptism is one of the Holy Ghost and fire. (Revelations 3:16)

291 Churton, *The Mysteries of John the Baptist*, 248.

attested sect to survive the first great Gnostic movement on Earth...'[292] They are the "*Nasuraiah*" (Arabic), the *Nasoreans*. They are the '"Guardians"[...] of a primal revelation...'[293] Tobias Churton argues that the term "Nazarene" does not refer to a place, as commonly interpreted, but comes from the Hebrew word meaning "to keep" and "to watch". The word NATZARIM (נצרים) is from *natzar* – "watchers". 'When we join the respective meanings of the words *keeper* and *watcher*, we produce, in English, the word *guardian*, and that may be the best sense for us to understand the nature of the original, authentic movement of John and Jesus.'[294]

> Not aloud shall they praise thee; but in the night watch one shall steal close, and grip thee with the secret grip...
>
> *Liber LXV*, I:23[295]

> "We do wash with water, in this world."
> And Life triumphs! John teaches in the night, Johannes in the evenings of the night, John teaches in the night...[296]

The above quotation is taken from *The Mandaean Book of John*, which is more properly called *Teachings of the Kings*. These "kings" are 'spirits who have descended from the world of light and govern the material world.'[297] The supreme being of the Mandaeans is the Great Life and sits above the cosmic

---

292 Churton, 252.

293 Churton, 252.

294 Churton, 202.

295 Crowley, *The Holy Books of Thelema*, 55.

296 Häberl and McGrath, *The Mandaean Book of John*, 71.

297 Häberl and McGrath, *The Mandaean Book of John*.

drama of their sacred texts, and of mortals. Taking pride of place in *Teachings of the Kings* is John, son of Zechariah – John the Baptist.

In Mandaean teaching, Jesus is not portrayed in a positive light. They teach that *Miriai* (sometimes equated with Mary) was made pregnant either through witchcraft, or by a man who was not her husband. *Miriai* is portrayed positively by the Mandaeans, but 'Jesus deviated from the truth and his Mandaean heritage.'[298]

One of the creation stories (the other is an emanation model) taught by the Mandaeans is based on opposing poles (the Lightworld and the Darkworld). There is additionally a middle world called *Tibil*, which is the habitation of humanity, on the lowest plane, the surface of the earth. 'Inhabitants of the Lightworld are known as *utras* (angels, guardians), along with other beings, who were involved in creation of the dark and light worlds, and they continue to look after the earthly and Lightworld and keep in touch with Mandaeans of earth.'[299] The Darkworld, in contrast, houses dark beings with an evil nature. These dark beings were defeated at the beginning of the world, but can still be a source of disturbance. Because of the Darkworld's proximity to Tibil, it can still touch humanity; so Mandaean ritual is focused on ritual purity and avoiding contagions.

To the Mandaeans the good is light, and *Nhora* (flowing and living water), whereas the bad is dark, is *Maia Tahmi* (dead and salty water). However, these two opposing forces are balanced on Earth, 'where there is a mixture to be found in all things.'[300] This middle or "mixedworld" covers the Lightworld

---

298 Shirazi, 'Iranian Mandaeans'.

299 Shirazi.

300 Churton, *The Mysteries of John the Baptist*, 256.

to the earth and is the place of all physical beings (including planets and stars).

The Mandaeans also teach that humanity is mixed in its nature and origin. 'The human essence comes from the light world and is called *nashamtā* or human soul; it is restricted in the physical body made from *ṭinā* (mud), which is part of *tibel* (earth).'[301] As one would expect from a gnostic tradition, the physical body is seen as a restrictive element infringing on their human essence. The brightest place for the Mandaeans is the cosmological North, and the darkest is the cosmological South. 'The Gnostic opposition of light and darkness forms the fundamental structural basis of Mandaic cosmology.'[302] The principle of life in opposition to material existence.

When discussing the Mandaeans, Churton makes the interesting observation that, 'standing and facing the sun is a persistent motif of what we may call broadly the John tradition.'[303] The sun is seen as a visible object of worship or contemplation that hides the invisible God. The worldly manifestation of the Mandaeans transcendental, impersonal God is running water (*yardenā*). This water is life, and from this "Life" comes the source of John's wisdom. This resonates with other traditions and connections that can be made with John – that he is 'linked to life and life eternal.'[304] This connection to the Sun can also be seen in the ritual practices of Thelema, especially *Liber Resh*, where the practitioner faces the Sun at different stations throughout the day, showing a continuity with ancient practice and the connection between the Sun and God.

---

301 Arabestani, 'Ritual Purity and the Mandaeans' Identity', 159.

302 Arabestani, 161.

303 Churton, *The Mysteries of John the Baptist*, 254.

304 Churton, 249.

'It is perhaps the Sun, the exoteric object of worship of all sensible cults…'[305]

Johannesschüssel

The use of the head of John the Baptist as an object of worship, as associated with the Templars, and their suspected ritual practices, is certainly not without well documented precedent. In the case of the *Johannesschüssel*, this is the head in conjunction with the platter. The *Johannesschüssel* is also called *Caput Iohannis in Disco* ("Saint John's head on a platter") and is from the late medieval/early modern period, found commonly in some parts of Europe and North of the Alps. The very nature of the platter and head as a three-dimensional object seems to induce a meditative state in the worshippers, and form a link between the symbolism of the body of Christ and the head of the Baptist. The veneration of the head was also believed to confer protection against various ailments, most notably – given the fertility symbolism associated with John the Baptist – male sexual dysfunction.

These objects refer to the descriptions in Mark 6:14–29 and Matthew 14:1–12 concerning the death of John the Baptist, where his decapitated head is presented on a platter. Although images related to this story had existed, the particular representation of it in the form of the *Johannesschüssel* appeared in the 13th century. Their appearance may be linked to the influx of skulls of John the Baptist; '[A]fter the Fourth Crusade of 1204, a small deluge of supposed skulls of St John flowed westwards:

---

305 Crowley, *The Book of Lies*, 77.

no fewer than twelve skulls were venerated as John the Baptist's by the end of the Middle Ages.'[306]

As Barbara Baert points out, in Indo-European the root for "head" and "skull" is the same as that of dish, platter, pan, recipient and frame. 'Heads and skulls are archetypically speaking hollow tools for keeping liquids in a cultic context.'[307] In this way there is a direct link between the head and the platter – they are equal and associated with "roundness".

The platter is required to catch the head; it presents and frames it within a form of the *temenos*[308] – it places the head within a sacred space. Without the platter 'the head is suspended in a vacuum'[309] – not grounded, framed, and presented to the viewer. Without this framing 'the snapshot of the decapitation could not have remained crystallized in the fraction of a moment, on the threshold, and consequently the head could not have become (image) because it was never (captured). The severed head bleeds out onto the ground, decomposes, and is eventually forgotten unless it is retrieved as a relic or re-established as an image.'[310]

In some ways the *Johannesschüssel* creates a mask to cover the root object at the core of this worship – the skull of John the Baptist in the Amiens Cathedral – making it more acceptable to the conscious mind. 'The wax in the relic of Amiens is not used as one would expect, to reconstruct the outward appearance of the face. The wax bears the imprint of the secret:

---

306 Baert, 'The Spinning Head: Round Forms and the Phenomenon of the Johannesschüssel', 45.

307 Baert, 45.

308 This Greek word represents a sacred and protected space.

309 Baert, 'The Spinning Head: Round Forms and the Phenomenon of the Johannesschüssel', 46.

310 Baert, 46–47.

the interior of the skull… Ce qui fascine d'abord, dans le crâne humain, c'est son côté interne; c'est la ›cavité des orbites‹, avec sa ›profondeur‹ dissimulée; c'est, en général, tous les ›trous visibles‹[311] ("That which fascinates first of all, in the human skull, is its internal side; it is the cavity of the orbits, with its 'depth' concealed; it is, in general, all the 'visible holes'")

The magical effect of the image is the result of the secret held by the skull - 'The terrible – visual penetration… of the black tunnels that John's head possesses – mouth, throat, ears,

---

311 Baert, 47.

nostrils – looses upon the viewer the precipitate energy of the evil averting *apotropaion*,[312] yet, now framed, controlled, channelled in the hypnotic round of the platter.'[313]

The *Johannesschüssel* were sometimes displayed on or in the Church altar, hanging on a wall or kept within the tabernacle niche; 'if hanging, John looked down upon the faithful; if lying prone, he looked into their eyes. This dynamic also reflects the dynamics of absence and presence, of a cult object in passivity and a cult object in action.'[314] The Head of John the Baptist in the *Johannesschüssel* projects and absorbs – it affects the consciousness of the viewer through both active and passive meditation in an exchange of gazes.

Because the blood is the life, and the blood of the sacrificed must not be lost, the platter receives and contains the blood, and therefore it is also representative of the recipient of it during the eucharist. The Baptist himself is recorded in John 1:29 to have said "*Ecce agnus Dei qui tollit peccata mundi*" ("Behold the Lamb of God who takes away the sins of the world") when he saw Jesus approaching, and these are the words spoken by the priest during the Mass before receiving the Eucharist.

---

312 Something that wards off evil.

313 Baert, 'The Spinning Head: Round Forms and the Phenomenon of the Johannesschüssel', 48.

314 Baert, 48.

Johannesschüssel (1500), Köln, Museum Schnütgen

We see another link between the Baptist and the Eucharist from a reading on the Feasts of Decollation (August 29). From the York breviary[315] – '*Caput Johannis in disco: signat corpus Christi: quo passimur in sancto altari: Et quod ecclesie gentium tribuitur in salutem ac remedium animarum.*' ("The head of John on the platter signifies the body of Christ with which we suffer on the holy altar. This head grants the church of the

---

315 A book containing the service for each day, to be recited by those in orders of the Roman Catholic Church.

people salvation and the healing of souls").[316] Additionally, from both York and Sarum,[317] liturgical manuscripts contain, '*O Beatum caput dignum reverentia,/Quod in disco matris tulit feralis bellua,/Quod tam multos instruxerat de Christi notitia*' ("O holy head, worthy of (our) reverence! A terrible beast has taken the head on the platter from the mother, a head that had taught so many (the knowledge) of Christ")'.[318] Here we have the severed head of the saint equated with the body of Christ and seen as an object of reverence used in liturgical services. 'The analogy extends from head to body, from dish to altar. According to A.A. Barb the association originated in Celtic tradition, where the concepts of the skull and blood still flourished in the myth of the Holy Grail. This pagan practice was redeemed by the Church, in the same way the "bleeding Head on the Dish was taken from the unholy hands of Herodias' daughter."'[319]

'*Conferat nobis, Domine, sancti Ioannis Baptistae utrumque solemnitas: ut et magnifica sacramenta quae sumpsimus patribus nostris significata veneremur, et in nobis potius edita gaudeamus*' ("Lord, grant us the worthiness of John the Baptist so that we may venerate the greatest sacraments we ever received in the name of our fathers, and so that we may rejoice that they were already accomplished in us"). This shows a recognition of the origins of these Eucharistic mysteries in the Celtic Grail traditions, but that (from the perspective of the Church) they now had the true vehicle to salvation through Christ.

---

316 Baert, 'The Spinning Head: Round Forms and the Phenomenon of the Johannesschüssel', 49.

317 An old name for Salisbury

318 Baert, 'The Spinning Head: Round Forms and the Phenomenon of the Johannesschüssel', 49.

319 Baert, 50.

The "round form" can be seen in both the platter and the Eucharist. The head could never be the Eucharist itself, but stands close to its mysteries.

An alabaster plaque dated from 1470–1485, now in the Burrell Collection of the Glasgow Museums, depicts a scene where 'John's praying soul escapes through his crown, accompanied by angels. At the time it was believed that the head was indeed the seat of the soul.'[320] Below this image is Christ in his tomb, depicted as the "Man of Sorrows". Both John and Christ share a vertical axis, with the head on the platter serving 'as the host on the round paten...'.[321] This vertical line then includes the soul of John, exiting through the top of his head. Likening the Eucharistic mysteries, John's sacrifice, and the promise of salvation (but John's death prefiguring that of Christ's).

The following example from the Victoria and Albert Museum also depicts the ascension of John's soul, but this time borne within a cloth, held on either side by angels, perhaps in reference to the burial shroud of Christ. Below the head is the "Lamb of God". 'The escaping soul seals a mysterious pact between the Forerunner and his Successor. In the sacrifice of the platter as *momentum* is contained imminent salvation, that which will transcend the momentary and bring about a cosmic revolution.'[322]

---

320 Baert, 51.

321 Baert, 51.

322 Baert, 52.

Alabaster John's head, 15th century
(London, Victoria and Albert Museum)

The Feast of Saint John included the burning of what were called "St. John's wheels". These wheels were associated with the *Johannesschüssel*, which Baert described as star shaped or floral wheels 'that generates a rotating effect.' 'From time immemorial the circle (the wheel, the disc, the platter) has constituted an image of the cosmos and the planets. The whirling effect of this universal form has been compared to the hypnotic impact of the gaze, and in fact reflects the central image of the *Johannesschüssel*.'[323] These ritual practices with St John's wheels must have similarly had an effect on the consciousness of the participants, drawing their minds within the whirling round forms, as they were drawn into the form of the severed head of John.

The burning of the St. John's wheels,[324] and the dancing around the altar 'with *Johannesschüsseln* and the platter itself was associated with the cycle of the cosmos. The alabaster plaque of John in Glasgow combines two forms of expression: refined, carved figurative language on the one hand, and abstract, associative pictorial language on the other, which appeals to universal symbols and ritual archetypes. It is precisely this doubling that allows the viewer to experience the layered dimensions of the decapitation. The beheading takes place on a cosmological plane, and lifts the *Johannesschüssel* into the mystery of the threshold and the revolution: the solstice, the toppling of the Old Covenant into New, etc. It is the revolution that clings fast as the deepest, most centrifugal message of the platter.'[325] The platter was linked to the dance, and the dance to the movement of the Sun.

So in the *Johannesschüssel* we have essentially a magical object, an icon that creates a hypnotic effect in the worshipper; it causes a change in their consciousness, and this, through the effects of rotation, and the cosmic symbolism embedded in

---

323 Baert, 52.

324 In Poitou in France, there used to be a custom on St. John's eve to set fire to a wheel wrapped in straw and roll it over fields in order to fertilise them. Additionally, 'Archives inform us that at the summer solstice outdoor processions took place across Europe to ensure the regeneration of the land and the fertility of women.' (Baert, 'The Johannesschüssel as Andachtsbild: The Gaze, the Medium and the Senses ', 123.)

325 Baert, 'The Spinning Head: Round Forms and the Phenomenon of the Johannesschüssel', 52–53.

some of the *Johannesschüssel,* and the associated rites, lifts the individual beyond themselves, as John's soul is seen rising up through the top of his head. The head is both a negation, and a powerful presence.

It is the platter, the round, the *temenos* that makes this engagement with the head possible. 'The round format makes the consuming gaze possible' and it 'activates, defines, yet perverts this potentiality of power.' Without being bordered the head 'would rotate into a self-destructive vacuum.'[326] It also entices the gaze of the worshipper – John calls on them to look.

Erhard Altdorfer, Veneration of a Johannesschüssel, Gutenstetten (1511), Gutenstetten parish church

---

326 Baert, 54.

The possible outcome of this altered state may be indicated in a different reading of the Gospel of John 3:30 (in John's last testimony) – 'He must increase, but I *must* decrease.' In the opinion of Churton this represents 'a straightforward piece of mystical advice… "He" (God) must increase, but "I" (ego) must decrease.'[327] Perhaps the image of the severed head of John can act as a medium for this experience – a decrease of the self, so that the Self might be experienced. Importantly, as Baert argues, the image actively engages the senses, and 'the phenomenological tension between head and visage […] leads to a reflection on the role of silence in the revelation of divine, cosmic truth.'[328] This then also connects to the archetypal dimension of the cycle of the year; the movement and the decrease of the sunlight, from June 24th to December 25th – from the Feast of John the Baptist to the celebration of the birth of Christ on Christmas Day. For there to be life, or new life, there must be a death – a decrease, so that the light may increase. This is an inward, mystical process reflected in outward, cultural practice. 'Because John has to decrease, in order that Christ can increase, an important cycle was recognised in the solstice of June (when the light decreases) and the solstice of December (when with the coming of Christ the light increases).'[329]

Unlike Christ, who is depicted as whole (although wounded and therefore open), John's body is divided; yet it is through this image of the moment of death, Baert argues, that we see Christ, just as in 'The moment John dies, he shall look upon the face of Christ.'[330]

---

327 Churton, *The Mysteries of John the Baptist*, 123.

328 Baert, 'Vox Clamantis in Deserto', 77.

329 Baert, 82.

330 Baert, 'The Johannesschüssel as Andachtsbild: The Gaze, the Medium and the Senses', 132.

The act of meditating on the *Johannesschüssel*, of looking, is 'an act of seeing that swells until it is near the face of God, the *beata visio*[331]…that looking at the *Johannesschüssel* likewise channels a longing to see the impossible. The decapitated head must bring us to the visage: *In conspectu domini*[332].'[333]

Johannesschüssel (15th century), Hamburg,
Museum für Kunst und Gewerbe

---

331 "Happy vision"

332 "In front of the Lord"

333 Baert, 'Vox Clamantis in Deserto', 78.

Baert explains further – 'Perhaps we should rather speak of a specifically inward-turned gaze. Looking at the *Johannesschüssel* brings about a tumbling into a black hole, into an abyss. Hence, in John's absorbing gaze we can reach that which cannot be seen physically: the indication of the invisible visage of God…Where Christ as living image has become an icon – the vera icon – John's iconic image is seized at the moment when he is flung out of time. From this nuclear fuel an incredible energy was released (I call it all-absorbing), an energy that quite fascinated the medieval and early modern individual, whether consciously or unconsciously.'[334]

Baert describes the connection between the prominence of the mouth and tongue, and the ruach, breath and prophecy in the *Johannesschüssel*. It is an image that invokes both life and death[335] - the live viewer is confronted by an image of brutal death frozen in time. 'The mouth is a portal into the dizzying depths of the body. It introduces us to the interiority of the body, which is taboo.'[336] In a legend associated with the execution of John, his tongue[337] is pierced by Herodias, perhaps

---

334 Baert, 80.

335 Baert also shows an archetypal connection between the *Johannesschüssel* and the iconography of the Medusa. 'Like the Medusa there is the physical analogy with respect to the face: the open mouth, the eyes of death, the gushing neck and, last but not least, the snakes and hair fanning out from the head. Many *Johannesschüssel* have pointed tendrils that project on all sides.' (Baert, 83.)

336 Baert, 81.

337 The tongue (especially a protruding tongue) is also seen as a phallic symbol in different cultures; sometimes kept as a trophy of an enemy through which their power can be transferred. The tongue has also been seen as a totem to ward off evil. Baert argues there is an equivalence between the head in the *Johannesschüssel* and the tongue. (Baert, 'The Johannesschüssel as Andachtsbild: The Gaze, the Medium and the Senses', 143.)

an attempt to silence the prophetic voice, the voice "crying in the wilderness", a voice now experienced in the silence. The 'silencing of the vox [...] leaves room for the Logos.'[338]

The decapitated head, revealing the neck and throat, is powerful and confronting. The throat is *gula* in Latin and 'in most languages makes use of the sound pattern GRG... in Indo European etymology this phonetic root also means "passage". The throat is a tube, a tunnel, a passage, a transition... the throat also reflects the uterus, or the dynamics of what has been "swallowed up" and can be vomited forth again'[339] The word *nephesh*[340] also had an original meaning of throat, one of the physical gateways of the breath, and 'thus related to the meaning of rûach.'[341] To decapitate someone, or cut the throat, separated the person from life – to cut them off. 'The connection between throat, John, solstice and silence is in fact already anchored in the passage from the first chapter of Luke (1:5–45)...'[342] This is where Zechariah becomes mute when he hears the news that he will be a father. 'Silence is truth and recommended to the seekers of that truth...The sacral silence is attributed in several cultures to the divine, to the epitheton[343] of God, to the locus where God can be encountered, hence to the zone or to a medium that allows the traffic between man and God, between humankind and the world beyond. It is the individual silence of concentration, interiority and meditation... In archaic Mediterranean culture the moment at which the Sun passes the meridian at its zenith is a mysterium... Midday is the

---

338 Baert, 'Vox Clamantis in Deserto', 82.

339 Baert, 83.

340 Soul or life.

341 Baert, 'Vox Clamantis in Deserto', 83.

342 Baert, 84.

343 Attributing to a person or thing a quality or description.

anxious moment of transition, of the motionless hour, when everything is enveloped in a net of light and astonishing quiet... There is scarcely a shadow. Pan is asleep now and everything and everybody must rest. In the landscape all is quiet, because nature has been struck dumb. The silence acquires the thickness of a holy place; the silence becomes a frightening *Gefühlsraum*[344, 345] It is in this silent "emotional space" that the *mysterium tremendum,* the awe-inspiring mystery, is experienced.

Again, beyond the personal, revelatory nature of silence, there is also a cosmic silence, the silence of the process of the universe and nature. 'Nature astonishes us with such powerful silences in two ways: the silence of zenith and the silence of solstice...The solstice goes through the cosmic 'throat' which needs the mediation by silence... The oral mastery of nature also implied the interval of sound and silence.'[346]

The head induces a response in the viewer by engaging speech, sight and hearing, represented by the tongue, the eyes, and the silence. This silence is '[t]he interval that possesses the secret of allowing something to pass – the tube, the transit, the throat, the uterus – makes use of cosmic silence in the fraction of a second: just before the turn. The *Johannesschüssel* seeks the vortex of all the senses, but at the end it demands us a vanishing point, an interval, a pause: silence indeed.'[347]

We can return the confessions made by Templars, during their interrogation, of having worshipped a head. This does not now seem so unusual considering the known practice of venerating the head of John the Baptist openly within some parishes in Europe (noting how widespread the presence of the Templars

---

344 Emotional space.

345 Baert, 'Vox Clamantis in Deserto', 84.

346 Baert, 84.

347 Baert, 84.

was). If we accept that the creation of the *Johannesschüssel* began in the 13th century, then it would have been contemporary with the Templars, and it must also be assumed that their creation did not appear from a vacuum but was a development of some existing practice (and it may be that the oldest examples are only the oldest still remaining in existence). Additionally, as stated by Baert, 'It is precisely this moment, during the age of the crusades, that the new image type comes into being, simulating St John's head on a platter.'[348] This may also be a link between the *Johannesschüssel* and the painting presented earlier of the Head of Christ from Templecombe (which has been carbon dated to the early 13th Century). Could this be a work with its origins in similar iconography, but rendered in only two dimensions? Although the head is not captured in a round frame, its similarity is striking.[349]

Like the image of Baphomet the *Johannesschüssel* presents to the viewer opposing concepts, two conflicting ideas that seek resolution. The head conjures life and death, and it sits in suspension between the old and the new (John 'belongs to the Old and the New Covenant').[350] He was the last of the Prophets and the first martyr. It exists between the static individual and the promise of transformation. It is both positive and negative (face and void), between the speech and the silence, and male and female – a male face with a womb-like interior.[351] The head has the potential to absorb, to draw the individual into its secrets, its mystery, its silence, but then cast them forth again,

---

348 Baert, 76.

349 The *Johannesschüssel* were also known to sometimes be modelled on images of Christ.

350 Baert, 'The Johannesschüssel as Andachtsbild: The Gaze, the Medium and the Senses', 121.

351 The head is also sometimes depicted as wounded, with an open gash.

reborn. In its function as an amulet against evil, the head is also dual; 'the *apotropaion*[352] terrifies, but at the same time swallows that terror. The *apotropaion* is 'homeopathic': it kills with its own negativity,[353] which turns the *apotropaion* into a 'positive' function.'[354] The *Johannesschüssel* simultaneously repels, but also draws in the gaze – look! This act of looking, this creation of an absorbing spectacle has the effect of 'provoking thought and nestling itself in the mind as the ultimate *compassio*.'[355] Meditating on the *Johannesschüssel* creates a transcendent state of compassion. The disk, like a mirror, reflects as well as absorbs, and there is a state that exists between these – between the horror of the image, and its simultaneous ecstatic beauty.

This old aeonic meditation on suffering and martyrdom could perhaps be viewed through the lens of the new aeon, if we refer to the 12th Aethyr of *Liber CDXVIII The Vision and the Voice* (noting the symbolic equivalence between wine and blood, and the function of the platter and the cup, and the possible connection in the iconography between the head of the Baptist, and the Eucharist).

This wine is such that its virtue radiateth through the cup, and I reel under the intoxication of it. And every thought is

---

352 Something that wards off evil

353 Baert interestingly links these concepts with that of obscenity (*obscenitas*), and an etymology of the word given as '*obs+cano*: what sounds, what is prophecy.' (Baert, 'Cutting the Throat. Obscenity and the Case of the Johannesschüssel, in "Scenes of the Obscene. The Non-Representable in Art and Visual Culture, Middle Ages to Today", Eds. Kassandra Nakas & Jessica Ullrich, Weimar, 2014, p. 127-147.', 128.)

354 Baert, 138.

355 Baert, 'The Johannesschüssel as Andachtsbild: The Gaze, the Medium and the Senses', 134.

destroyed by it. It abideth alone, and its name is Compassion. I understand by "Compassion," the sacrament of suffering, partaken of by the true worshippers of the Highest. And it is an ecstasy in which there is no trace of pain. Its passivity (= passion) is like the giving up of the self to the beloved.[356]

This self, in one sense, could be represented by the head. Giving up the self, the head to the round – the beloved.

This dissonance within the image of the decapitated John is also reflected in the vision of the Baptist experienced by Gertrude of Helfta (1256–1301/02).[357] Her vision was one of beauty; of a young and handsome man. This, perhaps, has an echo of the concept of Adam before the fall (initially male-and-female). In the late second temple period Adam is described as a 'youthful man, beautiful, wonderful'.[358] The Adam before the fall was clothed in glory. Adam and Eve wore 'garments of light', were 'clothed in glory and shining with praise.'[359] The possible implications (or interpretations) of these descriptions is discussed in more detail in the earlier section of this work related to the Shroud of Turin and the Rainbow Body.

Wisdom summons you in her goodness, saying…I am giving you a high-priestly garment woven from (every kind) of wisdom… Do not become desirous of gold or silver, which are

---

356 Crowley, Neuburg, and Desti, *The Vision & the Voice with Commentary and Other Papers: The Collected Diaries of Aleister Crowley, 1909-1914 E.V.*, 149.

357 Saint Gertrude lived in a state she called "nuptial mysticism", where she considered herself the bride of Christ, and the Mass was the 'wedding banquet at which a chaste self-giving consummated the sacred bond of lover and beloved.' ('Memorial of Saint Gertrude the Great'.)

358 Barker, 'Dominion Of Adam'.

359 Barker.

without profit, but clothe yourself with Wisdom like a robe, put knowledge upon you like a crown and be seated upon the throne of perception. ...Return to your divine nature.'[360]

Teaching of Silvanus

We could also interpret the relationship between John the Baptist and Jesus in a similar way to the relationship between Set (Seth) and Horus. John is the wild, unrestricted, creative impulse (The Devil), whereas Jesus, as Christ, as the King, shows this power, controlled and directed for the benefit of his people. Both were required for the new revelation.

Additionally, in relation to John and the revelation of Thelema, we can read in *The Vision and the Voice* (15th Aethyr):

As the dancer whirls, she chants in a strange, slow voice, quickening as she goes: Lo! I gather up every spirit that is pure and weave him into my vesture of flame. I lick up the lives of men and their souls sparkle from mine eyes. I am the mighty sorceress, the lust of the spirit. And by my dancing I gather up for my mother Nuit the heads of all them that are baptised in the waters of life. I am the lust of the spirit that eateth up the soul of man. I have prepared a feast for the adepts, and they that partake thereof shall see God.[361]

---

360 'The Teachings of Silvanus – The Nag Hammadi Library'.

361 Crowley, Neuburg, and Desti, *The Vision & the Voice with Commentary and Other Papers: The Collected Diaries of Aleister Crowley, 1909-1914 E.V.*, 131.

The Stomach Dance by Aubrey Beardsley (1894)

The above makes clear reference to the story of John, but here, in the New Aeon, Salome 'is a form of BABALON.'[362] Salome is transformed into something quite different; she becomes that to which we seek to attain. Initiates of the OTO[363]

---

362 Crowley, Neuburg, and Desti, 131.

363 It is tempting to see in the name of the Aethyr (OXO) a reference to the mysteries of the OTO. Crowley also assigns to this Aethyr the colour "olive for Salome, & of Malkuth." (Crowley, Neuburg, and Desti, 117.) As written by Ian Drummond, 'Like the olive oil which serves as the basis of the holy

should also consider Crowley's commentary to this section. 'There is a reference to the story of Salome in the Lesser Mysteries of the Dagger and Disk, in the cult of "the God John." "John" is "ON" – Oannes, Nu, Noah, Johah, etc., the Sun entering the watery sign of Cancer (the sign of the Whale, Ark, etc.) at the Summer Solstice.'[364] The God "ON", the headless or bornless God, as the Sun enters the waters, the waters of Binah.

> Now it is clear that what she has woven in her dance; it is the Crimson Rose of 49 Petals,[365] and the Pillars are the Cross with which it is conjoined. And between the pillars shoot out rays of pure green fire; and now all the pillars are golden.[366]

Here we see a clear connection between the mysteries of John the Baptist, the experience of the loss of the head, the extinguishing of ego consciousness and the Attainment to BABA-

---

oil, the Minerval ceremony is the base of the Mysteria Mystica Maxima...' (Walls, *Ora et Labora Vol 4*, 2023, 7.)

364 Crowley, Neuburg, and Desti, *The Vision & the Voice with Commentary and Other Papers: The Collected Diaries of Aleister Crowley, 1909-1914 E.V.*, 131.

365 I would also consider here the connection between this vision and Chapter 49 of *The Book of Lies*. In this vision the Rose is shown as 'a vast amphitheatre, with seven tiers, each tier divided into seven partitions. And they that sit in the Amphitheatre are the seven grades of the Order of the Rosy Cross.' (Crowley, Neuburg, and Desti, 131.) In Chapter 49 we should note that the "Dance of the Seven Veils" is not directly biblical, but found in the English translation of Oscar Wilde's play "Salome". Aubrey Beardsley also produced a work called "The Stomach Dance" in 1894, which was an interpretation of the dance. Beardsley was known to Crowley, and his lover Jerome Pollitt (1871-1942) was a collector of his works. I would also tentatively propose that Chapter 49 alludes to certain mysteries connected to the seven-fold chakra system, but this needs a great deal of further research and consideration.

366 Crowley, Neuburg, and Desti, 131.

LON in the form of Salome. John shows us that in order to make way for something else, something beyond ourselves, we must give up ourselves.

The Beheading of Saint John the Baptist by Hendrick ter Brugghen (1617)

The Black Man

"Le Grand Negre"

There is an entity in Germanic folklore who is, very un-threateningly, called Leonard, but is the demon inspector-general of sorcery or, as described by Collin de Plancy in his Infernal Dictionary, '*grand maitre de sabbats...*'[1] Leonard, 'is often called "Le Grand Negre" (The Black Man)...' he presides over the sabbath in the form of a goat.' Leonard also has a face on his backside, and '[w]itches adore him by kissing this lower face while holding a green candle in their hand.'[2] In the *Dictionary of Phrase and Fable* he is 'Grand-master of the nocturnal orgies of demons. He is represented as a three-horned goat with black human face. He marked his novitiates with one of his horns.'[3]

---

1 Jacques Collin de Plancy, *Dictionnaire Infernal*, 404.

2 A parallel could perhaps be drawn here with the accusations against the rituals of the Templars that involved the kissing of the anus or the base of the spine. The green candle could be a symbol of fertility.

3 Brewer, *Dictionary of Phrase and Fable*, 818.

Leonard is mentioned by Lévi in *Transcendental Magic*: 'To Sabbaths dreamed in this manner we must refer the accounts of a goat issuing from pitchers and going back into them after the ceremony; infernal powders obtained from the ordure of this goat, who is called Master Leonard; banquets where abortions are eaten without salt and boiled with serpents and toads; dances, in which monstrous animals or men and women with impossible shapes take part; unbridled debauches where incubi project cold sperm. Nightmare alone could produce or explain such scenes.'[4] Here Lévi is referring to visions induced by the taking of narcotics with 'black magical ceremonies…'.[5] There is a clear indication in the above that the archetype of the black man has a connection to sexual mysteries, here framed by Lévi in a negative way. Some have made a link between

---

4   Lévi, *Transcendental Magic*, 312.

5   Lévi, 312.

the descriptions of Leonard, the sacrificial goats, and Azazel in Leviticus.

The atmosphere around Leonard as described by Lévi is reminiscent of Jung writing about the *prima materia* – 'Once an unconscious content is constellated, it tends to [create], through projection, an atmosphere of illusion...[6] The situation is enveloped in a kind of fog, and this fully accords with the nature of the unconscious content: It is a "black blacker than black" (*nigrum, nigrius nigro*), as the alchemists rightly say, and in addition is charged with dangerous polar tensions, with the *inimicitia elementorum*.[7] One finds oneself in an impenetrable chaos, which is indeed one of the synonyms for the mysterious *prima materia*. The latter corresponds to the nature of the unconscious content in every respect, with one exception: this time it does not appear in the alchemical substance but in man himself...'[8]

Jung here associates blackness with the *prima materia*, and the unconscious and the "polar tensions" that this produces following the constellation and projection of this unconscious content. The attendance at the Sabbath with "*Le Grand Negre*" represents an active engagement with this process. It is to invite the unconscious into consciousness through projection; to actively invoke (or evoke) this "enmity of the elements" for the purpose of transformation, change and eventual return to harmony. The alchemical opus is essentially that of a union of opposites; a resolving of the polar tensions. The *prima materia*, or *massa confusa*, contains warring elements that must be separated and sublimated. As it states in the Gloria Mundi

---

6   Here Jung also describes the relationship between doctor and patient during this process, and the possible breakdown of trust.

7   The enmity of the elements

8   Jung, *The Practice of Psychotherapy*, 187.

from the sixteenth century, 'melted into a unity purified of all opposition and therefore incorruptible.'[9] The opus of alchemy is, in essence, one of the union of opposites, a resolving of these tensions. 'After violent oscillations at the beginning, the opposites equalize one another, and gradually a new attitude develops, the final stability of which is the greater in proportion to the magnitude of the initial differences. The greater the tension between the pairs of opposites, the greater will be the energy that comes from them; and the greater the energy, the stronger will be its constellating, attracting power.'[10]

There is an interesting theory (which I am not necessarily endorsing) based on the writings of Elijah Muhammad (1897–1975),[11] which suggests that black people are the original humans, and therefore, due to some elements of quantum physics (found in the work of Stephen Hawking and Leonard Mlodinow), are the "lords of creation". Because it was black people who first gained consciousness, and therefore were the first to consciously observe the universe, they were therefore 'responsible for the quantum collapse of the so-called multi-verse (wave-function) into the universe that we live in today...'[12] As Muhammad writes, 'You are the only man who needed light to light up **Your Universe.** You brought forth that light. You are walking around looking for a God to bow to and worship. **You Are the God!**'[13] If there is any truth to this idea, it could speak to the psychological and genetic roots of the image of the

----

9   Williams, 'The Origin of Alchemy and the Image of God in Man'.

10   Jung, 'Volume 8 Collected Works of C.G. Jung, Volume 8', 48–49.

11   Leader of the Nation of Islam from 1932 till 1975 and was the teacher of Malcolm X and Muhammad Ali among many others.

12   Muhammad, 'The Secret Hidden in Modern Science: Is the Black Man God'.

13   Muhammad, 'Our Savior Has Arrived'.

black man, and its presence in different religions and mystery traditions. The black man speaks to our very origins, or at least the dawn of our conscious existence.

Something of the essence described in the legends of Leonard may be seen in the 4th Aethyr of *The Vision and the Voice*:

Yea, as in a looking-glass, so in thy mind, that is backed with the false metal of lying, is every symbol read averse. Lo! everything wherein thou hast trusted must confound thee, and that thou didst flee from was thy saviour. So therefore didst thou shriek in the Black Sabbath when thou didst kiss the hairy buttocks of the goat, when the gnarled god tore thee asunder, when the icy cataract of death swept thee away.

Shriek, therefore, shriek aloud; mingle the roar of the gored lion and the moan of the torn bull, and the cry of the man that is torn by the claws of the Eagle, and the scream of the Eagle that is strangled by the hands of the Man. Mingle all these in the death-shriek of the Sphinx, for the blind man hath profaned her mystery. Who is this, Oedipus, Tiresias, Erinyes? Who is this, that is blind and a seer, a fool above wisdom? Whom do the hounds of heaven follow, and the crocodiles of hell await? *Aleph, Vau, Yod, Ayin, Resh, Tau,* is his name.

Beneath his feet is the Kingdom, and upon his head the Crown. He is spirit and matter; he is peace and power; in him is Chaos and Night and Pan; and upon BABALON his concubine, that hath made him drunk upon the blood of the saints that she hath gathered in her golden cup, hath he begotten the virgin that now he doth deflower. And this is that which is written: Malkuth shall be uplifted and set upon the throne of Binah. And this is the stone of the philosophers that is set as a seal upon the Tomb of Tetragrammaton, and the elixir of life that is distilled from the blood of the saints, and the red powder that is the grinding up of the bones of Choronzon.

Terrible and wonderful is the Mystery thereof, O thou Titan that hast climbed into the bed of Juno! Surely thou art bound unto, and broken upon, the wheel; yet hast thou uncovered the nakedness of the Holy One, and the Queen of Heaven is in travail of child, and his name shall be called Vir, and Vis, and Virus, and Virtus, and Viridis, in one name that is all these, and above all these.

After all has been broken, after the Adept has partaken of the true Black Sabbath, as described in the legends of Leonard, a Messiah is born – V.V.V.V.V. – 'one name that is all these, and above all these.[14]

In this blackness there is a certain mystery, introduced previously, articulated by Crowley in The Book of Thoth:

It becomes then reasonable to argue from analogy that since the end must beget the beginning, the symbolism will follow; hence, blackness is also attributed to the sun, according to a certain long-hidden tradition. One of the shocks for candidates in the "Mysteries" was the revelation "Osiris is a black god".[15]

The Sabbath, the Sabbath of Baphomet, is a necessary initiatic process that the Master must endure. Everything that was truth is now falsehood, everything that once supported the

---

14 Crowley, Neuburg, and Desti, *The Vision & the Voice with Commentary and Other Papers: The Collected Diaries of Aleister Crowley, 1909-1914 E.V.,* 209–10.

15 Crowley, *The Book of Thoth,* 118.

aspirant dissolves and they are lost in confusion. This is the approach to the primordial chaos that the adept must accept fully or, holding onto the illusion of themselves, they become shut up.

THE STONE

Levi writes in *Transcendental Magic*, 'The ancients adored the sun under the figure of a black stone, which they named Elagabalus, or Heliogabalus.'[1] Keep in mind Crowley's attribution of the Sun to Blackness above, and the many references to the black stone at the Kaaba, and its association with Mohammad, and references to stones or rocks which have featured throughout this work. I have also discussed the cubic stone forming the throne on which Baphomet sits, and the concept of the stone in relation to Baphomet.

Lévi's statement above is curious, Elagabalus or Heliogabalus was the Roman emperor Marcus Aurelius Antoninus (218 to 222), and Elagabalus or Heliogabalus are the Latinised names of his god. Antoninus was from a hereditary line of high priests who served the Arab-Roman sun god Elagabal. This is derived from the Arabic "Ilah Al-Gabal" (إله الجبل), which translates as "God of the Mountain".

In relation to the emperor Elagabalus, 'The name evokes an image of a depraved sybarite "treading in silver dust and sand of gold, his head crowned with a tiara and his clothes studded with jewels, working at women's tasks in the midst of his eunuchs, calling himself Empress and bedding every night with a new Emperor, picked for choice from among his barbers, scullions, and charioteers...". Such portraits of Elagabalus derive, ultimately, from the accounts of the emperor's reign (218-22 C.E.) provided by Dio Cassius, Herodian, and the author of the Historia Augusta. These historians represent Elagabalus as

---

1   Lévi, *Transcendental Magic*, 164.

an oriental despot prone to extravagance of all sorts and as a religious fanatic determined to impose a Syrian god upon the Roman populace. They also report that the emperor cultivated a feminine appearance; that he married three women (including a Vestal Virgin) and one man; that he had a sexual predilection for well-endowed males; and that he asked his court physicians to construct a vagina in his body. Elagabalus, if these sources are to be credited, was an emperor gone wild.'[2] It could also be said that this sexually ambiguous character (reliability of historical sources aside) seems an interesting association for the androgynous Baphomet, in light of Lévi's reference to this historical figure.[3]

In relation to the stone (as the *prima materia*) Jung writes 'Mercurius, it is generally affirmed, is the arcanum, the *prima materia*, the "father of all metals", the primeval chaos, the earth of paradise, the "material upon which nature worked a little, but nevertheless left imperfect." He is also the *ultima materia*,[4] the goal of his own transformation, the stone, the tincture, the philosophic gold, the carbuncle, the philosophic man, the second Adam, the analogue of Christ, the king, the light of lights, the *deus terrestris*,[5] indeed the divinity itself or its perfect counterpart.'[6]

Just as Gurnemanz pushes Parsifal out the door, considering him nothing but a fool, we are reminded that 'the Stone that the Builder has rejected is destined to become the Head

---

2   Nugent, 'From "Filthy Catamite" to "Queer Icon": Elagabalus and the Politics of Sexuality (1960–1975)', 171.

3   It should also be noted that representations of Elagabalus from coins of the period, show him with an eight-pointed star.

4   Last material.

5   Terrestrial God.

6   Jung, *Alchemical Studies*, 13:235.

of the corner.'[7] The gold or elixir can be produced from the imperfect. 'The stone, the *lumen novum*,[8] arising from the *coniunctio* of the reconciled opposites *Sol et Luna* was personified as the rounded, bisexual Anthropos and proclaimed as the *filius macrocosmi*,[9] the saviour of the macrocosm and counterpart to Christ.'[10] Body and soul, the passive and the active are reunited in this *coniunctio*, the *hieros gamos*, the cohabitation of the Sun and the Moon. As again described by Jung, '[f]rom this union sprang the *filius sapientiae*[11] or *filius philosophorum*,[12] the transformed Mercurius, who was thought of as hermaphroditic in token of his rounded perfection.'[13] This archetype of "roundness" is captured in the myths of the Holy Grail, and the trials and adventures of its servants. Like the alchemists, by reconciling with the grail, by healing the division between mind and body, they sought to come to wholeness. 'In alchemy, Mercurius is "a world creating spirit", an integration of light and dark, good and bad, the beginning and the end of the alchemist's quest. An animating principle, a vital force. Mercurius encourages us to keep on living, exploring, and learning from experience.'[14]

A final word on Baphomet as stone. As discussed earlier, by Gematria Crowley came to the spelling BAFOMIThR, which equals 729. This has the same value as *Kēphas* (Πέτρος) or

---

7   Leighton Cleather and Crump, *Parsifal Lohengrin and the Legend of the Holy Grail*, 132.

8   New light.

9   The son of the macrocosm.

10   Williams, 'The Origin of Alchemy and the Image of God in Man'.

11   The son of wisdom.

12   The son of the philosophers.

13   Williams, 'The Origin of Alchemy and the Image of God in Man'.

14   Mercurius, 'Who Is Mercurius?'

rock, which is the name Jesus is said to have given the apostle Peter as the foundation of his Church.

> You are Peter, and on this rock I will build my Church, and the gates of hell will not prevail against it.
>
> *Matthew* 16:18

In his Confessions, Crowley writes 'Already he had shown me that I, in my office as Baphomet, was the rock on which the New Temple should be built.'[15]

---

15   Crowley, Confessions, 833. For more on this see my original essay, "Baphomet", in *Ora Et Labora* Vol. 1, published in 2021 by In Perpetuity Publishing.

CONCLUSION

So where are we? We have moved from the simple to the complex, and the complex to the simple; from the past to the present; from the East to the West, and from the West to the East. From understanding to confusion and from confusion to understanding. We have explored some obvious ground for understanding Baphomet, but also wandered onto some unexpected paths.

If we want to understand the extent of this mystery, the mystery of Baphomet, both the force and the transformed consciousness that it represents (both required to effectively wield it) we need look no further than some of Lévi's closing remarks in *The Key of the Mysteries*, as translated by Crowley.

> The great arcanum – that is to say, the unutterable and inexplicable secret – is the absolute knowledge of good and evil.
>
> "When you have eaten the fruit of this tree, you will be as the gods," said the Serpent.
>
> "If you eat of it, you will die," replied Divine Wisdom.
>
> Thus good and evil bear fruit on one same tree, and from one same root.
>
> Good personifies God.
>
> Evil Personifies the Devil.
>
> To know the secret or formula of God is to be God.
>
> To know the secret or the formula of the Devil is to be the Devil.

To wish to be at the same time God and Devil is to absorb in one's self the most absolute antinomy, the two most strained contrary forces; it is the wish to shut up in one's self an infinite antagonism.

It is to drink a poison which would extinguish the suns and consume the worlds.

It is to put on the consuming robe of Deianira.[1]

It is to devote one's self to the promptest and most terrible of all deaths.

Woe to him who wishes to know too much! For if excessive and rash knowledge does not kill him it will make him mad.

To eat the fruit of the Tree of Knowledge of Good and Evil, is to associate evil with good, and to assimilate one to the other.

It is to cover the radiant countenance of Osiris with the mask of Typhon.

It is to raise the sacred veil of Isis; it is to profane the sanctuary.

The rash man who dares to look at the sun without protection becomes blind, and from that moment for him the sun is black.

We are forbidden to say more on this subject…'[2] This passage serves to make explicit what is required to be a true Master

---

1   Deianira translates as "man killer" or "killer of her husband". She killed her husband (Hercules) unwittingly with the "Nessus-robe".

2   Levi, 'The Key of the Mysteries', 285–87.

of these mysteries, and a warning – No One can truly understand what is required.

The Key of the Mysteries

Baphomet, as a form of the Cherubim, is a 'guardian of
all that is Holy' but also 'shows the way to the righteous.'[3]
Baphomet depicts both the state, and the mysteries of how to
achieve that state. A state of consciousness that stands between
contending forces – a stillness in motion – a speech in silence
– a wholeness. But there is more to this; having devoted 'one's
self to the promptest and most terrible of all deaths', one is also
reborn. And this new birth is a great Mystery of Redemption,
and of the Redeemer.

> And: This child danceth not, but it is because he is the soul of
> the two dances, - the right hand and the left hand, and in him
> they are one dance, the dance without motion.
>
> *The Vision and the Voice* (The First Aethyr)[4]

Also, as articulated by Edinger in his exploration of the
Apocalypse, 'Humanity is now in the role of "son of God."
And God is bringing about his own transformation by another
self-destruction while incarnated in the "mortal body" of humankind. There will follow necessarily, archetypally, the same
sequence of events as occurred in the life of a single individual
but now in a larger arena. And this second act of incarnation
likewise will bring about the same goal, a transformation of the
God-image. The image of a totally good God – albeit pestered
by a dissociated evil Satan – is no longer viable. Instead, the

---

3   *Mend Me This Shoe, That I May Walk.*

4   Crowley, Neuburg, and Desti, *The Vision & the Voice with Commentary
and Other Papers: The Collected Diaries of Aleister Crowley, 1909-1914 E.V.*,
248.

new God-image coming into conscious realization is that of a paradoxical union of opposites; and with it comes a healing of the metaphysical split that has characterized the entire Christian aeon.'[5] I would argue that one form of this new God-image becoming conscious in humanity is reflected in Lévi's Baphomet – a symbol of healing, a symbol of redemption.

The glyph of Baphomet provides us with a link into our deepest, archetypal past and our ancient sanctuaries, but also provides us with a key to the future, and demonstrates how to build the new Temple. If we see Baphomet as a form of the Sphinx, we can be reminded of Crowley's statement in *Liber Aleph*, 'It is now expedient that I instruct thee concerning the Four Powers of the Sphinx, the Strangler, and firstly, that this most arcane of the Mysteries of Antiquity was never at any Period the Tool of the Slave-Gods, but a Witness of Horus through the dark Aeon of Osiris to His Light and Truth, His Force and Fire.'[6]

The figure shows us the way to personal transformation, but also (as Lévi says) a way to transform society (the "larger arena" described by Edinger), and find a new way of living free from the errors of the past and the present. To transform the world, we need to transform individuals, and to transform individuals we also need to transform the world. We must create an environment in which each can pursue their Great Work – we must protect the pilgrims; we must be Templars.

> When the field of vision has been unified, the inner being comes to rest, and that inner peaceableness flows into the outer world as harmony and compassion[7]

---

5   Edinger, *Archetype of the Apocalypse*, 177.

6   Crowley, *Liber Aleph Vel CXI: The Book of Wisdom or Folly*, 151.

7   Bourgeault, 'Cynthia Bourgeault'.

So then its seed is in truth nothing else
But its own water, which in fetters lies
So chain'd within its centre where it dwells
That it is not apparent to the eyes,
       Ne to the minde, but of a mental man
       Who knows a Key this lock which open can.[8]

So therefore the beginning is delight, and the End is delight, and delight is in the midst, even as the Indus is water in the cavern of the glacier, and water among the greater hills and the lesser hills and through the ramparts of the hills and through the plains, and water at the mouth thereof when it leaps forth into the mighty sea, yea, into the mighty sea.

Liber CCCLXX, 39

One ghost succeeds the other like waves on the illusory sea of birth and death. In the course of life, there is nothing but the rise and fall of material and mental forms, while the unfathomable reality remains. In every creature sleeps an infinite intelligence, hidden and unknown, but destined to awaken, to tear the volatile web of the sensory mind, break the chrysalis of flesh, and conquer time and space.[9]

Godspeed

8   Philalethes, *Alchemical Works: Eirenaeus Philalethes Compiled*, 18.
9   Labatut, *When We Cease to Understand the World*, 135.

BIBLIOGRAPHY

Abreu, Jose Luis. *Zoroastrianism in China*. Los Angeles: Spenta Graduate Institute, 2016.

Achad, Frater. 'Bread of Stones?: Part I', n.d. https://www.100thmonkeypress.com/biblio/achad/texts/bread_or_stones_1/1923_02_00_occult_press.pdf.

———. 'Living in the Sunlight'. *The Fenris Wolf*, no. 7 (2014).

———. 'Stepping Out of the Old Aeon and Into the New'. The 100th Monkey Press, n.d. https://www.100thmonkeypress.com/biblio/achad/texts/stepping/aeon_text.pdf.

Adlington, William, and Lucius Apuleius, trans. 'The Project Gutenberg eBook of The Golden Asse, by Lucius Apuleius'. Accessed 24 December 2024. https://www.gutenberg.org/files/1666/1666-h/1666-h.htm.

Albanese, Luciano. 'Porphyry, the Cave of the Nymphs, and the Mysteries of Mithras'. *Acta Antiqua Academiae Scientiarum Hungaricae* 58, no. 1–4 (December 2018): 681–91. https://doi.org/10.1556/068.2018.58.1-4.39.

Apple, Rabbi Raymond. 'The Challenge of Yom Kippur'. Opinion. ABC Religion & Ethics. Australian Broadcasting Corporation, 8 October 2019. https://www.abc.net.au/religion/the-challenge-of-yom-kippur/11582690.

Arabestani, Mehrdad. 'Ritual Purity and the Mandaeans' Identity'. *Iran and the Caucasus* 16 (2012): 153–68.

Armstrong, Karen. *Jerusalem: One City, Three Faiths*. Alfred A. Knopf, 1996.

Arp-Neumann, Janne. 'Negating Seth: Destruction as Vitality'. *Numen* 68, no. 2–3 (2021): 157.

Bacher, Wilhelm, and Ludwig Blau. 'SANDALFON – JewishEncyclopedia.Com'. Accessed 20 October 2021. https://www.jewishencyclopedia.com/articles/13172-sandalfon.

Baert, Barbara. 'Cutting the Throat. Obscenity and the Case of the Johannesschüssel, in "Scenes of the Obscene. The Non-Representable in Art and Visual Culture, Middle Ages to Today", Eds. Kassandra Nakas & Jessica Ullrich, Weimar, 2014, p. 127-147.' Accessed 17 January 2022. https://www.academia.edu/9024084/Cutting_the_throat_Obscenity_and_the_case_of_the_Johannessch%C3%BCssel_in_Scenes_of_the_Obscene_The_Non_Representable_in_Art_and_Visual_Culture_Middle_Ages_to_Today_eds_Kassandra_Nakas_and_Jessica_Ullrich_Weimar_2014_p_127_147.

———. 'The Johannesschüssel as Andachtsbild: The Gaze, the Medium and the Senses', n.d., 44.

———. 'The Spinning Head: Round Forms and the Phenomenon of the Johannesschüssel'. Accessed 13 January 2022. https://www.academia.edu/40356414/The_spinning_head_Round_forms_and_the_Phenomenon_of_the_Johannessch%C3%BCssel?auto=download&email_work_card=download-paper.

———. 'Vox Clamantis in Deserto: The Johannesschüssel: Senses and Silences'. *Open Arts Journal*, no. 4 (February 2015). https://doi.org/10.5456/issn.2050-3679/2015w05.

Bajpai, Rajendra. 'Tinkering with the Unbearable Lightness of Being: Meditation, Mind-Body Medicine and Placebo in the Quantum Biology Age'. *Journal of Nonlocality* II, no. 2 (December 2013). https://www.academia.edu/5605281/Tinkering_with_the_Unbearable_Lightness_of_Being_Meditation_Mind_Body_Medicine_and_Placebo_in_the_Quantum_Biology_Age.

Barber, Malcolm. *The Trial of the Templars*. Cambridge: Cambridge University Press, 1993.

Barker, Margaret. *An Extraordinary Gathering of Angels*. London: MQ Publications Ltd, 2004.

———. 'Dominion Of Adam', 2009. http://www.margaretbarker.com/Papers/DominionOfAdam2009.pdf.

———. 'Jesus the Nazorean', 2014. http://www.margaretbarker.com/Papers/TemenosJesusintheGospelofJohn.pdf.

———. *Temple Mysticism: An Introduction*. London: SPCK, 2011.

———. *Temple Theology: An Introduction*. London: SPCK Publishing, 2004.

———. *The Great Angel: A Study of Israel's Second God*. Kentucky: Westminster John Knox Press, 1992.

———. *The Lost Prophet: The Book of Enoch and Its Influence on Christianity*. London: SPCK, 1988.

———. 'Where Shall Wisdom be Found? (Job 28.12)', 2001.

Beck, Roger. 'Mithraism'. Accessed 9 October 2021. https://iranicaonline.org.

Beckworth, D Houston. 'Are We Wrong: The Symbolic Identity of the Goat for Azazel (the Scapegoat)', n.d.

Beta, Hymenaeus, ed. *The Equinox*. Vol. III. 10 vols. Samuel Weiser, INC, 1991.

Beta, Hymenaeus, and Frater A.E.N., eds. 'The Magical Link' 9, no. 3 (1995).

Bhikkhu, Thanissaro. 'Selves & Not-Self: The Buddhist Teaching on Anatta'. Accessed 19 January 2022. https://www.accesstoinsight.org/lib/authors/thanissaro/selvesnotself.html.

Biale, David. 'The God with Breasts: El Shaddai in the Bible', n.d.

Bible Study Tools. 'Mesites Meaning – Greek Lexicon | New Testament (NAS)'. Accessed 25 June 2024. https://www.biblestudytools.com/lexicons/greek/nas/mesites.html.

Blavatsky, H.P. 'Life Principle – Blavatsky.Net'. Accessed 24 April 2022. https://www.blavatsky.net/index.php/life-principle.

———. *The Inner Group Teachings of H.P. Blavatsky*. Point Loma Publications, Inc, 1985.

———. *The Secret Doctrine*. Vol. 1. London: The Theosophical Publishing House, 2019.

Blech, Benjamin. 'Understanding Judaism : The Basics of Deed and Creed'. Accessed 20 July 2023. https://archive.org/details/understandingjud0000blec/mode/2up.

Blofeld, John. *Bodhisattva of Compassion: The Mystical Tradition of Kuan Yin*. Boston: Shambhala, 1988.

Bogdan, Henrik, and Jan A.M. Snoek, eds. *Handbook of Freemasonry*. Leiden | Boston: Brill, 2014.

Bogdan, Henrik, and Martin P. Starr, eds. *Aleister Crowley and Western Esotericism*. New York: Oxford University Press, 2012.

Bonner, John. *Qabalah: A Magical Primer*. York Beach, ME: Weiser Books, 2002.

Boodberg, Peter A. 'Philological Notes on Chapter One of the Lao Tzu'. *Harvard Journal of Asiatic Studies* 20, no. 3 and 4 (December 1957): 598–618.

Bourgeault, Cynthia. 'Cynthia Bourgeault'. Accessed 23 September 2022. https://cynthiabourgeault.org/.

Brand, Miryam T. 'Belial, Free Will, and Identity-Building in the Community Rule.' *Das Böse, Der Teufel Und Dämonen – Evil, the Devil, and Demons*, 2016, 77–92.

Bree, Tom. 'Symbolism as Marriage and the Symbolism of Marriage'. *Eye of the Heart: A Journal of Traditional Wisdom*, no. 3 (2009).

Brewer, E. Cobham. *Dictionary of Phrase and Fable*. London: Cassell and Company, Limited, 1900.

Browne, Laurence. 'Examining Coincidences: Towards an Integrated Approach'. PhD Thesis, The University of Queensland, 2014. https://doi.org/10.14264/uql.2015.119.

Browning, Robert. 'The Ring and the Book', n.d. Wikisource.

'Buddha'. Accessed 17 March 2022. https://www.palikanon.com/english/pali_names/b/buddha.htm.

Butler, Edward P. 'The Nature and Functions of Thoth in Egyptian Theology'. In *A Silver Sun and Inky Clouds: A Devotional for Djehuty and Set*. Asheville, North Carolina: Bibliotheca Alexandrina, n.d.

Campbell, Joseph. *The Inner Reaches of Outer Space*. New York: Harper & Row, 1988.

Carus, Paul. 'Anubis, Seth, and Christ: The Significance of the "Spott-Crucifix"'. *The Open Court* XV, no. 2 (February 1901): 65–97.

Cave. 'Nick Cave – The Red Hand Files – Issue #181 – How or When or Do You Shut the Voices of All Your Influences (Your Heroes, Your Parents, Your Jesus, Your Music) to Listen to Yourself, to Become You or to Believe That What You Create Is Your Own?' The Red Hand Files, 18 January 2022. https://www.theredhandfiles.com/voices-of-all-your-influences/.

Cavendish, Richard. *The Tarot*. London: Chancellor Press, 1988.

'Chaos – Theosophy Wiki'. Accessed 10 April 2022. https://theosophy.wiki/en/Chaos.

Churton, Tobias. *Occult Paris*. Rochester, Vermont: Inner Traditions, 2016.

———. *The Mysteries of John the Baptist*. Rochester, Vermont: Inner Traditions, 2012.

Cicero, Charles. 'The Rosicrucian Vault'. Societas Rosicruciana in America®. Accessed 5 November 2022. https://sria.org/the-rosicrucian-vault/.

Cleary, Thomas, trans. *The Secret of the Golden Flower: The Classic Chinese Book of Life*. New York: HarperOne, 1991.

Cohn, Norman. *Europe's Inner Demons*. St Albans: Paladin, 1976.

Crenshaw, James L. *Samson : A Secret Betrayed, a Vow Ignored*. Atlanta : John Knox Press, 1978. http://archive.org/details/samsonsecretbetr0000cren.

Criddle, Andrew, and Roger Pearse. 'The "Body and Blood of Mithras" Myth'. *The Tertullian Project* (blog), 19 May 2021. https://tertullian.org/rpearse/mithras_body_and_blood/

mithras_myth1.htm#:~:text=A%20common%20supposed %20quotation%20came%20my%20way%20in,usual%20 source%20seems%20to%20be%20Freke%20and%20Gandy.

Crowley, Aleister. *777 and Other Qabalistic Writings of Aleister Crowley*. Edited by Israel Regardie. York Beach, Maine: Samuel Weiser, Inc, 1994.

———. *Aleister Crowley and the Practice of the Magical Diary*. Edited by James Wasserman. New York: Sekmet Books, 2003.

———. *Amrita*. Edited by Martin P. Starr. Kings Beach, California: Thelema Publications, 1990.

———. *Collected Works of Aleister Crowley*. Vol. II. III vols. Des Plaines, Illinois: Yogi Publication Society, 1974.

———. *Liber Aleph Vel CXI: The Book of Wisdom or Folly*. York Beach, Maine: Samuel Weiser, Inc, 1995.

———. 'Liber CXCIV, An Intimation with Reference to the Constitution of the Order'. *The Equinox* III, no. 10 (1991).

———. 'Liber Librae Sub Figura XXX'. *The Equinox* III, no. 10 (1991).

———. 'Liber Pyramidos Sub Figurâ DCLXXI – Technical Libers of Thelema – The Libri of Aleister Crowley – Hermetic Library'. Accessed 5 November 2022. https://hermetic.com/ crowley/libers/lib671.

———. *Magick Without Tears*. Edited by Israel Regardie. Tempe, AZ: New Falcon Publications, 1997.

———. *Olla: An Anthology of Sixty Years of Song*. London: O.T.O., 1946.

———. *Tao Te King*. York Beach, Maine: Samuel Weiser, Inc, 1995.

———. 'The Attainment of Happiness | Vanity Fair'. Vanity Fair | The Complete Archive. Accessed 30 June 2024. https://archive. vanityfair.com/article/1916/11/the-attainment-of-happiness.

———. *The Book of Lies*. York Beach, Maine: Samuel Weiser Inc, 1995.

———. *The Book of Thoth*. York Beach, Maine: Samuel Weiser, INC, 1993.

———. *The Collected Works of Aleister Crowley*. Vol. I. Des Plaines, Illinois: Yogi Publication Society, 1974.

———. *The Confessions of Aleister Crowley*. London: Jonathan Cape, 1969.

———. *The Equinox of the Gods*. London: Ordo Templi Orientis, 1936.

———, ed. *The Goetia: The Lesser Key of Solomon the King – Clavicula Salomonis Regis*. Translated by Samuel Liddell MacGregor Mathers. York Beach, Maine: Samuel Weiser, Inc, 1995.

———. *The Heart of the Master & Other Papers by Aleister Crowley*. Edited by Hymenaeus Beta. Tempe, AZ: New Falcon Publications, 1997.

———. *The Holy Books of Thelema*. York Beach, Maine: Samuel Weiser, Inc, 1988.

———. *The Law Is for All*. Edited by Louis Wilkinson and Hymenaeus Beta. Tempe, AZ: New Falcon Publications, 1996.

———. *The Magical Diaries of Aleister Crowley: Tunisia 1923*. Edited by Stephen Skinner. York Beach, ME: Samuel Weiser, Inc, 1996.

———. *The Magical Record of the Beast 666*. Edited by John Symonds and Kenneth Grant. London: Gerald Duckworth & Co. Ltd., 1972.

———. 'The Temple of Solomon the King'. *The Equinox* I, no. 5 (1998).

Crowley, Aleister, and Evangeline Adams. *The General Principles of Astrology*. Edited by Hymenaeus Beta. York Beach, Maine: Weiser Books, 2002.

Crowley, Aleister, Mary Desti, and Leila Waddell. *Magick. Liber ABA. Book Four. Parts I-IV*. York Beach, Maine: Samuel Weiser, Inc, 1997.

Crowley, Aleister, and Roddie Minor. 'Liber DCCXXIX : The Amalantrah Working'. Ordo Templi Orientis, 1990.

———. 'The Amalantrah Working – Liber XCVII'. Ordo Templi Orientis, 1990.

Crowley, Aleister, Victor. B Neuburg, and Mary Desti. *The Vision & the Voice with Commentary and Other Papers: The Collected Diaries of Aleister Crowley, 1909-1914 E.V.* York Beach, Maine: Samuel Weiser, INC, 1998.

Crowley, Aleister, Charles Stansfeld Jones, J.F.C. Fuller, and H.P. Blavatsky. *Commentaries of the Holy Books and Other Papers*. Vol. 4. The Equinox 1. York Beach, Maine: Samuel Weiser, Inc, 1996.

'De Lege Libellum'. Accessed 15 June 2023. https://lib.oto-usa. org/libri/liber0150.html.

De Nieuwe kerk Amsterdam. 'Background Story: The Life of the Buddha, Path to the Present'. Accessed 20 May 2023. https:// www.nieuwekerk.nl/en/background-story-the-life-of-the-buddha-path-to-the-present/.

DeFrancisco, James J. 'Mithraism and Blood Sacrifice in Christian Belief and Practice and Its Relationship to Christianity', 2015. 05/09/2021.

Demurger, Alain. *The Last Templar*. London: Profile Books Ltd, 2009.

Dieter Betz, Hans, ed. *The Greek Magical Papyri in Translation*. Chicago & London: The University of Chicago Press, 1986.

Duncan, Jonathan. *The Religions of Profane Antiquity; Their Mythology, Fables, Hieroglyphics and Doctrines. Founded on Astronomical Principles*. London: Joseph Rickerby, 1830.

Edinger, Edward. F. *Archetype of the Apocalypse*. Edited by George F. Elder. Chicago: Open Court, 2002.

———. *Ego and Archetype*. Baltimore, Maryland: Penguin Books Inc., 1973.

Ellicott, Charles John, ed. *A Bible Commentary for English*

Readers by Various Writers. Vol. 1. New York: Cassell and Company, Limited, 1905.

Elshamy, Mostafa. 'Ancient Egypt: The Primal Age of Divine Revelation Volume I Genesis (Revised Edition)'. Accessed 22 April 2023. https://www.academia.edu/7377563/Ancient_Egypt_The_Primal_Age_of_Divine_Revelation_Volume_I_Genesis_Revised_Edition_.

Everett, Derrick. 'Parsifal under the Bodhi Tree', 2001.

Fortune, Dion. *The Mystical Qabalah*. London: Williams and Norgate, Ltd, 1948.

Frale, Barbara. *The Templars and the Shroud of Christ*. Ireland: Maverick House, 2011.

Frater Achad. *The Chalice of Ecstasy Being the Inmost Secret of Parzival*. Chicago: Yogi Publication Society, 1923.

Friday, Karl. 'The Historical Foundations of Bushido'. Accessed 29 September 2021. https://koryu.com/library/kfriday2.html.

Fuller, J.F.C. 'Liber DCCCCLXIII: The Treasure House of Images'. *The Equinox* I, no. 3 (1998).

GalEinai, Imry. 'From Essence to Actualization: The Secret of the Staff of Aaron'. GalEinai - Revealing the Torah's Inner Dimension, 6 April 2014. https://www.inner.org/audio/aid/E_023.htm.

Garfinkel, Yosef. 'The Face of Yahweh?' The BAS Library, 29 June 2020. https://www.baslibrary.org/biblical-archaeology-review/46/4/2.

Germer, Karl. Typed Letter. 'Karl Germer to Brother Williams'. Typed Letter, 24 June 1958.

Gilliam, Scott D. 'The Angels Call: The Angel and the Individuation Process'. Accessed 8 August 2022. https://www.academia.edu/8001140/THE_ANGELS_CALL_THE_ANGEL_AND_THE_INDIVIDUATION_PROCESS.

'Glory | Origin and Meaning of Glory by Online Etymology Dictionary'. Accessed 15 October 2021. https://www.etymonline.com/word/glory.

Godwin, Joscelyn. *The Theosophical Enlightenment*. New York: State University of New York Press, 1994.

Goodart. 'The Lesser Mysteries of Eleusis', n.d.

'Guillaume Postel'. In *Wikipedia*, 3 November 2021. https://en.wikipedia.org/w/index.php?title=Guillaume_ Postel&oldid=1053410732.

Guillaumont, A., H.-Ch Puech, G. Quispel, W. Till, and Yassah 'Abd Al Masih, trans. *The Gospel According to Thomas*. London: Brill, 1959.

Gunther, J. Daniel. *Initiation In the Aeon of the Child*. Lake Worth, FL: Ibis Books, 2009.

———. *The Angel and the Abyss*. Lake Worth, FL: Ibis Press, 2014.

Gunther, J. Daniel, and Gwen Gunther. *I Am the Heart: A Commentary on Liber LXV Chapter I, Ever the Heart: An Essay on the Symbolism of The Heart of Blood*. Wennoffer House, 2024.

Guppy, Shusha. 'A Paean to Kingship'. *The Guardian*, 18 February 2008, sec. Opinion. https://www.theguardian.com/ commentisfree/2008/feb/18/monarchy.iran.

Häberl, Charles G., and James F. McGrath, eds. *The Mandaean Book of John*. Berlin/Boston: De Gruyter, 2019.

Hamilton, Erik P. 'The Palindrome Paradox: A Multicultural Perspective to Uncovering the Mysteries of the ROTAS-SATOR Square'. *The Palindrome Paradox*, 1 January 2021. https://www.academia.edu/47890292/The_Palindrome_ Paradox_A_Multicultural_Perspective_to_Uncovering_the_ Mysteries_of_the_ROTAS_SATOR_Square.

Harding, D. E. *On Having No Head*. Arkana – Penguin Books, 1991.

Harford, Tim. 'Why Big Companies Squander Good Ideas'. *Financial Times*, 6 September 2018, sec. Undercover Economist. https://www.ft.com/content/3c1ab748-b09b-11e8-8d14-6f049d06439c.

Haring, Walter. 'The Winged St. John the Baptist Two Examples in American Collections'. *The Art Bulletin* 5, no. 2 (1922): 35–40.

Hegarty, Siobhan. 'Meet the Mandaeans: Australian Followers of John the Baptist Celebrate New Year'. *ABC News*, 21 July 2017. https://www.abc.net.au/news/2017-07-21/meet-the-mandaeans-sydneys-followers-of-john-the-baptist/8727720.

Heidrick, Bill. 'HEBREW GEMATRIA: Values from 10 – 19'. Accessed 2 July 2024. https://www.billheidrick.com/works/hgm1/hg0010.htm.

Hodson, Geoffrey. *At the Sign of the Square and Compass*. Adyar: The Eastern Federation International Co-Freemasonry, 1986.

Internal Arts International. 'Monks, Meditation, and Mountains: The Body as a Sacred Landscape in Daoism: Part 1', 28 February 2017. https://www.internalartsinternational.com/free/monks-meditation-mountains-body-sacred-landscape-daoism-part-1/.

Ishaq, Ibin. *The Life of Muhammad*. Translated by Alfred Guillaume. Oxford: Oxford University Press, 1967.

Jacques Collin de Plancy, Jacques. *Dictionnaire Infernal*. Paris: Henri Plon, 1863.

Jung, C. G. 'Volume 8 Collected Works of C.G. Jung, Volume 8: Structure & Dynamics of the Psyche'. In *Volume 8 Collected Works of C.G. Jung, Volume 8*. Princeton University Press, 2014. https://doi.org/10.1515/9781400850952.

Jung, C. G., and C. G. Jung. *Mysterium Coniunctionis: An Inquiry into the Separation and Synthesis of Psychic Opposites in Alchemy*. 2d ed. The Collected Works of C.G. Jung, v. 14. Princeton, N.J: Princeton University Press, 1977.

Jung, C.G. *Aion*. Princeton University Press, 1979.

———. *Alchemical Studies*. Translated by R.F.C. Hull. Vol. 13. Bollingen Series. Princeton: Princeton University Press, 1983.

———. *The Practice of Psychotherapy*. Translated by R.F.C. Hull. New York: Pantheon Books, 1954.

Kaczynski, Richard. *Forgotten Templars*. Published for the author, 2012.

Karlsson, Mattias. 'From Sumer to Assyria: The Term Black-Headed People in Assyrian Texts'. *In Akkadica 141/2 (2020), Pp. 127-139*, 1 January 2020. https://www.academia.edu/44744218/From_Sumer_to_Assyria_The_Term_Black_headed_People_in_Assyrian_Texts.

Kastner, L. E. 'Gavaudan's Crusade Song. (Bartsch, Grundriss, 174, 10)'. *The Modern Language Review* 26, no. 2 (1931): 142–50. https://doi.org/10.2307/3715447.

King, Steve. *Living in the Sunlight*. Canberra: In Perpetuity Publishing, 2022.

Kinsley, David. *Tantric Visions of the Divine Feminine*. Delhi: Motilal Banarsidass Publishers, 2003.

Labatut, Benjamin. *When We Cease to Understand the World*. Translated by Adrian Nathan West. London: Pushkin Press, 2020.

Laboury, Dimitri. *Akhénaton*. Pygmalion - Flammarion, 2010. https://orbi.uliege.be/handle/2268/7965.

Lamb, Jaime Paul. 'The Mystery of Baphomet'. Phoenix Commandery no. 3, Knights Templar, n.d.

Laneri, Nicola. 'Why Ancient Mesopotamians Buried Their Dead beneath the Floor | Psyche Ideas'. Psyche. Accessed 3 June 2023. https://psyche.co/ideas/why-ancient-mesopotamians-buried-their-dead-beneath-the-floor.

Lansberry, Joan Ann. 'Egyptian Serpent Power'. Accessed 1 December 2021. http://joanlansberry.com/setfind/s-power2.pdf.

———. 'May Set Possess His Power'. Accessed 30 November 2021. http://www.joanlansberry.com/setfind/set-hold.html.

Laycock, Joseph P. 'What The Satanic Temple Is and Why It's Opening a Debate about Religion'. The Conversation. Accessed 27 June 2021. http://theconversation.com/what-the-satanic-temple-is-and-why-its-opening-a-debate-about-religion-131283.

Leighton Cleather, Alice, and Basil Crump. *Parsifal Lohengrin and the Legend of the Holy Grail*. London: Methuen & Co., 1904.

Levi, Eliphas. *The Book of Splendours*. York Beach, Maine: Samuel Weiser Inc, 1984.

———. *The History of Magic: Including a Clear and Precise Exposition of Its Procedure, Its Rites and Its Mysteries*. Translated by Arthur Edward Waite. London: William Rider & Son, Limited, 1922.

———. *The Kabalistic and Occult Philosophy of Eliphas Levi*. Vol. 1. USA: Daath Gnostic Publishing (A.S.P.M.), 2018.

———. *The Kabalistic and Occult Tarot of Eliphas Levi: A Study Guide*. Daath Gnostic Publishing (A.S.P.M.), 2018.

———. 'The Key of the Mysteries'. Translated by Aleister Crowley. *The Equinox* I, no. X (1998).

Lévi, Eliphas. *The Mysteries of Magic: A Digest of the Writings of Eliphas Lévi*. Kila, MT: Kessinger Publishing Company, Unknown.

Lévi, Éliphas. *The Mysteries of the Qabalah or Occult Agreement of the Two Testaments*. York Beach, ME: Samuel Weiser, 2000.

Lévi, Eliphas. *Transcendental Magic*. Translated by A.E. Waite. York Beach, Maine: Samuel Weiser, Inc, 1992.

Li, Xiaoping. 'Gu Xiong'. Accessed 30 October 2022. http://guxiong.ca/en/reviews/the-symbol-of-the-mountains/.

Lucarelli, Rita. 'The Donkey in the Graeco-Egyptian Papyri', n.d., 16.

Luna, José R. 'Pairs and Pluralism in Yom Kippur: A Perspective', 2019.

MacGregor Mathers, S. Liddell. *The Kabbalah Unveiled*. York Beach, Maine: Samuel Weiser, Inc, 1993.

MacGregor Mathers, S. Liddell, trans. *The Key of Solomon the King (Clavicula Salomonis)*. York Beach, Maine: Samuel Weiser, Inc, 1989.

Mackey, Albert, and Robert Clegg. *Mackey's Symbolism of Freemasonry: Its Science, Philosophy, Legends, Myths and Symbols*. Chicago: The Masonic History Company, n.d.

Mackey, Albert G. *Encyclopedia of Freemasonry and Its Kindred Sciences Comprising the Whole Range of Arts, Sciences and Literature as Connected with the Institution*. Philadelphia: McLure Publishing Co., 1917.

Mahdihassan, S. 'Lead and Mercury Each as Prime Matter in Alchemy'. *Ancient Science of Life* VII, no. 3 & 4 (1988): 134–38.

Mark, Joshua J. 'The Lamentations of Isis and Nephthys'. World History Encyclopedia. Accessed 14 August 2022. https://www.worldhistory.org/article/878/the-lamentations-of-isis-and-nephthys/.

Marlow, Louis. *Seven Friends*. Thame: Mandrake Press Ltd, 1992.

Marshall, Taylor. 'The Horns of Moses – Defending Michelangelo's Horned Moses'. Taylor Marshall, 7 August 2013. https://taylormarshall.com/2013/08/the-horns-of-moses-defending-michelangelos-horned-moses.html.

Martone, Corrado. 'Evil or Devil? Belial Between the Bible and Qumran'. *Henoch* XXVI (2004): 115–27.

'Maruf Al-Karkhi – Sufiwiki'. Accessed 3 June 2023. https://sufiwiki.com/content/maruf_al-karkhi/.

Marvell, Leon. *Leonardo Electronic Almanac* 20, no. 2 (2014): 60–71.

Masaaki Hatsumi: Kuden Vol. 1. DVD. Quest, 2006.

Masahiro, Sato. 'Nitobe Inazo and Bushido'. Journal of Japanese Trade & Industry, February 2002.

Masciandaro. 'Non Potest Hoc Corpus Decollari: Beheading and the Impossible'. *Heads Will Roll*, 2012, 15.

Masciandaro, Nicola. 'John the Baptist and the Symbolism of Decapitation'. Accessed 17 November 2022. https://www.academia.edu/43433930/John_the_Baptist_and_the_Symbolism_of_Decapitation.

Maspero, G. *The Dawn of Civilisation*. Edited by A.H. Sayce. Fourth. London: Society for Promoting Christian Knowledge, 1901.

McClenechan, Charles T. 'AASR – 1884 – 28th Degree: Knight of the Sun (or Prince Adept)'. Accessed 13 November 2021. http://www.phoenixmasonry.org/AASR_1884_/28th_degree_knight_of_the_sun.htm.

McIntosh, Christopher. *Eliphas Levi and the French Occult Revival*. New York: Suny Press, 2011.

McPeters, Jim. 'The Demiurge and the Primeval Serpent Motif within Classical Thought and Its Culmination within Gnosticism and Early Christianity'. Fort Hays State University, 2022. https://doi.org/10.58809/HFXQ8377.

Melamed, Yitzhak Y. 'Eternity in Early Modern Philosophy'. In *Eternity*, edited by Yitzhak Y. Melamed, 129–67. Oxford University Press, 2016. https://doi.org/10.1093/acprof:oso/9780199781874.003.0009.

Mend Me This Shoe, That I May Walk. Initiation in the Aeon of the Child: The Path of the Great Return. Sydney, 2010.

Mercurius. 'Who Is Mercurius?' Accessed 15 June 2024. https://www.mercurius.one/home/who-is-mercurius.

Michael, Thomas. 'Mountains and Early Daoism in the Writings of Ge Hong'. *History of Religions* 56, no. 1 (2016): 23.

Middenway, Ralph. 'Parsifal, Kundry and the Dance of the Seven Veils'. State Opera of South Australia, 2012.

Mindnich, Percy A. 'That I May Follow and Dispel the Night: Wagner's Parsifal and Liber XV'. *Ora et Labora* 3 (2022).

Moneme, Nnamdi. 'John the Baptist: Witnessing to The Truth and to Truth'. Catholic Exchange, 30 August 2017. https://catholicexchange.com/witnessing-truth-truth/.

Morrisson, Mark. *Modern Alchemy: Occultism and the Emergence of Atomic Theory*. Oxford University Press, 2007. https://doi.org/10.1093/acprof:oso/9780195306965.001.0001.

Muhammad, Elijah. 'Our Savior Has Arrived'. GaryNoi.com. Accessed 2 October 2021. https://garynoi.com/our-savior-has-arrived/.

Muhammad, Robert. 'The Secret Hidden in Modern Science: Is the Black Man God', n.d. Accessed 2 October 2021.

My Catholic Life! 'Memorial of Saint Gertrude the Great'. Accessed 21 January 2022. https://mycatholic.life/saints/saints-of-the-liturgical-year/november-16-saint-gertrude-the-great-virgin/.

'Nabataean | Arabian, Petra & Trade | Britannica'. Accessed 18 June 2024. https://www.britannica.com/topic/Nabataean-people.

Nematollahi, Narges. 'The True Meaning of the Cup of Jamshid: Medieval and Pre-Modern Symbolic Readings of the Sh hn meh', n.d.

Nicholson, Helen J. 'The Changing Face of the Templars: Current Trends in Historiography'. *History Compass* 8, no. 7 (2010): 653–67.

Nugent, Mark. 'From "Filthy Catamite" to "Queer Icon": Elagabalus and the Politics of Sexuality (1960–1975)'. *HELIOS* 35, no. 2 (2008).

Orlov, Andrei. 'Azazel as the Serpent and the Tree of Knowledge'. Accessed 11 June 2024. https://www.academia.edu/58489466/Azazel_as_the_Serpent_and_the_Tree_of_Knowledge.

'O.T.O. and A A Libri by Class'. Accessed 16 October 2021. https://lib.oto-usa.org/libri/byclass.html.

Paracelsus, Theophrastus. 'Theophrastus Paracelsus: Alchemical Catechism'. Accessed 2 January 2022. http://www.rexresearch.com/ALCHEMYARCHIVES/zalchhtm/paracate.htm.

Partner, Peter. *The Murdered Magicians: The Templars and Their Myth*. Oxford University Press, 1982.

Payne Knight, Richard. *Book A Discourse on the Worship of Priapus and Its Connection to the Mystic Theology of the Ancients*. London: Privately Printed, 1894.

Pearse, Roger. 'Did Mithras Say "He Who Will Not Eat of My Body and Drink of My Blood…"?' *Roger Pearce: Thoughts on Antiquity Patristics, Information Access and More* (blog), 21 December 2020. https://www.roger-pearse.com/weblog/2020/12/21/did-mithras-say-he-who-will-not-eat-of-my-body-and-drink-of-my-blood/.

———. 'Mithras: All the Passages in Graeco-Roman Literature'. Accessed 25 September 2022. https://www.tertullian.org/rpearse/mithras/literary_sources.htm#Jerome.

Pearson, Birger A. 'The Figure of Seth in Gnostic Literature'. *The Rediscovery of Gnosticism (2 Vols.)*, 1 January 1980, 472–504. https://doi.org/10.1163/9789004378599_029.

Philalethes, Eirenaeus. *Alchemical Works: Eirenaeus Philalethes Compiled*. Edited by S. Merrow Broddle. Boulder, Colorado: Cinnabar, 1994.

Pike, Albert. *Morals and Dogma of the Accepted and Ancient Scottish Rite of Freemasonry*. Charleston: The Supreme Council of the Southern Jurisdiction, 1905.

Popova, Maria. 'The Dalai Lama on Science and Spirituality'. *The Marginalian* (blog), 16 October 2018. https://www.themarginalian.org/2018/10/16/dalai-lama-science-spirituality-destructive-emotions/.

Pryse, James. M. *The Apocalypse Unsealed: Being an Interpretation of the Initiation of Ioannes*. London: John M. Watkins, 1910.

Pullella, Philip. 'Knights Templar Win Heresy Reprieve after 700 Years'. *Reuters*, 12 October 2007, sec. Lifestyle. https://www.reuters.com/article/us-vatican-templars-idUSL093422320071012.

Read, Piers Paul. *The Templars*. London: Weidenfeld & Nicolson, 1999.

Richard H. Wilkinson. *The Complete Gods and Goddesses of Ancient Egypt*. Thames & Hudson, 2003. http://archive.org/details/completegodsgodd00wilk_0.

Rodkinson, Michael L., trans. *The Babylonian Talmud*. Vol. 1–10.

Boston New Talmud Publishing Company, 1903. http://www. ultimatebiblereferencelibrary.com/.

Roig, Alexandre. 'The Headless Body', 2015. https://www. academia.edu/27399301/The_Headless_body.

Römer, Thomas. 'The Horns of Moses. Setting the Bible in Its Historical Context : Inaugural Lecture Delivered on 5 February 2009'. In *The Horns of Moses. Setting the Bible in Its Historical Context*. Leçons Inaugurales. Paris: Collège de France, 2013. http://books.openedition.org/cdf/3048.

Russell, J. R. *Heredom*. Vol. 4. Scottish Rite Research Society, Washington D. C., 1995.

Sabazius. 'Parzival'. Accessed 4 October 2021. https://hermetic. com/sabazius/parzival.

———. 'Sir Richard Payne Knight | The Invisible Basilica of Sabazius | Essays, Speeches, Commentary, and Rituals by the National Grand Master of OTO USA'. The Invisible Basilica of Sabazius. Accessed 23 September 2021. https://sabazius. oto-usa.org/sir-richard-payne-knight/.

Sacks, Jonathan. 'Covenant & Conversation'. *Toras Aish* XXII, no. 32 (n.d.). https://www.aishdas.org/ta/5775/acharei.pdf.

Schwartz, Ellen C. 'Russian Icons and Byzantine Legacy; The Angel of Wilderness'. *Byzantinoslavica Revue Internationale Des Etudes Byzantines* LVIII (1997): 169–85.

Sebottendorff, Rudolf von. *Secret Practices of the Sufi Freemasons*. Translated by Stephen. E Flowers. Vermont: Inner Traditions, 2013.

Seligmann, Kurt. *The History of Magic*. New York: Pantheon Books, 1948.

'Seventh Principle – Theosophy Wiki'. Accessed 13 April 2022. https://theosophy.wiki/en/Seventh_Principle#cite_note-1.

Shah, Idries. *The Sufis*. London: ISF Publishing, 2015.

Shakespeare, William. 'Macbeth – Entire Play | Folger Shakespeare Library'. Accessed 11 September 2024. https://www.folger. edu/explore/shakespeares-works/read/.

Shirazi, Faegheh. 'Iranian Mandaeans'. *Iran Today, An Encyclopedia of Life in the Islamic Republic*, 2008.

Shiva X°. 'Aspiring to the Holy Order', 2016.

———. 'Australia: The Land of Sun Worshippers – Part IV: The OTO Living in the Sunlight Meditation'. Ordo Templi Orientis Australia, 2021.

Silk, Jonathan A, Richard Bowring, Vincent Eltschinger, and Michael Radich, eds. 'Brill's Encyclopedia of Buddhism'. Vol. II. Lives. Leiden: Brill, n.d.

Simard LaForêt, Elaine. *Descent from the Cross: Transformations of a Masochistic Woman*, 2024.

Simeoni, Gabriel. 'From Mithraism to Freemasonry. A History of Ideas'. *The New Mithraeum*, 1 January 2021. https://www.academia.edu/50982456/From_Mithraism_to_Freemasonry_A_history_of_ideas.

Soudavar, Abolala. *The Aura of Kings*. California: Mazda Publishers, Inc, 2003.

Stantonian, Jamie. 'Witch Hunts and the Weaponisation of Moral Panic'. *Medium* (blog), 27 February 2015. https://medium.com/@jamiestantonian/witch-hunts-and-the-weaponisation-of-moral-panic-892e6be0c82d.

Stephensen, P.R., and Aleister Crowley. *The Legend of Aleister Crowley*. Enmore, NSW: Helios Books, 2007.

Stratton-Kent, Jake. *The Trve Grimoire: The Encyclopedia Goetica Volume One*. London: Scarlet Imprint, 2009.

Strawn, Brent A. 'Moses' Shining or Horned Face? - TheTorah.Com'. Accessed 9 February 2022. https://www.thetorah.com/article/moses-shining-or-horned-face.

Strube, Julian. 'Occultist Identity Formations Between Theosophy and Socialism in Fin-de-Siècle France'. *Numen* 64, no. 5–6 (1 January 2017): 568.

———. 'Socialist Religion and the Emergence of Occultism: A Genealogical Approach to Socialism and Secularization in

19th-Century France'. *Religion* 46, no. 3 (2 July 2016): 359–88. https://doi.org/10.1080/0048721X.2016.1146926.

———. 'The "Baphomet" of Eliphas Lévi: Its Meaning and Historical Context'. *Correspondences* 4 (2016). https://correspondencesjournal.com/15303-2/.

'Susanoo | Description & Mythology | Britannica', 26 April 2024. https://www.britannica.com/topic/Susanoo.

Tay, C. N. 'Kuan-Yin: The Cult of Half Asia'. *History of Religions* 16, no. 2 (1976): 147–77.

The British Museum. 'Drawing | British Museum'. Accessed 23 September 2021. https://www.britishmuseum.org/collection/object/G_2010-5006-1152.

'The Contendings of Horus and Set'. Accessed 10 December 2021. http://courses.missouristate.edu/ECarawan/HorusSeth.htm.

'The Embryonic Generation of the Perfect Body: Ritual Embryology from Japanese Tantric Sources'. *Transforming the Void*, 2016, 253.

The KJV Study Bible. Uhrichsville, Ohio: Barbour Publishing, Inc, 2016.

'The Teachings of Silvanus – The Nag Hammadi Library'. Accessed 31 May 2025. http://www.gnosis.org/naghamm/silvanus.html.

Tinaz, I ık Eflan. 'The Winged Figure of Saint John the Baptist', n.d. Accessed 17 October 2021.

Tiso, Francis V. *Rainbow Body and Resurrection*. Berkeley, California: North Atlantic Books, 2016.

———. 'Taking the Next Step in Rainbow Body Research: Anthropological and Neurophysiological Objectives', n.d.

Toorn, Karel van der, Bob Becking, and Pieter W. van der Horst, eds. *Dictionary of Deities and Demons in the Bible*. Second. Leiden: Brill, 1999.

Torrens, R.G. *The Golden Dawn: The Inner Teachings*. New York: Samuel Weiser Inc, 1980.

Turnbull, Michael. 'Who Were the Templars?' *Open House*, no. 198 (2009).

Turner, Philip John. 'Seth: A Misrepresented God in the Egyptian Pantheon?', 2012.

Tyson Wils. 'Ora et Labora', 25 March 2021.

Ulansey, David. 'David Ulansey, "The Mithraic Mysteries," Scientific American, December 1989'. Accessed 9 October 2021. http://www.mysterium.com/sciam.html.

———. *The Origins of the Mithraic Mysteries*. New York: Oxford University Press, 1991.

Urban, Hugh. B. 'Magia Sexualis : Sex, Secrecy, and Liberation in Modern Western Esotericism'. *Journal of the American Academy of Religion* 72, no. 3 (September 2004): 695–731.

Uzzel, Robert L. *Eliphas Levi and the Kabbalah: The Masonic and French Connection of the American Mystery Tradition*. New Orleans, LA: Cornerstone Book Publishers, 2015.

Vandenbeusch, Marie. 'Thinking and Writing "Donkey" in Ancient Egypt: Examples from the Religious Literature'. *Altorientalische Forschungen* 46, no. 1 (2019): 135–46.

Vrhovnik, Dimitrij Mlekuz. 'Approaching Weird: Psychoanalysis and Archaeology of Caves'. *Academia Letters*, 2021. https://www.academia.edu/44995065/Approaching_weird_psychoanalysis_and_archaeology_of_caves.

Wallis Budge, E.A. *The Gods of the Egyptians: Studies in Egyptian Mythology*. New York: Dover Publications, Inc, 1969.

Walls, Brendan, ed. *Ora et Labora*. Vol. 3. Canberra: In Perpetuity Publishing, 2022.

———, ed. *Ora et Labora*. Vol. 4. Canberra: In Perpetuity Publishing, 2023.

Weiss, Judith. '"BL MS Sloane 1410: Some Paleographical Issues Relating Guillaume Postel's First Latin Zohar Translation and Commentary," Revue Des Études Juives 175, 1–2, 2016: 135–146'. Accessed 16 July 2023. https://www.academia.

edu/43272592/_BL_MS_Sloane_1410_Some_Paleographical_
Issues_Relating_Guillaume_Postel_s_First_Latin_Zohar_
Translation_and_Commentary_Revue_des_%C3%A9tudes_
juives_175_1_2_2016_135_146.

———. 'Guillaume Postel's Kabbalistic Notion of Marriage, Sex, and
Family'. *Marriage, Families & Spirituality* 26 (2020): 74–92.

Wen, Benebell. 'Postel's Key of Things Kept Secret (1547)'.
Benebell Wen (blog), 24 November 2019. https://benebellwen.
com/2019/11/24/postels-key-of-things-kept-secret-1547/.

Wilhelm, Richard, trans. *The Secret of the Golden Flower: A
Chinese Book of Life*. London: Kegan Paul, Trench, Trubner
& Co., Ltd, 1947.

Williams, Phil. 'The Origin of Alchemy and the Image of God in
Man'. Accessed 10 August 2022. http://www.jungpage.org/
learn/articles/analytical-psychology/52-the-origin-of-alchemy-
and-the-image-of-god-in-man.

Winter, Dr Jay. *The Complete Book of Enoch: Standard English
Version*. Winter Publications, 2015.

Winter, Franz. 'Looking out for Magic in Ancient China: The
Yijing, Its Trigrams and the Figurist Tradition in Eliphas
Levi'. *Appropriating the Dao: The Euro-American Esoteric
Reception of China*, 2024.

Wojtowicz, Robert T. 'The Original Rule of the Knights Templar: A
Translation with Introduction'. Western Michigan University,
1991. https://scholarworks.wmich.edu/masters_theses/1007.

Young, Emma. 'West Australian-Found Buddha Is a Ming
Dynasty Treasure: Antiques Roadshow'. The Sydney Morning
Herald, 5 March 2023. https://www.smh.com.au/national/
west-australian-found-buddha-is-a-ming-dynasty-treasure-
antiques-roadshow-20230227-p5cnwd.html.

Zada, John. 'On Contemporary Sufism and the Works of Idries
Shah'. *BLARB* (blog). Accessed 12 September 2021. http://
blog.lareviewofbooks.org/essays/beacon-sanity-age-polarity-
contemporary-sufism-works-idries-shah/.

Zalewski, Wojciech Maria. *The Crucible of Religion*. Oregon: Wipf and Stock, 2012.

Zsengellér, József. 'Does Wisdom Come from the Temple?' *Supplements to the Journal for the Study of Judaism* 127 (2008).

In Perpetuity Publishing

For more information about our publications please visit

https://inperpetuitypublishing.com/publications/

Available through all good online booksellers.

DESCENT FROM THE CROSS

TRANSFORMATION OF A MASOCHISTIC WOMAN

by Elaine Simard LaForêt

https://inperpetuitypublishing.com/publications/descent-from-the-cross/

ISBN 978-0645103953

Elaine's thesis *"Descent from the Cross: Transformation of a Masochistic Woman"* marked the completion of her psychoanalytic degree at the C.G. Jung Institute of New York. She has practised psychoanalysis for many years, taught at the C. G. Jung Institute of New Mexico, and presented public lectures (one is entitled "The Symbol of the Cross: Revitalizing the Balanced Cross of Nature") and classes and workshops for the public. She has a BA from Wellesley College and an MA from Harvard University in literature, psychology, and teaching.

ORA ET LABORA

https://inperpetuitypublishing.com/publications/ora-et-labora/

Wide-ranging and highly eclectic essays from around the world related to the OTO and to Thelema distributed through 57 articles across five volumes. Ora Et Labora gathers together the research and findings of the practitioner-scholars of Thelema.

ISBN 978-0645103908   Vol I   2021 e.v.
ISBN 978-0645103915   Vol II   2021 e.v.
ISBN 978-0645103922   Vol III   2022 e.v.
ISBN 978-06451039-7-7 Vol IV   2023 e.v.
ISBN 978-0645103960   Vol V   2025 e.v.

The topics from Volume V – Thelema and the East

The Balance of Opposites · Nibbana, Annihilation and Return to the Eye in the Triangle · (Tenchijin) · The Goddess and the Serpent · Aye! Feast! Rejoice! · Kundalini and The Book of the Law · The Wish Fulfilling Vase

THE LEGEND OF ALEISTER CROWLEY

https://inperpetuitypublishing.com/publications/the-legend-of-aleister-crowley/

ISBN 978-0645103939

This facsimile edition of P. R. Stephensen's 1930 broadside against the 'Campaign of Personal Vilification Unparalleled in Literary History' arrives in 2021 as the mainstream media thrashes in its death throes.

Quality digital scans of the original book, never before published material from the Australian OTO archives, as well as a new essay examining the politics of conspiracy and the pathologies of Fake News, make this an indispensable case study of media malfeasance and moral panic.

THE BEST OF OZ

https://inperpetuitypublishing.com/publications/
the-best-of-oz/

ISBN 978-0646815770

After 13 years and 50 Issues, OTO Grand Lodge of Australia is making its member-only OZ magazine available to the public in this 'best of' compilation. Inspiring and provocative, OZ chronicles the birth and early development of the Australian Grand Lodge experiment in thought leadership, scholarship, culture and magical design.

Origins of the modern O.T.O in Australia · Aurora Australis: topological reflections on the modern M.M.M. in Australia · 'New Commentary' Theology: Notes towards reorganising the EGC Part 1 & Part 2 · 'From the GM' (AUGL in Japan) · Toiling in the (local) fields of Our Lord · Remembering Parsi Krumm-Heller (1925-2008 e.v.) Obituary · Grand Master Shiva's Introduction to J. Daniel Gunther's 'Initiation in the Aeon of the Child: the Path of the Great Return' · Veni Cooper-Mathieson · Woman Girt with a Sword · EGC Retreat Keynote Address · Our Church – the Clarity of Vocation · Shadow of the Thelemites: the Abbot, the Abbey and the Nightmare · In the Flesh – Manifesting Liber 194 · Battle of the Ants · Apokalypsis 418 – The Temple of Christ, the Angelic priesthood and the Great Return of the Queen of Heaven · Temple Mount: The Oriental Templar crusade for Verità · Living In The Sunlight

Living in the Sunlight

Making a Forgotten Meditation an Atomic Habit

https://livinginthesunlight.site/

by Steve King

ISBN 978-0645103946

Living in the Sunlight by Steve King is a little gem of a book that is welcome and much needed, perhaps never as much as right now. Dedicated to the exposition of a deceptively simple meditation practice, the book's clear and unassuming narrative is brimful with initiated knowledge, and steeped in the esoteric lore of Ordo Templi Orientis and Aleister Crowley's Thelema. The practice of "Living in the Sunlight," however, originates not with Crowley but with his "scarlet woman" Hilarion (Jeanne Robert Foster) and can be adopted by anyone, irrespective of denominational affiliations and ideological convictions. In essence, it is a method of identifying one's deepest awareness with the Sun, for the ultimate purpose of radiating its light unto others. An antidote to the present culture of cynicism and ennui, Living in the Sunlight is based on a simple yet profound notion that happiness is contagious and grows by sharing. This book, and the method of putting it into practice, is rooted in a most radical idea, that the point of life is joy. Highly recommended.

- Gordan Djurdjevic, author of India and the Occult, and co-translator of Sayings of Gorakhnāth

IF YOU WANT
FREEDOM
YOU MUST FIGHT FOR IT

IF YOU WANT
TO FIGHT
YOU MUST ORGANISE

IF YOU WANT
TO ORGANISE
JOIN US

ORDO TEMPLI ORIENTIS
GRAND LODGE OF AUSTRALIA

• SYDNEY • MELBOURNE • BRISBANE •
• HOBART • PERTH • ADELAIDE •

www.otoaustralia.org.au

ORDO TEMPLI ORIENTIS
INTERNATIONAL CONTACT

www.oto.org

The OTO does not include the A∴A∴ with which body it is, however, in close alliance. While the curricula of A∴A∴ and OTO interpenetrate at points, this is more by nature than design, and the exception, not the rule. The respective systems and their methods are distinct. One follows the Path in Eternity. The other, the Path of the Great Return. The Grand Lodge of Australia openly supports the work of the Great Order by providing resources to its Outer College, hosting lecture tours to Australia by its senior instructors, and collaborating on joint projects and learning events.

Those of you whose will is to communicate with the A∴A∴ should apply by letter to the Cancellarius of the A∴A∴

www.outercol.org
secretary@outercol.org